GREENHOUSE
GOVERNANCE

GREENHOUSE GOVERNANCE

Addressing Climate Change in America

Barry G. Rabe

editor

BROOKINGS INSTITUTION PRESS
Washington, D.C.

Copyright © 2010
THE BROOKINGS INSTITUTION
1775 Massachusetts Avenue, N.W., Washington, DC 20036
www.brookings.edu

Library of Congress Cataloging-in-Publication data
Greenhouse governance : addressing climate change in America / Barry G. Rabe, editor.
    p.   cm.
  Includes bibliographical references and index.
  Summary: "Examines national and international laws and institutions governing human-mediated climate change. Issues examined include public perceptions and economic effects of climate change and policies to mitigate it, renewable electricity standards, vehicle fuel economy standards, cap-and-trade regimes, carbon taxes, and the adaptation-versus-mitigation debate"—Provided by publisher.
  ISBN 978-0-8157-0331-0 (pbk. : alk. paper)
  1. Environmental policy—United States. 2. Climatic changes—Government policy—United States. 3. Climatic changes—Environmental aspects—United States. I. Rabe, Barry George, 1957- II. Brookings Institution. III. Title.
  GE180.G7537 2010
  363.738'7405610973—dc22   2010019408

9 8 7 6 5 4 3 2 1

Printed on acid-free paper

Typeset in Adobe Garamond

Composition by R. Lynn Rivenbark
Macon, Georgia

Printed by R. R. Donnelley
Harrisonburg, Virginia

Contents

III   ARE FEDERAL INSTITUTIONS UP TO THE CHALLENGE OF CLIMATE CHANGE?

IV   RECONNECTING THE UNITED STATES WITH THE WORLD

Preface

This book was launched in a discussion at a national treasure, the Miller Center of Public Affairs at the University of Virginia. Gerald L. Baliles, director of the Miller Center, and Sidney Milkis, assistant director for academic programs, convened a gathering to begin to explore the challenges of "governing the climate" and how the Miller Center might bring together leading scholars and policymakers for serious consideration of this issue. With that, the National Conference on Climate Governance was born and the framework for this book was established.

The Miller Center, which became my academic home for the 2008–09 period, provided a unique blend of intellectual engagement and collegiality. Governor Baliles and Sid Milkis were exemplary leaders throughout, and they were backed by an exceptional set of colleagues. Anne Carter Mulligan provided superb support for all aspects of the project. I benefited also from collaboration with other members of the Miller Center team, including Brian Balogh, Michael Greco, Rose Marie Owen, Taylor Reveley, Joseph Taylor, and Lisa Todorovich Porter. Generous financial support was provided by Altria Group, Inc., the Emily Hall Tremaine Foundation, the WestWind Foundation, an anonymous Charlottesville foundation, the Center for Local, State and Urban Policy at the Gerald R. Ford School of Public Policy at the University of Michigan, and Muhlenberg College. Valuable research assistance was provided by Sourav Guha, Margaret McCarthy, Daniel McDowell, and Matthew Rabe. Roxanne Balmas reviewed early versions of the full manuscript and offered excellent editorial support while Joshua Keyes and Allison Wachter provided valuable technical assistance.

The transition from conference to draft papers to an edited book was capably facilitated by Brookings Institution Press. Christopher Kelaher provided support and good judgment throughout the process, and the book benefited greatly from the involvement of Robert Faherty, Eileen Hughes, Janet Walker, and Susan Woollen. In addition to helpful comments from external reviewers commissioned by Brookings, the authors received valued early feedback from our conference discussants, Timothy Conlan, Daniel Fiorino, Susan Gander, Kathryn Harrison, Christopher James, Suellen Keiner, Anne Khademian, Judith Layzer, and Alastair Totty. Valuable input was also provided by other colleagues, including Jonathan Cannon, Donald Kettl, Daniel Plafcan, Ed Russell, Vivian Thomson, and David Vogel.

BARRY G. RABE

Ann Arbor, Michigan
June 2010

PART I

Framing the Issue
of Climate Governance

1

Introduction:
The Challenges of U.S. Climate Governance

BARRY G. RABE

Policy analysts and policymakers continue to search for metaphors to describe the unique complexities posed by climate change. According to economist William Nordhaus, "If global warming is the mother of all public goods, it may also be the father of decision making under uncertainty."[1] Other policy analysts have referred to climate change as "perhaps the most hotly debated and controversial area of environmental policy ever" and as "one of the most complex challenges that the human race has ever created."[2] In the final days of a federal government career that spanned five decades and included a leading role in many foreign and domestic policy challenges during thirty years in the U.S. Senate, Republican John Warner of Virginia put it more simply: "Without question, this is the most complex problem I have ever faced."[3] Most of those comments were uttered prior to the tumultuous climate policy events of 2009–10, which included prolonged political combat over dauntingly complex legislative proposals before Congress, fallout over revelations from hacked e-mails that raised questions about the integrity of some high-profile climate scientists, and the melodramatic albeit largely inconclusive Copenhagen climate summit.

The discovery that accumulating levels of carbon dioxide, methane, and other gases in the atmosphere could cause a "greenhouse effect" that both elevated global temperatures and disrupted the climate is not new, though its saliency has grown markedly in recent years. In the United States, "rapid climate warming" first arose as an issue for the Domestic Policy Council in 1976, as the Gerald Ford administration responded to concerns raised by counterparts in the Soviet Union.[4] Ronald Reagan signed the first federal climate change legislation, the Global Climate Protection Act (P.L. 100-204), into law in 1987. This authorized the State Department to develop an approach to address global warming and established an intergovernmental task force to develop a national strategy. One year later, governors in California (George Deukmejian) and New Jersey (Thomas Kean) signed the first of many state laws designed to respond to climate change, none of which were capable of "solving" the problem or reversing the threat of climate change. But they initiated a process of "greenhouse governance" that has reached new prominence in the twenty-first century.

A domestic path to policy exploration was also established in other national and subnational capitals and moved rapidly into the arena of international policy. Well before the 1997 Kyoto Protocol to the United Nations Convention on Climate Change, which has triggered much controversy and proven such an abject failure of global governance, international agreements on different aspects of climate change were reached. The United States has been a participant in the vast majority of those agreements. In fact, it was among the first of more than 170 nations to ratify the 1992 UN Framework Convention on Climate Change, which formally pledged to attain "stabilization of greenhouse gas concentrations in the atmosphere at a level that would prevent dangerous anthropogenic interference with the climate system."

Between the first indicators of concern and the December 2009 United Nations Climate Change Conference in Copenhagen, it is impossible to calculate how much has been said and written about this topic. But we clearly know much more about climate change than in prior decades, and the vast preponderance of relevant evidence from the natural and physical sciences indicates a diverse and alarming set of threats to future generations. Former U.S. vice president Al Gore won the 2007 Nobel Peace Prize for his advocacy on this issue in his post-political career, during which he produced an award-winning film on climate change. Gore shared that award with a veritable army of international climate scientists, known as the Intergovernmental Panel on Climate Change (IPCC), which has brought new focus to what we know about this issue from virtually every discipline in the natural and physical sciences. The ongoing IPCC project remains only one piece of a massive effort that involves the work of countless scientists from around the world. For example, in November 2008 the American Geophysical Union, an international body of 50,000 members who study the earth and its environment, presented a number of major new studies on climate change, ranging from ice-melting patterns to temperature trends. This ever-growing body of scientific analysis has been explored in the hundreds of congressional hearings on climate science held between 1975 and 2009. It resonates with research findings from leading scholars on every continent, creating a consistently disturbing portrait of a staggering challenge. Although policy responses to climate change vary markedly, no national government in the world disputes the core scientific findings. Even the histrionics surrounding "Climategate" and the sophisticated effort to use a select set of purloined e-mails to challenge the existence of human-induced climate change do not reverse the veritable avalanche of evidence on this issue. That said, the best scientific practice remains limited in its ability to predict the future of the planet with any degree of exactitude. That leaves policymakers with considerable uncertainty as they weigh various strategies to reduce greenhouse gas emissions and evaluate the possible impact of the steps taken on global temperatures in future years and future decades.

While the community of natural and physical scientists has weighed in intensively on this issue, more modest contributions have emerged from the social and policy sciences. Within those disciplines, economists have clearly been the most active players on climate change, as reflected in a large body of publications and in active engagement in congressional and state legislative policy hearings and formal reports such as the 2006 *Stern Review on the Economics of Climate Change*. They have played a valuable role in shaping policy options and generally making the case in favor of market-based approaches, such as those that would allow for the trading of emissions among regulated parties or taxing directly the carbon content of fossil fuels. But economic analyses often confront serious limitations, such as weighing the most efficient strategy against political and institutional realities and constraints.

Other social science disciplines have been far more marginal players, including political science and allied fields that address public management and public policy concerns. A content analysis of the leading political science and public management journals over the past decade suggests a rather stunning absence of scholarly engagement on the topic of climate change. For example, between 1998 and 2009, the twenty-seven top-ranked public management journals published in English produced only a pair of articles on the application of management theory to the challenge of climate change. In more than 400 congressional hearings on climate change between 1975 and 2009, only two political science or public management scholars appear to have ever testified on climate change, in contrast to the far more substantial participation from economists, legal analysts, scholars in numerous natural or physical science disciplines, and representatives of diverse interest and environmental advocacy groups.

Consequently, we know far less than we should about what we will term "greenhouse governance," which involves the intersection of politics, history, public policy, and public management. Recognition of that void was an animating force behind the development of this book, which took shape through the National Conference on Climate Governance, held at the Miller Center of Public Affairs at the University of Virginia in December 2008. The intent was to convene leading scholars, drawn primarily from political science but with significant links to history, law, and other social science disciplines. All of the scholars had distinguished records in public policy, public management, or both. About one-half of the invited scholars had launched research programs that focused heavily on climate change; the other half had not but had completed work in other policy areas that was highly relevant to climate governance. They were joined at the conference by a diverse mix of additional scholars as well as policymakers from the public, nonprofit, and private sectors in the United States and abroad, some of whom served as formal commentators on initial papers and all of whom added to the debate over the course of two days. Comments from those exchanges inform this chapter and are cited frequently in subsequent pages. While the chapters that follow make robust analyses and point toward important considerations for future policy development, there was no effort to impose uniformity of viewpoint or to conclude with a memorandum of understanding that presented bullet points marking the next steps to take. Presidents and Congresses had long before been inundated with such "action lists"; we wanted instead to focus on larger and longer-term considerations.

Most of our analysis examines the United States. The conference took place at the midpoint of the transition between the November 2008 national election and the January 2009 inauguration of the 44th president and installation of the 111th Congress. There is, of course, a vast array of issues facing national elected leaders, as well as their counterparts in other nations and at the state and local levels. Some new policy steps have been taken in the United States since our gathering, others remain under consideration, and innumerable implementation challenges lie ahead. Climate change is both competing for attention and intermingled with other current issues, such as economic recovery, health care reform, energy diversification, infrastructure repair, and the redirection of U.S. foreign policy. It is our collective intent to reflect on some of the most serious challenges to developing a coherent set of policies in order to reverse the long-standing trend of growth in U.S. greenhouse gas emissions, to avoid causing economic harm through the implementation of climate change policies, and to re-engage the United States effectively in future international deliberations.

We offer our reflections with full awareness that unilateral action by any one government, even a nation as large as the United States or a state as large as California or Texas, has limited capacity to influence global concentrations of greenhouse gases. But we take seriously the fact that the past two decades have witnessed considerable policy experimentation, both in the United States and abroad. That experimentation provides us a unique opportunity to consider the likely challenges facing future policy alternatives by relying on real experience rather than estimates, models, and projections. It allows us to weigh the capacity of various levels of the federal system to engage on this issue, the political and institutional feasibility of various policy options to reduce greenhouse gas emissions, the capacity of existing federal government institutions to play coherent roles, and possible routes whereby the United States might reconnect with other nations, including its North American neighbors, in search of opportunities for international collaboration. Several key themes, discussed below, animate much of the discussion in subsequent chapters.

U.S. Climate Policy Already Is Operational

Many analysts contend that President Barack Obama and the 111th Congress were the first political actors in the United States to "do something" about climate change. President Obama quickly signaled his views on the federal role through high-level appointments and a pledge from the new leadership of the U.S. Environmental Protection Agency (EPA) to revisit an earlier decision to reject the designation of carbon dioxide as an air pollutant. Moreover, approximately 10 percent of the $787 billion American Recovery and Reinvestment Act signed into law in February 2009 will ultimately be devoted to a range of energy efficiency and renewable energy projects, which could serve to reduce U.S. greenhouse gas emissions. In his first address to Congress, on February 24, 2009, the president called for "this Congress to send me legislation that places a market-based cap on carbon pollution and drives the production of more renewable energy in America." All of this reflected a shift toward more energetic engagement on climate change, thereby reversing the Bush administration's stance, which was epitomized by the 2001 decision to withdraw the United States from the Kyoto Protocol. Indeed, the United States has been widely denounced in the European Union and around the world for its seeming indifference to climate change, best reflected in the slow pace of federal government action.

Along with those steps, a series of major climate policy initiatives were indeed taken in Washington during the first year of the Obama presidency. The EPA not only deemed carbon dioxide and other greenhouse gases to be air pollutants but moved beyond that step to issue an "endangerment finding" that could lead to unilateral executive branch steps to restrict future emissions to protect public health. A far-reaching agreement was reached in May 2009 to attempt to reduce greenhouse gas emissions from the transportation sector through substantial increases in mandatory fuel economy standards for future vehicle fleets. One month later, legislation that stretched to nearly 1,500 pages passed narrowly in the House of Representatives; its intent was to reduce U.S. emissions by 17 percent of 2005 levels by 2020, with more dramatic targets set for subsequent decades. The so-called American Clean Energy and Security Act would establish an exceedingly complex form of a cap-and-trade program for carbon, based loosely on earlier experience with more conventional air pollutants. This legislation included provisions to allow for the purchase of carbon offsets as an alternative to reducing emissions outright, through an elaborate system for regulating newly created carbon markets; for border tariffs to protect energy-intensive domestic industries; and for a maze of additional renewable energy and energy efficiency mandates and subsidies. The legislation stalled in the Senate, leaving its future uncertain in the remainder of the term of the 111th Congress. These domestic steps set the stage for nearly two weeks of international diplomacy in Copenhagen, in which a seeming collapse of the negotiation process was partially allayed by a last-minute agreement by a set of large national players that included a very general statement of future principles.

Despite the frenetic activity that occurred during 2009, one often-overlooked reality is that climate policy development has already been quite active in the United States, albeit at the state and local levels rather than the federal. That reflects the unique political dynamics of recent federal institutions but also a time-honored pattern for bottom-up development of U.S. public policy. In fact, many of the most prominent policy tools under consideration around the world for possible reduction of greenhouse gas emissions have their origins in one or more U.S. states and in many instances have been adopted by many other states. Mandates to increase the level of electricity derived from renewable sources are in operation in portions of nearly every continent. So-called renewable portfolio standards (RPSs), which were first developed in Iowa in 1991, are now in operation in twenty-nine states, with some presence in every region of the nation. In 2001, New Hampshire became the world's first government to enact carbon cap-and-trade legislation. That expanded into a ten-state regional network, the Regional Greenhouse Gas Initiative (RGGI), which in 2008 became the first zone in the world to auction nearly all of its carbon allowances. Some twenty-three states, concentrated in the Northeast, Pacific West, and Midwest, have committed to their own version of a regional cap-and-trade program that also includes four neighboring Canadian provinces. In 2002, California became the world's first government to enact carbon emission limits on new vehicles. It was formally joined by fourteen other states in seeking federal authority to implement its policy, and it became in effect the model for the 2009 national program on mandatory fuel economy. Wisconsin became the world's first government to mandate disclosure of carbon emissions from a wide set of sources, through an administrative change in 1993, and thirty-nine states have since negotiated the terms of a national emissions disclosure system. Local governments such as municipalities and counties have also launched far-reaching climate policy innovations.[5]

One can consider virtually every conceivable strategy to reduce greenhouse gas emissions and find one or more examples of it in operation somewhere in the U.S. federal system. Many of those efforts are modest and, as subsequent chapters suggest, many face significant implementation challenges. But collectively they demonstrate that there has been at least some degree of political will in most regions of the United States to take the initial steps in policy development. That squares with Christopher Borick's findings in chapter 2, which draw on the National Survey of American Public Opinion on Climate Change, a survey commissioned for this book that questioned more than 2,000 Americans in September 2008. Borick found strong evidence, even in very different states, that majorities of Americans considered climate change to be a serious problem, believed that both federal and state governments should respond with policies, and supported many (but not all) of a menu of policy options presented to them. A companion survey completed in late 2009 found some decline in the perceived severity of the problem since the previous year but revealed continued support for many forms of policy engagement across the different levels of government. Translating public sentiments into policy decisions and drawing careful lessons from the vast laboratory of policy experiments poses both challenges and opportunities for U.S. political leaders.

Climate Change Remains a Federalism Issue

The U.S. legacy of subnational policies gave President Barack Obama and the 111th Congress something other than a blank canvas on which to expand the federal role. On one hand, it offers innumerable models and lessons, allowing the federal government to build on the real experience of policy successes—and failures—at the state and local levels. It also ushers in the very real possibility of some formal intergovernmental sharing of responsibility for climate policy, consistent with other areas of U.S. public policy that entail joint jurisdiction. Done effectively, that could result in a creative strategy that plays to the respective strengths of the various levels of government and of policy alternatives, ultimately resulting in a dynamic federalist response to climate change. Chapter 3, by Martha Derthick, and chapter 4, by Paul Posner, explore the evolving relationship among the various levels of government, outlining points of possible contention and opportunities for building on the strengths and weaknesses of each level. A number of other chapters also consider collaborative intergovernmental strategies.

But such strategies have hardly been a hallmark of U.S. federalism in the last quarter-century, as both Derthick and Posner note. Federal engagement with states on climate change thus far has been limited, whether involving collaboration between executive agencies (as discussed by Walter Rosenbaum in chapter 12) or congressional consideration of state experience in guiding federal legislative options (as I discuss in chapter 11). Indeed, much intergovernmental interaction thus far has been adversarial, and it has required the involvement of the judiciary to try to resolve state-federal disputes, as in the 2007 *Massachusetts* v. *U.S. Environmental Protection Agency* case. The adversarial approach also is reflected in a growing body of other legal and political challenges involving an ever-expanding set of intergovernmental disputes, as explored by Kirsten Engel in chapter 10.

Any future federal effort to devise climate policy will require deft navigation between competing interests. That will invariably include collisions between proponents of competing energy sources and transportation modes as well as between representatives of different states. The odyssey of "homegrown" ethanol derived from American corn is one early indicator of likely dividing lines. Domestic ethanol production has long been propelled by generous federal subsidies and import restrictions, which were expanded into a renewable fuel mandate through 2007 federal legislation. The ethanol program has now generated enormous controversy over its actual impact on emissions as well as commodity prices, with considerable tension between various agricultural interests and consumers of transportation fuels. But there is also an increasingly tense interstate struggle, with some state leaders adamant about maintaining federal support for ethanol production while another set of governors calls for repeal of the existing policy.

The issue of biofuels looks straightforward compared with efforts to develop a national carbon cap-and-trade system, as reflected in the combat between organized interests, political parties, and regions of the nation in the months of battle that resulted in House passage of the American Clean Energy and Security Act in 2009. Even the seemingly simple task of allocating allowances was quickly transformed from a straightforward analytical task based on a measure of emissions derived from a previous annual baseline into an extraordinarily complex effort to reward allies and punish foes. Electric utilities generally got a much better deal, based on each unit of emissions released, than oil refineries, for example, but in the quest for political allies, treatment of individual sectors tended to further divide firms into net winners and losers. Even the issue of incorporating existing state cap-and-trade policies into a new national trading regime involved a unique formula that would freeze all operating state programs for five years, but only in the unlikely event that the federal regime was up and running by 2012. All of that would be revisited after the launch of the federal program, however, with the possibility of thawing out the state policies at a later time. As in this case, each and every provision of the so-called Waxman-Markey legislation that emerged in June represented a masterful political effort to accommodate key constituents and hold in place a narrow legislative majority. In the process, however, proponents produced a package with so many loopholes, and of such staggering complexity, that it was not at all clear that it would even approach its emission reduction targets in the event that the legislation were passed by the Senate and then signed into law by the president.

Regardless of the policy option considered, no two states will begin a future federal climate regime from the same starting point. Their state political leaders as well as their representatives in Congress will be increasingly forced to confront the very dramatic differences between individual states. Table 1-1 illustrates this phenomenon, considering both greenhouse gas emission trends between 1990 and 2007 and the level of state climate policy development as of 2009. The national average for emissions growth was 16 percent during that period, though it was expected to decline by about one-third by the end of the decade due to the economic contraction and the related reduction in energy use. Between 1990 and 2007, growth in state emissions ranged from a low of –5 percent in Delaware and Massachusetts and –4 percent in New York to a high of 62 percent in Arizona, 46 percent in Colorado, and 45 percent in South Carolina.[6] In the table, states

Table 1-1. *State Climate Policies and GHG Emissions Growth*

		Emissions growth, 1990–2007	
		High (>16 percent)	Low (<16 percent)
Number of policies, 2009	*High (12–20 policies)*	Arizona, Colorado, Illinois, Iowa, Maine, Minnesota, Montana, Nevada, New Hampshire, New Jersey, Oregon, Rhode Island, Utah, Vermont, Wisconsin	California, Connecticut, Delaware, Hawaii, Maryland, Massachusetts, New Mexico, New York, Pennsylvania, Texas, Washington
	Low (0–11 policies)	Alabama, Alaska, Arkansas, Florida, Georgia, Idaho, Kansas, Kentucky, Mississippi, Missouri, Nebraska, North Carolina, North Dakota, Oklahoma, South Carolina, Tennessee, Virginia	District of Columbia, Indiana, Louisiana, Michigan, Ohio, South Dakota, West Virginia, Wyoming

Sources: U.S. Environmental Protection Agency, *Inventory of U.S. Greenhouse Gas Emissions and Sinks 1990–2007*, EPA 430-R-09-004 (Washington: 2009); Barry G. Rabe, "Racing to the Top, the Bottom, or the Middle of the Pack? The Evolving State Government Role in Environmental Protection," in *Environmental Policy: New Directions for the Twenty-First Century*, edited by Norman J. Vig and Michael E. Kraft (Washington: CQ Press, 2010), p. 32.

are clustered depending on whether they are above or below the national emissions average. In turn, state engagement in climate policy varies just as dramatically. States were given a score ranging from 0 to 20 points as a proxy measure of their policy development to date based on twenty possible climate policy options established by 2009.[7] In some cases, such as California, Connecticut, Oregon, and Rhode Island, perfect or near-perfect scores are evident, reflecting extensive policy engagement. Mississippi receives the lowest score (3 points), and many Southeastern states are well below the national mean of 11 points.

Placing the fifty states into four separate cells serves to illustrate the competing state concerns and claims that state representatives are likely to carry into any debate over federal policy development and implementation.[8] In the case of California, there has been a high degree of policy engagement and the rate of emissions growth is about one-half the national average. Indeed, the state has already laid claim to national and even global preeminence on this issue, as indicated in a number of subsequent chapters. California will clearly want to be rewarded for its early actions and emissions record. In the case of Michigan, there was minimal climate policy development until 2008, making it impossible for it to seek credit for early efforts. But its emissions rate increased less than 1 percent between 1990 and 2007, due in large part to a 32 percent emissions decline in the manufacturing sector. All of that decline was registered prior to the near collapse of the auto manufacturing industry in Michigan in the final years of the 2000s, suggesting an emissions decline in that sector similar to that of Eastern European nations following the end of the cold war. Michigan's representatives in Washington will likely seek some form of credit or compensation for its emissions trend, even though realistically it had nothing to do with state policy, while also seeking maximum economic development assistance to rebuild its economy.

In contrast, many other states have experienced much higher emissions growth rates. Minnesota, for example, has experienced a 26 percent increase in emissions, although that increase has corresponded with high policy engagement, including renewable portfolio standards, pioneering efforts to price the environmental impact of carbon emissions in the electricity sector, and leadership in the Midwestern partnership designing a regional cap-and-trade program. Such a state would likely prefer to see its last decade and a half of emission trends ignored, while receiving credit for all of its policy initiatives. At the same time, another subset of states, such as Mississippi and its neighbors, is in a very different bargaining position. These states have very high emissions growth rates; high per capita emissions, reflecting intensive fossil fuel use; and little if any evidence of serious policy engagement. They would also like to overlook recent trends and may also be the most resistant to any federal engagement in this area given their potentially very high adjustment costs.

Each possible federal policy option presents a somewhat different intergovernmental challenge—and opportunity. A federal version of a renewable portfolio standard (explored by Ian Rowlands in chapter 8) is likely to present intergovernmental design challenges that are very different from those of a federal cap-and-trade program (examined by Leigh Raymond in chapter 5). Perhaps the most straightforward policy to implement on an intergovernmental basis, a carbon tax, appears likely to have the highest state and federal political opposition (a likelihood that I discuss in chapter 6 and that is reflected in the national survey findings presented in chapter 2), leading to policy options that involve a federal-state tug-of-war. The issue of preemption, whereby Washington periodically marches into a state-occupied policy area and takes the eraser to existing state efforts, would likely be received very differently in various state capitals. But that is the reality of working within a bottom-up intergovernmental system, one that is hardly unique to the United States. A similar dynamic is evident in other federal systems that have ratified Kyoto—for example, in the experiences of different Canadian provinces and Australian states. And as Henrik Selin noted, an "uneven response" is highly evident among member states of the European Union, in terms of both attainment of the emissions reductions that they pledged under Kyoto and the type and intensity of policy development.[9] So variation in the extent of policy engagement is not confined to the United States or even to formal federations.

Once Established, Climate Policy Does Not Self-Implement

Perhaps one reason that political scientists and scholars of policy implementation have played such a modest role in the climate policy debate thus far is the conventional wisdom that has emerged in recent decades asserting that market-based systems involving emissions trading would essentially self-implement upon creation. A U.S. program for trading sulfur dioxide emissions established in the 1990 Clean Air Act Amendments has been promoted repeatedly as a model to guide both domestic and international climate policy deliberations. The program—which was established for coal-burning utilities, building on some earlier experiments—is widely heralded as a success, having produced the desired emission reductions at a cost lower than anticipated and having taken advantage of the ready availability of low-sulfur coal. It has been heralded by many policy analysts as one of the great public policy breakthroughs of the modern era.[10] This case history has been trundled out repeatedly in congressional hearings in recent years, but with minimal consideration of the challenges of adapting the program to the far more numerous and complex set of sources that generate carbon dioxide.

The United States earlier carried this policy option into international negotiations leading up to Kyoto, arguing that it could be readily transferred to greenhouse gases through an international trading system. Ironically, the European Union initially balked at this strategy, although it accepted it as part of a larger bargain that it thought that it was striking with the United States.[11] The EU has since moved away from its earlier focus on carbon taxation and instead embraced the emissions trading approach, developing the EU Emission Trading System (ETS). The ETS began operation in 2005, although it left selection of policies for attaining a substantial portion of Kyoto-required reductions to the discretion of individual member states. Every recent Congress has been flooded with proposals for some variant of a carbon cap-and-trade system for the United States, including the one that was a cornerstone of the American Clean Energy and Security Act, which passed the House in June 2009 but faced substantial opposition in the Senate.

In theory, an emissions trading regime for greenhouse gases has enormous promise, even if it is an infinitely more complex undertaking than trading emissions from a limited number of sulfur dioxide sources. Early experience with this model underscores numerous challenges of policy design and implementation. In the EU ETS case, early design flaws included inadequate data on emissions and inequities in allocating emission allowances across member states, leading to considerable early controversy. ETS proponents have made significant modifications and contend that needed reforms have been made. It remains too early to discern how effective subsequent implementation will be.

As Leigh Raymond observed, there is a "daunting complexity" inherent in any such program for greenhouse gases. In the case of the Regional Greenhouse Gas Initiative in the U.S. Northeast, more than four years of careful interagency and interstate negotiations were required before the launch of initial auctioning in late 2008, with many key design elements still to be considered. RGGI, if anything, remains an "easy case," involving states with abundant experience with emissions trading, unusually close relations between neighboring states and agencies, and a focus on only the very kinds of facilities that had been covered under the sulfur dioxide trading system for nearly two decades. The Western and Midwestern versions of RGGI have set ambitious goals but have struggled to resolve basic design features, much less approach the point where they could begin implementation. Any national expansion, especially reaching beyond the RGGI target of coal-fired power plants, will be much more complicated, and most of the leading federal cap-and-trade bills that surfaced in the 111th Congress called for such broader scope. As Raymond observed, there can be a "danger of a cap-and-trade fetish," whereby a tool has been sold so aggressively that it may be tempting to look past likely problems and complexities in the rush to get something enacted.[12] That can include, for starters, such matters as compensatory offsets, leakage that makes the import of non-capped energy sources more attractive, and questions of allocating revenue generated by auctions. In many respects, a federal cap-and-trade bill would be among the most complicated pieces of legislation ever enacted by Congress, and it would also have to navigate numerous interstate differences. It remains, as Raymond noted, an intriguing and promising policy option, but will require careful consideration of numerous governance details if it is to be effective.

Proposals to tax the fossil content of fuels represent an alternative form of a market-based strategy. Like the cap-and-trade approach, carbon taxes are designed to deter consumption and hence reduce greenhouse gas emissions by increasing the cost of energy. Such an approach has long had support in the economics community and has been endorsed by a diverse group of analysts and commentators, as well as governments ranging from British Columbia to Sweden. It offers the clear advantage of relative simplicity, working from existing provisions in the federal tax code. Indeed, existing carbon tax proposals are relatively brief and remarkably simple in administrative detail, and they could go into operation almost immediately. At the same time, these taxes face steep political hurdles in that the costs are far more direct and visible than under cap-and-trade, and they might require adjustments in order to meet specific emission reduction goals given the uncertain consumer response to various prices. Ironically, carbon taxes, perhaps the most desirable approach from a policy perspective, may face the steepest climb politically, as explored in chapter 6 and in the analysis of public opinion in chapter 2.

Other climate policy options present significant implementation challenges of their own, and early experiences give one some pause. As Pietro Nivola notes in chapter 7, efforts to regulate vehicles for fuel economy (and, in effect, carbon emissions) have a very shaky track record despite decades of experience. Nivola compares the U.S. experience with that of the European Union and notes that steep taxation of transportation fuels has produced far greater fuel efficiency in the latter case, even in the continued absence of vehicle mandates. This is a sobering reminder of possible limitations facing such an approach, including President Obama's 2009 embrace on a national basis of efforts by California and like-minded states to, in effect, accelerate current vehicle fuel efficiency mandates.

Ian Rowlands observes in chapter 8 that a range of policies exists in the electricity sector to promote renewable energy and energy efficiency but that each presents different implementation challenges. The popular renewable portfolio standards, as he notes, have been "successful in catalyzing technologies and moving large-scale renewable energy projects" but have been "less successful at engaging individual or community groups" and face enormous legal and regulatory complexities. He also considers the interplay between regulatory tools such as the RPS and other policy options, such as "feed-in tariffs," which can be used to make renewable energy more cost-competitive with traditional sources but present their own governance challenges. As Marc Landy explains in chapter 9, adaptation strategies are only in their infancy but they are likely to entail many technical and ethical challenges, with very different framing depending on the region and the climate threat likely to take precedence.

Such complexities may help explain why so many governments, from nations that have ratified Kyoto to those that have set their own unilateral emission reduction targets, have failed miserably in their early efforts. Many nations that ratified Kyoto clearly will miss their pledged 2012 targets, including many EU member states whose efforts have been somewhat overshadowed by the outsized reductions achieved in Germany and the United Kingdom. Some will only begin to approach their target due to the economic collapse in the late 2000s and the attendant emissions decline, hardly a model for long-term climate policy.

In the United States, a number of individual policies have indeed succeeded, including a number of well-designed RPSs such as the one launched in Texas in 1999 and expanded in 2005. But a great many policies have struggled, with statewide as well as local targets frequently missed. For example, as highlighted in chapter 3, New Jersey issued an executive order in 1998 to reduce its emissions in accord with Kyoto targets and developed a series of policies under various governors to attempt to achieve its goals. But between 1990 and 2007, its emissions moved in the opposite direction, slightly exceeding the national rate.

Even California's 2006 statutory commitment for far-reaching emission reductions and renewable energy expansion in the coming decades has been veering in a direction that suggests that it is likely to miss early targets, despite considerable state policy expertise and broad public support for an active state response and pursuit of multiple policy options, as noted in chapter 2. A number of states have begun to follow the California model and may be heading in a similar direction. In turn, a number of state renewable portfolio standards appear unlikely to approach their mandated levels of renewable energy generation, in part due to policy design problems. Consequently, an early lesson from the past decade of experience with state climate policies is that emissions trading as well as other climate-friendly policies come with no guarantees that simply setting bold reduction targets and enacting climate legislation will reduce greenhouse gas emissions at all, much less in a timely and cost-effective manner.[13] That lesson applies with force at the federal level, where an aggressive effort to cut a deal in Congress could generate policies so loaded with exemptions and complex provisions to reward various stakeholders that they cannot be implemented over the near or long term. As a result, it is essential to give careful attention to key design elements and to establish institutions capable of effective implementation. Yet those prerequisites often get overlooked in the rush to get something through the political system when the opportunity arises.

Federal Institutions Are Not Ready for Prime Time

It may be telling that the first branch of the U.S. government to establish a clear position on climate change is the judiciary. Associate justice John Paul Stevens's opinion in *Massachusetts* v. *U.S. Environmental Protection Agency* speaks very clearly to the issues of climate science and the likely risks posed by policy inaction.[14] The decision also placed a clear set of challenges before the executive branch in revisiting its reluctance to engage with the issue. Combined with the minority opinion and the competing briefs, the outputs from this case may represent the high-water mark of federal deliberation on climate change thus far. As Kirsten Engel noted, the decision "has had some impact in terms of depoliticizing the science surrounding climate change" and thereby enabled increased focus on public policy questions.

In contrast, the executive and legislative branches have been stunningly ineffective in engaging with climate change, both in response to the Supreme Court case and more generally. The Bush EPA ran out the clock on its term and essentially evaded the Court's challenge, even going so far as to make the EPA administrator regularly unavailable for congressional hearings. And repeated Congresses have chosen to pass on the straightforward question at the heart of the 2007 case, namely whether or not the 1990 Clean Air Act Amendments were designed with sufficient elasticity to allow for inclusion of carbon dioxide. Many of the key architects of that legislative achievement remain in office, and yet Congress has remained silent. That left the Obama administration the option of a unilateral interpretation of what the legislative branch really meant. Carol Browner began that process toward the end of her tenure as EPA administrator in the 1990s without issuing a formal decision before leaving office, but she returned to the matter in her subsequent incarnation in 2009 as "climate czar." During 2009, the administration did resolve the definitional debate in declaring carbon dioxide an air pollutant. On the verge of the December 2009 Copenhagen meetings, EPA administrator Lisa Jackson issued an "endangerment finding," designating greenhouse gas emissions a human health threat, which could propel some forms of agency regulation under the umbrella of clean air legislation in the absence of new climate legislation.

Beyond these important definitional steps are sobering questions about the capacity of executive entities such as the EPA and the legislative branch to play constructive roles in coming years and decades. In the former case, Walter Rosenbaum notes in chapter 12 that EPA may well be woefully unprepared for dealing with climate change, a reflection of an agency resource base that is actually smaller in constant dollars than it was when it was cobbled together during an administrative reorganization by Richard Nixon. The agency was also formally constrained from taking a constructive role on climate change for more than a decade, whether hampered by congressional restrictions on funding in the Clinton years or by the Bush-era aversion to involving EPA staff in climate policy development internally or in collaboration with the states. Both unilateral regulatory steps through the endangerment findings and implementation of federal climate legislation would likely impose a staggering new workload, in terms of both sheer volume and technical complexity.

Moreover, the EPA continues to operate under the traditional division of environmental media into air and water as well as along the functional fault lines established at its inception, which analysts have lamented for decades as a barrier to effective performance. Ironically, as Rosenbaum notes, climate change represents "a magnitude of issues that are fundamentally different" from those that the EPA was designed to address and therefore the basic governance structure of the agency may be uniquely ill-suited for such a challenge. The agency will clearly need new resources but also new tools and skills to promote inter-unit collaboration. New agency leadership and the presidential appointment of an overarching czar may help increase its focus on climate change, but there has been no serious consideration of how EPA may need to be reconfigured to play a constructive role in dealing with the issue. All of this underscores the risks inherent in any agency-led effort to reinterpret the 1990 clean air legislation and advance a range of climate-related regulations in the event that Congress fails to act.

Beyond internal machinations within the EPA, there is the larger reality that climate change cannot be neatly compartmentalized under any single unit of the executive branch. That has been a clear lesson from the states and nations that have launched climate policies without attention to design or redesign of the institutions responsible for implementation. Many leading legislative proposals in the 110th and 111th Congresses called for sweeping collaboration between the EPA and virtually every other unit of the federal government, including the departments of energy, agriculture, transportation, commerce, and defense. They also have tended to call for the creation of a series of new institutions, many modeled on the agencies and boards that have regulated U.S. banking and finance, to oversee any transition toward an emissions trading system. These new entities have never been well-defined in legislative proposals and are all the more suspect given serious concerns about the performance of the existing financial regulatory bodies with respect to the banking and financing practices that led to the severe downturn of the economy. Collectively, that suggests that careful attention needs to be paid to the federal entities that will be responsible for any implementation of future climate policy, a task that will involve far more than simply expanding budgets and adding staff.

Thus far, Congress has shown little if any appetite for this task or the other vital challenges of climate governance. As I noted, recent Congresses have shown a proclivity to either "pass the buck, pass the pork, or pass the microphone" on climate change rather than demonstrate a serious capacity to assume a leadership role. Buck-passing has resulted in a steady pattern of failure to enact legislation that would provide a basic infrastructure for climate governance, such as an emissions disclosure system or even a definition of whether carbon dioxide is a pollutant, much less a comprehensive legislative strategy. Pork-passing is reflected in the gargantuan energy bills of 2005 and 2007, which allocated a stunning array of subsidies and incentives to every conceivable energy source; a serious assessment of the carbon impact of those bills probably is impossible (and would likely be disconcerting it if could be undertaken). In both laws, the notion of "energy independence" has provided a broad fig leaf to evade serious consideration of how best to transition to less dependence on carbon-based energy sources.[15] There is considerable risk that the provisions of the 2009 American Recovery and Reinvestment Act that have an energy and environment focus will simply move the decimal point on provisions included in the earlier bills, throwing more money at multiple sources rather than systematically pursuing the most viable paths to minimizing carbon emissions.

Microphone-passing refers not only to the staggering number of congressional hearings on climate change, with more than 200 being held in the 110th Congress alone, but to a disturbing lack of anything approaching serious deliberation over difficult climate policy choices. Congress will have to confront a series of continuing challenges if it is to play a more constructive policy development role. They include both navigating the proliferation of committees in both chambers competing for jurisdiction and avoiding a tendency to gravitate toward policy options and design elements that may be appealing to special interests but ultimately prove expensive and minimally effective in reducing greenhouse gas emissions. Previous cases of environmental and other public policies suggest that those hurdles can be cleared, but not easily. As Daniel Fiorino warned, "Environmental responsibilities at the federal level alone are so fragmented and divided up amongst so many different organizations, and the whole congressional oversight system is very fragmented, and yet climate, by definition, is an integrating problem that requires integrating responses." The first session of the 111th Congress demonstrated such characteristics. Through the American Clean Energy and Security Act, the House of Representatives indicated that it was possible to secure a majority vote in favor of a far-reaching climate bill, albeit one that posed numerous governance concerns and did not match the policy preferences of the Senate, suggesting that it faces a highly uncertain future.

The Uphill Climb to a Global Regime

Much of the scholarly and popular discourse on climate change has assumed that it would involve exclusively nation-states engaging in international bargaining that would lead to a global regime. Perhaps that assumption was based on some prior cases in international environmental policy, such as the relative success of establishing an international regime to guide the transition to reduced use of substances that endanger the earth's ozone layer. In that instance, a relatively small number of national actors worked cooperatively with key industries to forge a pact that phased out ozone-depleting substances in favor of other alternatives; they also devised mechanisms to begin to share those alternatives with emerging nations. That was indeed a great success, but it remains an anomaly in the environmental policy area; moreover, it does not translate well to the far more complicated arena of emissions of carbon dioxide and other greenhouse gases. In turn, the continued hope that "the next" international gathering of nations to debate climate governance will represent the "turning point" toward a global regime may simply be unrealistic. Indeed, the much-anticipated December 2009 Copenhagen summit appears to have followed this pattern. Despite President Obama's contention that the event produced "an unprecedented breakthrough," Copenhagen adjourned with only a vague and nonbinding agreement by five large nations on a set of future goals. There was no formal endorsement from the dozens of other participants, including the European Union, much less a clear plan for translating those goals into concrete policy steps.[16] Instead, Copenhagen simply kept alive the possibility that the issues might be more fully addressed down the road at some other international conclave, such as the 2010 version in Cancun.

Stacy VanDeveer and Henrik Selin explained the limited applicability of an international regime approach to the climate arena, at least at this stage. Instead, other kinds of multilevel governance arrangements have begun to emerge, some of which are especially promising. They often begin with ad hoc coalitions, alliances among nations in a geographic region, such as North America, or among an established network, as in various trade regimes. Fostering collaboration across national borders should build on "existing forums which actually do things," in VanDeveer's terms. That idea suggests many possible routes toward a more bottom-up approach to development of international capacity, perhaps generally following the paths taken by trade and public health policy rather than the once-anticipated "ozone blueprint." In turn, comparative analysis can yield considerable insights for the United States. Despite their divergent views on Kyoto ratification, the European Union and the United States may actually be laboratories for mutual learning with respect to policy options rather than polar extremes, as may be the case for other governmental systems that formally divide powers, such as Australia, Canada, and India.

Plan of the Book

The subsequent chapters in this volume, which develop these themes in greater detail, are divided into four parts. Part 1 helps frame the climate change issue in the U.S. context. Chapter 2, Christopher Borick's analysis of key findings from the 2008 and 2009 versions of the National Survey of American Public Opinion on Climate Change, devotes particular attention to public views of the roles of different levels of government in climate change policy and public receptivity to many policy options, including those explored in individual chapters in part 2. Chapters 3 and 4 present distinct analyses of federalism issues, by Martha Derthick and Paul Posner respectively. Derthick develops the idea of "compensatory federalism," considering the respective strengths and weaknesses of the federal and state governments in evaluating the bottom-up nature of climate policy development that has dominated in the United States thus far. Posner follows with an analysis of methods of "vertical diffusion," the process whereby a policy area initially dominated by states ultimately shifts toward either a balanced intergovernmental role or federal domination through preemption. He examines a range of previous environmental policy cases and considers them as possible models for climate change policy.

That sets the stage for part 2, five chapters that consider a series of leading climate policy options. Some of the chapters focus on a specific policy tool, such as the cap-and-trade model, whereas others explore options within an entire sector, such as alternative methods for promoting renewable energy. Chapters 5 and 6 consider a pair of market-based options: Leigh Raymond examines the cap-and-trade issue, and I explore carbon taxes. Both of these tools involve some effort to use pricing mechanisms to allow adjustments to a more carbon-constrained society, though they use very different methods and seem to have somewhat varied levels of political support. The two subsequent chapters focus on options that would tend to fall into the realm of "command-and-control"–type approaches. In chapter 7, Pietro Nivola navigates "the long and winding road" of U.S. experimentation with setting federal standards for vehicle fuel efficiency. He notes many ways in which this policy has only marginally reduced fuel consumption and greenhouse gas emissions, and he is fairly skeptical of the likely impact of the 2007 or 2009 federal expansions of the program. In chapter 8, Ian Rowlands reviews renewable portfolio standards and a range of subsidy programs to expand the supply of renewable electricity. He draws on the considerable experience in the U.S. states and around the world and also explores variants on this approach, such as "feed-in tariffs," which guarantee a long-term price to providers of renewable energy. In chapter 9, Marc Landy concludes part 2 by exploring an increasingly salient consideration in climate policy: shifting from mitigating greenhouse gas emissions toward adapting to their consequences. Such a strategy would entail a very different set of policy challenges and responses to climate change as it plays out in coming years. Landy does not dismiss mitigation efforts, but his chapter underscores another key dimension of climate policy: the likely need to adjust to a climate that is already changing and is likely to do so to varying degrees regardless of near-term reductions in emissions.

Part 3 considers the capacity of the three branches of the federal government to assume an expanding role in addressing climate change. Although each chapter focuses on a federal institution, each takes account of intergovernmental considerations, given the inevitable interaction of the federal and state governments. In chapter 10, Kirsten Engel provides an extensive review of existing climate litigation, including *Massachusetts v. U.S. Environmental Protection Agency*, the prominent Supreme Court case noted previously. She demonstrates that much of the expanding body of cases that have some degree of climate content involves substantive differences between state, federal, and local governments. She also offers an examination of the varying types and amount of litigation that might be anticipated in response to alternative climate policies if they are adopted. In chapter 11, I explore Congress, which, after decades of inertia, began to take center stage in formulating federal climate policy in 2009. I review the many impediments to congressional deliberation and decisionmaking—some with particular salience to the issue of climate change—which cross many social and economic boundaries as well as the lines that demarcate the turf of individual congressional committees and subcommittees. In chapter 12 Walter Rosenbaum examines the Environmental Protection Agency, a federal body that Congress repeatedly harangues in public hearings but that is likely to be assigned a pivotal role in the implementation of future climate legislation. Rosenbaum refrains from the popular sport of EPA-bashing but notes the woeful lack of resources and support that the agency has received from Congress to prepare for what may be its greatest challenge in four decades of operation. He also raises sobering questions about the preparedness of other key bureaucratic players on climate, such as the Department of Energy. The chapters on both Congress and the EPA note enormous intergovernmental divides and tensions, indicating potential collisions between early-mover states and federal institutions that enter the game belatedly but with considerable clout.

Part 4 considers ways in which the United States might "reconnect with the world" after the fallout over Kyoto, the failure to achieve major agreements in Copenhagen, and extended U.S. conflict with other nations over climate change. Stacy VanDeveer and Henrik Selin team up for a pair of chapters that consider alternative models that might constitute building blocks for U.S. re-engagement and movement toward greater multinational and international collaboration. They also draw heavily on experience from outside the United States, most notably in the European Union, in considering possible lessons for U.S. (and North American) leadership on the world stage. Collectively, these four sections set the stage for the concluding chapter, which reflects on early developments in the Obama administration and the 111th Congress. The final chapter also returns to the key themes introduced above with a brief set of recommendations to guide future policy development in the area of climate change and environmental governance.

Notes

1. William Nordhaus, *A Question of Balance: Weighing the Options on Global Warming Policies* (Yale University Press, 2008), p. 62.

2. Carlos Pascual and Evie Zambetakis, "The Geopolitics of Energy: From Security to Survival," in *Energy Security: Economics, Politics, Strategies, and Implications*, edited by Carlos Pascual and Jonathan Elkind (Brookings, 2010), p. 23.

3. This is a direct quotation of a comment at the National Conference on Climate Governance, held at the Miller Center of Public Affairs, University of Virginia, December 11–12, 2008. All subsequent quotes in this chapter from authors in this volume are drawn from comments that they made at the conference rather than in their respective chapters.

4. As Robert M. White, administrator of the National Oceanic and Atmospheric Administration, wrote to George W. Humphreys, associate director of the Domestic Policy Council, in July 1976, "I still believe that we need to undertake a lot more work on climate problems." I am grateful to David Horrocks, chief archivist of the Gerald R. Ford Presidential Library, for introducing me to this exchange.

5. This book focuses primarily on the state and federal levels, given their broad constitutional powers in policy design and implementation. Attention is given to local issues as appropriate in some chapters. For a broad overview of the evolving local government role in the United States and Canada, see Christopher Gore and Pamela Robinson, "Local Government Response to Climate Change: Our Last, Best Hope?" in *Changing Climates in North American Politics*, edited by Henrik Selin and Stacy VanDeveer (MIT Press, 2009), pp. 137–58.

6. Environmental Protection Agency, *Inventory of U.S. Greenhouse Gas Emissions and Sinks, 1990–2007*, EPA 430-R-09-004 (Washington: 2009).

7. Barry G. Rabe, "Racing to the Top, the Bottom, or the Middle of the Pack? The Evolving State Government Role in Environmental Protection," in *Environmental Policy: New Directions for the Twenty-First Century*, edited by Norman J. Vig and Michael E. Kraft (Washington: CQ Press, 2010), p. 32.

8. An earlier version of this discussion appears in Barry G. Rabe, "States on Steroids: The Intergovernmental Odyssey of American Climate Change Policy," *Review of Policy Research* 25, no. 2 (March 2008), pp. 105–28.

9. This is a direct quotation of a comment at the National Conference on Climate Governance.

10. The program and the expansive literatures that examine it are explored in Dallas Burtraw and Karen Palmer, "SO_2 Cap-and-Trade Program in the United States: A 'Living Legend' of Market Effectiveness," in *Choosing Environmental Policy: Comparing Instruments and Outcomes in the United States and Europe*, edited by Winston Harrington, Richard D. Morgenstern, and Thomas Sterner (Washington: Resources for the Future Press, 2004), pp. 41–66.

11. For an excellent analysis of the evolving U.S. and European positions on climate change over multiple decades, see Loren Cass, *The Failure of American and European Climate Change Policy* (State University of New York Press, 2006).

12. This is a direct quotation of a comment at the National Conference on Climate Governance.

13. In one early effort to analyze the performance of state and local climate policies that emerged from broad commissions or planning processes, numerous problems were identified in achieving pledged reductions or moving successfully from policy design into policy implementation. See Stephen M. Wheeler, "State and Municipal Climate Change Plans: The First Generation," *Journal of the American Planning Association* 74, no. 4 (September 2008), pp. 481–96.

14. As the majority opinion noted, "The harms associated with climate change are serious and well recognized. The Government's own objective assessment of the relevant science and a strong consensus among qualified experts indicate that global warming threatens . . . a precipitate rise in sea levels, severe and irreversible changes to natural ecosystems, a significant reduction in winter snowpack with direct and important economic consequences, and increases in the spread of disease and the ferocity of winter events."

15. Pietro S. Nivola, "Rethinking 'Energy Independence,'" *Governance Studies at Brookings* (December 30, 2008).

16. John M. Broder, "Many Goals Remain Unmet in 5 Nations' Climate Deal," *New York Times,* December 19, 2009.

2

American Public Opinion and Climate Change

CHRISTOPHER P. BORICK

Within the realm of democratic political systems, the relationship between public opinion and public policy is of paramount interest. At its core, democracy is a mechanism to translate the wants of citizens into public policy. While factors besides citizens' desires may indeed influence government actions, there is little debate that the public's preferences should play the preeminent role in determining the behavior of government institutions. As the issue of global warming has emerged as one of the most significant challenges facing policymakers both in the United States and abroad, it has become increasingly important to understand the attitudes and beliefs of citizens regarding this issue.

This chapter examines American public opinion on global warming from a number of perspectives. After a brief discussion of the literature on the effect of public opinion on public policy, the chapter explores public acceptance of the phenomenon of global warming through an examination of polling data over the past two decades. Data are presented from the 2008 and 2009 National Surveys of American Public Opinion on Climate Change, which explore the underlying factors determining individual belief and disbelief in global warming. Attention then turns to public perceptions of the role of government in addressing climate change, including preferences regarding governance within the U.S. federal system. Finally, support for various policy options to address climate change is examined, with additional attention given to the public's willingness to pay for efforts to reduce global warming.

The Relationship between Public Opinion and Public Policy

The role of public opinion in shaping government policies has always been a central interest in the field of political science. Given the theoretical importance of responsive government within the framework of a democratic system, it should not be surprising to see considerable scholarly attention paid to this matter. It should also be fairly reassuring to proponents of democratic rule that many national-level studies have shown that public policies do reflect the views of the broader electorate.[1] Indeed, there is now little debate within the field of political science about whether or not public opinion affects public policy. Instead, contemporary questions of value focus on the degree to which the preferences of the people shape the outputs of government and the conditions under which government is most responsive.

While there is a general consensus that public opinion does affect government action, the relationship between opinion and policy within particular policy areas is less clear. A central question is whether public attitudes and beliefs regarding environmental issues play a role in shaping government efforts to address environmental matters. In their article on the determinants of environmental attitudes, Johnson, Brace, and Arceneux find evidence that public support for increased efforts to protect the environment are related to the adoption of environmental policies in at least the area of water quality protection and that public opinion on this matter is also shaped by existing environmental conditions and previous policy efforts.[2]

While their article provides the clearest evidence of a relationship between environmental perspectives and policy output, it suffers from some of the same limitations as other efforts to isolate the impact of public opinion on public policy. More specifically, the lack of refined measures of public opinion requires the use of very general approximations of public support for environmental protection efforts. In the Johnson, Brace, and Arceneux study, the measure of public support for increased government efforts to protect the environment was pooled data from a national survey that asked respondents to rate their level of agreement with the statement "I support pollution standards even if it means shutting down some factories." That measure was then compared to an index of state water policy interventions in order to ascertain the relationship between opinion and policy. Although valuable in demonstrating the general relationships between public preferences and policy adoption in the area of environmental protection, the very general nature of the measures raises questions about the actual correlation between opinion and policy. For example, does support for pollution standards in general correspond with equal support for the various spheres of environmental protection, such as those pertaining to air, land, and water?

Of particular interest in this chapter is the connection between pubic opinion regarding global warming and the level of effort that states have made to address

climate change. As with other areas of public policy, the ability to connect attitudes with policy output on the issue of global warming has been limited by the
paucity of comparable state-level opinion research on the topic. While there is a
growing body of research on the attitudes and beliefs of Americans in general
regarding global warming,[3] very little effort has been made to measure the opinions of individuals at the state level. And as is often the case, the few studies that
have focused on state-level opinion on global warming have focused only on a single state, thus making direct comparison impossible.[4]

    To address the absence of comparable state-level data on public opinion regard-
ing global warming, the 2008 National Survey of American Public Opinion on
Climate Change (NSAPOCC) involved both national and state-level samples. In
2008 this project surveyed more than 2,000 Americans on the subject of global
warming and energy policy, with samples of at least 300 residents in four states:
California; Virginia; Pennsylvania; and Mississippi (a full methodological statement can be found in appendix 2A). These states were chosen because of their
extremely varied levels of effort in the areas of global warming policy and alternative energy development. As highlighted in numerous ways throughout this volume, California has consistently been a national leader in climate and energy policy, often developing pathbreaking policy alternatives in these areas. While not as
active as California, Pennsylvania has emerged as one of the more progressive states
in requiring alternative energy use. Virginia has been slow to act on the issue of climate change and renewable energy development but has taken tentative steps to
increase its efforts in this area during recent years. Finally, Mississippi has been
among the least active states in the areas of climate and energy policy, having
undertaken very few substantial initiatives. This substantial variation in policy
effort across states and the corresponding state-level public opinion data provide
added insight into the nexus between public opinion and public policy in the
realm of climate and energy policy.

    In 2009 many of the questions from the 2008 NSAPOCC were repeated in a
canvass of nearly 1,000 Americans in a national sample. The findings from the
2009 survey were beneficial in capturing changes in national attitudes toward
global warming in a year in which Congress became more active in considering
climate policy, the world considered action on global warming at the United
Nations Climate Change Conference in Copenhagen, and the national and world
economies were mired in a deep recession. Throughout this chapter, both the
2008 and 2009 NSAPOCC, along with results from other national surveys, are
used to paint a picture of where Americans stand on the issues of global warming,
alternative energy, and myriad policy options related to climate policy in the
United States.

Public Perceptions of Global Warming

What do Americans know about global warming, and how concerned are they about the issue? Those questions underlie any effort to understand the broader role that public opinion has in shaping climate policy in the United States. For opinion to play a meaningful role in leading government to action, it must be broad-based and display at least a moderate degree of intensity. If only a few citizens care about an issue and their attachment to the issue is not very strong, the likelihood of government action on that issue is low.[5] Therefore, any examination of the effect of public opinion on government efforts to address global warming should start with an analysis of public awareness of the problem and the level of public concern regarding the impacts of climate change.

When global warming first emerged as an issue during the 1980s, the public reaction was fairly limited. In 1986 only 4 in 10 Americans acknowledged having heard about "the greenhouse effect," or global warming. However, after the record-setting heat and drought of the summer of 1988, along with the massive fires in Yellowstone National Park, 7 in 10 Americans reported that they had heard of this issue. By the time of the Earth Summit in 1992, the percentage of Americans who knew about global warming had surpassed 80 percent, and in the most recent surveys, researchers found that 9 in 10 Americans had heard about this phenomenon (see table 2-1).[6]

Interestingly, while Americans have become increasingly aware of the concept of global warming, their comprehension of the problem has grown more slowly. Since 1992, the Gallup Organization has been polling individuals in the United States to determine how well they understand the issue of global warming.[7] The survey results indicate that there has been slow growth in the percentage of Americans who feel that they understand global warming, with the percentage who claim that they understand the issue "very well" growing from 11 percent to only 21 percent between 1992 and 2008, as reflected in table 2-2.

A related and crucial element of public opinion on global warming is whether the public believes that global warming is actually occurring. As the issue has evolved over the past two decades, there has been significant debate in the public forum regarding the reality of the phenomenon. While the scientific community has become more uniform in its acceptance of anthropogenic (human-induced) climate change, debates within the political realm and the media have continued. As shown in table 2-3, the 2008 NSAPOCC found that more than 7 in 10 Americans believed that there is solid evidence that the earth is warming.[8] However, the 2009 version of the survey revealed a 6 percent drop, with only 66 percent of Americans indicating that they believe that the planet has been warming over the past four decades. Other 2009 national surveys (ABC News/Washington Post, Pew Research Center, and Gallup) found a similar decline in level of belief. Those

Table 2-1. *Percent of Americans Who Have Heard of the Greenhouse Effect or Global Warming, by Year*

Year	Percent
1986	39
1989	68
1992	82
2000	89
2006	91

Source: 1986, 1989, and 1992 surveys from Cambridge; 2000 survey from Harris; 2006 survey from Pew, compiled in Teresa Myers and Matthew C. Nisbet, "Trends: Twenty Years and Public Opinion about Global Warming," *Public Opinion Quarterly* 71, no. 3 (Fall 2007).

Table 2-2. *Responses to "How Well Do You Understand the Issue of Global Warming?" by Year*

Percent responding

Response	1992	1997	2002	2007	2008
Very well	11	16	17	22	21
Fairly well	42	45	52	54	59
Not very well/not at all	44	38	31	23	20
No opinion	3	1	<1	<1	<1

Source: Gallup Organization, "Did Hollywood's Glare Heat Up Public Concern about Global Warming?" March 21, 2007 (www.gallup.com/poll/26932/Did-Hollywoods-Glare-Heat-Public-Concern-About-Global-Warming.aspx).

Table 2-3. *Responses to "Is There Solid Evidence That the Earth Is Warming?" by Survey and Year*

Percent responding

Response	Yes	No	Not sure
Pew June 2006	70	20	10
Pew Jan 2007	77	17	6
Pew April 2008	71	21	8
NSAPOCC September 2008	72	17	11
Pew October 2009	57	33	10
NSAPOCC November 2009	66	20	14

Source: Pew Research Center, "A Deeper Partsian Divide over Global Warming," May 8, 2008 (http://people-press.org/report/417/a-deeper-partisan-divide-over-global-warming); NSAPOCC.

Table 2-4. *Responses to "Is There Solid Evidence That the Earth Is Warming?"
for the Nation and Selected States*

Percent responding

Sample	Yes	No	Not sure
Nation	72	17	11
Pennsylvania	69	16	15
Virginia	75	13	12
Mississippi	69	16	14
California	74	12	13

Source: NSAPOCC, 2008.

findings suggest that while a majority of Americans continue to believe that global warming is real, public opinion on the matter remains unsettled.

While public opinion nationwide remains unstable, the 2008 NSAPOCC found that belief in the warming of the planet is fairly consistent across various regions of the United States. More specifically, residents from four different states (Virginia, California, Mississippi, and Pennsylvania) maintained very similar views on the issue of global warming, with about 7 in 10 residents in those states indicating their belief that the earth's temperature is rising. Given the fairly significant economic, social, and political differences across these states, the regional consistency of public opinion on the existence of global warming is noteworthy (see table 2-4).

While there is a substantial and widespread belief in global warming among Americans, there is significant variation in their views on the underlying factors. For most individuals who believe in global warming, the activities of humans play at least a partial role. The 2008 and 2009 NSAPOCC national surveys found that a large majority of Americans who believed in global warming attributed the increased temperatures either completely to anthropogenic activities or to a combination of human activities and natural cycles. Less than 1 in 5 of those who believed in global warming attributed the environmental changes to natural causes entirely. These findings are generally consistent with Stanford/ABC surveys in 2006 and 2007 that indicate that a substantial majority of believers in global warming attribute climate change at least in part to the activities of humans (table 2-5).[9]

As Americans have increasingly acknowledged that climate change is human-induced, there has been significant growth in their level of concern regarding global warming. But unlike awareness of and belief in the phenomenon itself, which increased fairly gradually, concern regarding climate change increased sharply over a one-year period. A comparison of polls conducted jointly by the *Washington Post*, ABC News, and Stanford University in 2006 and 2007 found an increase of more than double the number (16 percent to 33 percent) of Americans who identified global warming as the biggest environmental threat facing the world.[10]

Table 2-5. *Perceived Causes of Global Warming, by Year and Survey*[a]

Percent responding

Year and survey	Things people do	Natural causes	About equal
2006 ABC News/Washington Post/Stanford	31	19	49
2007 ABC News/Washington Post/Stanford	41	17	42
2008 NSAPOCC	36	18	41
2009 NSAPOCC	36	12	51

Source: ABC News/*Washington Post*/Stanford University, "Concern Soars about Global Warming as World's Top Environmental Threat," April 20, 2007 (http://woods.stanford.edu/docs/surveys/Global-Warming-2007-ABC-News-Release.pdf); NSAPOCC.

a. Responses only of those who believe in global warming.

Similarly, the 2008 and 2009 NSAPOCC results indicate that Americans who believe that global warming is occurring also feel that it is a serious problem. As reflected in table 2-6, more than 9 in 10 residents of the United States who believe that the planet is warming consider the increase in temperatures to be a very serious or somewhat serious problem. (However, the survey results do show a decline in the number of those believing that global warming is a very serious problem, with 60 percent holding that view in 2008 but only 51 percent in 2009.) Yet while there are some differences across states in terms of public perception of the severity of the problem, majorities from states as diverse as California and Mississippi persist in their belief that global warming is a pressing issue facing the nation.

Although a majority of Americans indicate that they are concerned about the impact of global warming, public understanding of the scientific basis of the phenomenon appears to be less developed. The General Social Survey (GSS) presented almost 3,000 Americans with true and false statements regarding the sci-

Table 2-6. *Public Perceptions of the Seriousness of Global Warming for the Nation and Selected States*[a]

Percent responding

Sample	Very serious	Somewhat serious	Not too serious	Not a problem	Not sure
Nation 2008	60	32	5	2	<1
Nation 2009	51	40	8	<1	<1
Pennsylvania 2008	52	38	6	2	2
Virginia 2008	61	28	6	4	1
Mississippi 2008	56	32	6	3	2
California 2008	73	20	4	2	2

Source: NSAPOCC, 2008 and 2009.

a. Responses only of those who believe in global warming.

Table 2-7. *Public Perceptions of the Causes of the Greenhouse Effect, 2000*
Percent responding

Cause	Definitely true	Probably true	Probably not true	Definitely not true	Cannot choose
"Every time we use coal or oil or gas, we contribute to the greenhouse effect."	18	44	19	5	15
"The greenhouse effect is caused by a hole in the earth's atmosphere."	17	37	18	12	16

Source: National Opinion Research Center, "General Social Survey," 2000 (www.norc.org/GSS+ Website/).

entific underpinnings of global warming, shown in table 2-7. The results from the 2000 GSS[11] (the last in which these statements were included) found that most Americans (62 percent) correctly responded that the use of coal, oil, and gas contributes to the greenhouse effect. However, a majority (54 percent) incorrectly attributed the greenhouse effect to a hole in the earth's atmosphere. The dated nature of the data may not reflect current public awareness of the scientific arguments for climate change, but the responses demonstrate considerable misperceptions nationwide regarding global warming.

Thus, public opinion research in the United States paints a picture of a nation that generally acknowledges the existence and perils associated with a global increase in temperatures despite some misperceptions about the issue.[12] What has *not* been fully explored, however, are the reasons underlying that belief, along with what levels of government should be responsible for addressing the problem.

The Determinants of Belief in Global Warming

As indicated, most Americans not only believe in global warming but also view it as a serious threat. That belief is quite important in terms of its potential impact on the political process, yet it remains unclear what facts or evidence are responsible for the position of most residents of the United States on this matter. As in many areas of public opinion, there are underlying demographic factors that appear to affect the likelihood that an individual believes in global warming. As can be seen in table 2-8, factors such as gender, age, educational attainment, and race have a moderate effect on an individual's belief; in general, being younger, college-educated, female, and nonwhite marginally increases the likelihood that an American believes that global temperatures are increasing. However, by far the strongest factor in predicting belief in global warming is partisan affiliation. Self-identified Democrats are significantly more likely than Republicans to believe that the average temperature on earth is getting warmer,

Table 2-8. *Responses to "Is There Solid Evidence That the Average Temperature on Earth Has Been Increasing over the Past Four Decades?" by Demographic Group*
Percent responding

Group	Yes	No	Not sure
Overall	66	20	14
Male	66	23	11
Female	66	17	17
White	61	25	14
Nonwhite	78	8	14
18–44	68	17	15
45–64	68	20	13
65+	56	29	15
Democrat	80	6	14
Republican	49	36	15
Independent	61	25	14
College graduate	67	20	13
Not college graduate	64	20	15

Source: NSAPOCC, 2009.

with politically independent Americans positioned between their partisan counterparts on this issue.

While table 2-8 provides a glimpse into the correlates of belief in global warming, it does not provide insight into the reasons for individuals' views on the issue. In particular, there has been very little research to examine what arguments have been most persuasive in convincing individuals that global warming is actually occurring. Thus, the 2008 NSAPOCC included a battery of questions that asked respondents why they believe in the phenomenon. Among the questions was an open-ended query in which respondents were asked to identify the primary reason for their belief that temperatures on earth are increasing. The results show that Americans give three reasons as most responsible for their belief in global warming. About 1 in 5 individuals who believed that the planet is warming indicated that the melting of glaciers and polar ice has had the largest role in establishing their views on the matter, while another 1 in 5 identified personal observations of warmer temperatures in their local communities as the biggest reason for their belief. Just under one-fifth of Americans cited changing weather patterns and more intense storms as the key reasons for their beliefs. A full breakdown of the reasons identified is given in table 2-9.

As reflected in table 2-10, when individuals were asked to indicate the impact of various events on their belief in global warming, a similar trend was observed. Declines in glaciers and polar ice and warmer local temperatures were among the issues most strongly identified as affecting individual beliefs on the subject. Individuals also noted weather events and patterns, such as severe droughts and hurricanes, as having a strong impact on their acceptance of the phenomenon.

Table 2-9. *Responses to "What Is the Primary Factor That Has Caused You to Believe That Temperatures on Earth Are Increasing?"*

Factor	Percent responding
Melting glaciers and polar ice	19
Warmer local temperatures/personal observation	19
Changing weather patterns/stronger storms	18
Media coverage/literature on the issue	15
Scientific research	9
Al Gore documentary	2
Pollution/human activity	4
Declining species	<1
Natural patterns	<1
Not sure/no specific reason	12
Other	<1

Source: NSAPOCC, 2008.

The results of the 2008 state-level NSAPOCC, however, indicated a number of significant differences in terms of the factors that led individuals across the nation to believe in climate change. For example, residents of Mississippi were significantly more likely than the national average to report that the strength of hurricanes hitting the United States had a strong effect on their beliefs, which might be expected given the recent history of large hurricanes on the Gulf Coast. Similarly, residents of states such as California and Mississippi, which have been hit with severe droughts in recent years, were much more likely than the national average to cite droughts as a strong reason for their belief in a warming planet. Conversely, Mississippi residents were less likely than the national average to note

Table 2-10. *Factors Strongly Affecting Individual Belief in Global Warming for the Nation and Selected States*
Percent responding

Factor	Nation	Pennsylvania	Virginia	Mississippi	California
Declining glaciers and polar ice	63	58	63	48	68
Warmer temperatures in your area	42	37	39	56	44
Computer models that indicate warming	30	31	30	23	32
Strength of hurricanes	47	50	46	64	51
Al Gore documentary	21	22	20	17	30
Milder winters in your area	36	45	40	54	29
Declining numbers of polar bears	40	42	35	34	44
Severe droughts in areas of the United States	47	49	45	55	58

Source: NSAPOCC, 2008.

Table 2-11. *Responses to "My State Has Already Felt Negative Effects Attributable to Global Warming," 2008 and 2009*

Percent responding

Response	2008	2009
Strongly agree	28	16
Somewhat agree	27	30
Somewhat disagree	12	19
Strongly disagree	17	15
Not sure	16	19

Source: NSAPOCC, 2008 and 2009.

that computer models strongly affected their belief in global warming, while Californians were more likely than other Americans to claim that Al Gore's documentary *An Inconvenient Truth* had a major impact on their views about the reality of climate change.

The strong impact of individual experience in shaping public perceptions of global warming can also be observed in table 2-11, which shows the percentage of Americans who feel that their state is already feeling its negative effects. In 2008, 55 percent of the American adult population believed that their state has seen negative effects of the trend; however, that number dropped to 46 percent in 2009. As noted earlier, we found that personal experiences with hotter temperatures in a respondent's home community were among the most important factors in determining belief in global warming. Thus the decline in the percentage of Americans who strongly believe that their state has already experienced global warming effects may be contributing to the lower percentage of those believing that the planet is warming.

Although a majority of Americans now believe in global warming, about 1 in 5 do not. In the 2008 NSAPOCC, respondents who did not were asked the primary reason for their beliefs, and 4 in 10 cited their personal observations of stable temperatures. In addition, 19 percent of individuals who did not believe in global warming cited a belief that any warming reflects natural fluctuations and not a long-term trend (see table 2-12). Thus, as with those who believe in global warming, personal experience appears to be an important driver of disbelief regarding this phenomenon.

The 2008 and 2009 NSAPOCC further examined the factors that determined public attitudes toward climate change through a series of statements with which respondents could agree or disagree. The statements were drawn from media accounts that portrayed different controversies that have arisen in U.S. and international deliberations over climate change. To further refine public sentiment, each was a declarative statement about some aspect of global warming. The findings in each cell of table 2-13 reflect the 2009 results, with the 2008 data included

Table 2-12. Primary Factor for Disbelief of Individuals Who Do Not Believe in Global Warming

Factor	Percent responding
Personal observations	42
Natural patterns explain change	19
Not enough scientific evidence	11
Evidence that disproves global warming	8
No particular reason	5
Media has misled the public	3
Other reason	12

Source: NSAPOCC, 2008.

below in parentheses. In most cases, respondents were less likely to "strongly disagree" with statements that questioned the validity of global warming in 2009 than they were in 2008. The results indicate a modest increase in skepticism regarding the evidence and the role of scientists. For example, a comparison of survey results from both years shows that Americans were less likely to disagree with the statement that "there is not enough scientific evidence to support claims

Table 2-13. Responses to Various Statements on Climate Change, 2008 and 2009[a]

Percent responding

Statement	Strongly agree	Somewhat agree	Somewhat disagree	Strongly disagree	Not sure
"There is not enough scientific evidence to support claims that the earth is getting warmer."	19 (20)	23 (18)	24 (19)	29 (39)	6 (4)
"Scientists are overstating evidence about global warming for their own interests."	17 (19)	25 (19)	20 (20)	29 (38)	8 (5)
"Any recent warming on earth is the result of natural trends and not the activities of man."	16 (21)	27 (19)	25 (22)	26 (31)	6 (8)
"The media are overstating the evidence about global warming."	27 (24)	22 (22)	20 (20)	27 (31)	5 (4)
"Instead of trying to stop global warming from occurring we should focus on adapting to a warmer climate."[b]	10	21	25	36	9

Source: NSAPOCC, 2008 and 2009.

a. Results for 2008 are in parentheses.

b. Statement was not included in the 2008 survey.

Table 2-14. *Agreement with Various Statements on Global Warming,*
by Respondent's View on Global Warming
Percent responding

Statement	Respondent believes in global warming	Respondent does not believe in global warming
"There is not enough evidence to support claims that the earth is getting warmer."	23	92
"Scientists are overstating evidence about global warming for their own interest."	26	83
"Any recent warming on earth is the result of natural trends and not the activity of man."	27	84
"The media are overstating the evidence about global warming."	32	94

Source: NSAPOCC, 2009.

that the earth is getting warmer." Similarly, Americans were less likely to disagree that "scientists are overstating evidence about global warming for their own interests" than they were in 2008. It is important to note that this increased skepticism was measured before the e-mail hacking incident known as "Climategate" became widely publicized in December 2009.

Table 2-14 reflects agreement with various statements by individuals who believe in global warming and by those who do not. While a plurality of Americans disagreed with all of the statements presented in the table, there appears to be a very significant difference between the two categories. More specifically, among U.S. residents who did not believe that the earth is warming, there were high levels of "agreement" with the various statements presented to them. Conversely, relatively few Americans who believe in global warming offered strong agreement with any of these statements regarding climate issues.

Public Attitudes Regarding the Role of Government

With the American public's growing acceptance of the reality of global warming and its threats to the nation, greater attention has been given to the role of government in addressing the problem. As noted, about 2 in 3 Americans now believe in global warming, and among them there is strong support for immediate government action to address the problem. The 2008 NSAPOCC shows that 70 percent of Americans who believe in global warming feel that the issue requires an immediate government response. Although there is generally high support for government action across key demographic groups, such as those defined by gender, race, age, and educational attainment, there are significant differences in support for government intervention across party affiliations. As shown in table 2-15, among individ-

Table 2-15. *Responses to "Does Global Warming Require Immediate Government Action?" by Demographic Group*
Percent responding

Group	Yes	No	Not sure
Overall	70	20	10
Republican	49	44	7
Democrat	83	12	6
Independent	67	20	13
Male	68	24	8
Female	71	18	12
White	67	24	9
Nonwhite	75	13	12
College educated	70	22	8
Not college educated	70	18	12
18–44	75	18	8
45–64	70	20	10
65 and older	64	24	12

Source: NSAPOCC, 2008.

uals who acknowledge the existence of global warming, there is a 34 percent difference between Democrats and Republicans in terms of their preference for immediate government action to address climate change, and Independents are almost perfectly situated between them. When combined with the results in table 2-8, which demonstrate a strong partisan divide in terms of belief in climate change, the prominent role of partisanship in this policy area is clearly observable.

The fairly extensive level of support for immediate government action to address global warming does not necessarily imply unconditional support for government intervention, however. The various forms of action that are available to the government may entail significant costs to individuals, and therefore public support for government efforts may be considered conditional. The Program on International Policy Attitudes (PIPA) asked Americans to reveal their preferences on government action to address global warming given certain conditions.[13] The PIPA survey results presented in table 2-16 reveal that in 2005, while about 3 in 4 Americans preferred government action to address increasing temperatures on earth, the costs of the various actions significantly affected their preferences. Although 34 percent of Americans wanted government to take immediate actions to address global warming even if those actions involved significant costs, 42 percent preferred gradual steps entailing lower costs. Only 1 in 5 Americans indicated that they would oppose any actions to address climate change that entailed economic costs.

While previous public opinion research has shown that the American public supports at least some degree of government action to mitigate global warming,

Table 2-16. *Preferences for Government Policy to Address Global Warming, by Various Years*

Percent responding

Policy	1998	2004	2005
"Government should begin taking steps now even if it involves significant costs."	39	31	34
"Government should address global warming by taking steps that are low in cost."	44	45	42
"Government should not take any steps to address global warming that would have economic costs."	15	23	21
Not sure	2	1	2

Source: Program on International Policy Attitudes, "Americans on Climate Change," July 5, 2005 (www.worldpublicopinion.org/pipa/articles/btenvironmentra/79.php?lb=brusc&pnt=79&nid=&id=).

there has been scant evidence regarding the public's preferences for which levels of government should be involved in doing so. A number of studies in 2007 and 2008 have shown that residents of Michigan, Pennsylvania, California, Florida, and Virginia believe that their states should be active in addressing the issue of climate change,[14] and the 2009 NSAPOCC provided additional insight into the American public's perceptions of the relative responsibility of governments within the U.S. federal system in dealing with global warming. The results show that the public places the largest responsibility for dealing with climate change in the hands of the federal government, but it also places substantial responsibility on both state and local governments. Only 10 percent of Americans indicated that state governments had no responsibility for dealing with global warming, while just 14 percent stated that local governments were devoid of responsibility on this matter (see table 2-17).

Since the late 1990s, state governments have taken the lead in many areas of climate and energy policy, as is discussed in chapter 1. From the development of

Table 2-17. *Public Perceptions of Government Responsibility for Addressing Global Warming, by Level of Government*

Percent responding

Level of government	A great deal of responsibility	Some responsibility	No responsibility	Not sure
Federal	55	31	10	4
State	37	49	10	4
Local	34	47	14	6

Source: NSAPOCC, 2009.

renewable energy requirements to the adoption of energy efficiency goals, state governments have directly addressed the underlying causes of climate change. However, there has been substantial debate surrounding their efforts, focused on both the economic impact of unilateral state initiatives to reduce greenhouse emissions and the relationship between state and federal government policies in this area. Critics of state efforts to reduce greenhouse gases regularly contend that states put themselves at a competitive disadvantage by placing strict standards on emissions. Conversely, proponents of state efforts to increase energy efficiency and alternative energy production have made the case that state governments can enhance their economies through policies that support the reduction of green-house gas emissions.

In that vein, the 2008 and 2009 NSAPOCC asked individuals for their level of agreement with a series of statements regarding the impact of state-level initia-tives to address global warming. In general, we find considerable support for allowing individual states to adopt standards on greenhouse gas emissions that are stricter than any established by the federal government. There also is support for unilateral state efforts in the absence of comparable action by neighboring states or the federal government, though there were some shifts between 2008 and 2009 in the intensity with which those views were held. Moreover, most Americans continued to believe that their state economies would be bolstered by expanded use of renewable energy, although there was a 20 percent decline between 2008 and 2009 in the number of Americans who strongly agreed with that proposition. Americans also have become more divided on the economic effects of renewable energy requirements in states where neighboring states lack similar requirements.

These results indicate that most Americans want their states to address global warming even if their actions come without similar efforts on the part of neigh-boring states or the federal government. Indeed, in 2009 half of Americans believed that their state should adopt anti–global warming policies even when neighboring states failed to take action. Meanwhile, 2 in 3 adults in the United States felt that their state was responsible for dealing with climate change even if the federal government abdicated its role on this matter. Even with these high lev-els of support for state action to address climate change, it is notable that public support for unilateral state efforts did decrease between 2008 and 2009, as seen in table 2-18.

Americans also overwhelmingly (70 percent) believed that state governments could boost their economies by requiring greater use of renewable energy. How-ever, they were more divided on the impact of such efforts without similar efforts in adjacent states. While 41 percent of Americans disagreed that their state's econ-omy would be damaged by requiring greater use of renewables when neighboring states did not adopt such requirements, 41 percent believed that the economy of their state would be hurt by unilateral adoption of renewable energy requirements. Once again there were notable differences in agreement with those statements

Table 2-18. *Responses to Various Statements Regarding State Efforts to Address Climate Change, 2008 and 2009*[a]

Percent responding

Statement	Strongly agree	Somewhat agree	Somewhat disagree	Strongly disagree	Not sure
"The federal government should allow state governments to adopt standards for the emission of greenhouse gases that are stricter than any federal standards."[b]	35	40	11	8	6
"My state should not adopt anti–global warming policies unless neighboring states also adopt similar policies."	11 (19)	21 (15)	27 (22)	33 (40)	8 (5)
"If the federal government fails to address the issue of global warming it is my state's responsibility to address the problem."	26 (41)	40 (29)	16 (9)	11 (17)	7 (5)
"State governments will boost their economies by requiring greater use of renewable energy."	27 (47)	43 (30)	12 (6)	8 (8)	10 (9)
"My state's economy will be damaged if it requires greater use of renewable energy while neighboring states don't have such requirements."	16 (13)	25 (24)	25 (20)	16 (31)	18 (13)

Source: NSAPOCC, 2008 and 2009.
a. Results for 2008 in parentheses.
b. Statement was not included in the 2008 survey.

between 2008 and 2009, with Americans less likely to see renewable energy as being as economically beneficial in 2009 as they did in 2008. (For further discussion on the role of renewable energy in climate change mitigation, see chapter 8 in this volume.)

The 2008 NSAPOCC state surveys also indicate significant differences across states when it comes to perceptions of the economic impact of renewable energy requirements. As shown in table 2-19, a plurality of Mississippians agreed that their state's adoption of renewable energy requirements would damage the Mississippi economy if neighboring states did not take similar actions. Conversely, most Californians do not believe that the inaction of their neighbors would harm their state's economic well-being.

The contrast between public opinion in the two states is especially interesting given the dramatically different policies that have been adopted by each state. Dur-

Table 2-19. *Responses to "My State Economy Will Be Damaged if It Requires Greater Use of Renewable Energy While Neighboring States Do Not," for the Nation and Selected States*

Percent responding

State	Strongly agree	Somewhat agree	Somewhat disagree	Strongly disagree	Not sure
Nation	13	24	20	31	13
Pennsylvania	20	24	21	24	11
Virginia	14	23	25	24	13
Mississippi	22	27	19	18	15
California	16	14	18	34	17

Source: NSAPOCC, 2008.

ing the last quarter-century, California has established itself as a national leader in promulgating regulations to promote alternative energy use, while Mississippi is one of only fifteen states that currently has neither any mandatory renewable energy requirements nor any explicit state goal for the use of renewable energy.[15] In addition, Mississippi is the only state in the nation in which no neighboring state has either a mandatory or voluntary renewable energy standard (see figure 2-1). Thus, it may not be surprising that Mississippi residents are significantly more likely than the rest of the nation to believe that action on the part of their state without similar action in Louisiana, Alabama, Tennessee, and Arkansas may place Mississippi at a competitive disadvantage.

One other notable aspect of state public opinion regarding government efforts to promote use of renewable energy involves public knowledge of the actual adoption by their home state of policies in this area. Do Americans in fact know what efforts their states have made to promote alternative energy use? The 2008 NSAPOCC state surveys found mixed results: most Americans were unsure whether their state had adopted requirements for use of renewable energy sources. In only 1 of the 4 states (Mississippi) in which surveys were conducted did a majority of residents indicate knowledge regarding their state's policy in the area of climate change. As shown in table 2-20, almost half of the respondents (47 percent) in Mississippi correctly stated that their state did not have a renewable energy requirement and only 6 percent incorrectly claimed that their state had such a policy. In California, a state with an aggressive renewable energy standard, only 1 in 3 residents knew that the state had adopted such a policy, with over half (51 percent) unsure of their state's policy in this area. The results from the Virginia survey found that 6 in 10 Virginians did not know whether their state had a renewable requirement; as Virginia is 1 of 5 states that have renewable energy goals but not requirements, however, the state's policies are essentially voluntary.

Figure 2-1. *State Adoption of Renewable Portfolio Standards and Renewable Energy Goals*

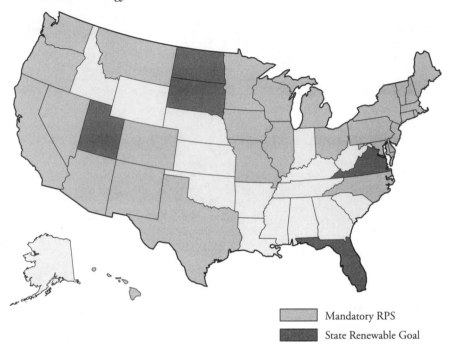

Mandatory RPS

State Renewable Goal

Source: Pew Research Center, "The Pew Global Attitudes Project," June 13, 2006 (http://pew global.org/reports/pdf/252.pdf).

In the survey, 32 percent of Virginians correctly claimed that the state did not have a requirement, with only 8 percent indicating that the state did have such a rule. Perhaps most interesting were the results from Pennsylvania. Only 15 percent of residents could accurately claim that the state had a renewable requirement, 20 percent indicated that no such policy existed, and an astounding 65 percent were not sure of the status of state efforts in this area. That lack of public

Table 2-20. *Percent of Respondents Indicating That Their State Has a Requirement for the Production of Renewable Energy, by Selected States*

State	Yes	No	Not sure
Pennsylvania	15	20	65
Virginia	8	32	60
Mississippi	6	47	46
California	33	15	51

Source: NSAPOCC, 2008.

knowledge prevailed despite the prominent emphasis placed on energy policy by Governor Edward Rendell throughout his tenure in office.

Public Preferences for Policy Options to Address Climate Change

Public opinion research has shown that Americans largely favor government action at the federal, state, and local levels to address rising global temperatures. However, such general support should not be construed as public endorsement of all available policy options to combat global warming: the array of policies being used or considered is extensive, and the direct impact on the public of one can vary considerably from the impact of another. The many options can be placed in three broad categories: regulatory mandates; economic incentives and disincentives; and markets for greenhouse gases. A number of significant national studies over recent years have shown great variance in public support for the various policy options,[16] affected as it is by numerous social, political, economic, and geographic factors.

Regulatory Mandates

The following sections outline various options for confronting climate change within the realm of regulatory mandates and Americans' opinions regarding them. Several of these options are explored in greater detail in part 2 of this volume.

STRONGER EMISSION AND EFFICIENCY STANDARDS

One of the most commonly employed methods of addressing climate change is to reduce greenhouse gas emissions through laws and regulations that either require lower emissions from pollutant sources (for example, cars and factories) or greater use of alternative energy sources (for example, nuclear, solar, and wind energy). A number of national surveys have shown that the American public has a generally favorable view of government regulations on carbon emissions. The Gallup polls from the last decade have consistently shown that approximately 3 in 4 Americans favor higher emission standards for automobiles and industries (see table 2-21).[17] (See chapter 7 in this volume for a fuller discussion of the U.S. experience with federal standards for vehicular fuel efficiency).

The 2008 and 2009 NSAPOCC also asked Americans about their support for government regulations of emissions, but it focused on state-level efforts. The surveys' results, shown in table 2-22, are very similar to those of the Gallup surveys: more than 3 in 4 Americans supported increased auto efficiency standards, even if the increased efficiency would add to the cost of the vehicle. There was a 17 percent drop in "strong support" for this policy approach between 2008 and 2009, perhaps reflecting the deep recession that engulfed the United States during the 2009 fielding of the survey.

Table 2-21. *Public Opinion on Increased Emission Standards for Automobiles and Industry, by Selected Years*

Percent responding

Opinion	2001	2003	2007
Automobiles			
Favor	75	73	79
Oppose	23	24	18
Not sure	2	3	3
Industry			
Favor	75	73	79
Oppose	23	24	18
Not sure	2	3	3

Source: Lydia Saad, "Most Americans Back Curbs on Auto Emissions, Other Environmental Proposals," Gallup News Service, April 5, 2007 (www.gallup.com/poll/27100/most-americans-back-curbs-auto-emissions-other-environmental-proposals.aspx).

RENEWABLE ENERGY STANDARDS

In addition to supporting improved energy efficiency standards, Americans strongly support government efforts to increase the use of renewable energy sources. Numerous surveys since 2000 have substantiated that finding through strong evidence that the public advocates greater government support for the development of such resources. Among the most popular alternative energy options are renewables such as solar and wind power. According to Gallup, in 2007 nearly 8 in 10 Americans favored higher government expenditures to develop these technologies. In addition to support for greater government outlays, the public highly favored the adoption of renewable energy requirements. With twenty-nine states currently employing mandates for the use of renewable energy in the production of electricity, the regulatory approach is a centerpiece of many state efforts (see chapter 8 in this volume). As reflected in table 2-23, in 2009

Table 2-22. *Responses to "State Governments Should Require Automakers to Increase the Fuel Efficiency of Vehicles Even if It Increases the Cost of the Vehicle," 2008 and 2009*

Percent responding

Year	Strongly support	Somewhat support	Somewhat oppose	Strongly oppose	Not sure
2008	52	35	8	11	4
2009	35	40	11	11	4

Source: NSAPOCC, 2008 and 2009.

Table 2-23. *Public Opinion on State Renewable Energy Requirements, for Nation and by Partisan Affiliation, 2008 and 2009*[a]

Percent responding

Party affiliation	Strongly support	Somewhat support	Somewhat oppose	Strongly oppose	Not sure
Nation	41	35	9	9	6
	(59)	(23)	(6)	(8)	(4)
Republican	32	35	13	15	5
	(52)	(22)	(5)	(20)	(2)
Democrat	51	37	5	3	5
	(68)	(20)	(5)	(3)	(4)
Independent	36	35	10	11	9
	(58)	(24)	(8)	(6)	(4)

Source: NSAPOCC, 2008 and 2009.
a. Results for 2008 are in parentheses.

more than 3 in 4 U.S. residents offered support for state regulations that require a set portion of electricity to come from renewable energy sources, with more than 4 in 10 Americans offering strong support for that option. However, partisan affiliation does appear to have a significant impact on individual preferences regarding the development of standards. The 2009 NSAPOCC results indicate that Republicans are significantly more likely than Democrats or Independents to oppose state laws that require a set portion of electricity to come from sources such as wind, solar, or geothermal power. Nevertheless, more than 2 in 3 GOP loyalists offer support for state renewable energy requirements.

At the state level, support for renewable energy standards in 2008 was quite strong, although there were some moderate differences in terms of the intensity of support. While just under 2 in 3 Californians strongly supported state requirements for the use of renewable energy sources for the production of electricity, less than half (49 percent) of Mississippi residents maintained similar positions on the matter (see table 2-24). Strong support for renewable standards is similar in Pennsylvania and Virginia, with 53 percent and 55 percent of state residents respectively indicating that they were highly supportive. These moderately varied levels of support are positively correlated with state efforts to increase alternative energy use.

ALTERNATIVE ENERGY

While renewable sources of energy such as wind and solar energy draw overwhelming support from the American public, other alternative energy sources, such as nuclear energy, ethanol, and "clean coal," receive less favorable responses.

—*Nuclear energy.* With its lack of carbon emissions, nuclear power has been advocated as a primary means of addressing global warming; however, it remains

Table 2-24. *Existing State Renewable Energy Requirements and Public Support for State Renewable Energy Requirements, by Selected States*
Percent responding

State	Existing requirements for use of renewable energy	Strong support for requirements
California	Aggressive statewide requirement	64
Pennsylvania	Moderate statewide requirement	53
Virginia	Voluntary statewide standard	55
Mississippi	No statewide requirement	49

Source: NSAPOCC, 2008.

highly controversial due to safety risks and waste-storage issues. Nonetheless, there has been a moderate increase in public support for the use of this policy option, reflected in table 2-25.

As table 2-26 demonstrates, the 2008 NSAPOCC found similar support for state efforts to increase nuclear power as a means of reducing greenhouse gas emissions. Almost 60 percent of Americans wanted states to support increased use of nuclear power in order to reduce the emissions of gases that cause global warming, with about 1 in 3 strongly supporting such efforts. Support for nuclear power as part of the fight against climate change was also strong across the states themselves, with nearly identical levels of support in states as diverse as California and Mississippi. The major demographic divides in support for nuclear power as a means of addressing global warming were gender and age. Support for nuclear power was highest among men and senior citizens, with women significantly more unsure than men regarding efforts to increase nuclear power use.

—*Ethanol.* In addition to nuclear power, ethanol has become a controversial option in the public debate over energy policy in the United States. While it originally received significant positive public attention, ethanol has become a much more divisive issue in recent years. During the 2007 congressional debates on

Table 2-25. *Public Opinion on Expanding the Use of Nuclear Energy, by Selected Years*
Percent responding

Opinion	2001	2003	2007
Favor	41	45	50
Oppose	55	51	46
Not sure	5	6	4

Source: Lydia Saad, "Most Americans Back Curbs on Auto Emissions, Other Environmental Proposals," Gallup News Service, April 5, 2007 (www.gallup.com/poll/27100/most-americans-back-curbs-auto-emissions-other-environmental-proposals.aspx).

Table 2-26. *Public Opinion on Increased Use of Nuclear Power to Reduce Greenhouse Gas Emissions, by Nation, State, and Demographic Group*
Percent responding

State or group	Strongly support	Somewhat support	Somewhat oppose	Strongly oppose	Not sure
Nation	34	25	12	17	12
Pennsylvania	38	21	14	14	13
Virginia	30	29	15	14	12
Mississippi	31	29	13	12	16
California	36	24	8	17	16
Male	46	25	8	17	5
Female	25	25	15	17	18
18–44	31	24	15	18	12
45–64	31	29	12	17	12
65 and Older	47	20	7	15	12

Source: NSAPOCC, 2008.

energy and climate issues, members of Congress frequently cited estimates that corn-based ethanol produced 20 percent less greenhouse gas than gasoline and that cellulosic ethanol reduced emissions by up to 70 percent.[18] However, a 2008 Princeton University study contradicted those claims, arguing that increased ethanol use would actually exacerbate the problem by increasing greenhouse gas emissions.[19]

When asked whether state governments should increase their support for the development of ethanol, more than half of Americans (58 percent) indicated that they supported such efforts (see table 2-27). However, about one-third of Americans were opposed to increased state support for ethanol development, with 1 in 5 strongly opposed. It has been found that support for this option is moderately affected by educational attainment, with college graduates more likely to oppose government support for ethanol than their counterparts without college degrees.

Table 2-27. *Public Opinion on Increased Government Support for Ethanol, by Level of Education*
Percent responding

Level of education	Strongly support	Somewhat support	Somewhat oppose	Strongly oppose	Not sure
Overall	32	26	12	20	11
College educated	28	24	13	24	11
Not college educated	35	27	11	16	11

Source: NSAPOCC, 2008.

—*Clean coal technology.* Controversy also surrounds government efforts to develop clean coal technology. The concept of clean coal has been trumpeted by many as a means to exploit the nation's vast coal resources in a way that mitigates coal's impact on global warming and air quality in general. While claims of clean coal's benefits have helped draw the support of many elected officials, there has been substantial criticism of the science behind this effort.[20] Among the most common criticisms is that the technology to capture, transport, and store carbon from the use of coal is simply not viable and that the cost of such efforts is excessive.[21] While controversy has raged in policy debates, there seems to be far less division toward the proposal among the broader American public. The 2008 NSAPOCC found that nearly 80 percent of Americans supported increased government support for clean coal technology (see table 2-28). The highest levels of support for this policy option were found in coal-rich Pennsylvania, with only about half of the residents of Virginia, Mississippi, and California indicating strong support. Support for clean coal technology does not seem to be affected by the partisan divide found for most policies aimed at fighting climate change. As seen in table 2-28, the levels of support for clean coal are almost identical among Democrats, Republicans, and Independents.

Economic Incentives and Disincentives

The following sections outline a variety of market-based policy options on climate change mitigation and their level of support among the American public. These policy options are explored in greater detail in chapters 5 and 6 of this volume.

TAXES

The relatively high level of support that Americans show for regulatory approaches to reducing fossil fuel consumption stands in stark contrast to their opinion of tax-based methods to address climate change. All major public opinion polls since 2000 have found evidence of deep public opposition to tax-oriented efforts to reduce greenhouse gas emissions.[22] As noted in chapter 6, while economists regularly cite the use of taxes as the most efficient way to reduce carbon emissions, the public has not viewed tax mechanisms favorably.[23] Polls conducted by both ABC News and the *Washington Post* have found that vast majorities of Americans oppose increased taxes on electricity or gasoline in order to reduce global warming. In particular, 8 in 10 individuals in the United States oppose raising taxes on electricity to combat climate change, with roughly 2 in 3 opposed to higher taxes on gasoline for that purpose (see table 2-29).

The 2009 NSAPOCC found similar levels of public aversion to tax-based mitigation of global warming, although opposition to increased gasoline taxes was marginally lower in 2009, at 62 percent, than it was in 2006 (67 percent), 2007 (68 percent), and 2008 (73 percent). The nation's near-record gas prices, which

Table 2-28. *Public Opinion on Increased Government Support of Clean Coal Technology, by Nation, State, and Partisan Affiliation*
Percent responding

State or group	Strongly support	Somewhat support	Somewhat oppose	Strongly oppose	Not sure
Nation	51	28	5	7	9
Pennsylvania	58	26	5	5	6
Virginia	51	31	6	5	8
Mississippi	46	32	7	5	9
California	51	26	4	7	12
Republican	48	28	5	9	10
Democrat	53	26	4	7	10
Independent	50	32	4	8	7

Source: NSAPOCC, 2008.

occurred just before the fielding of the survey during September 2008, may have helped intensify the negative public sentiment on this approach, while lower prices in 2009 may have decreased opposition. One of the most striking elements of public opposition to reducing gasoline consumption through tax mechanisms was the consistency of negative opinion across important demographic divisions. As seen in table 2-30, a majority of Americans in each political, gender, race, educational attainment, and age category opposed using higher gas taxes to fight climate change. Such overwhelming disfavor helps explain the near total lack of consideration that elected officials have given to this option, despite the recommendations of policy analysts and economists.[24]

While the ABC and NSAPOCC surveys demonstrate strong opposition to the general concept of raising taxes to reduce global warming, the instruments

Table 2-29. *Public Opinion on Taxes to Reduce Global Warming, 2006 and 2007*
Percent responding

Opinion	2006		2007	
	Taxes on Electricity	Taxes on Gasoline	Taxes on Electricity	Taxes on Gasoline
Favor	19	32	20	31
Oppose	81	67	79	68
No opinion	<1	1	1	1

Source: ABC News/*Washington Post*/Stanford University, "Concern Soars about Global Warming as World's Top Environmental Threat," April 20, 2007 (http://woods.stanford.edu/docs/surveys/Global-Warming-2007-ABC-News-Release.pdf).

Table 2-30. *Public Opinion on Increasing State Taxes on Gasoline to Reduce Consumption, by Demographic Group*

Percent responding

Group	Strongly support	Somewhat support	Somewhat oppose	Strongly oppose	Not sure
Overall	11	20	22	40	7
Male	14	18	22	43	4
Female	9	20	23	37	10
White	10	16	20	45	7
Nonwhite	14	29	29	23	5
18–44	12	24	22	33	9
45–64	13	14	21	44	8
65+	6	18	27	48	0
Democrat	20	24	21	28	7
Republican	4	13	24	53	6
Independent	9	18	22	43	8
College graduate	13	28	22	32	4
Not college graduate	9	12	23	46	9

Source: NSAPOCC, 2009.

employed do not capture public reaction to various levels of taxation. Indeed, what is the marginal impact of a one-cent increase in gasoline taxes on overall opinion regarding the use of taxes to address climate change? In 2007 a team of researchers at Stanford University undertook an Internet-based experiment in which individuals were asked to express their support for various tax scenarios.[25] The researchers presented participants with various situations in which oil companies could produce gasoline that would result in a 5 percent reduction in greenhouse gas emissions by 2020. They then provided respondents with annual price increases of 10, 30, or 70 cents for a gallon of gasoline, leading up to prices of $4, $7, and $15 a gallon in 2020. The results indicate that support for this policy option diminished significantly as the price increased (see table 2-31).

Another way to view public support for renewable energy is to find out how much extra money individuals would be willing to pay each year to produce green energy. The 2008 and 2009 NSAPOCC included such a question, with results that demonstrate fairly limited public willingness to accept financial burdens in the name of greater renewable energy production. The percentage of Americans who were unwilling to pay anything for more renewable energy increased from 22 percent to 33 percent between 2008 and 2009. Among those willing to pay some amount of money to get more renewable energy, there was a notable decline in the percentage of those willing to pay $250 or more a year. In 2008, 17 percent of Americans said that they would be willing to pay at least $250 each year

Table 2-31. *Public Opinion on Increasing Gasoline Prices to Reduce Greenhouse Gas Emissions, under Various Price Scenarios*[a]
Percent responding

Opinion	$4 per gallon	$7 per gallon	$15 per gallon
For	37	28	22
Against	63	72	78

Source: Brent Bannon, Ray Kopp, and John Krosnick, "Americans' Evaluations of Policies to Reduce Greenhouse Gas Emissions," *New Scientist* (June 2007).

a. A hypothetical 5 percent reduction in greenhouse gas emissions in 2020 was offered in exchange for various gas prices in that year.

to increase renewable energy production, but in 2009, only 5 percent held that view. While many factors may have contributed to the decline, the struggling national economy was a likely candidate (see table 2-32).

One interesting facet of the public's willingness to pay for renewable energy is the relationship between individual opposition to taxes as a means of reducing fossil fuel consumption and the level of financial support that individuals find acceptable. In essence, the willingness of the public to pay for alternative energy development significantly outpaces its support for using taxes to reduce consumption of fossil fuels. As discussed further in chapter 8, individuals who oppose increasing taxes on fossil fuels are willing to pay some amount to produce more renewable energy. Notably, a majority (51 percent) of Americans who strongly opposed increasing fossil fuel taxes in 2008 displayed at least some degree of willingness to pay for greater production of energy from renewable sources.

Table 2-32. *Public Support for Paying Extra Money Each Year for Greater Production of Renewable Energy, under Various Cost Scenarios, 2008 and 2009*
Percent responding

Additional annual amount	Support	
	2008	2009
$0	22	33
$1–$49	16	31
$50–$99	17	15
$100–$249	13	13
$250–$499	10	3
$500 or more	7	2
Not sure	15	7

Source: NSAPOCC, 2008 and 2009.

Table 2-33. *Public Opinion on Hybrid Vehicle Tax Credit, by Year and Survey*[a]
Percent responding

Opinion	2004 (PIPA)	2005 (PIPA)	2008 UVA/Miller Center
Favor/support	78	77	71
Oppose	20	19	24
Not sure	2	4	5

Source: Program on International Policy Attitudes, "Americans on Climate Change," July 5, 2005 (www.worldpublicopinion.org/pipa/articles/btenvironmentra/79.php?lb=brusc&pnt=79&nid=&id=) and NSAPOCC.

a. Question was worded slightly differently in the PIPA and NSAPOCC.

Tax Incentives

The heavy public opposition seen with increasing taxes as a means of combating global warming is not seen when it comes to using tax incentives to *increase* environmentally desirable behaviors. In 2008, nearly 350,000 hybrid gasoline-electric vehicles were purchased within the United States, with many Americans claiming credits on their federal income taxes for their purchases. Under the Energy Policy Act of 2005, individuals who purchased a hybrid vehicle could subtract a specified amount directly from the total amount of their federal taxes owed, thus reducing (or even eliminating) their tax obligation.[26] As shown in table 2-33, approximately 75 percent of Americans reported that they support government tax breaks for individuals who purchase hybrid fuel vehicles.

Cap and Trade

The final policy approach often considered as a means of fighting global warming is commonly referred to as cap and trade. It involves creating a market whereby emission permits are allocated and can be traded among sources, leading, in theory, to a more cost-effective approach than mandating the same standard or technology for every source. As further discussed in chapter 5 in this volume, in 2009 cap-and-trade options played a prominent role in climate change deliberations in the 111th Congress and are likely to remain a significant alternative that Congress will consider as further efforts to address global warming are pursued during the Obama administration.

It is unclear, however, if the general public can readily understand the comparatively complex cap-and-trade mechanism as easily as it can the regulatory and tax-based policy approaches already discussed. When the 2008 NSAPOCC asked Americans whether or not state governments should allow businesses to buy and sell permits to release greenhouse gases if doing so would result in an overall decrease in emissions, more Americans were supportive of the proposal than were opposed to it, by about a 2-to-1 margin. However, as table 2-34 suggests, about 1 in 5 respondents were uncertain about this option. When the same question

Table 2-34. *Public Opinion on a Cap-and-Trade Program to Reduce Emissions, 2008 and 2009*

Percent responding

Opinion	2008	2009
Strongly support	25	14
Somewhat support	30	25
Somewhat oppose	9	23
Strongly oppose	18	28
Not sure	18	9

Source: NSAPOCC, 2008 and 2009.

was presented to respondents in the 2009 NSAPOCC, support for cap and trade had fallen by 15 percent and opposition had increased by 24 percent, while the percentage of Americans who were unsure about the option had halved, from 18 percent to 9 percent. It appears that the high profile of this policy alternative, which included a number of ads opposing it,[27] helped both to form opinion among formerly undecided Americans and to increase opposition.

Last, support for cap and trade also appears to be greatly affected by the financial impact that adoption of the policy would have on individuals. In the 2009 NSAPOCC respondents were asked their level of support for a cap-and-trade scenario in which there was no specified financial burden; a $15 per month cost to the individual; or a $50 per month cost to the individual. The results, presented in table 2-35, demonstrate substantial loss of support for cap and trade as the financial burden increased, with only about 4 in 10 Americans supporting cap and trade with a $15 monthly price tag and just over 1 in 5 respondents favoring cap and trade if it cost them $50 each month.

Table 2-35. *Public Opinion on a Cap-and-Trade Program to Reduce Emissions, under Various Individual Cost Scenarios*

Percent responding

Opinion	Cap and trade without a specified financial cost to the individual	Cap and trade with a $15 a month cost to the individual	Cap and trade with a $50 a month cost to the individual
Strongly support	17	14	7
Somewhat support	36	28	15
Somewhat oppose	14	22	18
Strongly oppose	20	29	54
Not sure	12	8	6

Source: NSAPOCC, 2009.

Conclusions

It is difficult to underestimate the importance of public opinion within a democratic system of government. While many factors besides citizens' preferences may affect the decisions of elected officials, public opinion plays crucial theoretical and practical roles in the dynamics of a functioning democratic state. As global warming continues to rise in prominence as a threat to the well-being of both the nation and the world, the beliefs, attitudes, and preferences of Americans regarding the problem become ever more important. Given its role as one of the planet's largest emitters of greenhouse gases, the United States must take the lead in any effort to manage climate change. Of course, such a commitment will come to fruition only if the American public believes that global warming is indeed a real threat and that the results are worth the cost of implementing corrective policies.

The growing body of evidence on American public opinion on climate change allows us to reach some fairly clear conclusions. Most U.S. citizens believe not only that global warming exists but also that it is a serious problem facing the nation. Their beliefs are drawn from a combination of personal observations of changes in the physical environment and images of altered global environments (for example, melting polar ice). Most Americans believe that immediate government action is needed to deal with climate change and that governments at all levels of the federal system have a responsibility to deal with it. U.S. citizens generally embrace regulatory means whereby alternative energy sources can be developed and energy efficiency achieved, although a substantial and growing partisan divide challenges consensus on this matter.

Survey results from 2009 provide evidence that the steadily increasing levels of belief in the United States in global warming have begun to decline and that support for government efforts to address climate change has declined modestly. It is against this backdrop that the Obama administration, Congress, state governments, and municipalities must attempt to move the nation forward in tackling this elusive policy problem. While any imposition of direct costs on the American public will likely face strong opposition, there appear to be a number of areas in which the public will likely offer significant support. The 2008 and 2009 NSAPOCC indicate that state efforts to develop alternative energy sources are seen as a means to boost state economies. If states and the federal government can package alternative energy programs as engines for economic development and the revenue generation for such efforts is not seen as either punitive or excessive, significant progress on climate policy may be achieved. The high level of public support for the development of green technologies may help to explain the Obama administration's decision to use alternative energy and energy efficiency as a cornerstone of its economic stimulus plan in 2009.[28] Similarly, the public's favorable view of government investment in green energy has helped propel alternative energy policies to the forefront of some state economic recovery plans.[29] Ultimately, such policies may be well-suited to a public that wants action on energy and climate change but does not want to pay directly for such advances.

Appendix 2A

The 2008 and 2009 National Surveys of American Public Opinion on Climate Change (NSAPOCC) provided many of the findings that are included in this chapter. The NSAPOCC was created to measure American public opinion on global warming, with emphasis on state and local government policies and underlying determinants of individual beliefs. The first NSAPOCC was developed in conjunction with the National Conference on Climate Governance at the Miller Center of Public Affairs at the University of Virginia and was conducted by telephone between September 8 and 24, 2008. The survey results are based on a random sample of households in the United States at large and in four particular states: California, Pennsylvania, Virginia, and Mississippi. Table 2A-1 presents the sample size and margin of error for each of the samples. The margin of error was calculated at the 95 percent confidence level.

The second NSAPOCC was conducted by telephone between September 21 and November 24, 2009. The survey results are based on a random sample of 988 households throughout the United States. The margin of error for the 2009 study is plus or minus 3 percentage points, calculated at the 95 percent confidence level.

Percentages for both surveys were rounded upward at the .5 mark; thus many totals in the results will not equal 100 percent. All data were weighted to reflect U.S. Census Bureau population estimates. Margins of error for subgroups (for example, women, Republicans, college-educated individuals) are larger than for the overall sample because of smaller sample sizes. Interviews were conducted by the Muhlenberg College Institute of Public Opinion in Allentown, Pennsylvania. The survey instruments were designed by Barry Rabe of the University of Michigan and

Table 2A-1. *Sample Characteristics, 2008 National Survey of American Public Opinion on Climate Change*

Sample	Sample size	Margin of error (percentage points)
National	603	+/– 4
Virginia	660	+/– 4
Pennsylvania	307	+/– 5
California	304	+/– 5
Mississippi	302	+/– 5

Christopher Borick of Muhlenberg College. The 2008 survey was funded by the WestWind Foundation, the Miller Center at the University of Virginia, the Muhlenberg College Institute of Public Opinion, and the Center for Local, State, and Urban Policy at the University of Michigan. The 2009 survey was funded by the Muhlenberg College Institute of Public Opinion.

Notes

1. A prime example includes Benjamin I. Page and Robert Y. Shapiro, "Effects of Public Opinion on Policy," *American Political Science Review* 77, no. 1 (March 1983), pp. 175–90.

2. Kevin Arceneaux, Paul Brace, and Martin Johnson, "Public Opinion and Dynamic Representation in the American States: The Case of Environmental Attitudes," *Social Science Quarterly* 86, no. 1 (March 2005), pp. 87–108.

3. Riley E. Dunlap and Aaron M. McCright, "A Widening Gap: Republican and Democratic Views on Climate Change," *Environment* (September-October 2008); Teresa Myers and Matthew C. Nisbet, "Trends: Twenty Years and Public Opinion about Global Warming," *Public Opinion Quarterly* 71, no. 3 (Fall 2007), pp. 444–70.

4. Mark Baldassare and others, *Californians and the Environment* (San Francisco: Public Policy Institute of California, 2008); Kenneth Broad and Anthony Leiserowitz, *Florida Public Opinion on Climate Change* (Yale University, School of Forestry and Environmental Studies, 2008).

5. Malcolm Goggin and Christopher Wlezien, "Abortion Opinion and Policy in the American States," in *Understanding the New Politics of Abortion*, edited by Malcolm Goggin (Newbury Park, Calif.: Sage, 1993); Fay Lomax Cook and Jeff Manza, "A Democratic Polity? Three Views of Policy Responsiveness to Public Opinion in the United States," *American Politics Research* 30, no. 6 (2002), pp. 630–67.

6. Myers and Nisbet, "Trends: Twenty Years and Public Opinion about Global Warming."

7. Gallup Organization, "Did Hollywood's Glare Heat Up Public Concern about Global Warming?" March 21, 2007 (www.gallup.com/poll/26932/Did-Hollywoods-Glare-Heat-Public-Concern-About-Global-Warming.aspx).

8. Pew Research Center, "A Deeper Partsian Divide over Global Warming," May 8, 2008 (http://people-press.org/report/417/a-deeper-partisan-divide-over-global-warming).

9. ABC News/*Washington Post*/Stanford University, "Concern Soars about Global Warming as World's Top Environmental Threat," April 20, 2007 (http://woods.stanford.edu/docs/surveys/Global-Warming-2007-ABC-News-Release.pdf).

10. Juliet Eilperin and Jon Cohen, "Growing Number of Americans See Warming as Leading Threat," *Washington Post*, April 20, 2007.

11. National Opinion Research Center, "General Social Survey," 2000 (www.norc.org/GSS+Website/).

12. Myers and Nisbet, "Trends: Twenty Years and Public Opinion about Global Warming."

13. Program on International Policy Attitudes, "Americans on Climate Change," July 5, 2005 (www.worldpublicopinion.org/pipa/articles/btenvironmentra/79.php?lb=brusc&pnt=79&nid=&id=).

14. Christopher P. Borick and Barry G. Rabe, "Survey of Michigan Residents on the Issue of Global Warming and Climate Policy Options: Key Findings Report," *Policy Report of the University of Michigan Center for Local, State, and Urban Policy* 11 (February 2008), pp. 1–12;

Christopher P. Borick and Barry G. Rabe, "A Reason to Believe: Examining the Factors That Determine Americans' Views on Global Warming," Brookings, *Issues in Governance Studies* 18 (July 2008), pp. 1–14; Broad and Leiserowitz, *Florida Public Opinion on Climate Change.*

15. Pew Research Center for the People and the Press, "An Increase in GOP Doubt" (Washington: May 8, 2008).

16. Brent Bannon, Ray Kopp, and John Krosnick, "Americans' Evaluations of Policies to Reduce Greenhouse Gas Emissions," *New Scientist Magazine* (June 2007); Myers and Nisbet, "Trends: Twenty Years and Public Opinion about Global Warming."

17. Lydia Saad, "Most Americans Back Curbs on Auto Emissions, Other Environmental Proposals," Gallup News Service, April 5, 2007 (www.gallup.com/poll/27100/most-americans-back-curbs-auto-emissions-other-environmental-proposals.aspx).

18. Joseph H. Herbert, "Study: Ethanol May Add to Global Warming," *Washington Post,* February 2, 2008.

19. Fengxia Dong and others, "Use of U.S. Croplands for Biofuels Increases Greenhouse Gases through Emissions from Land-Use Change," *Science*, February 29, 2008, pp. 1238–240.

20. Matthew L. Wald, "Mounting Costs Slow the Push for Clean Coal," *New York Times,* May 20, 2008.

21. Stephen Ansolabehere and others, *The Future of Coal: Options for a Carbon Constrained World* (Massachusetts Institute of Technology, 2007) (web.mit.edu/coal/The_Future_of_Coal.pdf).

22. Myers and Nisbet, "Trends: Twenty Years and Public Opinion about Global Warming."

23. Gilbert E. Metcalf, "Using Tax Expenditures to Achieve Energy Policy Goals," *American Economic Review* 98, no. 2 (May 2008), pp. 90–94.

24. Andrew C. Revkin, "On Global Warming, McCain and Obama Agree: Urgent Action Is Needed," *New York Times,* October 18, 2008.

25 Bannon, Kopp, and Krosnick, "Americans' Evaluations of Policies to Reduce Greenhouse Gas Emissions."

26. Internal Revenue Service, "Alternative Motor Vehicle Credit" (U.S. Department of the Treasury) (www.irs.gov/newsroom/article/0,,id=157632,00.html).

27. Ben Smith, "Groups Target GOP on Cap-and-Trade," *Politico,* August 25, 2009.

28. Kate Galbraith, "Obama Pushes Clean Energy," *New York Times,* January 8, 2009.

29. Jon Corzine, "Governor Corzine's Address to the Joint Session of the Legislature" (Trenton, N.J.: October 16, 2008) (www.nj.gov/governor/news/speeches/economic_plan.html).

3

Compensatory Federalism

MARTHA DERTHICK

Always confounding, federalism has also become controversial in recent
years, at least in academic circles. We owe that to the Rehnquist court,
which, in attempting to construct a constitutionally grounded defense of federalism, aroused an opposition.[1] But the views of the court's academic critics are far
from uniform. At an iconoclastic extreme is the work of Malcolm Feeley and
Edward Rubin at the University of California, Berkeley, who tell us that we no
longer have federalism inasmuch as no one is willing to sacrifice his life in defense
of a state. Rather, we have "managerial decentralization." "When there is a consensus, national norms swamp state prerogatives. What at times appears to be a
manifestation of federalism is the absence of national norms; when there is disagreement, states are permitted discretion."[2]

The formidable Michael Greve at the American Enterprise Institute argues
that we no longer have, but could conceivably recapture, "real" federalism, which
protects liberty with an institutional design that encourages governments to compete with one another—states with other states, and states with the federal government.[3] Instead, he says, since the New Deal we have constructed a cartelized
system in which governments collude and, by colluding, grow. On the left is
Erwin Chemerinsky, who argues, in sharp contrast to Greve, for empowerment
federalism, which unleashes all governments to solve today's wide array of public
problems. He would empower the federal government by rejecting the limits that
the Rehnquist court attempted to construct on federalism principles (he says that

it failed to define any principles), and he would empower the states with a presumption against preemption.[4]

Policy analysts with a pragmatic focus do not necessarily have to choose among these competing theoretical and normative views. They can be content to ask one question: When does federalism "work"? With that approach, it is fair to say that the standard answer is that federalism works when the many governments in the federal system cooperate. I recall, for example, the Brookings study by James L. Sundquist, published in 1969, entitled *Making Federalism Work: A Study of Program Coordination at the Community Level.* The theoretically sophisticated work of Peterson, Rabe, and Wong, *When Federalism Works,* which examined nine federal grant-in-aid programs in four cities in the early 1980s, rested on the premise that intergovernmental conflict in such programs is dysfunctional and offers an analytically insightful explanation of when and why conflict occurs.[5] It occurs because local and state governments on one hand and the federal government on the other specialize in different types of policies. State and local governments specialize in "developmental policies," which are intended to improve the economic position of a community in its competition with others. The federal government is better able to embrace "redistributive" policies, which benefit needy groups. No local government will provide redistributive services on its own initiative for fear that it will be unduly burdened by a social problem while others escape responsibility for it. Without explicitly invoking the need for cooperation, Alice Rivlin, in her foreword to Tim Conlan and Paul Posner's recent volume on intergovernmental management, implores policymakers at all levels to keep the intergovernmental machinery in repair and operating smoothly.[6]

I propose a different criterion. For the ideal of cooperative federalism, I would substitute "compensatory federalism," at the risk of adding yet one more catchphrase to a subject that is already afflicted with too many of them. After giving myself a crash course in environmental policy, I came to the conclusion that one could argue that federalism works when governments at one level of the system are able to compensate for weaknesses or defects at another level. That turns upside down the argument of Paul Manna in *School's In*, which asserts that governments at different levels "borrow strength" from one another.[7] More cynically, I want to suggest that they counteract weaknesses.

On the state and local side, arguably the gravest defects have consisted of deviations from constitutional norms. The leading historical case would, of course, be slavery in the South and the discriminatory laws and exploitative customs that were its post–Civil War successors. Less grave but still arguably threatening to constitutional integrity would be barriers erected by states to interstate commerce, the subject of the Supreme Court's negative commerce clause jurisprudence and, at least in principle, Congress's statutory preemptions. In general, it is a function of the Supreme Court to guard against constitutional deviations. It performs constitutional corrections, which are not what I have in mind when I speak of compensation; my focus is on less momentous matters of policy and practicality. At this level, the defects of state and local governments are the large numbers of such governments and their very uneven capacities to perform basic public functions.

Multiple governments are inherent in the structure of a federal system, and scholars who embrace competitive federalism as a value argue that the existence of many units increases consumer satisfaction. Free to move, citizens can choose to live in jurisdictions that offer what they judge to be an optimal mix of taxes and services. Whether many citizens actually do that—apart from parents, who have a propensity to discriminate among school districts—may be doubted.[8] Fewer than 12 percent of Americans moved in 2008, and 57 percent had never moved outside their home state. Most movers are responding to better jobs. One suspects that movers also are influenced by climate as well as family considerations, such as the desire of retirees to be near children as their health deteriorates with age, but family attachments often cut the other way. Most people who do not move give as the reason that they are tied to their families.[9]

Even persons who argue the value of competitive federalism do not usually cast the argument as a defense of the government-rich polity that the United States actually is. Also, there is another side. Whereas some students of federalism detect citizen satisfaction in interjurisdictional competition, others see a destructive race to the bottom, as governments compete in pursuit of self-serving ends. They shrink from supporting the poor and lure corporations with tax privileges and freedom from regulation. Welfare, corporate chartering, and pollution control are policy terrains often thought to be affected by such competition. That corporations would move in response to differences in state policies is more plausible than that individuals would do so. But while the logic of a race to the bottom seems compelling in the abstract, empirical support is thin in contemporary American government.[10]

Whatever the pros and cons of competition among governments—whether the race is of taxpaying citizens to liberty and efficiency, of revenue-hungry governments to laxity, or of some mix of the two—there is no denying that very many governments exist in the United States and that what happens in any one of them may affect its immediate neighbors or even the nation as a whole. The fifty U.S. states are a large number when compared with Canada's ten provinces, Australia's six states, Germany's sixteen *länder*, or even Mexico's thirty-one *estados*—not to mention the country's 39,000 general-purpose local governments, 13,800 school districts, and 35,000 other special districts. Effects of public action or inaction spill over boundaries and invite the attention of more encompassing jurisdictions. Differences in policy outcomes and levels of public service, which are persistent and widespread, typically are deplored by public policy analysts and journalistic commentators rather than being accepted as an inevitable, even desirable, badge of federalism. We are by now quite accustomed to being told that the failure of lagging schools to teach children to read, write, and calculate is, besides an injustice, a threat to national security. Policymakers in the more encompassing governments, the federal government above all, strive to reduce differences and elevate government performance everywhere. For a long time, and at an accelerating pace as the twentieth century advanced, the federal government has been giving financial and technical aid, issuing regulations, and setting standards to bolster the weak and the wanting. That is its contribution to compensatory federalism.

On the federal side, I see five weaknesses or defects, which are less widely acknowledged. One is the arrogance of power. Thanks both to the Constitution and the dynamics of political development, the federal government is the 400-pound gorilla in our governmental zoo. Despite the putative function of state governments as policy laboratories, national legislators have not developed the habit of routinely and systematically inquiring into what can be learned from state-level experience, and both legislators and administrators often proceed with limited regard for the consequences of their actions for state governments.

The textbook theory of American government stipulates that federalism provides checks and balances, but checks on the federal government issuing from the states are hard to find in modern times. Greve's cartelization is more in evidence. Yet environmental protection provides what I take to be a bona fide example of state power checking federal power. I take at face value the ability of state governments to sue the federal government to clean up toxic sites. An essay on state attorneys general and the environment says:

> Some of the most dangerous waste disposal sites in this country are associated with facilities owned by the United States. . . . Arguing that federal facilities should be held to the same standards as privately owned facilities, states have filed litigation at numerous sites throughout the country. The Attorneys General have brought suit under every major environmental act to compel compliance with state law on a site-by-site basis.[11]

The Environmental Protection Agency (EPA) presumably collaborates with the state attorneys general (AGs) in these cases. For example, the *Washington Post* reported in August 2008 that the Maryland attorney general had announced plans to sue the U.S. Army to clean up pollution at Fort Meade and added that EPA and Maryland officials had been working for years to remedy the site.[12] A follow-up story in the *Post* six months later said that the Department of Justice had informed the Department of Defense that it could not legally resist orders from the EPA to clean up Fort Meade. Maryland's environmental secretary said that the state intended to proceed with its legal action.[13]

As of November 2008, Washington state was threatening to sue the federal government over a failure to meet deadlines for cleaning up the Hanford nuclear reservation, which is the nation's most contaminated nuclear site. Hanford is the subject of a pact signed in 1989 by the Washington State Department of Ecology, the U.S. Department of Energy, and the EPA. The state threatened to sue when negotiations over revision of the pact's deadlines failed to reach an agreement.[14]

A rather different yet still pertinent example would be a lawsuit filed by the attorney general of North Carolina against the Tennessee Valley Authority, asking that it be required to cap sulfur dioxide and other pollutants that drift across state lines from its coal-burning plants in Tennessee, Alabama, and Georgia. A twelve-day trial in a federal district court wrapped up late in July 2008, and in January 2009 the judge ruled that TVA must reduce emissions at four coal-fired plants within 100 miles of North Carolina. TVA filed an appeal with the Fourth Circuit Court.[15] (For further review of climate-related litigation within the courts, refer to chapter 10, this volume.)

A second trait of the federal government that I regard as a defect is the tendency of its legislature to issue statutory commands that are unrealistic, even utopian, with little regard for the costs or strain on implementing agencies. Hence there are yawning gaps between ends and means in our nation's policy endeavors (see also chapter 12, this volume, on the capacity of agencies to implement and oversee future climate change legislation). The leading current case is surely No Child Left Behind, with its command that every American school child attain proficiency in language arts and math by 2014. Environmental policy produced by the great wave of legislation in the 1970s is another case of congressional overreach. To support the point, I have cherry-picked the following passages from Shep Melnick's 1999 essay, "Risky Business: Government and the Environment after Earth Day":

—The 1970 Clean Air Act contained specific, "technology-forcing" auto-emission standards. It required the EPA to set air-quality standards for major pollutants and nationally uniform emission limitations for newly constructed sources of pollution. . . . The sponsors of the legislation expected key industries—auto, steel, coal-burning utilities, smelters—to develop new technology to meet these standards quickly and cheaply. To a large extent this was an exercise in wishful thinking.

—In the early days of the environmental era Congress set ambitious goals for pollution reduction without knowing what it was getting into. Although few of the original deadlines were met, the restrictions imposed on polluters became ever more extensive and costly. . . . Meanwhile, new problems . . . produced new programs. The government's reach and responsibility grew in ways most citizens—and most politicians—could hardly fathom.

—The more unrealistic the deadline, the surer the opportunity for inquisitorial oversight hearings. . . . [P]arty competition . . . created a dynamic that has . . . produced rigid, demanding environmental statutes.

—With each reauthorization the laws became more detailed and more demanding. . . . The 1990 law included 90 specific emission limitations for motor vehicles alone. . . . In 1986 Congress rewrote the Safe Drinking Water Law to require the EPA to establish forty new standards over the next two years and twenty-five additional standards every three years after that. . . . The Water Quality Act of 1987 required the EPA to issue twenty-five rules, produce forty policy documents, prepare thirty-one reports to Congress, and meet ninety deadlines—all within three years.

—A 1985 study found the EPA to be subject to more than three hundred statutory deadlines—most of which it had failed to meet.[16]

How does a law-abiding society respond to a legislature like that? One answer, of course, is that it sues. There is a great deal of litigation. But that does not alleviate the overreach. To cite Melnick again, this time his classic work on courts and the Clean Air Act:

—Court action has encouraged legislators and administrators to establish goals without considering how they can be achieved, exacerbating the tendency of these institutions to promise far more than they can deliver.

—The major failing of the federal courts has been their inability to recognize the overriding need to bring the agency's goals and authority into better balance.[17]

But litigation is only one way of responding to the legislative overreach. Most fundamentally, the problem and the burden are exported to other governments, the states, which—in this field and others such as education and welfare—bear much of the responsibility for implementing federal statutes, albeit under federal supervision. That does not reduce the great gap between Congress's laws and administrative capacity, but hides it in one of the least visible venues of American government—the intergovernmental relations of administrative agencies. In large measure, it becomes the responsibility of state officials to practice compensatory federalism by adjusting the aspirations of Washington's elected politicians to the realities of the economy and society. One of the notable features of environmental policy has been the earnest attempts, undertaken mostly in the 1990s, to reconcile the resulting intergovernmental tensions through such initiatives as the National Environmental Performance Partnership System.

Many of the tensions that arise in intergovernmental relations result from a third defect of the federal government—its propensity to impose uniform standards on a diverse society, economy, and ecology. Perhaps that should not be counted a defect, but merely the inescapable other side of its own compensatory coin. In seeking to attain minimum standards and bring other governments up to par on a nationwide scale, it imposes one-size-fits-all solutions. To what extent that happens has varied over time and with the policy subject and policy instrument. A case in which it famously did not happen was that of grants for public assistance in the Social Security Act of 1935. The Roosevelt administration had proposed that state governments, as the recipients of federal grants, be required to pay the poor "a reasonable subsistence compatible with decency and health." That attempt to define—at least in words, if not in currency—a national standard of payment died in Congress, which preferred to give aid "for the purpose of enabling each State to furnish financial assistance, as far as practicable under the conditions in each State."[18]

Half a century later, in the wave of environmental regulation, the federal government has been prone to giving direct, detailed, and unqualified commands—"command and control," as this approach is usually called. Here are two examples, chosen at random, from a brief study by Pietro S. Nivola and Jon A. Shields that describes irrational impositions on local places:[19]

> [U]nder the Resource Conservation and Recovery Act (RCRA), the Environmental Protection Agency's standards for landfills create unjustifiable costs for some southwestern cities. Double liners for landfills are a reasonable precaution in wet climates in which rainfall can cause pollutants to leach into the water table, but they are less crucial in places where there is little rain. Double-lined sites also may be a waste of money where subsurface soils impede liquid percolation. RCRA compliance for Midland, Michigan, has multiplied unnecessarily the costs of disposing of solid waste; this locality's landfill, which sits on 75 feet of clay, probably is safe with no liner at all. . . .
>
> Under the rules of the Safe Drinking Water Act, localities everywhere have been busy examining their water supplies for pesticides and other toxic residues that pose substantial risks only in particular areas. Before it was finally relieved from some of this duty in the mid-1990s, Columbus, Ohio, found itself guarding against approximately 40 pesticides, many of which had long since been discontinued in the vicinity—including one product used chiefly on pineapple plantations in Hawaii.

That sort of mismatch is not an inevitable result of national regulation. Exceptions are sometimes made to command and control. A well-known, because successful, example is the cap-and-trade regime enacted by Congress in the Clean Air Act Amendments of 1990 to curb sulfur dioxide emissions.[20] Some statutes authorize federal administrators to use waivers to permit state and local discretion. Waivers were a critical instrument in fostering the state-level experiments that culminated in welfare reform in the mid-1990s.[21] They can be found in the laws governing Medicaid grants, SCHIP (State Children's Health Insurance Program), grants for elementary and secondary education, and in the Telecommunications Act of 1996, wherein Congress acknowledged the difficulty of creating a uniform regulatory structure for the fast-changing telecommunications industry. Waivers are not completely unknown in environmental protection law. Although federal law preempts state regulation of motor vehicle emissions, California is allowed to apply to EPA for waivers of federal preemption and other states may follow California if EPA approves, but California is a unique case.[22]

Jonathan Adler of Case Western Reserve University Law School has proposed a policy of "ecological forbearance," under which states could petition the EPA administrator to seek the forbearance of a standard or requirement imposed by or pursuant to an environmental statute administered by EPA. Once a petition was received, the EPA would be required to determine whether granting states added regulatory flexibility would be consistent with the protection of public health and the environment in the context of a notice-and-comment rulemaking. One of Adler's goals is to broaden debate over the roles of the federal and state governments, which he argues have been allocated arbitrarily, as the result of historical accident rather than conscious design.[23]

A fourth defect of the federal government is the capital city's *insularity*. That is ironic, for the city has become more insular as it has grown from a provincial town into an international capital, now even preferred by some intellectuals over New York as a place to live. Washington was a provincial town for a long time, lacking glamour, fine restaurants, and a rich cultural life. It emptied out in the summer as members of Congress went home to their jobs, for in the old days they did have jobs in their home towns. Now they are full-time professional politicians, and even after they leave Congress they do not leave Washington—they become lobbyists. There is a self-absorbed world "inside the Beltway," as the stock phrase has it.

Compensatory federalism consists of drawing people into this world from the farm teams in state and local governments. Newly arrived congressmen often come with fresh experience in those venues, and political appointees in the executive branch often do so as well. Thus, directors of EPA frequently have had experience in state government as chief executives (say, Christine Todd Whitman, who had been governor of New Jersey, and Michael Leavitt, who had been governor of Utah, before joining the administration of George W. Bush) or as directors of state environmental agencies (say, Carol Browner, who had directed environmental protection in Florida before joining the Clinton administration).

A final weakness of the federal government is its susceptibility to paralysis. It is not just the institutional design—separation of powers and a bicameral legislature—that contributes to this, which would not distinguish it from the states, other than Nebraska. It's the extremely crowded agenda, the high stakes, the high visibility, a swarming sea of expertly staffed and well-financed advocacy groups (Washington contains 16,000 registered lobbyists), the need for a supermajority to avoid filibusters in the Senate, and the distraction of legislators who invest large amounts of time in fundraising for their next campaigns, in flying home and back, and in holding hearings with more show than substance even when they are in Washington. Dispersion of power through the multiplication of subcommittees has increased the number of show horses; workhorses who are willing and able to take the lead in building coalitions and getting bills passed find that such work is very hard and less rewarding than it once was. I'm not sure that the term "workhorse" even has currency today.

When Washington is hesitant, uncertain, distracted, and in disagreement over what to do, states, having governments of their own, may step into the breach. Washington's failure becomes their ferment. There is no clearer case than that of states' action on climate change and control of greenhouse gases beginning in the late 1990s and extending through the George W. Bush administration, a record that has been extensively chronicled and analyzed by Barry G. Rabe. While Washington has dawdled, states, in Rabe's phrase, have been "on steroids." In 2008 he reported that twenty-two states representing about half of the U.S. population had enacted two or more of eight possible climate policy options.[24] A few of those states, including California, Massachusetts, Connecticut, and New York, had adopted six or seven of the eight. The remaining twenty-eight states, representing the other half of the population, had one or no policies in operation, indicating a lack of support, yet the overall trend was toward more adoptions in more places.[25]

Among states, there are always leaders and laggards in policy innovation. In *Statehouse and Greenhouse*, published in 2004, Rabe singled out New Jersey as a leader, identifying it as the only government in North America that had embraced both the Rio Declaration on Environment and Development (1992) and the Kyoto Protocol (1997) and had taken formal steps to ensure implementation.[26] Conscious of a threat from rising sea levels, New Jersey in 1998 made a formal pledge under Governor Whitman to achieve by 2005 a 3.5 percent reduction of greenhouse gas emissions below the levels of 1990. That would put it on track to reach Kyoto-level targets.

A core element of New Jersey's action plan was "covenants of sustainability," an idea borrowed from the Netherlands, which was its partner in climate control. The covenants were pledges to reduce emissions by specified percentages by specified dates. They were signed by Johnson and Johnson, the pharmaceutical giant in New Brunswick; the Public Service Enterprise Group, which is the state's largest electric utility; all fifty-five of the state's colleges and universities; a number of public school districts; a consortium representing more than 6,000 religious congregations; and even some of the major departments of state government.

Rabe's later work places emphasis on New York as another leader. In 2003 Governor George Pataki sent a letter to neighboring governors inviting them to take part in a regional system for cap-and-trade regulation of carbon emissions. As discussed in other chapters throughout this volume, that initiative would evolve by 2007 into RGGI—the Regional Greenhouse Gas Initiative—in which ten states are participating (Connecticut, Delaware, Maine, New Hampshire, New Jersey, New York, Vermont, Maryland, Massachusetts, and Rhode Island). The memorandum of understanding that is RGGI's founding document declares that the signatories "wish to establish themselves and their industries as world leaders in the creation, development, and deployment of carbon emission control technologies."[27] "Reggie," as it is called, held its first auction of carbon emission allowances late in September 2008, with six of the organization's ten states participating. Most of the bidders were generators of electric power whose emissions the states had capped. The auction raised $40 million for the states, which pledged to spend it on renewable energy technologies and energy efficiency programs.[28]

Meanwhile, on the West Coast, California was expanding its always-strong claim to environmental leadership. California, according to Rabe in 2008, "has surpassed any other U.S. state in the sheer range of climate policies enacted and the boldness of its overall emissions reduction plan."[29] Among California's many acts, the standout is the Global Warming Solutions Act, signed by Governor Arnold Schwarzenegger in September 2006 in a ceremony on Treasure Island, surrounded by international celebrities from the worlds of politics, industry, and entertainment. The act calls for a range of strategies to reduce the state's greenhouse gas emissions to 1990 levels by 2020 despite projections of economic and population growth, and it sets a target for reducing emissions by 80 percent of levels during the 1990s by 2050. It was, the governor said, "the most radical climate policy in the world."[30]

Given that New York and California are big, populous states with active, wide-ranging governments and legislatures that often battle internally by party and externally with their governors, one wonders why they are not, like the federal government, inclined to paralysis. In both places, politics is heated and intense. There are plenty of lobbyists. Yet even the biggest states are not preoccupied with defense and national security, as is the federal government, and they are more homogeneous politically. Public opinion in California exhibits strong concern over the potential effects of climate change on the state, as indicated in chapter 2 in this volume, and support for unilateral action to reduce emissions. Public concern is aggravated by a series of events that, whether rightly or wrongly, are increasingly associated with climate change: proliferation and intensification of wildfires, elevated temperatures in portions of the state, drought in some key agricultural zones, and declining productivity from large dams that produce more than 15 percent of the state's electricity. Also, it is possible to argue more cogently in California than elsewhere that what is good for the environment will also be good for the economy. The state contains relatively little heavy manufacturing but much clean, high-tech industry that could flourish in a carbon-constrained economy. It has few coal-fired power plants. "I say unquestionably it is good for business," the governor said on signing the Global Warming Solutions Act.

In explaining the vitality of the states, Rabe in 2004 emphasized the role of upper-level bureaucrats—policy entrepreneurs with environmental expertise who operate just below the level of political appointees but with the appointees' support.[31] As long ago as the 1930s, when state governments lacked the reputation many would acquire later in the century for competence and energy, Louis Brandeis liked to recommend that young people with a desire for accomplishment through public service look to the states. His daughter and son-in-law worked in Wisconsin.[32] Half a century after Brandeis, Justice William H. Rehnquist would tell his clerks the same thing: "Go home" if they wanted to get something done. States offered the best opportunities for a career.[33] The more manageable venue, the easier access to elected chief executives, and proximity to concrete circumstances have combined to appeal to aspiring public servants who were frustrated by the grinding pace and paper-shuffling of Washington's marble corridors. Rabe detected the influential presence of such persons when he set out to explain the states' entrepreneurship. But only a few years later, with a greater focus on California, he found it necessary to acknowledge "the dramatic expansion and intensification of entrepreneurial activity in many states." The entrepreneurs now included "a range of elected officials, agency and department heads, and a cavalcade of other individuals from foundations, consulting firms, environmental groups, and industry who perceive (then seize) opportunity to influence the shape of climate policy for a given jurisdiction."[34] Leading states began to look more like Washington, and as they acquired the greater complexity associated with innovative policymaking they also exhibited difficulty in implementing their innovations. Evidence mounts that the gap between ends and means that so bedevils the federal government is appearing also in leading states.

New Jersey, which in 2004 Rabe had portrayed as a leader in policy innovation, had become a laggard in implementation by 2008, as noted in chapter 1 in this volume. The sustainability plan was in disarray. Instead of following the declining emissions trajectory pledged by Whitman in 1998, New Jersey's emissions had increased by 9 percent between 1990 and 2003, putting it below twelve other states and the District of Columbia. As of 2007, New Jersey was reinventing its climate change wheel. Governor Jon Corzine signed into law the New Jersey Global Warming Response Act, which set California-like goals for emission reduction. The commissioner of the Department of Environmental Protection was given a lead role in implementation, but Rabe notes that "many of the initial duties imposed on the department and its partners resemble what was long since supposed to have been completed through the 2000 Action Plan."[35] California, he added, was moving forward "with the most ambitious set of climate policies of any government on the globe but no clear models of successful governance to follow from other states or nations."

The democratic governments of the United States, headed by elected, publicity-seeking chief executives and legislatures whose members have little incentive to take public management seriously, appear to share a tendency to act boldly when setting goals for popular causes but to postpone reflection on how to pay the costs or organize the means for getting to their proclaimed destinations. It is not at all clear that leading states, when stepping as policymakers into the inviting breach of federal inaction, do so with any greater ability to balance ends and means.

Conclusion

The role of state governments as innovators is not new. Historically, federal domestic policy has usually had state-level antecedents. Lord Bryce, Justice Brandeis, and President Franklin Roosevelt are among the notable historic figures who asserted that the capacity to try measures out on a small scale before adopting them on a large scale is an advantage of the federal system. Nonetheless, the function of the states as laboratories, in the stock phrase, is not uniformly appreciated. Feeley and Rubin spend three pages dismissing it as irrelevant and overblown, mainly because today the states are too constrained by national norms to be free to experiment. No state can experiment with denying health care to children or deliberately increasing emissions. In their eyes, a federalism that does not provide for variation in norms—fundamental values—is not federalism at all. But it certainly is possible to argue that in a world where policymaking contains many uncertainties—about priorities, pace, cost-benefit calculations, implementation strategies, the validity of scientific data—there is plenty of room for experiment even when goals are stipulated and norms widely embraced. Granted, the language of science—"laboratories of experiment"—is misleading and invites skepticism. There is more politics than science in what the states do. But that does not vitiate it. Public policy in any setting must pass political tests. Also, Feeley and Rubin overlook the extent to which national norms emerge through action at the state level. They do not come full blown from Congress.

The state-level activity regarding climate change vividly illustrates the central paradox of American federalism. Centralization advances relentlessly; that is the powerful secular trend. And yet the states refuse to die. They have a vigorous governmental life. With the exception of civil rights, no area of domestic policy experienced more centralization or more rapid centralization than environmental protection in the 1970s. Congress passed dozens of laws, most of them either regulating the states directly or using the newly invented technique of partial preemption, through which Congress occupied a field but gave the states the choice of adopting and implementing federal standards—the Kool-Aid that most of them took. Now, thirty years later, we are witness to states that are not passive, that are not thoroughly subordinated—states on steroids, as Rabe puts it. States have taken initiatives as Washington, for better or worse, has hesitated, and in doing so have demonstrated one of the leading features of compensatory federalism.

Notes

1. For more than a decade beginning in the early 1990s, a narrow majority of the Rehnquist court rendered decisions that purported to protect state governments against national power. Those decisions sought to impose limits on Congress's power to regulate interstate commerce and to enforce the Fourteenth Amendment; to limit the power of Congress to "commandeer" state governments in order to implement federal law; to broaden the immunity of state governments to lawsuits under the Eleventh Amendment to the Constitution; to show increased deference to state courts; and to reduce judicial supervision of state and local institutions such as schools and prisons. That effort inspired a large scholarly literature, of which the following are only a few examples: Frank Goodman, "The Supreme Court's Federalism: Real or Imagined?" *Annals of the American Academy of Political and Social Science* 574, no. 1 (2001); R. Shep Melnick, "Deregulating the States: Federalism in the Rehnquist Court," in *Evolving Federalisms: The Intergovernmental Balance of Power in Europe and America* (Maxwell School, Syracuse University, 2003); Mark Tushnet, *A Court Divided: The Rehnquist Court and the Future of Constitutional Law* (New York: W. W. Norton, 2005), chapter 10; and Ernest A. Young, "The Rehnquist Court's Two Federalisms," *Texas Law Review* 64 (2004), p. 1.

2. Malcolm M. Feeley and Edward Rubin, *Federalism: Political Identity and Tragic Compromise* (University of Michigan Press, 2008), p. ix.

3. Michael S. Greve, *Real Federalism: Why It Matters, How It Could Happen* (Washington: AEI Press, 1999).

4. Erwin Chemerinsky, *Enhancing Government: Federalism for the 21st Century* (Stanford University Press, 2008).

5. Paul E. Peterson, Barry G. Rabe, and Kenneth K. Wong, *When Federalism Works* (Brookings, 1986).

6. Timothy J. Conlan and Paul L. Posner, *Intergovernmental Management for the Twenty-First Century* (Brookings, 2008).

7. Paul Manna, *School's In: Federalism and the National Education Agenda* (Georgetown University Press, 2006).

8. But note the case of New Jersey. Much analysis of the state's experience of both in-migration and out-migration has appeared in recent years. Scholars at Rutgers University, Princeton University, and Boston College all have produced studies. For findings, see John Havens, "Migration of Wealth in New Jersey and the Impact on Wealth and Philanthropy," January 22, 2010 (www.bc.edu/research/cwp/meta-elements/pdf/njreport.pdf [March 5, 2010]). Havens does not attempt to explain his main factual finding—that there was an outflow of wealthy households between 2004 and 2008—but both the state's Chamber of Commerce and the *Wall Street Journal* editorial page confidently conclude that a sharp rise in the state's top marginal income tax rate is the cause. The rate went from 6.37 percent in 1996 to 8.97 percent in 2004 and to 10.75 percent in 2009. "Escape from Taxation," *Wall Street Journal*, February 13–14, 2010, A12.

9. Sam Roberts, "Data Show Steady Drop in Americans on the Move," *New York Times* (December 21, 2008), p. 27.

10. Compare Roberta Romano, *The Advantage of Competitive Federalism for Securities Regulation* (Washington: AEI Press, 2002); Richard L. Revesz, "Federalism and Environmental Regulation: A Public Choice Analysis," *Harvard Law Review* 115 (2001), p. 115; and Paul E. Peterson, *The Price of Federalism* (Brookings, 1995).

11. Paula Cotter, "Environment," in *State Attorneys General: Powers and Responsibilities,* 2nd ed., edited by Emily Myers and Lynne Ross (Washington: National Association of Attorneys General), pp. 143–44.

12. William Wan, "Attorney General Announces Suit to Enforce Cleanup," *Washington Post,* August 20, 2008, p. B4.

13. Lyndsey Layton, "Justice Dept. Says Pentagon Must Comply with EPA Cleanup Orders," *Washington Post,* December 5, 2008, p. A23.

14. Shannon Dininny, "AP Source: Washington State to Sue Feds over Hanford," November 25, 2008 (www.theolympian.com/stategovernment/story/674124.html).

15. Associated Press, "N.C. Lawsuit against TVA Pollution in Federal Court" (www.news-record.com/content/2008/07/30/article/nc_lawsuit_against_tva_pollution); Bruce Henderson, "Judge to TVA: Curb Emissions near N. C. Line," *Charlotte Observer,* January 14, 2009 (www.lexisnexis.com/us/lnacademic), and Dave Flessner, "TVA to Appeal Clean Air Order," *Chattanooga Times Free Press,* May 30, 2009 (www.lexisnexis.com/us/lnacademic).

16. Morton Keller and R. Shep Melnick, *Taking Stock: American Government in the Twentieth Century* (Washington: Woodrow Wilson Center Press and Cambridge University Press, 1999). The quotations are from pages 164–69.

17. R. Shep Melnick, *Regulation and the Courts: The Case of the Clean Air Act* (Brookings, 1983), pp. 344, 393.

18. Martha Derthick, *Keeping the Compound Republic: Essays on American Federalism* (Brookings, 2001), p. 131.

19. Pietro S. Nivola and Jon A. Shields, *Managing Green Mandates: Local Rigors of U.S. Environmental Regulation* (Washington: AEI-Brookings Joint Center for Regulatory Studies, 2001), pp. 4–5.

20. Eric M. Patashnik, *Reforms at Risk: What Happens after Major Policy Changes Are Enacted* (Princeton University Press, 2008), chapter 8.

21. Steven M. Teles, *Whose Welfare? AFDC and Elite Politics* (University Press of Kansas, 1996), pp. 141–44.

22. James E. McCarthy and Robert Meltz, "California's Waiver Request to Control Greenhouse Gases under the Clean Air Act" (Washington: Congressional Research Service, March 4, 2008).

23. Jonathan H. Adler, "Hothouse Flowers: The Vices and Virtues of Climate Federalism," *Temple Political and Civil Rights Law Review* 17 (Spring 2008), p. 443.

24. The policy options are renewable electricity mandates or portfolio standards; carbon taxes; renewable fuel mandates or equivalent programs that mandate expanded use of biofuels; carbon cap-and-trade programs; statewide emissions reduction targets; mandatory reporting of carbon emissions; formal participation as a co-plaintiff in the Supreme Court case *Massachusetts* v. *EPA* concerning carbon dioxide regulation; and adoption of carbon emission standards for vehicles enacted by California. For an updated, expanded illustration of the relation between state climate policies and GHG emissions growth, see table 1-1 in chapter 1 of this volume.

25. Barry G. Rabe, "States on Steroids: The Intergovernmental Odyssey of American Climate Policy," *Review of Policy Research* 25, no. 2 (2008), pp. 105–28.

26. Barry G. Rabe, *Statehouse and Greenhouse: The Emerging Politics of American Climate Change Policy* (Brookings, 2004), chapter 4.

27. Barry G. Rabe, "Regionalism and Global Climate Change Policy: Revisiting Multistate Collaboration as an Intergovernmental Management Tool," in *Intergovernmental Management for the Twenty-First Century*, edited by Timothy J. Conlan and Paul L. Posner (Brookings, 2008).

28. Felicity Barringer and Kate Galbraith, "States Aim to Cut Gases by Making Polluters Pay," *New York Times,* September 16, 2008, p. A14; Robin Shulman, "Carbon Sale Raises $40 Million," *Washington Post,* September 30, 2008, p. A4.

29. Barry G. Rabe, "Governing the Climate from Sacramento," in *Unlocking the Power of Networks*, edited by Stephen Goldsmith and Donald F. Kettl (Brookings, 2009), p. 37.

30. Ibid.

31. Rabe, *Statehouse and Greenhouse,* chapter 1.

32. Derthick, *Keeping the Compound Republic*, p. 135.

33. John Yoo, "Election Was No Sweeping Mandate," *Philadelphia Inquirer,* December 7, 2008 (www.aei.org/include/pub_print.asp?pubID=29030).

34. Rabe, "Governing the Climate from Sacramento."

35. Ibid.

4

The Politics of Vertical Diffusion: The States and Climate Change

PAUL L. POSNER

Concerns about climate change and related environmental and energy issues have prompted a broad and diffuse set of policy responses in the United States. Following in their time-honored role as policy laboratories and innovators in the federal system, states have initiated a wide range of climate-related programs, including regional cap-and-trade regimes, state renewable energy portfolio mandates, emergent automobile tailpipe emissions standards, land use regulations, smart growth plans, and recycling incentives, among others. The federal system has provided a strong state-based pathway to policy reform that stands in stark contrast to the policy gridlock that has hamstrung full congressional approval of House and Senate climate change legislation in the 111th Congress.

While providing a safe harbor for policy innovation, the states' policy initiatives have also served to stoke the interest of national leaders in putting this issue squarely on the national agenda. The relationship between state initiatives and national policy formulation and adoption (vertical diffusion) is an important but little studied area of the federal system.[1] While not well understood, states' policy leadership often bears fruit on the national stage. Whether relating to the federal highway program, special education, or air quality standards themselves, major federal policy thrusts often have antecedents in the states. It is likely that without state initiatives, national programs would have taken longer to bloom and develop, if at all.

This chapter attempts to better understand the vertical diffusion process as it pertains to climate change. First, the political dynamic behind the expansion of state policies to the federal level is assessed: what forces are at work to expand state climate change initiatives to the national level—or to limit them?

Second, the implications of state initiatives for federal policymakers and designers is explored. Does the presence of substantial state policy leadership dispose federal leaders to accommodate states' interests when designing federal policies that build on state policies? Do federal officials defer to preexisting state policies, helping to guarantee substantial delegation or devolution to the states? Are there specific policy tools that enable federal officials to both accommodate the states while also promoting national values and priorities? How do federal leaders attempt to accommodate and balance the interests of states that adopted reforms early with those of states that have not yet embraced reforms?

Such questions are likely to increasingly preoccupy national leaders as they struggle to fashion a national climate change policy. Ironically, while standing on the shoulders of the states, Washington may very well adopt policies that outflank, curb, and even preempt those of the states that served as the midwives for policy reform at the outset.

Trends in State Policy Innovation

In some of the earlier debates surrounding the establishment of modern national policy, states were perceived to be recalcitrant actors, bucking national policy moods, values, and bandwagons. State limitations and deficiencies stemmed from their uneven fiscal and managerial capacities and their lack of incentives to adequately address the growing range of public problems whose benefits or costs spilled over state or even national boundaries. Many took note of the propensity of states in general to underfund policies that could erode their state's ability to compete with others for jobs and wealth—the so-called "race to the bottom."[2]

Against that backdrop, it is a turnabout indeed that states are now viewed as the policy innovators in the U.S. system. Frustrated by political and policy gridlock at the national level, many groups championing policy reforms find states to be hospitable and eager champions of new policy ideas and reforms. It is quite a conceptual reversal to view states as the catalyst for national policy change, influencing reluctant federal officials to adopt policy reforms. Not content to rest on their own policy laurels, state officials join with powerful advocacy groups to champion the nationalization of policies, realizing that in some sense the disparate actions of individual states are incomplete and suboptimal solutions to pressing national and global problems.

Important political realities underpin states' role as policy innovators. Most notably, many states are positioned to reach policy agreement and action well ahead of national policymakers on many issues. Compared to the national policymaking process, most states are more cohesive and homogeneous, thereby enabling them to achieve consensus on policy action in a more timely way. James Madison presciently observed that smaller units of government would be quicker to act; extending the "sphere" makes it more difficult to act in unison because of the greater number of interests and parties.[3] Over a century later, Louis Brandeis observed that states are the "laboratories of democracy," building a store of policy innovations that can be tapped by national officials when the time is ripe.[4]

The constitutional responsibilities for providing for public education, health, and safety, among other basic domestic services, ensures that states and local governments often will address emerging public issues and problems in their formative stages. John Teaford argues that states played the role of policy incubators as far back as the nineteenth century, hatching reforms in child labor, public assistance, and workers' compensation that were later nationalized during the Progressive Movement and the New Deal.[5]

It can be argued that the role of the states as policy incubators has intensified in recent years. The growth of state policy and governance capacity has prompted greater policy activism. Over the past 50 years, structural and political reforms such as the reapportionment of legislatures, growth of professional staffs, and enhanced revenue systems have transformed states into the workhorses of the U.S. federal system. Throwing off the yoke of segregation that clouded their national policy legitimacy, many states became more responsive to the broader range of groups and interests that found their way to state capitals. As states became more critical players in implementing the growing array of federal domestic programs, national advocacy groups joined the ranks of business and other traditional interest groups in organizing a state presence.[6] Thanks to many of those changes, ambitious state political leaders have become policy activists, often competing with one another to champion early adoption of many emerging policy ideas, whether relating to nonsmoking ordinances, stricter drinking-and-driving regulations, or more ambitious work requirements for welfare programs.

The Nationalization of State Policy Reforms

Ironically, greater state policy activism has also sparked greater federal policy ambition in its wake. Far from earning the states forbearance, state-based reforms have increasingly been seized on by federal officials to institute more centralized federal programs. While many such programs provide federal funds to hard-pressed states, they also often come laden with centralizing and coercive federal policies as well.

The national adoption of state initiatives results from both state push and national pull, as discussed in chapter 3 of this volume. In one recent study of the national expansion of state policy reforms, the advocacy of state officials proved to be the most important factor in nationalizing state initiatives.[7] Where state policies have external benefits or costs, the initiatives of leading states can often be undermined by the inaction or opposition by other states. For instance, states with strong gun control laws cannot effectively police their borders, as their regulatory regimes are undermined by the importation of guns purchased in states with weaker regulations. Similarly, states with strong air pollution regimes cannot achieve their goals in the absence of effective controls by upwind states. States with strong climate change programs could suffer as business relocates to states with weaker regulatory profiles. Accordingly, state leaders often seek federal policy action to save state initiatives from the downward spiral of intergovernmental competition, but their calls for federal action entail risks as well, since state leaders can lose control of their policies to contending national groups.

While states have become more fertile sources of policy innovation, shifts in national political institutions have ensured that state ideas gain national attention more quickly than ever before. Fundamental changes in the U.S. party system have converted national political officials from being ambassadors of state and local party officials into independent political entrepreneurs anxious to establish their own visible policy profiles to appeal for financing and votes from a diverse coalition of special interests, media organizations, and voters. In a nation with a "24/7" news cycle focused on Washington, a more diverse and aggressive media are likely to report and analyze state policies and place the underlying issues more readily on the policy agendas of national leaders.

More assertive and diverse national interest groups and policy entrepreneurs stand ready to capitalize on state innovations to promote the adoption of national policies. State initiatives are often used to illustrate that the new policies are feasible, effective, and popular. Moreover, state policy initiatives trigger the deployment of powerful equity arguments—as more states adopt a policy, the failure of all states to adopt the policy comes to be viewed as promoting inequitable treatment of citizens, businesses, or other entities based solely on their state of residence. Eventually, state policy initiatives reach a tipping point at which policy benefits are perceived to constitute a national minimum standard or even entitlement. In this kind of system, state policy innovations are not as much cause for celebration as for alarm by advocates seeking to nationalize policy and by opponents such as business interests seeking to slow the pace of policy innovation.[8]

The role of business as a force promoting nationalization of state policies is especially noteworthy. As business becomes more global, it has shifted from its traditional position of supporting decentralization of policy to the states to seeking national legislation to standardize, restrict, or actually prohibit state initiatives. Whether regarding initiatives in such areas as environmental protection, taxation of access to the Internet, or regulation of health benefits, many business interests have been busy seeking ways to limit states' policy flexibility and discretion.

Indeed, it is likely that the pace of vertical diffusion has grown over recent decades.[9] The greater penetration of nationalized media and Internet communications interact with increasingly organized and articulate interest groups and ambitious and anxious national political leaders to create a combustible critical mass of policy and political energy. Michael Greve argues, however, that the more rapid pace of dissemination and adoption means that the laboratories of democracy are not given sufficient time to test policy ideas.[10]

Richard Nathan argues that there has been a cyclical aspect to this process of policy expansion. States become more active when conservative regimes occupy Washington, which suggests that as liberal, activist regimes come to power, states' policy activism recedes.[11] While cyclical forces may have some influence, the forces propelling states to take on roles as national policy activists are more secular than cyclical. They are rooted in the fundamental changes that have occurred in state and national politics and institutions. They also are rooted in shifts in national media coverage and political parties. Indeed, as the Bush presidency reflects, even conservative ideological regimes are no longer shy about centralizing federal power and programs.[12]

Many who have studied the U.S. federal system in recent years have chronicled the secular growth of nationalizing and centralizing forces within the system. Policy areas from education to emergency preparedness that traditionally were the preserve of state and local governments have become subject to a seemingly inexorable process of federal policy centralization. Federal officials have been increasingly enticed and pressured to respond to a prodigious agenda of national problems through more centralized and nationalizing policy actions and tools, whether they take the form of mandates or other forms of preemptions. Regardless of how small or localized, seemingly no issue of domestic governance is off the table for a national policy response. Areas of long-standing local control, such as education, give way to national policy regimes in the face of leaders anxious to prove their policy and political mettle to their restive publics. Centrally, the impulse to nationalize policy has proven to be surprisingly bipartisan, as conservatives in the Bush era built new national mandates in such areas as education, homeland security, and election administration.[13] The secular trend toward greater federal preemption through 1999 is shown in figure 4-1.

Barry Rabe notes that in environmental policy, Washington has gradually shifted from a strategy emphasizing financial carrots to one laden with regulatory mandates.[14] Whereas federal grants covered approximately 70 percent of state environmental protection expenditures in the early 1980s, that figure had declined to about 30 percent by the beginning of the George W. Bush presidency. This transition occurred along with an accumulation of federal rules and mandates that expanded the state governments' workload and narrowed states' ability to pursue their own priorities.

Figure 4-1. *Trends in Federal Preemptions, 1791–1999*

Number

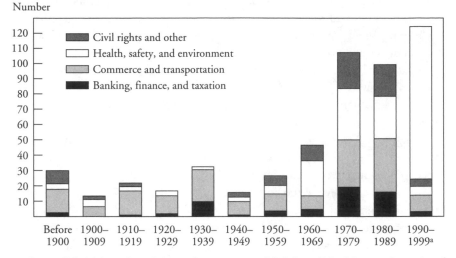

Source: U.S. Advisory Commission on Intergovernmental Relations, *Federal Statutory Preemption of State and Local Authority: History, Inventory, and Issues* (Washington, 1992), p. 7.

a. The 1990–91 rate was multiplied by 5 to estimate how many preemptions might be enacted during 1990–99.

The Emergence of State Leadership on Climate Change

State governments have emerged as the principal policy leaders in the U.S. system on climate change. The states have developed policy initiatives on their own—and, increasingly, in concert with other states in their region—that have garnered attention and greater diffusion across the states in the past decade. (Many of those policies are introduced in chapters 1 and 3 in this volume.)

Most notably, states have initiated their own cap-and-trade programs to control greenhouse gas emissions. As noted elsewhere in this volume, as of 2009, twenty-three states as well as four Canadian provinces were participating in three separate regional cap-and-trade systems: the Regional Greenhouse Gas Initiative (RGGI) in the Northeast, the Western Climate Initiative, and the Midwestern Greenhouse Gas Reduction Accord. In addition, California has instituted a separate cap-and-trade program in the Global Warming Solutions Act of 2006 (Assembly Bill 32, or AB 32). The only system actually in operation is RGGI, with a cap-and-trade system focusing on power plant emissions of carbon. The other regional agreements will be phased in beginning in 2012 and are scheduled to include other carbon sources in addition to power plants.

A November 2009 Resources for the Future study identifies the range of state initiatives, several of which are explored in greater detail in part 2 of this volume.[15] They include the following:

—*Emissions targets.* Twelve states have targets to reduce their emissions below a baseline level. California has committed the state to lower greenhouse gas emissions to 1990 levels by 2020. Twenty-eight other states have climate plans to identify strategies to reduce emissions over time.

—*Electricity policies.* Nearly thirty states require that specific amounts of electricity be generated from renewable sources, including wind, solar, geothermal, and biomass energy. Many states have dedicated funds for the support of energy efficiency projects, collected from utilities. Several states have gone further to require that new power plants meet a carbon performance standard, and several have required offsets for a portion of new emissions.

—*Transportation policies.* California has adopted a new requirement for tailpipe emissions of greenhouse gases from automobiles that became national policy in a May 2009 decision by President Barack Obama. In addition, states are working to develop transportation and land use planning that will save on energy consumption by providing for mass transit, reducing sprawl, and promoting rideshare programs and other congestion management strategies.

—*Agricultural policies.* Some states are working with farmers to improve soil conservation techniques to increase the amount of carbon stored in the soil.

—*Building energy codes.* States are establishing codes for residential and commercial buildings designed to reduce energy consumption.

Local governments also have taken initiatives to deal with climate change. Mayors of more than 710 cities participate in the Mayor's Climate Protection Agreement, which urges cities to institute programs to reduce emissions through efficient lighting, enforcement of building codes, carpooling, mass transit, and low-carbon vehicles and green buildings for government business.[16]

Despite the wide scope of state and local initiatives, many appear to be illogical from a public choice perspective. After all, states are asking for sacrifice from their businesses and residents in return for benefits that not only often spill over state and even national boundaries but that are apparent only over several decades. Rabe argues that many states have at least framed the issue in terms of economic development, making the case that developing green industries and renewable energy sources will create new jobs for state residents.[17] Indeed, state programs have inspired the creation of "green" markets that depend on stronger regulations for their survival. In effect, green companies' support for greenhouse gas emissions controls constitutes a form of rent seeking, under which the companies support government policies to bolster their own market position over those of competitors.[18] Anne Carlson argues that many state initiatives were prompted by what she calls a "strong nudge" from the federal government; for example, California's leadership in air standards is attributable in part to the push from federal clean air standards.[19]

While no doubt true, a good deal of the explanation for the states' proactive role in climate policy comes from the interplay of increasingly robust policy pathways within state politics and government that include input from experts and interest groups and symbolic efforts. Experts in environmental policy have become institutionalized within states over the years, thanks partly to federal programs, and they have become centers of advocacy for climate policy. Interest groups have become more robust as well, as environmental groups have found their way to state capitals.[20] And finally, political leaders have engaged in increasingly sophisticated campaigns to tap widespread public concern over climate change, resulting in a competitive "race to the top" with political competitors both within state government and across the nation.[21]

The Instability of State Innovations in Climate Change Policy

It should be noted that, notwithstanding the ambitious goals set by states, most climate change initiatives have not yet been implemented. Engel and Orbach suggest that the endorsement of these policies engenders immediate benefits to political leaders who can claim credit and position themselves as leaders on an important issue. However, the costs and many of the difficult trade-offs associated with climate policies, particularly cap and trade, are postponed.[22] Richard Stewart argues that the gains to each state are marginal at best—California's emissions represent a little more than 1 percent of global totals. He concludes that the benefits may not be sufficiently compelling to outweigh the costs of unilateral state action once the programs reach full implementation.[23]

Some have suggested that the state and local initiatives undertaken so far constitute pledges to reduce emissions at some distant date in the future, not robust programs to achieve results in the near term. One observer concluded that such state initiatives are reminiscent of the prayer of Saint Augustine: "Give me chastity and continence, but not yet."[24]

The disconnect between ambitious goals and the realities of implementation is a familiar dilemma in the federal system. Regional water commissions, such as the six state networks governing the cleanup of the Chesapeake Bay, have been prone to adopting "stretch" goals, only to be perennially disappointed as the diffuse actors responsible for nonpoint source pollution, such as farmers, developers, and local governments, fail to take the costly actions necessary to attain the goals.[25] Other national collective action initiatives pursued by state officials have proven to be vulnerable to free riders and defections by key states. State initiatives to harmonize the regulation of insurance protections for consumers, driver's license requirements, and sales taxes all failed to gain threshold levels of support from other states. Federal leadership was essential to gaining full participation in the insurance and driver's license cases.[26]

In the climate arena, many of the initiatives that states have piloted are vulnerable to slippage and challenges from other state and national actors. Subnational reforms may suffer from leakage, under which businesses in stronger states move transactions to states with weaker regulatory regimes, thereby undermining the political and economic sustainability of stronger state controls. Rabe shows that New York governor David Paterson caused a stir in September 2008 when he said that the state might withdraw from RGGI because of concerns that businesses in the state might move outside the region to search for cheaper power.[27] States also risk stirring opposition from national businesses due to the higher transaction costs associated with differing state programs and standards across the national economy. Moreover, state or regional cap-and-trade systems carry the potential to limit the liquidity and flexibility required for trading markets to work effectively. Ultimately, integrating the nation's climate control strategy with those of other nations is best facilitated by a common framework across the states.

Perhaps aware of their own limitations, state actors have not contented themselves with championing change in their own backyards. Rather, they have become national figures intent on expanding their initiatives to the nation itself. Many argue that the primary reason for state climate policies is not that they are ends in themselves but that they are part of a political strategy to secure federal adoption of national climate measures, including most notably a national cap-and-trade system.

Accordingly, climate change policy appears to be following a path taken by other policies.[28] Recognizing that state or regional efforts cannot contain spillovers and leakages, state officials have come to champion national policy adoption, albeit through policies that provide a robust role for the states. Specifically, state officials have championed a comprehensive climate program, featuring a national cap-and-trade program. However, they also have pushed for authority for individual states and regional compacts to exceed federal greenhouse gas standards. In addition, state organizations have argued for federal funding in the form of allowances and grants allocated to states as well as federal support for the pursuit of state regulatory policies in areas such as transportation and land use and economic development that complement cap-and-trade regimes.

State climate change policies have bolstered advocacy of a national program by other interests as well. Business groups have argued for a preemptive national program, arguing that the emergence of differing state regulatory and cap-and-trade policies are economically inefficient. Environmentalists also have used state programs to show the feasibility of fully national programs; while sympathetic to the right of states to go beyond national standards, environmentalists have nonetheless been leaders in arguing for a fully national policy.

A national climate change program was a main plank in the policy platform of President Obama as well as of the Democrats now controlling both houses of Congress. As noted throughout this volume, the Obama administration's support of a national greenhouse gas emissions program stands in marked contrast to the opposition evinced by the Bush administration. Moreover, the Obama administration appears to be more sympathetic to a role for the states as well. Its decision to base new nationwide motor vehicle tailpipe standards on California's standard went well beyond the traditional waiver that federal officials have granted to California and states adopting California's standard voluntarily. Moreover, in May 2009, the administration issued new policy guidance to federal agencies urging them to avoid preemption of states, calling on them to review Bush era preemptions of states to ascertain their fit with the new policy guidance.[29]

Federal Policy Responses to State-Led Changes

The questions facing federal policymakers confronting a cap-and-trade system are profound. They, of course, must deal with sensitive trade-offs among different energy sources and between various sectors of the economy. But either explicitly or implicitly, they essentially will be making decisions about how to deal with the states.

The states' role in climate change raises classic questions about the roles of federal and state governments in achieving environmental, economic, and political goals. Absent some kind of federal regulatory framework, the existence of unfettered state regulation and cap-and-trade programs can burden interstate commerce, complicate potential negotiations on a global climate change framework, and limit the liquidity of national carbon trading markets. As noted before, state initiatives are likely to be unstable, as first-mover states with strong climate rules become vulnerable to exploitation by "free rider" states with weaker regulations. Such intergovernmental competition can serve to undermine the environmental gains achieved by first movers.[30] Avoiding a "race to the bottom" requires a degree of intergovernmental collaboration among the states that is rare in the federal system.

While uniform federal regulations and cap-and-trade frameworks can ensure uniformity and bring about deeper and more liquid trading markets, they also have significant downsides. A single uniform federal set of standards threatens to impose a one-size-fits-all framework on states with vastly different energy markets and needs that should be taken into account if a cap-and-trade system is to work effectively. Even once the federal government adopts a cap-and-trade system, a continued strong role for independent state programs can be justified as an important feedback and learning mechanism that can continue to help national policymakers adjust to new developments and public expectations. States, moreover, have control over key complementary policies that have a direct bearing on climate change, including land use and transportation planning. Depending on its design, a single federal framework can also penalize states that served a vital function as first movers in innovating pioneering programs to deal with climate change in advance of the federal government.[31]

The decisions about how to deal with states occur across many different fronts. First, questions need to be resolved about whether and how to accommodate state

Figure 4-2. *Overlapping Policy Strategies*

Source: Author's illustration.

cap-and-trade programs that cover the same issues to be regulated in federal legislation. In addition, there is a wide range of complementary policies besides cap and trade in which states play primary roles. Here, functions traditionally controlled by state and local governments—such as land use, building codes, transportation planning, and regulation of utilities—play a critical role in determining the nation's output of carbon emissions. As figure 4-2 shows, those "complementary policies" go hand-in-hand with more explicit regulation of carbon emissions through cap-and-trade programs to constitute the policy portfolio available to deal with the climate change threat. One assessment concluded that complementary measures could achieve as much as half the reductions needed to meet federal emissions targets.[32]

Federal Policy Tools

Federal officials have a number of policy tools that could be considered in balancing federal and state roles, and their decisions will be influenced by their support for both the underlying policy goals and the states' role. Table 4-1 shows how these two variables together can inform federal policy tool choices.

Federal officials who favor a policy and who view states as policy allies would be disposed to select a categorical grant, which gains state involvement with accountability for specific, discrete federal goals. For instance, in the 1916 Federal-Aid-Road Act, Congress used a grant to encourage the states to create highway departments, which had already been adopted by thirty-three states at the time.[33] Federal champions of a policy who do not fully trust states to share their priorities might reach for more coercive tools, such as mandates.

National officials with qualms about the policy proposed might try to defeat it outright, but if they fail, they still have several strategies available. If they are

Table 4-1. *Choosing Federal-State Policy Strategies*

	Pro-policy	Anti-policy
Pro-state	Grant	Devolution
Anti-state	Mandate	Preemption

Source: Author's illustration.

comfortable with allowing the states to play a prominent role, they can devolve the policy to the states, enabling them to exercise their own priorities. The Reagan block grants of the 1980s, for instance, represented a conscious strategy to devolve decisionmaking to states for programs that the president felt were no longer top national priorities. Those opposed to policies can also preempt the states by enacting legislation preventing government action in the policy area. The prohibition of state taxation of access to the Internet is a case in which Congress did not feel that any level of government should levy taxes on access.

In the climate change area, each of these tools has already come into play in legislation considered in 2008 and 2009:[34]

—*Categorical grants.* Recognizing the importance of complementary policies such as those concerning land use and transportation, the federal government can provide categorical grants with conditions requiring states to use the funds to support strong complementary programs in such areas, with appropriate reporting and accountability. States already use funding from existing categorical grants such as those issued through the Department of Energy's State Energy Program to support green building upgrades of building codes and related activities. Leading cap-and-trade proposals award allowances to states that meet specific national policy goals, such as energy-efficient building codes and transportation planning.

—*Federal mandates.* Regulations can be imposed on both states and businesses in which specific activities have a more direct bearing on climate change. Mandates on states to implement renewable energy portfolio standards and national building code standards are two examples contained in pending House or Senate climate change bills under consideration in the 111th Congress.

—*Devolution.* In effect, the federal government has devolved authority to the states in recent years to develop their own standards and initiatives. While the federal government is unlikely to continue to take a passive leadership position in the future, it is possible that it will devolve authority to regulate or oversee particular areas contributing to climate change to the states under the rubric of a broad national regulatory program. That approach may be used in areas in which state and local control is firmly entrenched, such as in land use and building codes.

—*Preemption.* Preemption of the states can be employed by national officials who oppose any state government action on an issue. But in the U.S. federal system, it also has become a fallback or second-best option used by business interests to replace numerous stronger state regulatory programs with a single, weaker

Figure 4-3. *Preemption Dynamics*

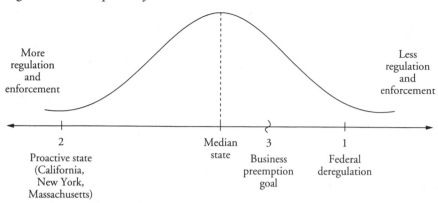

Source: Paul Teske, "Checks, Balances, and Thresholds: State Regulatory Reinforcement and Federal Preemptions," *PS: Political Science and Politics* 38, no. 3 (July 2005), p. 367.

federal standard. While viewed as a defeat for the states, federal preemption can actually constitute a triumph for state policy initiatives when they force business to accept a compromise in the form of federal standards that lie between no standards and the most stringent state standards. For instance, in the case of national energy appliance standards, state regulatory standards forced business interests to shift their position from opposition to any government regulation to support for national standards that preempted those of the states. In this case, states' initiatives, in effect, pushed the business community further down the road toward national standards than they originally wished to go. Ironically, then, while state policy initiatives can lead to their own preemption, the resulting national standards in fact constitute an expansion of some portion of earlier state policies, as illustrated by figure 4-3, from work by Paul Teske.[35]

Joint Federal-State Programs: The Partial Preemption Model

One approach that lies between preemption and grants is partial preemption, which often is used to share federal and state authority for environmental programs. Under this strategy, the federal government typically promulgates national standards but enables states to go beyond those standards to respond to unique state conditions and constituencies. From a political perspective alone, it is an effective approach to accommodate both national uniformity and state diversity. States also are typically assigned roles in implementing and enforcing the joint federal-state standards.

The partial preemption approach is well-suited to federal programs initiated by the states. The framework undergirding the Clean Air Program from its founding entails a shared federal-state policy implementation process. EPA sets national air quality standards, while states prepare implementation plans detailing their own strategies for reaching those standards, including initiatives to exceed the federal minimums.

The partial preemption approach recognizes that a partnership between federal and state governments can constitute a more effective approach to dealing with the broad sweeping challenges posed by climate change than either a purely state or federal strategy. One of the factors that augers well for a continuing state role in climate change is the strong tradition of state participation in EPA's regulatory programs. States continue to be called on to play a central role in most areas of environmental policy implementation. They operate about three-quarters of the federal environmental programs that can be delegated to states, which constitute about 90 percent of the environmental protection service workload. States also conduct approximately 90 percent of all environmental enforcement actions and collect nearly 95 percent of the data used by EPA.[36]

The states also can bring considerable assets to the implementation of climate change policy. As with other environmental policies, the ambitions of the federal government far exceed its administrative, legal, fiscal, and political capacity to implement its programs, mandates, and preemptions. Accordingly, states and local governments, along with a wide range of nonprofit and private corporations, are brought in as third parties to carry out federal initiatives through a host of government tools, including grants and loans, in addition to regulatory tools.[37] The states bring resources such as staff, expertise, legal authority, fiscal capacity, and the potential to provide political legitimacy to federal regulatory programs.

Moreover, thanks partly to four decades of federal programs, states have matured in their commitment to the environment and in their capacity to design and implement complex policies. The maturation of states as stewards of federal initiatives came full circle as states replaced many of the federal cuts in EPA programs in the 1980s with increased fees and taxes.[38]

Challenges in Deploying Partial Preemption Strategies

The partial preemption model that has served the nation so well in other environmental policy areas raises vexing challenges and tensions when applied to a national cap-and-trade system. The partial preemption model would enable states with more stringent climate cap-and-trade policies to continue them once a national program is approved. However, this time-honored formula may be undermined by powerful incentives favoring national trading of allowances under an economically efficient cap-and-trade program.

Most economists would argue that a national cap-and-trade system must cover as many emission sources as possible to produce the optimal outcomes for the climate and the economy. Broader coverage will promote more functional trading markets, promote the pricing of as many alternative reduction strategies as possible, and limit leakage from capped to uncapped sources.[39] Thus, cap-and-trade programs are a classic case of a policy that is more effectively used at the national than the state or regional level.[40] Accordingly, most congressional proposals under consideration provide for direct EPA regulation of individual sources of greenhouse gas emissions, skipping the states.

Most important, there are profound disincentives for states to employ stronger emissions controls in a national trading market. As articulated by former RGGI leader Franz Litz, a federal cap establishes both a ceiling and a floor on greenhouse gas emission reductions. That is, the federal program distributes allowances based on the total tonnage of emissions permitted from covered sources under the cap-and-trade program. States that impose more stringent emissions limits on their home state industries would reduce the total emissions from those sources but would not reduce the number of federal allowances. Accordingly, the allowances freed up by firms within the more stringent state would then be sold to firms in other states. As long as the total number of federal allowances remains unchanged nationwide, states with more stringent caps would, in effect, redistribute emissions but not lower them on net. Firms in the stringent state would reduce their emissions below federal caps only to enable firms in more lenient states to avoid reducing emissions by purchasing the freed-up allowances.[41] That would set up a prisoner's dilemma for stringent states—their consumers may face higher energy costs that would ease the compliance burden of consumers in other states through the creation of allowances.[42]

Litz articulates options for giving states meaningful roles in a federal trading program:

—Allow states to control all or a portion of allowances issued to firms within their borders. The states would receive allowance budgets, similar to those under RGGI. EPA's ozone program offers an example of a cap-and-trade program with an EPA-regulated national market in which emissions limits are based on emissions budgets assigned to the participating states. States are free to choose how they allocate their allowances to individual sources.[43]

—Allow states to impose restrictions on the sale or use of allowances. One way to ensure that more stringent targets stick would be to enable states to restrict the use or sale of allowances by firms within the state. Eliminating state allowances would, in effect, reduce the national cap.

—Distribute allowances or auction revenues to states to support complementary climate policies. As noted above, states could be enticed to increase support for energy efficiency, mass transit, and other low-carbon strategies by funds provided through auctions of allowances. Such allowances could be tied to actual reductions achieved through those strategies, assuming that reductions could be reliably measured.

—Permit states to opt out of the federal cap-and-trade program to join a single alternative state program. As in California's auto emissions program, states could collectively establish a single alternative program with lower caps.

Those alternatives, of course, generate concerns of their own. The dilemma stems from the fact that cap-and-trade systems rely on deep national markets to generate pricing signals that lead to the most economically efficient energy choices. Creating separate state markets based on different state standards would obviously limit the liquidity and efficiency of national trading markets for allowances generated from cap-and-trade programs. Even within a common national market, creating separate or stronger state caps risks creating transaction costs. Firms would have to keep track of different allowances issued on the same unit of emissions, as well as other rules on offsets and points of regulation that might differ across governments.

Placing state restrictions on the sale of allowances would possibly risk judicial action. In a comparable case, New York attempted to prevent in-state firms from selling excess allowances under the acid rain program to firms in "upwind states"—a process that encouraged dirtier air to float back to New York. A federal court ruled that the New York law was preempted by directly contradictory provisions of the federal acid rain program.[44]

The foregoing suggests that difficult trade-offs must be made in designing a national cap-and-trade bill that both optimizes national markets and gives states appropriate incentives. Deep national markets promote cost-effective choices and lower the nation's bill for achieving climate goals. However, the price for achieving that is to forgo the advantages of state engagement and innovations in the design and implementation of cap-and-trade programs.

Implications of Differences among States for Program Design

Dealing with differences among the states is endemic to policies featuring national expansions of state-led policy. Indeed, one of the purposes of national legislation is to achieve greater congruence in policy outcomes across the states. Dealing with tensions between first movers of policy innovations and late adopters is a perennial challenge for national policymakers that will become central to the politics of cap and trade.

As Barry Rabe suggests in chapter 11, climate change strategies create cleavages throughout the country that defy partisan fault lines. The effects on utilities that rely on nuclear or hydroelectric power will be different from those on companies that rely on coal. Even generators of renewable technologies, such as wind and solar power, compete with one another for scarce subsidies and market share. As Rabe notes, at the very least these fault lines complicate the process of assembling majorities to support particular types of climate change legislation.[45]

The politics of climate change will play out against major disparities in both emissions rates and regulatory programs among the states, as discussed in chapter 1. EPA data show that states varied significantly in their emissions growth rates, with Delaware, at the low end, reducing emissions by 5 percent from 1990 through 2007 while Nevada increased emissions by 45 percent over the same period. By mapping the disparate trends onto equally disparate levels of regulatory programs, Rabe defines four groupings of states—those with high emissions and high policy effort, high emissions and low policy effort, low emissions and high policy effort, and low emissions and low policy effort (see table 1-1).[46]

As noted previously, these differences have implications for states' support of climate change legislation. States in the low-emissions, high-effort quadrant will have far different positions on a national cap-and-trade program than states in the high-emissions, low-effort part. This variability among the states has already served to complicate their political stance on these issues in Washington. Staff of a leading organization representing the states report that their organization cannot take positions on federal climate change legislation due to the internal conflicts that doing so would create among its members.

First Movers and Late Adopters: Grants and Regulations

In the climate change arena, federal grants and payments among states could once again serve their time-honored role in building political support across the nation. The acid rain program in 1990 was facilitated by a series of strategic concessions to high-sulfur coal states, including distribution of free allowances based on historical rates of sulfur dioxide pollution.[47] As suggested by Leigh Raymond in chapter 5 of this volume, for climate change legislation, the allocation and distribution of allowances and/or auctioned permits constitutes a potential source of redistribution across sources and states that can either exacerbate or ameliorate tensions between winners and losers. Carbon credits are wealth—annual revenues from the sale of allowances are estimated to be between $50 billion and $300 billion a year by 2020.[48] Thus, for instance, allowances awarded on the basis of historical emissions will tend to reward firms and states with higher emissions while those awarded on the basis of population or total power consumption would have different distributional consequences.[49]

Resolving the tensions between first movers and late adopters is one of the perennial challenges of crafting federal legislation in many policy areas. On one hand, promoting innovation in any system, federal or not, has longer-term value to policymakers who recognize and reward early adopters. Policies that have the effect of penalizing those taking the initiative to address emergent public problems can bring about a form of moral hazard that can discourage the initiative and innovation that is the hallmark of a healthy federal system.

On the other hand, states or businesses that have not yet climbed the learning curve face marginal costs and other charges that are arguably far higher than those faced by early adopters. Since federal programs often serve to disseminate innovation from early adopters to late adopters, one could argue that the latter group has more leverage. As social scientist Helen Ingram noted many years ago, the first goal of many federal programs is to achieve universal participation, even at the expense of accountability for program goals. Gaining participation often requires compensating those late adopters who might be reluctant to join the national effort, thereby jeopardizing the process of nationalization.[50]

Federal grants often play a role in forging broad political support by accommodating late adopters, sometimes at the expense of first movers. For capital projects, communities that forged ahead on their own lose out, while those that delayed projects can, if their timing is right, get federal funds to cover all or part of their costs. For major capital projects, such as EPA's sewage treatment program in the 1970s, the implicit disincentive for first movers became explicit as local governments engaged in queuing behavior, forestalling their own water treatment projects while waiting for EPA to provide funding.[51]

Federal maintenance-of-effort provisions attached to many grants can also penalize those states and localities that take the initiative to start programs before federal aid becomes available. While having the noble intent of preventing state and local grantees from using federal funds to reduce their own effort, provisions requiring grantees to maintain their spending at the level they did prior to receiving the grant have the effect of penalizing recipients that adopted programs before federal funds became available. Entities that waited for federal aid are implicitly rewarded for their lack of effort because they can use the entire federal grant to establish a basic program.

This dilemma manifested itself with the creation of the State Children's Health Insurance Program in 1997. States like Rhode Island and Washington, which covered all children eligible under Medicaid prior to the program, were not allowed to use the new grant to cover those children. On the other hand, states like Texas, which had large numbers of uninsured children, were able to use the new grant with its higher federal match to extend coverage.[52] Ironically, the very states that provided models for the federal program found themselves locked into their disproportionately high level of effort, while states with no programs at all found themselves rewarded by being able to use federal funds for their entire program.

Federal regulatory programs can also affect first movers. In the area of climate change, the preemption issue will define winners and losers among first movers and late adopters. Partial preemption could diffuse tensions among the states—states with different regulatory programs would have the flexibility to pursue alternative policies as long as federal minimums were retained. Total preemption of the states, on the other hand, may penalize those states taking the initiative to adopt their own cap-and-trade policies. If preempted by the federal government, the value of the existing allowances granted by the state or regional entity will fall toward zero; such a price collapse could occur as preemption expectations grow even in advance of federal adoption of legislation. The consequences are that state emissions could increase unless the federal legislation gives credit for state allowances.[53]

Other regulatory decisions also have implications. The decision regarding which baseline to use to gauge state progress in achieving reductions will have a critical bearing on the relative positions of first movers and later adopters. Those that lead the nation with lower emissions and strong programs will likely favor a 1990 baseline, while later adopters will favor a 2000 benchmark.[54] The free provision of allowances based on historical records of emissions tends to disadvantage first movers, which are likely to have lower emissions than late adopters. Conversely, auctions disproportionately favor first movers since they will not have to purchase as many allowances as late adopters. As with grants, participation matters, so efforts will be redoubled to mollify and assist reluctant firms or states that have heretofore dragged their feet.

National Legislative Proposals

Recent legislation under consideration in Congress sheds some light on how federal officials are approaching sensitive issues triggered by the states' early leadership on climate change. As noted throughout this volume, 2009 looked like a propitious year for comprehensive climate change legislation. After years of gridlock, passage of legislation was a high priority for the new Obama administration. The House passed the American Clean Energy and Security Act (HR 2454) on June 26, 2009. In the fall of 2009, Senators John Kerry and Barbara Boxer introduced their Clean Energy Jobs and American Power Act (S 1733), which was reported out of the Senate Environment and Public Works Committee. However, as the effects of the recession deepened and the public mood soured on expansive federal policy initiatives, support for full congressional action began to erode. Moreover, deep-seated regional differences emerged that crossed party lines, undermining the prospects for gaining the necessary supermajority votes in the Senate.

Both bills, as well as predecessors considered in 2008, prescribe expansive federal roles across a wide range of activities. The proposals embrace strong new federal regulatory actions; there is no devolution of broad authority to the states to develop their own cap-and-trade programs. However, states are recognized as major players for a wide range of complementary programs, ranging from renewable energy and transportation planning to building codes and adaptation planning. In those areas, the proposals contain a mixed outlook for the states, with some provisions imposing new mandates and preemptions while others provide major new categorical assistance contingent on state compliance with new national policies.[55]

All major proposals are premised on a national cap-and-trade program with federal regulation and caps applying to individual sources. All major decisions on issues such as whether allowances will be free or sold at auction will made by EPA at the national level, not by the individual states. Unlike other EPA programs covered under the Clean Air Act, states are not given the authority to implement cap-and-trade policies or to go beyond the federal policy with more stringent programs.

Significantly, both the House and Senate bills preempt similar state cap-and-trade programs for five years. Holders of state allowances may exchange them for federal allowances, although not necessarily on a one-for-one basis. The preemption is narrowly defined to cover only the cap-and-trade program and not other state climate programs or regulation of greenhouse gases from individual facilities.

Both the House and Senate bills contain several features to recognize and reward the initiatives of states that were early adopters as well as states that wish to implement stronger climate regulations on their own. First, both bills provide for additional allowances for greenhouse gas reductions achieved in the years prior to the effective date of the new federal program. Second, states may require a source to surrender its federal allowances. That will enable states to control leakages when they require emissions lower than mandated under the federal cap. As noted earlier, without this authority, the gains from stronger state controls will be lost by simply freeing up federal allowances to enable facilities in other states to escape controls on their emissions.[56]

While helpful to the states, the preemption itself will have the effect of shutting down the existing state cap-and-trade programs and will discourage implementation of others. By spurning a partial preemption approach that has served other environmental programs well, the new legislative proposals have taken a decidedly federal turn toward a single uniform cap-and-trade program. That could mollify the business community, which is concerned about having to meet different state and federal standards and trading regimes, even while arousing the opposition of state officials.

Notably, the bills considered in 2009 were more prescriptive and preemptive than the leading Senate bill considered in 2008, the Lieberman-Warner-Boxer bill (S 3036), which would have allowed states to adopt more stringent cap-and-trade policies. States would have been encouraged but not required to embrace the federal cap-and-trade regime by the provision of additional free allowances should they retire their own cap-and-trade programs. By contrast, the leading bill considered but not passed by the House in 2008, the Dingell-Boucher bill, would have preempted state cap-and-trade programs as well as California's tailpipe emissions program for greenhouse gases.

The 2009 legislation also contained a number of new mandates on the states to control the complementary policies pursued under the states' traditional regulatory role in the U.S. system. Under both bills, states are required to update their state and local building codes to conform to new national energy efficiency building codes. States and local planning organizations are required to develop plans to reduce greenhouse gas emissions from the transportation sector. Under the House bill, a new national renewable electricity standard is imposed, requiring 20 percent of the electricity supply to be derived from energy efficiency and renewable energy measures by 2020. While states are given the flexibility to decide how to accomplish that goal and to go beyond the new federal standard, they are nonetheless mandated to achieve the new federal standards.

Significantly, the Congressional Budget Office found that both House and Senate bills would impose on states what would be considered an unfunded mandate under the Unfunded Mandates Reform Act of 1995. The principal fiscal impact on states arises from the preemption of state and regional cap-and-trade programs for five years, which would reduce states' revenues by several hundred million dollars annually, according to CBO estimates.[57]

Last, a wide range of categorical assistance is provided to the states and to local governments to advance greenhouse gas controls through complementary programs. In this, climate change legislation follows the rich tradition of cooperative federalism, and new categorical grant programs are authorized that are familiar to students of the federal system. However, this legislation provides most of its major new aid through a new vehicle—the provision of allowances to state and local governments that are conditioned on their working toward new federal goals and objectives. All told, states would get $60 billion in allowances under the Senate bill (S 1733), and $50 billion under the House bill (HR 2454), over five years. Federally issued allowances will support states and localities in implementing building retrofit programs, renewable energy and efficiency projects, climate change adaptation, health protection and promotion, green jobs development and training, home heating oil assistance, and building code reform.

Conclusions

There is much to celebrate in the unfolding story of climate change and the states. Innovative designers at the state level have built an astonishing record of well-crafted policies that are elegant and technically complex, befitting a complex economy and ecology. Even for a program with significant spillover effects and international implications, the states have succeeded in accelerating the movement of this issue onto the national agenda. In a tribute to their growing capacity and political ambition, state officials now claim the high ground, which federal officials are scrambling to reach to appease an electorate eager for climate policy victories.

However, we know that progress is by no means so linear. The recent centralization of policy in the U.S. system is testament to the many state-generated ideas that have been used as the foundation for the mandates and preemptions that now constrain their flexibility and governance capacity. State-driven policy expansions in fact present certain perennial dilemmas for national decisionmakers. How can the interests of more advanced states be rewarded while at the same time bringing weaker states into a national policy community? How can states continue to function as innovators and policy adapters once national policies become enacted? These questions are even more vexing in the climate change arena because of the tension between state involvement and the creation of national trading markets, a tension that could very well discourage states from exceeding federal standards.

Climate change legislation is bold and sweeping, affecting many areas of public policy at all levels of government. The complexity of the challenges is illustrated by the broad range and numerous policy design decisions embodied in major legislative proposals under consideration. The fact that even a popular new administration with control of both houses of Congress continues to struggle to gain passage of this legislation should remind us of the daunting political stakes and distributional consequences associated with such efforts. As the nation enters a new decade, the prospects for bold new national action on climate change have become mixed at best, as the different regional consequences of federal proposals divide members of Congress within each party. While the public appeared to embrace bold new federal action at the outset of the new administration, it appears that its ambivalence about federal power has resurfaced, undermining support for climate change legislation.

The sweeping nature of the changes involved should remind us of the role that the federal system historically has played in buffering conflict and enabling changes to be ushered in with less wrenching conflict and gridlock. In a culture that is historically ambivalent about the power and size of the federal government, state participation helps legitimize new programs and adapt them to differing conditions and priorities throughout the nation. Most critical, they can also play a time-honored role as a "political sink" to resolve and defuse conflicts over trade-offs that are simply too difficult to resolve in Washington. States enable the nation to enact broad policy while devolving and disaggregating wrenching choices to venues where they can be dealt with in ways that may generate greater consensus and less gridlock.

As the nation approaches the complex choices entailed in making climate policy, we have gained respect for one other important function served by a healthy federal system—learning. The experiences of the states—both successes and mistakes—help inform the nation about the economic, ecological, and political consequences of the daunting challenges involved in reducing global warming. It is to be hoped that, having learned much already, the nation will institutionalize a strong role for the states in implementing a new climate policy as the learning process will invariably continue as the nation moves into uncharted policy terrain.

As this chapter indicates, reconciling the interests of a national economy and climate trading market with those of the states will not be easy. But the benefits are substantial. Accordingly, policymakers would be advised to embrace the partial preemption model, with the goal of providing incentives for states to exceed federal standards where appropriate. Options for creating state markets or enabling states to bury credits earned for exceeding national floors on emissions need to be explored to make it work. Sensitive redistribution issues need to be worked out as well, particularly to ensure the political sustainability of climate change control regimes. While auctions are preferred on efficiency and budgetary grounds, providing a portion of credits as free allowances at the outset may help mitigate political opposition in those states and industries that would bear disproportionate costs.

Inviting states into the national policy dialogue is guaranteed to be messy and inefficient. As Frank Bane, former director of the U.S. Advisory Commission on Intergovernmental Relations, once said, the only thing that the states can guarantee is that "no damn fool at the top can screw it all up." As we face the "unknown unknowns" of climate change collectively, those are words that we need to remember.

Notes

1. Political scientists have not dealt with vertical diffusion nearly as much as horizontal diffusion across states. Little attention has been given to a systematic analysis of what policies are adopted, why they are adopted, and the factors that led to their adoption. Similarly, little attention has been given to the kinds of policy design issues raised by state experimentation for federal policymakers. For an exception, see Keith Boeckelman, "The Influence of States on Federal Policy Adoptions," *Policy Studies Journal* 20, no. 3 (1992), pp. 365–75.

2. Paul E. Peterson, *The Price of Federalism* (Brookings, 1995).

3. James Madison, *Federalist Papers Number 10* (New York: New American Library), p. 83.

4. *New State Ice Co. v. Liebmann*, 285 U.S. 262 (1932).

5. John C. Teaford, *The Rise of the State: Evolution of American State Government* (Johns Hopkins University Press, 2002), p. 34.

6. Clive S. Thomas and Ronald J. Hrebenar, "Interest Groups in the States," in *Politics in the American States,* edited by Virginia Gray, Russell L. Hanson, and Herbert Jacob (Washington: CQ Press, 1999), p. 113.

7. Andrew Aulisi and others, *Climate Policy in the State Laboratory: How States Influence Federal Regulation and the Implications for Climate Change Policy in the United States* (Washington: World Resources Institute, 2007).

8. Paul Posner, *The Politics of Unfunded Mandates: Whither Federalism?* (Georgetown University Press, 1998).

9. Robert L. Savage, "Diffusion Research: Traditions and the Spread of Policy Innovations in a Federal System," *Publius: The Journal of Federalism* 15 (Fall 1985), p. 9.

10. Michael S. Greve, *Laboratories of Democracy: Anatomy of a Metaphor* (Washington: American Enterprise Institute for Public Policy Research, May 2001).

11. Richard Nathan, "Updating Theories of Federalism," in *Intergovernmental Management in the 21st Century*, edited by Timothy J. Conlan and Paul L. Posner (Brookings, 2008), pp. 13–23.

12. See Timothy Conlan and John Dinan, "U.S. Federalism and the Bush Administration," *Publius* 37, no. 3 (Summer 2007).

13. Conlan and Posner, *Intergovernmental Management in the 21st Century*, chapter 15.

14. Barry G. Rabe, "Environmental Policy and the Bush Era: The Collision between the Administrative Presidency and State Experimentation," *Publius* 37, no. 3 (Summer 2007), p. 413.

15. Katherine N. Probst and Sarah Jo Szambelan, *The Role of the States in a Federal Climate Program* (Washington: Resources for the Future, 2009).

16. See U.S. Conference of Mayors Climate Protection Agreement (www.usmayors.org/climateprotection/agreement.htm).

17. Barry G. Rabe, "States on Steroids: The Intergovernmental Odyssey of American Climate Policy," *Review of Policy Research* 25, no. 2 (2008), pp. 105–28.

18. Henrik Selin and Stacy D. Van Deveer, "Political Science and Prediction: What's Next for U.S. Climate Change Policy?" *Review of Policy Research* 24, no. 1 (2007), p. 14.

19. Ann E. Carlson, "Iterative Federalism and Climate Change," UCLA School of Law Research Paper 08-09.

20. See Paul Teske, *Regulation in the States* (Brookings, 2004).

21. The concept of "policy pathways" was coined to explain the increasingly diverse ways that policy ideas take root in the public agenda. See David Beam, Timothy Conlan, and Paul Posner, "The Politics That Pathways Make," paper delivered at the Annual Meeting of the American Political Science Association, Boston, September 1–4, 2002.

22. Kirsten H. Engel and Barak Y. Orbach, "Micro-Motives and State and Local Climate Change Initiatives," *Harvard Law and Policy Review* 2 (2008), pp. 119–37.

23. Richard Stewart, "States and Cities as Actors in Global Climate Regulation: Unitary vs. Plural Architectures," *Arizona Law Review* 50, no. 681 (2008), p. 698.

24. Alan Greenblatt, "Confronting Warming," *Congressional Quarterly Researcher* 19, no. 1 (January 2009), p. 5.

25. Paul L. Posner, "Networks in the Shadow of Hierarchy: The Chesapeake Bay," in *Unlocking the Power of Networks*, edited by Donald Kettl and Stephen Goldsmith (Brookings, 2009). Also see National Academy of Public Administration, *Taking Environmental Protection to the Next Level* (Washington: NAPA, 2007).

26. Paul L. Posner, "The Politics of Preemption: Prospects for the States," *PS: Political Science and Politics* 38, no. 3 (July 2005), p. 374.

27. Barry G. Rabe, "The Complexities of Carbon Cap-and-Trade Policies: Early Lessons from the States," Governance Studies Paper (Brookings, October 2008).

28. Aulisi and others, *Climate Policy in the State Laboratory*.

29. White House, "Presidential Memorandum to the Heads of Departments and Agencies on Preemption," May 20, 2009.

30. House Committee on Energy and Commerce, "Climate Change Legislation Design: Appropriate Roles for Different Levels of Government," Staff Paper, February 2008.

31. An excellent framework for analyzing preemptions and the alternatives is found in the National Academy for Public Administration, *Beyond Preemption: Intergovernmental Partnerships to Enhance the New Economy* (Washington: NAPA, 2006).

32. William Andreen, "Federal Climate Change Legislation and Preemption," *Environmental and Energy Law and Policy Journal* 3 (2008), p. 261, cited in Probst and Szambelan, *The Role of the States in a Federal Climate Program*, p. 11.

33. Teaford, *The Rise of the State: Evolution of American State Government*, p. 34.

34. As is discussed later, the House passed its legislation (HR 2454), the American Clean Energy and Security Act. The Senate bill (S 1733), the Clean Energy Jobs and American Power Act, has been introduced by Senators Kerry and Boxer and reported by the Senate Committee on Environment and Public Works.

35. Paul Teske, "Checks, Balances, and Thresholds: State Regulatory Re-enforcement and Federal Preemption," *PS: Political Science and Politics* 38, no. 3 (July 2005), p. 367.

36. Barry G. Rabe, "Environmental Policy and the Bush Era: The Collision between the Administrative Presidency and State Experimentation," *Publius* 37, no. 3 (Summer 2007).

37. Paul Light, *The True Size of Government* (Brookings, 1999).

38. Penelope Lemov, "User Fees, Once the Answer to City Budget Prayers, May Have Reached Their Peak," *Governing* 2 (1989), pp. 24–35.

39. Pew Center for Global Climate Change, *Scope of a Greenhouse Gas Cap-and-Trade Program* (Washington: 2008).

40. Franz T. Litz, *Toward a Constructive Dialogue on Federal and State Roles in U.S. Climate Change Policy* (Washington: World Resources Institute, 2008), p. 27.

41. Franz Litz and Kathryn Zyla, *Federalism in the Greenhouse: Defining a Role for States in a Federal Cap-and-Trade Program* (Washington: World Resources Institute, 2008).

42. Another systematic analysis of federal-state relations under a cap-and-trade regime is Meghan McGuinness and A. Denny Ellerman, *The Effects of Interactions between Federal and State Climate Policies* (Center for Energy and Environmental Policy Research, MIT Energy Initiative and Sloan School of Management, 2008).

43. Andrew Aulisi and others, *Greenhouse Gas Emissions Trading in U.S. States: Observations and Lessons from the OTC NO$_x$ Budget Program* (Washington: World Resources Institute, 2005), p. 19.

44. *Clean Air Markets Group* v. *Pataki*, 194 F. Supp. 2nd 147 (N. Dist. NY 2002); affirmed, 338 F. 34d 82 (2nd Cir. 2003).

45. Barry G. Rabe, "Can Congress Govern the Climate?" paper presented at National Conference on Climate Governance, Miller Center of Public Affairs, University of Virginia, December 11–12, 2008.

46. Rabe, "States on Steroids."

47. See Eric M. Patashnik, *Reforms at Risk: What Happens after Major Policy Changes Are Enacted* (Princeton University Press, 2008), p. 142.

48. Congressional Budget Office, "Trade-Offs in Allocating Allowances for CO_2 Emissions" (Washington: 2007).

49. See National Association of Clean Air Agencies, "What Role Can States and Localities Play in Implementing a Federal Greenhouse Gas Reduction Program?" paper presented at "Defining the Role of States and Localities in Federal Global Warming Legislation," Arlington, Virginia, February 12–13, 2008.

50. Helen Ingram, "Policy Implementation through Bargaining: The Case of Federal Grants-in-Aid," *Public Policy* 25 (Fall 1977), pp. 499–526.

51. See Edward M. Gramlich, "Infrastructure Investment: A Review Essay," *Journal of Economic Literature* 32, no. 3 (September 1994), pp. 1176–96. Also, James M. Jondrow and Robert A. Levy, "The Displacement of Local Spending for Pollution Control by Federal Construction Grants," *American Economic Review* 74, no. 2 (1984), pp. 174–78

52. Marilyn Werber Serafini, "Looking for a Waiver," *National Journal* 30, no. 9 (1998), pp. 465–66.

53. McGuinness and Ellerman, *The Effects of Interactions between Federal and State Climate Policies*, p. 31.

54. Rabe, "States on Steroids."

55. See "Overview of State-Related Provisions in House and Senate Bills" (Georgetown State-Federal Climate Resource Center, Georgetown University, 2009).

56. See William Buzbee, "Boxer-Kerry: Measures to Address Error and Illegality," Center for Progressive Reform, October 5, 2009 (www.progressivereform.org/CPRBlog.cfm?idBlog= 26AA1345-C71B-3C79-0B6C7A24A8DEE099).

57. Congressional Budget Office, "Cost Estimate for S 1733," December 16, 2009.

PART II

Market and Regulatory Approaches to Climate Governance

5

The Emerging Revolution in Emissions Trading Policy

LEIGH RAYMOND

In the past twenty years we have witnessed a startling shift in what constitutes "acceptable" and "unthinkable" arguments regarding emissions trading and the allocation of emissions rights. We have moved from deep skepticism about creating a "right to pollute" to greater comfort with market-based approaches. At the same time, we have nearly abandoned "squatters' rights" norms of entitlement in favor of assertions of collective public ownership of the atmospheric commons. This chapter argues that these rapid changes represent an emergent revolution in terms of policy design, with important implications for the viability of future policies to address climate change and other environmental challenges.

The chapter begins with a review of the history of emissions trading programs, including a discussion of the "old model" of cap and trade represented in the design of the 1990 U.S. acid rain program. The chapter then documents the emergence of public ownership claims to the atmospheric sink capacity for greenhouse gases (GHGs) when the EU Emission Trading System (ETS) was initiated and the rapid ascendancy of those claims during the development of new U.S. cap-and-trade programs, including the Regional Greenhouse Gas Initiative (RGGI) and the Western Climate Initiative (WCI). The chapter also briefly addresses recent developments in federal cap-and-trade policy, including allocation proposals under the Climate Security Act of 2008 and the American Clean Energy and Security Act of 2009. The chapter concludes with a discussion of the broader policy design issues and dilemmas raised by this shift in understanding of who owns the resources that constitute the "global commons."

Background: Enclosing the Commons

A cap-and-trade program is, at its core, a new system of private rights to limit the use of an open-access resource or "commons."[1] By creating a limited number of these rights, society protects a vulnerable open-access resource from overuse. The idea works for "sources" of natural capital (where the problem is overextraction of a valuable product like minerals or timber) as well as "sinks" for environmental waste (where the problem is too much pollution to be absorbed safely).

Although some U.S. politicians claimed that the 1990 acid rain emissions trading program was unprecedented, in a larger sense that claim is not correct. Privatizing common or open-access resources has gone on for centuries, back to the enclosure movement in pre-modern England and earlier. More recently, authors have argued that private rights and "limited entry" are better solutions to a wide range of environmental problems, including overfishing and overgrazing.[2] Thus, the Taylor Grazing Act of 1934 is as much an intellectual predecessor of modern cap-and-trade programs as the individual transferable quota fisheries programs of the 1970s.[3] Garrett Hardin made such prescriptions famous with his 1968 article, "The Tragedy of the Commons," wherein he recommended private ownership as a solution to what he considered the inevitable overuse of common resources.[4] Meanwhile, economic historians have explored the development or atrophy of private rights to natural resources over time, to the benefit or detriment of the environment.[5] Throughout these varied efforts, the unifying notion that limiting resource access might prevent environmental damage while preserving efficiency and environmental quality has remained central.

Cap and trade as a method to control pollution dates back to academic work in the 1960s.[6] The concept is straightforward: policymakers set a limit on total pollution (or "critical load") and then assign private rights to emit shares of that pollution, usually on an annual basis. Those rights are often referred to as "allowances." Polluters must hold an emissions allowance for every unit that they emit in a given period of time, with the fixed number of allowances maintaining the overall cap. Polluters (and others, in many cases) may buy and sell allowances (the "trade" portion of the policy), so that those with high pollution abatement costs may save money by purchasing allowances from firms that can make emissions reductions more cheaply. The policy thereby lowers total regulatory costs by equalizing the marginal cost of compliance across firms, as well as by giving polluters more flexibility in meeting their emissions targets. In this way, cap-and-trade advocates argue, society can get more environmental "bang for the buck."

In sum, cap-and-trade policies represent not only the culmination of creative economic thinking in the late twentieth century but also another step in a long line of efforts to enclose, or privatize, the commons. Such enclosure efforts have always been controversial, especially due to concerns about giving public rights away to powerful private interests. Despite that concern, allocation of rights has frequently given way to the ownership claims of current resource users. Although some oversimplify its role, the idea that de facto possession or prior use of a resource entitles a user to some form of legal ownership has a long history in U.S. environmental policy, dating back to the Preemption Acts of the 1840s.

1990–2005: The "Old" Cap-and-Trade Model

Despite earlier academic treatments, it was not until the 1980s that environmental policymakers gave emissions trading serious consideration.[7] Early experiments included "bubbles" covering multiple sources and "netting" of emissions to allow new sources to be offset by the reduction of existing pollution sources under the Clean Air Act Amendments of 1977, as well as a program to trade rights to add lead to gasoline during the fuel additive's phase-out. Although the lead trading program was considered a success, substantial resistance remained to other, broader emissions trading programs, especially among environmental advocates.[8] Only after a complicated confluence of political events in the late 1980s did the nation get its first major cap-and-trade program: Title IV of the Clean Air Act Amendments of 1990, which was established to address the problem of acid rain.[9] This program created a national cap on sulfur dioxide (SO_2) emissions from large electricity generators, ultimately cutting annual emissions to approximately 50 percent of 1980 levels. The 1990 policy is summarized, in comparison with other cap-and-trade policies, in table 5-1.

Those supporting cap and trade as a solution to the acid rain problem had to overcome numerous political obstacles, including distrust of private "rights to pollute" as well as the thorny problem of allocating such rights. Ironically, many cap-and-trade advocates were largely uninterested in allocation; focused on creating a fixed cap on emissions, the small number of environmental groups supporting the policy declared themselves "agnostic" on the initial distribution of pollution rights. Academics also tended to pay relatively little attention to allocation at the time; some quietly advocated having the government auction the rights to polluters as the most efficient mechanism, but the idea gained little traction politically.

Indeed, a detailed review of the debate over the 1990 acid rain program shows that the idea of auctioning allowances was never seriously considered—there were no significant proposals for an auction beyond a very small annual sale of allowances to ensure liquidity, price discovery, and market access for new entrants. Instead, allowances were given away to existing polluters based on a combination of historical levels of energy use and benchmarked pollution rates. That system effectively gave whatever revenue or "rents" might be gained from the new emissions allowances to existing polluters.

Table 5-1. *Comparison of Cap-and-Trade Programs*

Program	Year	Cap reduction	Allocation rules	Auction provisions	Offsets	Major revenue recipients
U.S. acid rain program	1990	SO_2: 50 percent below 1980 levels by 2010	One component: historical energy use and benchmarks	Limited: New entrants only	None	Emitters
EU ETS Phase I	2005	CO_2: 10 percent below to 15 percent above 2003 levels	Two components: economic need and historical emissions	Limited: ≤ 5 percent of allowances	Limited: < 50 percent of reductions	Emitters
RGGI	2008	CO_2: 10 percent below 2008 levels by 2018	Two components: status quo and auction	Substantial: 60 percent to 100 percent of allowances	Limited: ≤ 3.3 percent to 10 percent of emissions	Consumers and government
WCI	2008	Six greenhouse gases: 15 percent below 2005 levels by 2020	Two components: status quo and auction	Substantial: ≥ 10 percent to 25 percent of allowances[a]	Limited: ≤ 49 percent of reductions	Government and perhaps consumers
ACESA	2009	Six greenhouse gases: 17 percent below 2005 levels by 2020	One component: auction and congressional choice	Substantial: ~40 percent of allowances	Limited: up to 50 percent (or more) of reductions by 2030	Government, emitters, and consumers

Sources: For the U.S. acid rain program: Leigh Raymond, *Private Rights in Public Resources* (Washington: Resources for the Future Press, 2003); for the EU ETS: Leigh Raymond, "Allocating the Global Commons: Theory and Practice," in *Political Theory and Global Climate Change*, edited by S. Vanderheiden (MIT Press, 2008) and Denny Ellerman, Barbara Buchner, and Carlo Carraro, *Rights, Rents, and Fairness: Allocation in the European Emissions Trading Scheme* (Cambridge University Press, 2007); for RGGI: Regional Greenhouse Gas Initiative (www.rggi.org) and Barry G. Rabe, "Regionalism and Global Climate Change Policy," in *Intergovernmental Management for the Twenty-First Century*, edited by T. J. Conlan and P. L. Posner (Brookings, 2008); for WCI: Western Climate Initiative (www.westernclimateinitiative.org); and for ACESA: HR 2454 and "Distribution of Allowances under the American Clean Energy and Security Act (Waxman-Markey)" (Pew Center on Global Climate Change, August 2009).

a. Jurisdictions without legal authority to auction allowances are exempt (WCI Design Document, section 8.7.3; p. 32).

The guiding principle in 1990 was consistent with previous allocations of private rights to formerly open-access resources: privilege current or prior users. This core principle was never seriously questioned during passage of the 1990 law, even by new electric power producers excluded from the free allowance pool. The idea that the government might sell allowances to the highest bidder, let alone use the revenue from such an auction for other purposes, appears to have been unthinkable. Even revenue from the small allowance auctions for new entrants was returned to existing allowance holders. Thus, the "old" model for cap and trade was based on a few basic principles:

—Private rights to public resources are created only with reluctance.

—The initial allocation is of little interest to environmental advocates.

—Auctions are largely unthinkable; "squatters' rights" is the default rule.

Those principles were grounded in the belief that existing users are a resource's rightful owners, rather than the government or the public at large. Such claims were justified either by a "Lockean" view of ownership based on a history of beneficial prior use or on a more ethically limited "Humean" notion of ownership based simply on current possession.[10] Regardless, the idea that the *public* might own the resources was absent from the conversation.

The implementation of the SO_2 cap-and-trade program was widely perceived as a success.[11] Compliance was nearly perfect, emissions dropped dramatically, and enforcement and administrative costs remained low.[12] The perception of success had several important consequences; for instance, it weakened resistance to market-based approaches using property-like policy instruments. In fact, where cap-and-trade programs had previously been considered with reluctance, by the end of the 1990s such programs threatened to become the holy grail of environmental policymaking, proposed even for inappropriate problems. Emissions trading can concentrate pollutants locally, so the policy is suspect for pollutants with toxicity at low levels of exposure. However, that fact did not prevent serious cap-and-trade proposals for toxic pollutants like mercury in the wake of the acid rain program's success.[13] Emissions trading also is vulnerable to the displacement of emissions to sources outside the cap, a problem sometimes referred to as "leakage." Yet again, the threat of leakage did not stop numerous regional groups from proposing regional U.S. cap-and-trade programs for GHGs vulnerable to just such a problem, as discussed further below.

Also building on the success of the acid rain program, the United States pushed other nations to accept market mechanisms to address climate change. Although the EU resisted at first, it eventually created a cap-and-trade system to help meet its collective emissions reduction commitment under the Kyoto Protocol even as the United States withdrew from the Kyoto process. That made the EU the home of the next major emissions trading program and the first to address the emissions responsible for the problem of global warming.

The EU Emission Trading System began operation in 2005. Patterned sub-stantially after the U.S. SO$_2$ program, the ETS covered emissions of CO$_2$ (see table 5-1). Caps varied by country, but ranged from 10 percent below to 15 percent above 2003 emissions for the first phase, ending in 2008.[14] Detailed allocations were left to individual nations, but the European Commission mandated that no more than 5 percent of phase 1 allowances be distributed by auction.[15] Few nations auctioned even that amount; the dominant allocation principles were historical emissions combined with projections of future economic needs.[16] As with the acid rain program, the primary revenue beneficiaries were current emitters.

Unlike the U.S. acid rain program, the ETS permitted sources to obtain addi-tional allowances through emissions reduction projects outside the EU. These "off-sets" were limited to two programs created under the Kyoto Protocol: Joint Imple-mentation (JI) and the Clean Development Mechanism (CDM).[17] The ETS limited offsets to no more than 50 percent of the total emissions reductions required (making them "supplemental" to domestic actions) and authorized lower national offset limits. Nevertheless, a number of countries considered CDM or JI credits an important way to meet their national emissions reduction goals.[18] Of course, offsets represent a sort of "back door" auction mechanism, since firms must pay for the projects that generate these offset credits or buy the credits on the open market. Nevertheless, offsets inspire a different sort of political controversy than the question of domestic allocation auctions and are usually treated separately.

Phase 1 of the ETS challenged two of the three prominent beliefs underwrit-ing the 1990 acid rain program. There was greater comfort with creating private rights to emit pollution in 2003–05 than in 1990 and greater interest in the allo-cation process. Indeed, allocation was a major topic of academic and political dis-cussion in the EU, with a heated dialogue continuing between the EU Commis-sion on the Environment and the national agencies writing the phase 1 "national allocation plan" for each participating country.[19] Think tanks and academics wrote numerous reports discussing allocation options for the ETS. Environmen-tal groups also were more invested in allocation issues, as the large volume of com-ments on draft national allocation plans in places like the United Kingdom attests. Thus, as political actors grew more comfortable with a policy relying on private rights, interest in allocation intensified.

The result, however, was not a radically different allocation approach, at least not initially. Instead, the EU allocations hewed closely to the status quo, consis-tent with the "old" cap-and-trade model. Most nations declined to set aggressive national emissions reduction targets within the ETS or to allocate allowances among firms without paying close attention to existing emissions patterns. The major change from the 1990 SO$_2$ allocation was the emphasis on economic pro-jections—trying to forecast the energy needs of different sectors of a national economy for the coming years and then allocating CO$_2$ emissions accordingly.[20] The principle of economic need was not widely used in the acid rain program (although there were modest allocation adjustments for utilities based on economic and population trends).

In sum, despite significant differences between the design of the cap-and-trade program in the ETS for phase 1 and the U.S. acid rain program, the basic tendency to favor the claims of current resource users remained as late as 2005, consistent with long-standing norms favoring possession and prior use as justifications for ownership. Although the ETS reflected some changes in public and elite thinking about cap-and-trade program design, including greater comfort with a "private rights" approach to solving environmental problems, the results were more significant in promoting allocations based on economic need than in furthering the idea of public resource ownership and allocation by auction. Although inklings of the more dramatic shifts to come in cap-and-trade policy design were apparent by 2005, the changes remained small and suggestive.

2005 to 2009: The "New" Cap-and-Trade Model

As noted above, by 2005 the acid rain program had become a "living legend,"[21] and it is only a slight exaggeration to say that cap and trade had changed by this time from a "grand policy experiment"[22] to an answer for nearly every pollution problem. Enthusiasm for cap and trade reached its apex at this point, despite the rather mixed experience of the ETS in phase 1 (2005–08), which included problems of overallocation, price volatility (driven by a surplus of allowances expiring at the end of 2008), and allegations of windfall profits for polluters.[23] The difficulties of the ETS shaped the design of newer emissions trading programs without initially diminishing enthusiasm for the cap-and-trade approach.

Indeed, emissions trading became almost a fetish among some policymakers and advocates at that time, to the detriment of other options like emissions taxes or even command-and-control regulations, which are highlighted in the subsequent three chapters in part 2 of this volume. That is ironic when one considers how close some cap-and-trade policies have moved toward an emissions tax through the addition of significant government revenue (from auctions) as well as "off ramps," "safety valves," "price collars," and other devices to limit the economic cost of a cap-and-trade program.[24] While there are more and less plausible methods for including price controls within a cap-and-trade framework, it can be an awkward marriage.[25]

That is not to suggest that no important differences exist between emissions taxes and cap-and-trade.[26] One key difference is that an emissions tax limits economic costs while letting environmental impacts vary (fixed cost per unit of pollution, no fixed pollution cap), while emissions trading does the opposite (fixed pollution cap, no fixed costs). One might ask, therefore, why some advocates and political actors have insisted on cap-and-trade policies as the solution to climate change problems in a U.S. political environment deeply concerned about economic costs. Although there are practical reasons to prefer cap and trade, including better integration into global programs for emissions reductions like the ETS and the CDM, it is hard to resist the conclusion that the situation is at least partially due in part to overinfatuation with the success of the acid rain program.[27] Political aversion to new taxes may also be an important reason to support cap and trade (see chapter 2 on public opinion in this regard, as well as chapter 6 with regard to the failure of the Canadian Liberal Party's 2008 carbon tax proposal), although the recent tendency of opponents to describe the policy as "cap and tax" weakens this rationale. (Indeed, the recent success of efforts to discredit cap and trade by name has led some to "rebrand" emissions trading proposals using terms like "reduction and refund").[28]

Several U.S. cap-and-trade programs were the leading innovators of this new emissions trading model. First among them was the Regional Greenhouse Gas Initiative, a partnership of northeastern states creating a cap-and-trade system for CO_2 starting in 2009. Soon to follow was the Western Climate Initiative, a similar regional emissions trading program for a number of western states and Canadian provinces, scheduled to come online in 2012. Finally, the governors of six Midwestern states and Manitoba have joined as full members of the Midwestern Greenhouse Gas Reduction Accord (MGGRA), created in November 2007. Similar to RGGI and WCI, MGGRA also proposes a regional cap-and-trade program for up to six greenhouse gases.[29] MGGRA is somewhat behind WCI and RGGI, having released a final advisory draft of basic design recommendations only in June 2009; although MGGRA will not be discussed in this chapter, its recommendations are broadly consistent with those of WCI and RGGI.[30]

The Regional Greenhouse Gas Initiative

RGGI began with a 2005 memorandum of understanding, eventually signed by the governors of ten states: New York, New Jersey, Connecticut, Maine, Vermont, New Hampshire, Maryland, Delaware, Massachusetts, and Rhode Island. Like the acid rain program, RGGI limits emissions from power plants with 25 megawatts or more generation capacity.[31] The RGGI cap stabilizes current CO_2 emissions through 2014, then reduces emissions by 2.5 percent every year from 2015 to 2018.[32] Participating states will review the program in 2012 and address the question of whether more reductions should be required after 2018.[33] (See table 5-1 for additional information on RGGI.)

The RGGI allocation occurred in two stages. First RGGI distributed allowances among the participating states on the basis of status quo emissions, with an egalitarian adjustment giving larger states a modest reduction and smaller states a slight increase.[34] States then decided how to distribute allowances to emitters within their borders. At present, RGGI states have committed to auctioning most or all of their allowances, even though that was not required by the original memorandum of understanding or model rule.[35] Auction revenues go to state energy-efficiency programs as well as programs to lower energy costs for low-income households.[36] Auctions are open to all bidders, with a reserve price that prevents allowances from being sold if demand is too low.[37] Any unsold allowances are carried forward to the next auction.

RGGI's decision not to give away most allowances to existing users was a substantial departure from previous emissions trading policies. The move to an auction-based system even surprised many who were involved in the RGGI design process.[38] Advocates justified auctions as "fairer" to consumers—a more transparent way to pass the cost of emissions controls to consumers and prevent windfalls for industry.[39] RGGI publications continue to promote auctions as a better means to a "fair and open carbon market."[40]

The idea that free allowances are a "windfall" for polluters is a fundamental rejection of the old model of emissions trading. From this new perspective, status quo users are no longer entitled to allowances based on prior use. Instead, free allocations to current users are unfair giveaways that prevent the public from getting its due. The underlying paradigm shift is profound: if current users are not entitled to free allowances, someone else must effectively "own" the resource in question. Environmental advocates also have taken up this idea of public ownership when writing about allowance auctions.[41]

Explaining why this sudden shift in perspective occurred at this moment requires further research, but it appears that the change grew out of the early stages of the ETS. EU officials designing and implementing the ETS spoke publicly about the atmosphere's CO_2 sink capacity as a "public resource" for the first time.[42] The shift also seems to have been driven in part by media reports of EU energy companies making significant and undeserved profits on their phase 1 allocations.[43] One leading environmentalist was quoted in 2007 as saying that in the wake of the EU experience the idea of giving away allowances was "teetering and almost dead."[44] While the reality of such alleged windfall profits may be more complex than usually reported, the perception was an important part of the discussion about U.S. programs like RGGI.[45]

As a final point, like the ETS, RGGI also permits limited use of offsets to meet emissions reduction targets. Under normal circumstances, affected RGGI sources can offset up to 3.3 percent of their total annual emissions.[46] Given that on average states have to reduce emissions by 2.5 percent annually, it appears that the average facility in a RGGI state could meet its full emissions reduction requirement with offsets. If the price of allowances goes above certain thresholds, the amount of offsets permitted also goes up.[47] Offsets must go beyond the existing legal requirements in any jurisdiction where the projects are located; no offsets are given for any action that is legally mandated.[48] Many offsets appear to be calculated against a status quo, or "business as usual" (BAU), baseline.[49]

These details suggest that RGGI's treatment of offsets is both complicated and somewhat contradictory. Calculating offsets based on status quo or BAU emissions seems inconsistent with the rejection of the same rationale for allocating allowances within the RGGI system. The RGGI offsets rule rewards profligate prior or current resource use, much like the "old" model of cap and trade. At the same time, RGGI imposes numerous limits on the use of offsets—only 3.3 percent of emissions can be covered by offset allowances under normal circumstances—and there are more than sixty pages of rules specifying minimum standards for offset projects.[50] As a result, the rules strictly limit how many and what kinds of offsets can be used, even as they perpetuate liberal assumptions about status quo entitlements for polluters.

The Western Climate Initiative

WCI currently includes seven U.S. states and four Canadian provinces as full participants: Washington, Oregon, California, Arizona, Montana, Utah, New Mexico, Quebec, Ontario, Manitoba, and British Columbia.[51] Its cap takes effect in 2012 with state/provincial limits at current status quo levels for emissions from electricity and some industrial processes.[52] WCI plans to cover almost 90 percent of all GHG emissions from six different greenhouse gases and a variety of energy sectors by 2015.[53] Ultimately, the cap will lower emissions to 15 percent below 2005 levels for those gases by 2020.[54] (The specifics of the WCI program are summarized in table 5-1.)

The WCI allocation system is similar to RGGI's, although the final details are yet to be worked out. State and provincial caps are to be based on status quo emissions levels combined with need-based projections of factors like population growth.[55] The WCI design document requires that some of the value of allowances be set aside for "public purposes," such as energy conservation and efficiency, mitigation efforts, and adaptation to climate impacts.[56] It also suggests, but does not require, set-asides for mitigating higher energy costs, especially for low-income households.[57] Allocation details are otherwise left to states and provinces, except for a requirement to auction at least 10 percent of allowances in the first compliance period and to increase that to at least 25 percent by 2020.[58] WCI's stated aspiration is to auction all allowances if possible, although that objective was subject to disagreement among WCI stakeholders.[59] Auctions will be held throughout the region and with a reserve price, much like RGGI auctions.[60]

WCI restricts the use of offsets more than RGGI does, requiring that they be "supplemental" to reductions under the cap, as the ETS program did in phase 1.[61] WCI designers "encourage" offset projects that are within WCI boundaries to capture the projects' "collateral benefits," but they seem willing to accept offset credits from other parts of the world, including CDM projects.[62] Unlike RGGI, WCI will not grant offsets for emissions reductions outside the WCI area in developed countries if the reductions would have been legally required by the WCI cap-and-trade program.[63] As with RGGI, WCI stakeholders were concerned that offsets be "rigorous" and of the "highest quality" to be accepted (although WCI had not spelled out offset requirements as of this writing, including formulas for calculating offset allowances created by a given project).[64] Stakeholders also disagreed about whether limits on the use of offsets were appropriate.[65] In the end, however, WCI designers recognized the need to allow some offsets as a low-cost compliance option.[66]

Thus, WCI is an ally of RGGI in the current cap-and-trade "revolution." Like RGGI, WCI rejects allocations to polluters based on existing or historical emissions levels in favor of public ownership of the atmospheric commons. Also like RGGI, it requires a substantial portion of any auction revenue to benefit public owners directly, albeit more through energy-efficiency programs than through consumer rebates. All of this demonstrates a new paradigm of public resource ownership, building presumably on the same momentum that drove the RGGI innovations in the first place. Public comments regarding WCI invoke the same sort of claims about "fair treatment" for all resource users and the need to generate revenue for environmental improvements and consumer rebates, among other public goods.[67]

Finally, it is worth noting that the design recommendations now emerging from the Midwestern Greenhouse Gas Reduction Accord also are consistent with the main principles of the "RGGI revolution." The MGGRA is farther from implementation, but its latest draft recommendations include similar emissions reduction goals, a commitment to cap and trade with few free allowances from the start, full auctioning of allowances by the fourth compliance period (around 2021), and a desire to limit offsets, especially from projects outside the cap.[68] The recommendation to charge for nearly all allowances and move quickly toward a 100 percent auction model is especially noteworthy for a program affecting several states with coal-intensive economies.

Federal Actions

Federal efforts to create a cap-and-trade program for greenhouse gases intensified in the wake of regional programs like RGGI and WCI. In the 110th and 111th Congresses, cap-and-trade bills gained more attention and votes than ever before. Although the recent federal proposals are complex and incorporate a wide variety of allocation rules in a rapidly changing political environment, they consistently reflect a shift toward allowances as a "public" resource.

The Climate Security Act (CSA) of 2008 (S 3036) was the most important federal GHG cap-and-trade proposal in the 110th Congress.[69] A spectacularly complicated program (the full bill was nearly 500 pages long, or approximately 10 times the length of Title IV of the Clean Air Act Amendments of 1990, which set up the SO_2 cap-and-trade program), the CSA set emissions caps for six greenhouses gases through 2050, including a 19 percent reduction from 2005 levels by 2020. The complexity of its allocation process was unprecedented: according to one analysis, approximately 43 percent of the allowances under the bill were to be auctioned, with the other 57 percent allocated without cost by Congress to a wide range of constituencies, including programs for energy efficiency and technology development, consumer benefits, public lands management, and deficit reduction.[70] Those percentages are somewhat misleading, however, because the bill permitted allowance recipients (including many who were not GHG emitters) to auction their allowances and receive a share of the revenue instead. Only about 15 percent of all allowances were to be given away to existing GHG emitters.[71] The bill also created a modest role for offsets, of up to 15 percent of all required reductions, including a small number of credits from other programs like CDM.

Following the failure of the Climate Security Act, a new Congress arrived in 2009 with new cap-and-trade proposals. An early leader was the American Clean Energy and Security Act (ACESA) of 2009 (HR 2454). Also known as the Waxman-Markey bill, after its sponsors, ACESA is similar to the CSA in many ways (summarized in table 5-1). It sets a slightly lower short-term reduction goal of 17 percent of 2005 emissions by 2020, and it auctions fewer allowances in the early years of the program than the CSA. At the same time, ACESA gives offsets a greater role, including international offsets that appear likely to serve as a primary compliance option in the early years of the program.[72] Although ACESA auctions only about 2 percent of allowances in the first few years, 70 percent of all allowances are to be auctioned annually by 2031. Over the life of the bill, approximately 40 percent of the allowances are to be auctioned and 60 percent given away, a proportion fairly close to that under the CSA approach.[73]

A companion bill introduced in the Senate, the Clean Energy Jobs and American Power Act (S 1733), auctions an even greater initial percentage of allowances (25 percent minimum).[74] Other leading Senate bills contemplate auctioning even larger percentages of allowances, with substantial portions of the revenue being returned directly to the public—for example, S 2877, the Carbon Limits and Energy for American Renewal (CLEAR) Act. The idea of returning revenue from the sale of allowances directly to citizens also appears to be gaining political importance even among Senate "moderates" on climate change and energy policy.[75]

All of these leading federal cap-and-trade bills follow RGGI and WCI in treating atmospheric GHG sinks as a public resource. This shift in perspective has forced industry to reframe its claims on allowances in terms of "compensation" for economic harm or as a benefit to its consumers rather than as an "entitlement" to emissions rights based on prior use.[76] Even some business-friendly Republicans now condemn free allowance distributions as potential "giveaways" to corporations.[77] Although few federal bills have equaled RGGI's example (or President Obama's stated goal) of nearly 100 percent auctioning, the paradigm shift remains evident as current emitters fight the allocation battle on radically different political terrain.

That being said, there is an important difference in the nature of public ownership as outlined in the CSA and ACESA. Unlike RGGI, the only federal bills to get through either house of Congress make *government* the owner of record, free to do what it will with the revenue from the sale of emissions allowances. Rather than using a "cap-and-dividend" design under which the public receives the benefits of ownership directly (through compensation by way of lower taxes or equal per capita payments), the CSA and ACESA treat emissions allowances as the property of the people's representatives, to be used for a variety of purposes, much like other tax revenue. Although a majority of the allowances in these bills (58 percent under ACESA, for instance) are dedicated to consumer price relief, they go to a wide range of industries as compensation for economic harms or otherwise serve a variety of interests besides those of consumers.[78] Recent political developments suggest that equal payments to citizens may be gaining support at the federal level, but as of this writing, no such bill has been adopted by either the Senate or House.

Thus, although the shift away from private entitlement based on prior use is consistent across all of these cases, the exact nature of the new form of "public" ownership is still contested and varies from program to program. It is the difference in the nature of public ownership that brings us to the final part of the discussion of these changes and their implications for future cap-and-trade policies to address climate change.

Discussion and Conclusions

Designers of future climate change policies must now confront a new ownership paradigm regarding atmospheric sinks to absorb greenhouse gases. After years of treating polluters as prior resource users entitled to private rights under any policy of limited entry, political actors are now witnessing (and in many cases encouraging) a remarkable normative shift in which the public is seen as the rightful owner of natural resource sinks and polluters as beneficiaries of a free ride at the public's expense. Existing emitters have tried to block the change, but their efforts continue to look like a losing rear-guard action. The idea that we should reward polluting behavior with free pollution rights was always a bit implausible, and it is now giving way to the principle of public ownership.[79]

This dramatic change has significant implications for the political viability and effects of any future climate change policy. Indeed, the paradigm shift has arguably become more influential in light of recent attempts to portray cap and trade unfavorably as "cap and tax" or as subject to corruption or fraud that have weakened public support for the policy. Such concerns have actually strengthened political support for, for example, the stronger notions of public ownership incorporated in "cap and dividend" proposals that auction 100 percent of emissions rights and refund the money to citizens on an equal per capita basis.[80] They have also appeared to make other policies that charge for private uses of a "public" resource, including a carbon tax on vehicle fuels, more politically palatable.

Why this shift occurred requires more investigation. Entitlement claims based on prior "abuse" of a resource run counter to another powerful norm in environmental politics: the "polluter pays" principle. At first, free allocations to polluters may have arisen by default from previous models of natural resource allocation, such as grazing and fishing rights, in which the resource uses were more easily framed as beneficial. At the same time, Congress significantly modified that allocation principle even as early as 1990, using technological benchmarks to reduce the SO_2 allowances awarded to dirtier power plants.[81] Still, the idea that polluters might have to bid competitively for the right to use a public resource was inconceivable until just a few years ago.

However, as policymakers and environmental advocates became more comfortable with cap and trade, policy entrepreneurs paid more attention to the allocation process.[82] Largely ignored by environmentalists in 1990, allocation is now recognized as a unique opportunity to generate revenue for environmental policy objectives, or at least to cushion the blow of higher energy prices. Meanwhile, the perception that European companies made significant profits on their free allowances under the Emission Trading System bolsters this new perspective. Other factors are surely at play—as noted, the full story behind this paradigm shift merits a detailed analysis of its own—but it is hard to dispute that we are witnessing the replacement of one dominant norm of entitlement based on possession and prior use with another based on public ownership.

The idea of public ownership is itself complex, however. One can identify at least two different perspectives on the idea. One is more populist, rooted in a belief that the public itself is entitled to certain common resources like the atmosphere. This idea underwrites programs that distribute equal shares of revenue from natural resources to all citizens, such as payments to Alaskans from oil development supported by individuals as diverse as environmentalist Peter Barnes and former Alaska governor Sarah Palin.[83] One might call this an "egalitarian" version of public ownership—one that appears in international climate policy as proposals for equal per capita shares of GHG emissions rights for all nations, as well as the common law Public Trust Doctrine that limits government's ability to restrict public rights to certain natural resources.[84]

Yet there is another way to assert public ownership of natural resources: one that favors government decisionmakers over individual citizens as the rightful "owners." This version of public ownership is more consistent with long-standing beliefs in enlightened government stewardship that have underwritten policies creating expert agencies to manage natural resources on behalf of the public. One might call this a "governmental" form of public ownership, in which political elites allocate natural resources on behalf of the public at large. Under this conception, revenues from natural resource ownership are still put to public use but not necessarily in a way that provides equal shares or direct revenue to all citizens as common owners.

It should be apparent that both versions of public ownership appear in the new models of cap-and-trade promulgated since 2005. Of the three, RGGI takes the most egalitarian stance, giving consumer rebates and price relief priority over other contenders for auction revenues such as alternative energy research and development.[85] WCI reverses these priorities in its draft regulations, mandating that auction revenue go toward energy efficiency programs and making consumer relief optional. Leading federal proposals such as the CSA and ACESA take the "governmental" form to an even greater degree, providing less direct transfer of auction revenues to consumers and allocating more auction revenue or allowances to a wider range of priorities, including deficit reduction and aid to energy-intensive industries. Other recent federal proposals promote the egalitarian perspective.

Neither approach is necessarily preferable, but the differences are significant. The original justification for auctions under RGGI included the argument that monetary relief to consumers would be an important part of any attempt to raise the price of energy to limit GHG emissions. The soon-to-be-elected governor of New York, Eliot Spitzer, spoke in favor of RGGI auctions in which revenue could be used to "minimize the burdens on the public at large in order to build public support for further reductions that will be needed in the future, both at the state and federal levels."[86] The RGGI executive summary also promotes auctions on the basis of being more "fair" to the consumer.[87] WCI makes similar claims, but does not yet mandate consumer relief.[88] The Climate Security Act, in contrast, proposed distributing only 23 percent of allowances or allowance revenue directly to consumers, and ACESA distributes many of its allowances for consumer price relief to electricity companies, not directly to citizens, creating potentially perverse price incentives.[89] Other leading federal proposals, including the aforementioned 2009 CLEAR Act, take a much more egalitarian approach to public ownership, refunding nearly all auction revenue to citizens equally.

Thus, the shift to public ownership of emissions sinks is only part of the story. The next step will be to determine to what degree we adopt a populist, egalitarian vision of collective public ownership or a more bureaucratic vision in which emissions sinks become another source of tax revenue for the government. That decision will have critical implications for the efficiency of future cap-and-trade policies as well as for their future political viability.

In terms of efficiency, there is a clear temptation in any auction-based system to fund research and development on low-carbon energy options (as well as other underfunded government programs) through the sale of GHG allowances.[90] Many analysts agree that this sort of R&D is a public good, likely to be underfunded by private firms without public intervention.[91] In addition, there is a lively debate in environmental policy circles over the advantages of higher energy prices relative to those of other approaches, such as R&D funding, in achieving sufficient GHG reductions. At the same time, efficiency gains from auctioning emissions allowances are maximized by lowering regressive taxes on labor such as the payroll tax. In this way, the recognized benefits of more funding for R&D and conservation programs are in tension with the regressive impacts of higher energy prices for lower-income consumers. How to allocate revenue among these various goals—as well as how to distribute revenue to consumers or to citizens to minimize the economic burden of higher energy prices while maintaining the correct price signal for conservation—is a critical design decision.

Two political risks of the government ownership model also come to mind: public backlash regarding higher energy prices and the political collapse of an allocation process that becomes too complex. One need look no further than calls for suspending the federal gasoline tax in the face of the 2008 spike in fuel prices to comprehend the seriousness of the first problem. Egalitarian cash rebates to the public might limit such a backlash. In addition, given the amount of potential income that allowances represent,[92] the temptation to direct some of that revenue to preferred programs and constituencies threatens to make the allocation process overwhelmingly complex, reducing transparency and trust in the program. The Climate Security Act was a good example of this process, in which dozens of constituencies were involved in negotiations over the allocation of billions of dollars of emissions allowances. When allocations become this complex and take place outside any widely recognized normative framework of entitlements, they risk creating a Gordian knot that any political process will struggle to untie.[93] They also create opportunities for opponents to frame cap-and-trade policies as overly complex and subject to gaming and fraud by elites. Supporters of a simpler and more egalitarian "cap and dividend" approach point to the transparency and simplicity of their model as a major political selling point.

Other questions emerge from the shift to a public ownership paradigm. What will happen to projections of "need" and historical baselines as a basis for allocation in the long run? How will arguments for compensating high-emitters play out over time in this new normative context? If we are going to compensate industry for losses due to new climate regulations, for example, are we also going to provide allowances to compensate those damaged by future climate change impacts? In an early example, the Climate Security Act and ACESA put a small percentage of allowances into funds to help groups affected by climate change to adapt (for a fuller discussion of adaptation, refer to chapter 9 of this volume).[94] Finally, how are regional or national cap-and-trade programs going to deal with the need for reductions outside existing emissions caps and with the challenge of ensuring "additionality, verifiability, and permanence" for offset programs that try to meet that need?[95] It is worth remembering, in this regard, that a major selling point of the original 1990 U.S. cap-and-trade program was its administrative simplicity and lower administrative and enforcement costs.[96] In the pursuit of offset quality assurances, we risk creating an administrative structure for future cap-and-trade programs that undermines one of the policy's original selling points, a problem that continues to beset international CDM offsets as well.[97]

Given the incomplete nature of regional cap-and-trade programs such as RGGI and WCI, it is understandable that providing credit for emissions reductions outside the affected region would be difficult. Indeed, a vital issue treated by other chapters in this volume is how various cap-and-trade regimes will fit together as new programs come online at the federal or international level. Under a complete auction system, the "trade" in cap and trade becomes almost moot—in theory, there should be little trading within such a system if parties buy the allowances that they need at auction (marginal costs of compliance are effectively equalized through the auction mechanism rather than the subsequent exchange of allowances among sources). As we move toward greater auctioning as an allocation mechanism, therefore, trading between different "capped" regions seems important to any future global solution to climate change—linking various regional and national carbon markets together to take advantage of greater differentials in the marginal costs of compliance across international borders.[98] One can look at precedents in which allowances from regions with weaker caps or enforcement standards might be discounted by another program—given only 75 percent or 50 percent of the credit of an "internal" allowance, for example.[99] This might address many concerns about weakening more stringent and ambitious programs by trading between regional and national caps.

Two more problems remain, however. One involves federalism and the potential for "caps within caps." Some suggest that any federal cap-and-trade program avoid preempting more stringent state and local climate policies, including regional cap-and-trade efforts like RGGI and WCI.[100] As explored more fully by Selin and VanDeveer in chapter 14 of this volume, while the idea of federal standards as "floors" leaving room for stricter state or local rules works well in many environmental regulations, the idea of a federal floor in the form of a cap-and-trade program would be unprecedented. Indeed, it is hard to imagine how a federal cap-and-trade program could function in this regard, and federal bills to date offer no clear solutions to this challenge beyond preemption.

Despite the risk of weakening regional efforts, one could argue that federal preemption might be a sensible solution to problems of offsets and emissions leakage, especially given the widespread buying and selling of electricity across state and national borders in today's electricity markets. In this scenario, the federal government could negotiate some sort of buyout or "currency exchange" for existing regional cap-and-trade allowances to avoid punishing those now taking early action.[101] Or, one could argue that the need to avoid preemption indicates a need for federal action that is more complementary to regional cap-and-trade approaches, like a national carbon tax or renewable portfolio standard, as discussed in this volume in chapter 6 and chapter 8 respectively.

The second problem concerns offsets. As discussed above, current cap-and-trade policies evince a substantial mistrust of offsets through a somewhat paradoxical set of rules.[102] Many programs continue to use historical or "business as usual" emissions as a baseline from which to calculate offset credits, even as they move away from historical pollution levels as a criterion for allocating emissions allowances inside the cap. That is understandable, perhaps, from a practical perspective—it is hard to imagine how else one could quantify offsets (although a system that relied more on technology-based benchmarks seems a reasonable alternative). At the same time, programs often require offsets to be supplemental, allowing them to count for only a minority of required emissions reductions inside the cap. That combination risks missing important opportunities to reduce compliance costs and emissions by effectively creating a "cheap currency" in the form of offsets calculated from BAU baselines and then limiting the ability to spend that currency.

The public ownership paradigm suggests that tougher rules for calculating offsets (that is, no longer rewarding "bad behavior" by polluters via BAU baselines) might make them less controversial. WCI's approach is worth highlighting in this respect—the draft regulations give no offset credit for actions that would be required for WCI generators or sources inside the WCI cap, even if the reductions were not legally required where undertaken.[103] Thus, the failure of the public ownership perspective to extend into offset policies makes those policies more controversial and potentially less effective. One might keep an eye on this aspect of future cap-and-trade programs going forward, assuming the public ownership paradigm continues to gain influence.

A related point concerns the issue of emissions reporting. The 1990 acid rain program required all sources to install continuous emissions monitoring systems (CEMS), providing constant and reliable data on their SO_2 emissions. Measuring GHG emissions from a wide range of sources is a considerably greater challenge, and it is uncertain how new cap-and-trade programs will handle the reporting issue. RGGI appears to require CEMS for affected sources, although the breadth and scope of that requirement remains a bit unclear from the regulations issued to date.[104] WCI is a more ambitious program covering multiple gases and upstream sources, including those importing electricity into the regulated area, so CEMS are not going to be able to measure all relevant emissions. WCI and RGGI designers have agreed that they will require third-party audits to help ensure the necessary accuracy and transparency of reporting.[105]

How these programs will ensure honest reporting of GHG emissions, especially from upstream sources with no obvious "smokestack" output to measure, therefore remains a vital question. Some have suggested upstream accounting based on the GHG content of various fossil fuels as introduced into the economy, but no cap-and-trade proposal to date has fully adopted that approach.[106] Without some sort of solution to the reporting challenge, it will be harder to develop links between various emissions trading "currencies" since no one will have a basis for trusting claims of reductions in other political jurisdictions. To that end, states have begun experimenting with voluntary registries for GHG emissions,[107] and experimental economists are working on how to ensure reliable emissions reporting with only spot auditing and inspections.[108]

Perhaps the most important conclusion, however, is that we must avoid the danger of either romanticizing or demonizing cap and trade as a policy solution. While there is little question that the 1990 SO_2 trading program has been a success, cap and trade has important limitations, including the risk of concentrating pollution in local areas through trading and uncertain economic costs. While most greenhouse gases create no local pollution problems, other pollutants commonly associated with GHG emissions (for example, mercury, nitrogen oxides, volatile organic compounds, and sulfur dioxide) have serious local health effects. Thus, cap-and-trade for climate change could create some risk of increased local pollution and public health problems. At the same time, the measurement issues for cap-and-trade compliance are significant. In addition, the opportunities for equalizing marginal costs of compliance may be smaller given the lack of currently viable technology for reducing CO_2 emissions "at the smokestack"—a problem that does not exist in the case of SO_2, for example.[109]

We therefore should not overestimate the suitability of cap and trade as a policy option for GHGs even as we recognize its many accomplishments and advantages. At the same time, cap and trade's high profile has inspired recent criticisms that have badly misrepresented the policy. Perhaps such a backlash was inevitable, but it is no more helpful than the initial exaggerations of the policy's utility. In sum, it is important that policy designers and decisionmakers step back to appreciate the strengths and weaknesses of the policy for what they are, rather than buying into the exaggerations and misrepresentations on either side of the discussion. That is especially true as the range of options in emissions trading design multiply in a manner that makes "cap and trade" a relatively poor description of several policies being contemplated under that name.

It also is important to note that the shift toward public ownership of natural resources like the atmospheric sink capacity for greenhouse gases has significance for more than the design of cap-and-trade policies. Many other climate policies, including a tax on the use of an emissions sink that benefits the public, are also well justified by the new public ownership paradigm. Thus, the apparent agreement that the public does indeed "own" some common resources, rather than those who happen to have been using them historically, has ramifications well beyond the world of cap-and-trade policy design. In the end, that may be the most important legacy of the recent series of changes and controversies in emissions trading policy.

Notes

1. Technically, "commons" is a misleading term since many commonly owned resources have been conserved and used sustainably for centuries. Unfortunately, the term "commons" is often used synonymously with a resource that is "unowned" and has no limits on use or access.

It is in this sense that I use the term here. See Daniel W. Bromley, "Comment: Testing for Common versus Private Property," *Journal of Environmental Economics and Management* 21 (1991), pp. 92–96.

2. Seth Macinko and Leigh Raymond, "Fish on the Range: The Perils of Crossing Conceptual Boundaries in Natural Resource Policy," *Marine Policy* 25, no. 2 (2001), pp. 123–31.

3. Leigh Raymond, *Private Rights in Public Resources* (Washington: Resources for the Future Press, 2003).

4. The other solution, of course, being government regulation—"mutual coercion, mutually agreed upon." Garrett Hardin, "The Tragedy of the Commons," *Science* 162, no. 3859 (1968), pp. 1243–48. A long line of research has since shown the inevitability of this "tragedy" to be wrong. See Elinor Ostrom, *Governing the Commons: The Evolution of Institutions for Collective Action* (Cambridge University Press, 1990).

5. Harold Demsetz, "Toward a Theory of Property Rights," *American Economic Review* 57, no. 347 (1967); Gary Libecap, *Contracting for Property Rights* (Cambridge University Press, 1989).

6. J. H. Dales, *Pollution, Property, and Prices* (University of Toronto Press, 1969).

7. The following discussion of the 1990 SO_2 emissions trading program draws substantially on a more detailed analysis in chapter 4 of Leigh Raymond, *Private Rights in Public Resources* (Washington: Resources for the Future Press, 2003).

8. Daniel J. Dudek and John Palmisano, "Emissions Trading: Why Is This Thoroughbred Hobbled?" *Columbia Journal of Environmental Law* 13 (1988), pp. 217–56.

9. See Richard E. Cohen, *Washington at Work: Back Rooms and Clean Air* (Boston: Allyn and Bacon, 1995).

10. For more on the Lockean and Humean approaches to ownership, see chapter 2 of Raymond, *Private Rights in Public Resources.*

11. Dallas Burtraw and Karen Palmer, "The Paparazzi Take a Look at a Living Legend: The SO_2 Cap-and-Trade Program for Power Plants in the United States" (Washington: Resources for the Future, 2003).

12. U.S. Environmental Protection Agency, "Acid Rain and Related Programs: 2007 Progress Report" (Washington, 2009).

13. Rena I. Steinzor and Lisa Heinzerling, "A Perfect Storm: Mercury and the Bush Administration, Part II?" *Environmental Law Reporter* 34 (2004), pp. 10485–97.

14. A. Denny Ellerman, Barbara Buchner, and Carlo Carraro, *Rights, Rents, and Fairness: Allocation in the European Emissions Trading Scheme* (Cambridge University Press, 2007), p. 354.

15. Directive 2003/87/EC of the European Parliament and of the Council, 10/13/2003, article 10.

16. Ellerman, Buchner, and Carraro, *Rights, Rents, and Fairness.*

17. Directive 2004/101/EC of the European Parliament and of the Council, 10/27/2004.

18. Ellerman, Buchner, and Carraro, *Rights, Rents, and Fairness,* p. 356.

19. Michael Grubb, Christian Azar, and U. Martin Persson, "Allowance Allocation in the European Emissions Trading System: A Commentary," *Climate Policy* 5 (2005), pp. 127–36.

20. Leigh Raymond, "Allocating the Global Commons: Theory and Practice," in *Political Theory and Global Climate Change*, edited by S. Vanderheiden (MIT Press, 2008).

21. Burtraw and Palmer, "The Paparazzi Take a Look at a Living Legend."

22. Robert N. Stavins, "What Can We Learn from the Grand Policy Experiment? Positive and Normative Lessons from the SO_2 Allowance Trading Program" (Washington: Resources for the Future, 1997).

23. A. Denny Ellerman and Paul Joskow, "The European Union's Emissions Trading System in Perspective" (Washington: Pew Center on Global Climate Change, 2008).

24. There are several versions of the idea, including simply capping the allowance price at a certain level, creating more allowances for distribution when prices hit a certain threshold (either by permitting more emissions or by "reserving" a small percentage of allowances annually for release only in the event of a price spike), or allowing firms to borrow allowances from the future or to expand their offset credits. Most radically, there have been proposals to suspend the cap-and-trade program entirely for a year or more if price thresholds are exceeded. Whatever the metaphor, all of these devices are versions of the same idea—trying to limit costs within a cap-and-trade framework by weakening or suspending the cap if allowance prices rise above a certain threshold.

25. For a price control scheme sensitive to some of these concerns that has yet to be implemented politically, see Robert N. Stavins, "Addressing Climate Change with a Comprehensive U.S. Cap-and-Trade System," *Oxford Review of Economic Policy* 24, no. 2 (2008), pp. 298–321.

26. The differences remain critical, as Coase famously pointed out in his critique of Pigouvian taxes in 1960. Ronald Coase, "The Problem of Social Cost," *Journal of Law and Economics* 3 (1960), pp. 1–44.

27. Stavins, "Addressing Climate Change with a Comprehensive U.S. Cap-and-Trade System."

28. "Senate Bill Allocation Fight Expected to Go down to the Wire," *E&E Daily*, March 26, 2010 (www.eenews.net/EEDaily/us_climate_debate/2010/03/26/1).

29. Although unlike RGGI and WCI, the Midwestern group explicitly states a preference for a federal program rather than a regional cap-and-trade policy. See Midwestern Greenhouse Gas Reduction Accord (MGGRA), "Advisory Group Draft Final Recommendations," June 2009, p. 3 (www.midwesternaccord.org/GHG%20Draft%20Advisory%20Group%20Recommendations. pdf).

30. Midwestern Greenhouse Gas Reduction Accord, "Preliminary Recommendations of the Advisory Group," updated 11/1/2008; MGGRA, "Advisory Group Draft Final Recommendations."

31. RGGI Executive Summary, updated 9/23/2008 (www.rggi.org/about/documents).

32. Ibid.

33. RGGI MOU 12/20/2005, section (6)(D) (www.rggi.org/about/history/mou).

34. Barry G. Rabe, "Regionalism and Global Climate Change Policy," in *Intergovernmental Management for the Twenty-First Century*, edited by T. J. Conlan and P. L. Posner (Brookings, 2008) p. 187.

35. RGGI MOU 12/20/2005, section (2)(G). The final model rule for the program required states to ensure that at least 25 percent of their allowances went toward consumer benefits or energy-efficiency programs annually. RGGI Model Rule, section XX-5.3(a) (www.rggi. org/about/history/model_rule).

36. RGGI Executive Summary, updated 9/23/2008.

37. Ibid.

38. Rabe, "Regionalism and Global Climate Change Policy," p. 198; see also "New York State Proposes Auctioning 100 Percent of RGGI Credits instead of 25 Percent," *Global Power Report* 25 (December 7, 2006).

39. "Spitzer Seeks GHG Allocation Sales in Previewing New York's RGGI Rules," *Inside Green Business Weekly Report,* September 13, 2006.

40. RGGI Executive Summary, updated 9/23/2008.

41. "Enviros See Carbon Auctioning as Key to Funding Mitigation Plans," *Platts Coal Outlook* 31, no. 11 (July 2, 2007); James Hansen, "Cap and Fade," *New York Times,* December 6, 2009; more generally, see Peter Barnes, *Who Owns the Sky?* (Washington: Island Press, 2001).

42. Leigh Raymond, "Allocating Greenhouse Gas Emissions under the EU ETS: The UK Experience," paper presented at 6th Open Meeting of the Human Dimensions of Global Environmental Change Research Community, University of Bonn, Germany, October 2005.

43. See, for example, "Spitzer Seeks GHG Allocation Sales in Previewing New York's RGGI Rules," and "States Aim to Cut Gases by Making Polluters Pay," *New York Times,* September 16, 2008, A, p. 17.

44. The quote is from NRDC's David Doniger, "EU Experience Seen as Leading U.S. to Auction, not Give Away, Carbon Emission Allowances," *Electric Utility Week,* April 16, 2007.

45. On the complexities of "windfall" profits in the EU ETS, see Ellerman and Joskow, "The European Union's Emissions Trading System in Perspective."

46. RGGI MOU 12/20/2005, section 2(F)(2); RGGI Executive Summary, updated 9/23/2008; RGGI Model Rule corrected 1/5/07, section XX-6.5.

47 RGGI MOU 12/20/2005, section 2(F)(3); RGGI Model Rule corrected 1/5/07, section XX-6.5 (a)(3).

48. RGGI Model Rule, section XX10.3(d)(1); section XX10.5(d)(3).

49. See RGGI Model Rule on landfill emissions, section XX10.5(a)(3)-(4); on SF6 emissions, section XX10.5(b)(4); on afforestation, section XX10.5(c)(4); on energy conservation, section XX10.5(d)(3); and on anaerobic digesters, section XX10.5(e)(4) (www.rggi.org/about/history/model_rule).

50. Including the remarkable requirement that any afforestation project have a permanent conservation easement to qualify. RGGI Model Rule, sections XX-10.1–XX-10.7.

51. Arizona announced in February 2010 that it would not participate in the WCI cap-and-trade program, but it remains a part of the initiative. See "Arizona Quits Western Climate Endeavor," *Arizona Republic*, February 11, 2010.

52. WCI Overview (www.westernclimateinitiative.org/the-wci-cap-and-trade-program); WCI Design Document section 6.2 (p. 4) (www.westernclimateinitiative.org/document-archives/wci-design-recommendations)

53. WCI Overview; WCI Design Document, p. 15.

54. WCI Overview.

55. WCI Design Document, section 7.2, pp. 5–6, and stakeholder comments, p. 30. It is important to note that not all WCI stakeholders supported allocating to states or provinces based on projections of need, however: see WCI Design Document, pp. 28–56.

56. WCI Design Document, section 8.2 (p. 7) and p. 32.

57. WCI Design Document, section 8.3 (p. 7).

58. WCI Design Document, pp. 8, 32. The document recognizes in the same sections, however, that some states may lack legal authority to auction allowances, which should not hold back the rest of the program.

59. WCI Design Document, pp. 8, 33.

60. WCI Design Document, section 8.10 (p. 8).

61. WCI Design Document, section 9.2 (p. 10).

62. WCI Design Document, sections 9.3, 9.8 (pp. 10, 11).

63. WCI Design Document, p. 41.

64. WCI Design Document, p. 40.

65. Ibid.

66. WCI Design Document, p. 41.

67. For example, see "Companies Oppose Proposals to Auction California GHG Credits," *Inside Green Business Weekly*, November 1, 2006.

68. MGGRA, "Advisory Group Draft Final Recommendations," June 2009 (www.midwesternaccord.org/).

69. It is important to note that the CSA was only one of many bills introduced in the 110th Congress to address climate change. Many of the leading bills were similar in important respects, including in addressing a full "basket" of six greenhouse gases and in most cases requir-

ing that a significant portion of allowances be auctioned under a cap-and-trade framework. Because the CSA was not adopted, the analysis will use the last version to gain serious consideration in Congress. That bill was the so-called Boxer-Lieberman-Warner amendment (S 3036), which failed a cloture vote on June 6, 2008; "Economy-Wide Cap-and-Trade Proposals in the 110th Congress" (Pew Center on Global Climate Change, December 1, 2008).

70. "Distribution of Allowances, S. 3036 Boxer-Lieberman-Warner Substitute Amendment" (Pew Center on Global Climate Change, June 3, 2008).

71. Ibid.

72. The final bill permits up to 2 billion tons of offset credits annually, which is more than required to meet the 17 percent reduction in emissions by 2020: House Committee on Energy and Commerce, *Committee Report, H.R. 2454,* June 23, 2009. The Congressional Budget Office estimated that up to 52 percent of all emissions reductions required by Waxman-Markey could be achieved through offsets by 2030: "The Use of Offsets to Reduce Greenhouse Gases," *Congressional Budget Office Economic and Budget Issue Brief,* August 3, 2009.

73. "Distribution of Allowances under the American Clean Energy and Security Act (Waxman-Markey)" (Pew Center on Global Climate Change, August 2009).

74. Clean Energy Jobs and American Power Act (S 1733), sec. 771(c)(2).

75. Republican Senator Lindsey Graham of South Carolina expressed this view in discussing his ideas for a new cap-and-trade program: "[T]he money we collect from [emitting firms] gets passed back to the consumer, which holds them harmless. Bill Gates may not get it, but most people in my state will." See "Senate Bill Allocation Fight Expected to Go Down to the Wire."

76. For example, see Thomas Content, "Climate Bill Costly for Midwest: Utility Group Says House Version Penalizes Coal," *Milwaukee Journal Sentinel,* August 23, 2009, D1; and testimony of Jeffry E. Sterba, Edison Electric Institute, U.S. House of Representatives Committee on Energy and Commerce, Subcommittee on Energy and Environment, *Hearing on Allocation of Emissions Allowances,* April 23, 2009. For an indication of the shift in the debate from the academic perspective, see Dallas Burtraw and Karen Palmer, "Compensation Rules for Climate Policy in the Electricity Sector," *Journal of Policy Analysis and Management* 27, no. 4 (2008), pp. 819–47.

77. For example, Senator Lisa Murkowski (R-Alaska) commented at a Senate hearing on allowance allocation: "Immediate decisions about who should receive them will have lasting consequences. Accordingly, we should view attempts to secure free permits with a healthy dose of skepticism and, frankly, concern." Another Republican senator, Bob Corker of Tennessee, expressed support at the same hearing for a full auction and "100 percent return of revenue to consumers" in any cap-and-trade bill. Darren Samuelsohn, "GOP Fence Sitters Voice Concerns over Allocations," *Greenwire,* October 22, 2009. See also comments of Senator Lindsey Graham already quoted from "Senate Bill Allocation Fight Expected to Go Down to the Wire."

78. "Distribution of Allowances under the American Clean Energy and Security Act (Waxman-Markey)"; "Distribution of Allowances, S. 3036 Boxer-Lieberman-Warner Substitute Amendment." At least one prominent environmental economist has publicly criticized the efficiency losses of such deviations from more equal per capita distributions of allowance revenue. See Testimony of Dallas Burtraw, Resources for the Future, Senate Committee on Finance, *Hearing on Climate Change Legislation: Allowance and Revenue Distribution,* August 4, 2009.

79. For more on the weakness of these claims, see Raymond, "Allocating the Global Commons: Theory and Practice."

80. "'Cap and Trade' Loses Its Standing as Energy Policy of Choice," *New York Times,* March 25, 2010.

81. Raymond, *Private Rights in Public Resources,* chapter 4.

82. On growing comfort with market-based regulations (although less among environmentalists in his data), see Brian J. Cook, "The Politics of Market-Based Environmental Regulation: Continuity and Change in Air Pollution Control Policy Conflict," *Social Science Quarterly* 83, no. 1 (2002), pp. 156–66.

83. Barnes, *Who Owns the Sky?*; James P. Lucier, "What Palin Really Did to the Oil Industry," *Wall Street Journal,* September 5, 2008.

84. Anil Agarwal and Sunita Narain, "Global Warming in an Unequal World: A Case of Environmental Colonialism" (New Delhi: Center for Science and Environment, 1991); Joseph L. Sax, "The Public Trust Doctrine in Natural Resource Law: Effective Judicial Intervention," *Michigan Law Review* 68 (1970), pp. 471–566.

85. However, some federal proposals have included substantial revenue sharing for consumers to defray higher energy costs. For some examples, see "Economy-Wide Cap-and-Trade Proposals in the 110th Congress."

86. "Spitzer Seeks GHG Allocation Sales in Previewing New York's RGGI Rules."

87. RGGI Executive Summary, updated 9/23/2008.

88. WCI Design Document, section 8.3.

89. "Distribution of Allowances, S. 3036 Boxer-Lieberman-Warner Substitute Amendment." For market distortions and welfare loss under the ACESA form of consumer relief, see testimony of Burtraw, *Hearing on Climate Change Legislation: Allowance and Revenue Distribution.*

90. As appears to be happening already in some RGGI states facing budget shortfalls: "Money to Fight Climate Change Gets Siphoned into Other Budgets," *Climatewire,* March 19, 2010 (www.eenews.net/climatewire/2010/03/19/6/)

91. For example, see Stephen H. Schneider and Lawrence H. Goulder, "Achieving Low-Cost Emissions Targets," *Nature* 389 (1997), pp. 13–14.

92. Allowances could be worth more than $100 billion annually. See Sergey Paltsev and others, "Assessment of U.S. Cap-and-Trade Proposals," Working Paper W13176 (Cambridge, Mass.: National Bureau of Economic Research, 2007).

93. David G. Victor, *The Collapse of the Kyoto Protocol and the Struggle to Slow Global Warming* (Princeton University Press, 2001); see also Leigh Raymond, "Viewpoint: Cutting the 'Gordian Knot' in Climate Change Policy," *Energy Policy* 34 (2006), pp. 655–58.

94. For example, see S 3036 Boxer-Lieberman-Warner Substitute Amendment, Title VI subtitle C; "Distribution of Allowances under the American Clean Energy and Security Act (Waxman-Markey)."

95. See "The Use of Offsets to Reduce Greenhouse Gases" and WCI Offsets Committee, "White Paper on Offset Definition and Eligibility Criteria," July 24, 2009.

96. Brian J. McLean, "Evolution of Marketable Permits: The U.S. Experience with Sulfur Dioxide Allowance Trading," *International Journal of Environment and Pollution* 8, no. 1/2 (1997), pp. 19–36; Burtraw and Palmer, "The Paparazzi Take a Look at a Living Legend."

97. For instance, see recent meeting of the Ad Hoc Working Group on Further Commitments for Annex I Parties under the Kyoto Protocol on September 29, 2009, as reported in "Further Division between Developed and Developing Countries in the Kyoto Protocol," *Third World Network Bangkok News Update 8,* October 1, 2009; and *Earth Negotiations Bulletin* 12, no. 430 (September 30, 2009). More generally, see Robert Repetto, "The Clean Development Mechanism: Institutional Breakthrough or Institutional Nightmare?" *Policy Sciences* 34 (2001), pp. 303–27.

98. As noted in International Emissions Trading Association, "IETA Report on Linking GHG Emissions Trading Systems," Executive Summary, for publication at the United Nations Climate Change Conference COP13/CMP3, Bali, Indonesia, December 2008 (http://www.ieta.org/ieta/www/pages/getfile.php?docID=2733).

99. ACESA, for example, requires 1.25 international offsets for a single domestic allowance. "The Use of Offsets to Reduce Greenhouse Gases."

100. William Andreen and others, "Cooperative Federalism and Climate Change," Center for Progressive Reform White Paper 803 (Washington: Center for Progressive Reform, 2008). See also Barry G. Rabe, *Statehouse and Greenhouse* (Washington: Brookings, 2004).

101. Such buyouts are not unprecedented in market-based policies; New Zealand negotiated a similar deal with private fishermen in the 1990s, and environmentalists have urged the purchase and retirement of U.S. federal grazing permits as another conservation effort.

102. As a recent example of this mistrust of offsets, see Derik Broekhoff and Kathryn Zyla, "Outside the Cap: Opportunities and Limitations of Greenhouse Gas Offsets," World Resources Institute Climate and Energy Policy Series (Washington: World Resources Institute, 2008).

103. WCI Design Document, p. 41.

104. RGGI Model Rule, corrected 1/5/2007, section XX-8.1(a)(1) (p. 72). Note that the rules permit alternatives to CEMS with approval in section XX-8.6 (p. 86).

105. WCI Design Document, section 10 (pp. 11–12); RGGI Model Rule, corrected 1/5/2007, section XX-8.2 and XX-8.3 (pp. 76–83).

106. Stavins, "Addressing Climate Change with a Comprehensive U.S. Cap-and-Trade System."

107. For a leading example, see the Climate Registry (www.theclimateregistry.org/). The Climate Security Act also required a federal greenhouse gas registry to be developed in two years, but did not specify any precise reporting requirements: S 3036 Boxer-Lieberman-Warner Substitute Amendment, section 102.

108. James J. Murphy and John K. Stranlund, "A Laboratory Investigation of Compliance Behavior under Tradable Emissions Rights: Implications for Targeted Enforcement," *Journal of Environmental Economics and Management* 53 (2007), pp. 196–212; John Stranlund, Carlos Chavez, and Barry Field, "Enforcing Emissions Trading Programs: Theory, Practice, and Performance," *Policy Studies Journal* 30 (2002), pp. 343–61.

109. I am grateful to Chris James for reminding me of this point.

6

The "Impossible Dream" of Carbon Taxes: Is the "Best Answer" a Political Non-Starter?

BARRY G. RABE

> I've talked to a number of economists on this issue. . . and every one of them says the same thing: a direct fee is the better approach—but for the politics. . . . Cap-and-trade is an easier sell because the costs are hidden—but they're still there. And the payoff is more uncertain.[1]
>
> —Michael Bloomberg, mayor of New York City

A veritable army of economists and policy advocates have locked arms and expressed their passionate belief that the direct taxation of the carbon content of fossil fuels trumps all other policy options for reducing greenhouse gas emissions. Mayor Bloomberg did not disclose the identity of his advisers on the matter, but one sees daily evidence of this outpouring of support, much of it crossing traditional divides. Gregory Mankiw chaired George W. Bush's Council of Economic Advisers between 2003 and 2005, not exactly a high-water mark for federal engagement on climate change. However, he has since returned to Harvard University, where he writes a blog, the "Pigou Club Manifesto," devoted to plugging energy and carbon taxes as the best way to confront climate change. The Nobel Prize laureates in economics Paul Krugman and Joseph Stiglitz, who fre-

I am grateful to Christopher Borick, Timothy Conlan, Christopher James, William Lowry, Pietro Nivola, David Uhlmann, and Henrik Selin for thoughtful comments on earlier versions of this chapter.

quently disagree with Mankiw, have happily joined this choir. In turn, other luminaries such as Gary Becker, Martin Feldstein, Alan Greenspan, Arthur Laffer, Anthony Lake, William Nordhaus, Richard Posner, and Murray Weidenbaum have formally expressed their support, and they have been joined by many others. Scholars from such disparate think tanks as the American Enterprise Institute, the Brookings Institution, the Hudson Institute, the Rand Corporation, and Resources for the Future, among many others, along with diverse columnists such as David Brooks, Thomas Friedman, and Charles Krauthammer, are on board with this remarkable train of convergent thought. The *Wall Street Journal*, one of the world's most prominent opponents of any regulatory steps to reduce greenhouse gases or virtually any form of a tax increase, offered Ralph Nader one-half of its op-ed page in November 2008 to make the case for carbon taxation, followed shortly thereafter by a similar endorsement from ExxonMobil CEO Rex Tillerson. Although President Obama has never endorsed the idea of a carbon tax, four of his most prominent senior advisers were outspoken in their support of this approach before assuming new duties in 2009: Energy Secretary Steven Chu; Office of Management and Budget director Peter Orszag; National Economic Council chair Lawrence Summers; and Economic Recovery Advisory Board chair Paul Volcker. Speaking for these masses, Nordhaus has written that "conceptually, the carbon tax is a dynamically efficient Pigouvian tax that balances the marginal social costs and marginal social benefits of additional emissions" of greenhouse gases.[2]

Despite Bloomberg's concern about "the politics," some prominent political officials also have joined this remarkable bandwagon. It is worth mentioning, however, that most of these individuals no longer hold elected office or that their support of the idea of a carbon tax did not assist them in winning elections. 2000 Democratic presidential rivals Al Gore and Bill Bradley, for example, had little to say about carbon taxation during their bitter campaign but now are effusive on the subject. Indeed, Gore had his personal epiphany on climate change more than a generation ago, as is well-known from his award-winning film *An Inconvenient Truth*, yet never seriously advanced a carbon tax proposal in any of his four campaigns for national executive office (1988, 1992, 1996, or 2000). He did endorse a form of energy taxation known as a BTU tax after election to the vice presidency, but only as part of a larger deficit reduction program. In this case, Gore had to quickly backtrack in the face of fierce opposition and settle for a modest increase in existing federal gasoline taxes. He now commonly exhorts the nation: "We should tax what we burn, not what we earn. This is the single most important policy change we can make."[3] Gore was especially outspoken on this issue in early 2009, including in multiple rounds of congressional testimony.

Although most public support for carbon taxation has been evident outside of political office, it has not been invisible at the highest levels of political campaigning. Two prominent political officials *did* attempt to parlay outspoken support for

expansive carbon taxation into election to two of the highest political offices in
North America. Senator Christopher Dodd (D-Connecticut) moved his family to
Iowa in 2007 to take his well-heeled presidential campaign into this key caucus
state. Once settled, he placed strong emphasis on his support for a "corporate carbon tax" that would generate more than $50 billion annually and use funds to pro-
mote renewable energy and the safe disposal of nuclear waste.[4] He ran what may
have been the first televised commercials for a carbon tax in U.S. history, rolling
globes on a lawn with Iowa children against a musical backdrop of "We've Got the
Whole World in Our Hands." Dodd never ascended to the rank of frontrunner
and indeed folded his campaign immediately after receiving less than 1 percent of
the Iowa caucus votes. A subsequent Canadian federal election campaign turned
at least in part on the decision by Liberal Party leader Stéphane Dion to make a
"green shift" toward carbon taxation a central plank in his campaign to oust Conservative Stephen Harper as prime minister. Dion sought an initial carbon tax of
$10 (Canadian) per ton that would rise to $40 per ton over a four-year period.
That would be imposed on the carbon content of all fossil fuels except gasoline,
which is already taxed federally in Canada at $42 per ton, well above combined
U.S. federal and state taxes for fuel. He further proposed to return the majority of
revenues through income tax cuts and dividend checks to all Canadians. That
approach received wide support among Canadian economists, think tank senior
fellows, and prominent columnists, but Harper derided it as a "green shaft" and
countered with a proposal to reduce some existing energy taxes. Dion ran a seriously flawed campaign, but carbon tax backlash contributed at least in part to the
worst showing by the Liberal Party in a national election in more than two generations. As former deputy prime minister and fellow Liberal Sheila Copps wrote
shortly after the debacle, "Whether Nobel Laureates embrace the green shift means
little to voters concerned about pocketbook politics."[5]

Similarly, a pair of carbon tax proposals did succeed in taking legislative form
in the 110th Congress but ultimately received little serious attention. Some interpreted that deafening silence as a final pronouncement on the fate of such policies in the United States. Representative Fortney "Pete" Stark (D-California),
dusting off legislation that he first introduced nearly two decades earlier, proposed
the "Save Our Climate Act," which called for a $10 per ton tax on carbon, not-
ing that "economists widely agree that a carbon tax is the best way to reduce carbon dioxide emissions and save our planet from catastrophic climate change."[6]
But neither his legislation nor a similar bill introduced by Representative John
Larson (D-Connecticut), which set a $15 per ton tax, received significant support
or attention beyond broad endorsement from carbon tax aficionados. Additional
proposals emerged during the 111th Congress and attracted support from Republicans such as Representative Bob Inglis (R-South Carolina). They were, however,
quickly overshadowed by proposals that relied instead on some form of carbon
cap and trade, as reviewed in chapter 5 of this volume.

Consequently, one might well dismiss carbon taxation as an idea that plays well in many corners of the academy and among many members of the chattering classes but lacks political traction in the real world of representative democracies. This chapter examines that issue and also explores some indicators that carbon taxation could play at least some role in evolving U.S. climate policy. First, the analytical case on behalf of carbon taxation as an optimal climate policy tool merits a more thorough review as well as an examination of the substantial political hurdles facing any federal or state effort to enact such a policy. In turn, the chapter examines recent developments in the European Union, where many member states have adopted carbon taxes and some have decades of experience with them, as a test of their performance once these taxes move beyond the blog and into the real world of policy implementation. That examination is combined with consideration of some recent state and local government experimentation with modest forms of carbon taxation, leading to a concluding analysis that considers their future viability and possible links with other policy tools.

The Policy Advantages

Perhaps the biggest attraction of carbon taxes is their anticipated efficiency. Unlike other policy options, carbon taxes do not try to mandate any particular technology, degree of energy efficiency, or level of emission reduction. Instead, they set a price on the carbon content of all fossil fuels and operate much like other specialized excise taxes, such as those for gasoline, beer, wine, spirits, and cigarettes (see figure 6-1). The tax does not prohibit purchase or use, leaving those decisions to producers and consumers, and in the process collects revenue that can be used for a range of purposes. By concentrating on the carbon content of various fuels, such a tax would respond to the variation in levels of carbon released and climate impacts of differing fossil fuels, hence placing a lighter burden on natural gas and gasoline than on coal. At a rate of $30 per ton of carbon, for example, such a tax would add approximately $.30 per gallon of gasoline and $.01 per kilowatt of coal-generated electricity, or approximately 10 percent of the current retail price. In turn, the tax burden would be considerably lower for natural gas, reflecting its relatively lower release of carbon dioxide per unit of energy generated. A $30 per ton carbon tax would produce an estimated $50 billion in revenue per year. A tax that was set at $700 per ton would increase the cost of coal-generated electricity by approximately 150 percent and add more than $2 to the price of a gallon of gas.

Behavioral Impacts

Carbon tax proponents contend that one undeniable result of increased price is reduced use. Whereas most other policy options are loaded with uncertain links, such as the impact on gasoline use that can be attributed to improvements in

Figure 6-1. *Rate Ranges for Various State "Sin" Taxes versus State Gasoline Taxes*

Dollars

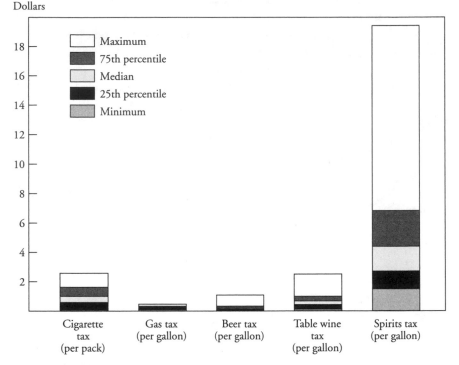

Source: Tax Foundation, "State Sales, Gasoline, Cigarette, and Alcohol Tax Rates by State, 2000–2008" (www.taxfoundation.org/taxdata/show/245.html).

vehicular fuel efficiency, abundant evidence is available from the natural cycle of energy prices (supplemented by a cottage industry of literature in economics journals) that behavior does respond significantly. Past spikes in gasoline prices in the 1970s and earlier in the 2000s produced unexpected declines in gasoline purchases. Of course, perhaps the most telling indicator of price sensitivity in gasoline involves the earlier months of 2008, when real prices soared to record highs. Not only did gasoline purchases decline during that period but the almost unthinkable occurred, an outright reduction in miles driven. According to the Federal Highway Administration, Americans drove 4.3 percent fewer miles in March 2008 than in the previous March. That pattern also was evident during other months in which prices were elevated, although it also overlapped with the onset of an unusually severe recession. This is very similar to the evidence available from Europe following major increases in various energy taxes and from prior U.S. experience during gasoline price spikes due to supply disruptions. While the debate over price elasticity for gasoline and other fossil fuel sources is endless, there can be no question that taxation is one direct way to reduce consumption.

Simplicity

Carbon taxes also offer the advantages, at least in theory, of relative simplicity and ease of implementation. Most other policy options entail considerable complexity in implementation and constitutional uncertainty, as pointed out in a number of other chapters in this volume. Even in the case of cap-and-trade programs, for which market features are a significant selling point, the process of sorting out issues such as setting baselines, determining allowance allocations, defining and measuring offsets, and monitoring compliance is highly convoluted. Initial experimentation with relatively simple carbon cap-and-trade policies, such as the Regional Greenhouse Gas Initiative (RGGI) in the northeastern United States, which applies only to fossil fuel–burning power plants, required four years of painstaking deliberation before the launch of its initial stages of operation. RGGI required considerable development of new institutional mechanisms for governance and unusually extensive cooperation across departmental lines (both environmental and energy), which are known around the world as common places for rivalry and turf wars.[7] Other regional cap-and-trade efforts, such as the Western Climate Initiative, that are more ambitious in scope are experiencing considerably greater early implementation difficulties.

In contrast, carbon taxes are easier to understand and put into operation, and few constitutional issues are likely to complicate their implementation. Whereas most federal cap-and-trade bills run to hundreds or even thousands of pages, two carbon tax proposals set forth in the U.S. House, one by Representative Stark and the other by Representative Larson, offer much more succinct propositions: the Stark proposal covered twelve pages beginning to end and the Larson proposal was only five pages longer. Their governance task is simpler; essentially, it lies in explaining the tax level and the sources on which the tax will be imposed and also in assigning responsibility for collecting the resulting revenue. Indeed, the main reason for the added length of the Larson proposal was that it further discussed how the revenues would be reallocated to the citizenry through the reduction of other taxes. As legal scholars Reuven Avi-Yonah and David Uhlmann have noted, the United States has "extensive experience with economy-wide excise taxes on a wide variety of products, including gasoline." Their interpretation of the Larson bill is that it would simply entail adding "three new relatively short sections to the existing excise tax part of the Internal Revenue Code"[8] and generate little if any need for additional staff or reorganization of the Internal Revenue Service.[9]

Such a tax would prove simplest to implement if imposed "upstream," closest to the points of most intensive fossil fuel use. One can envision other arrangements, depending on the structure of the tax, but they clearly offer a more streamlined path to implementation, and they can go into operation much more rapidly than either regulatory or cap-and-trade mechanisms that are likely to require years of complex rulemaking. As Larson asserted in December 2008, "there will be no need to create new agencies or bureaucracies to implement it. Just use the internal revenue code that already exists. Affected entities already pay taxes so the system is already there in place."[10]

Larson vowed in early 2009 to use his new post as chair of the Democratic House Caucus, where he replaced White House chief of staff Rahm Emanuel, as well as his seat on the House Ways and Means Committee to continue to push this option. In the early stages of the 111th Congress, he introduced one of four carbon tax proposals, HR 1337, which would begin by setting a $15 per ton tax on the carbon content of fossil fuels. Future increases would be linked to emission trends, with failure to meet designated reduction targets triggering larger increases. Most of the revenue generated through such a tax would be returned to the citizenry through payroll tax rebates, with small amounts reserved for development of clean energy technology and transition assistance to affected industries. However, Larson quietly downplayed his proposal as House deliberations intensified and said nothing at all about it during an impassioned June 2009 floor speech in which he declared his support for the American Clean Energy and Security Act.

At the same time, all fifty states have had somewhat similar experiences with and authority to establish carbon taxes, reflecting their own histories with gasoline and a wide range of other excise taxes. The states collectively operate more than 400 separate taxes and fees related to the environment, including a growing number of direct charges on emissions. For example, more than forty states currently tax the sale of vehicle tires, using the proceeds to cover tire recycling operations. The operation of these taxes and fees tends to be relatively straightforward. In turn, it is relatively easier to envision cross-state and international collaboration on establishing uniform taxation rates for carbon than reconciling competing versions of other programs, such as cap and trade. That would be especially evident in cases involving immediate U.S. neighbors such as Canada, given both nations' extensive history in seeking common ground on trade issues and various excise taxes.

Price Certainty and Intergovernmental Compatibility

A further advantage of carbon taxes is that they provide greater predictability concerning the price of energy, in vivid contrast to the tremendous volatility that has been found in cap-and-trade systems, whether highlighted by the U.S. experience with sulfur dioxide or by the early years of the EU Emission Trading System for carbon. Carbon taxes send clear signals regarding pricing and can be set up in such a way that they establish a floor below which energy prices do not fall. As a result, they are far more likely to shift the difference in prices between renewable and fossil fuels to a tipping point where the former become the more attractive alternative on economic as well as environmental grounds. Indeed, carbon taxes literally "fit" more effectively with other policy tools, such as renewable portfolio standards, than cap-and-trade strategies do. By elevating and clarifying the price of the continuing use of fossil fuels, carbon taxes allow consumers and firms to respond accordingly.

This adaptability extends also to intergovernmental relations, making a carbon tax likely to be the easiest form of federal policy to integrate with the evolving tapestry of state initiatives. Virtually every other possible climate policy option poses numerous challenges for federalism, particularly in those instances in which multiple states have already become active in policy development. In such instances, any subsequent federal involvement must address the difficult matters of sorting out early action and claims for differential treatment on the basis of policy capacity or emissions patterns to date. Indeed, the question of intergovernmental conflict is an abiding concern in many other areas of climate policy.

In contrast, the creation of a federal carbon tax would not require any sorting out of intergovernmental powers or raise questions of preemption. States would presumably retain the authority to keep their own energy tax levels, and the federal carbon tax would provide a further incentive to continue with their own climate policy experiments in order to reduce the burden that the new federal tax would impose on their citizens. Indeed, given the significant interstate differences in per capita rates of energy use and greenhouse gas emissions, a federal carbon tax would provide an immediate reward for those states that had already found ways to use energy more efficiently.

The Political Hurdles

Any discussion of the potential advantages of carbon taxes is almost inevitably coupled with the presumption that the political feasibility of imposing such taxes is extremely low. Carbon taxes pose a significant financial threat to all sectors of society that have developed a dependence on fossil fuels, particularly coal, given its relatively high carbon content. Political opposition to carbon tax proposals would likely cut across sectors such as electricity, transportation, and manufacturing. Perhaps more significant, the impact of the taxes would be highly visible to the general citizenry, whether through increased costs at the gas pump or in the monthly electricity bill. As a result, carbon taxes represent a form of direct loss that can be seen and felt rapidly across society.

From an economic standpoint, that has many advantages, but politically it would likely draw together a constituency affronted by the costs, unlike more popular climate policy options that are far less efficient but whose costs are veiled by a tapestry of mandates and subsidies that are far more difficult to trace to specific government actions. Many analysts note that there are some parallels between carbon taxes and cap and trade, in that both generate revenue derived from the use of fossil fuels. Although far more complicated to design and implement, one of the perceived political advantages of cap and trade is that it is easier to obscure the ways in which it would impose costs.

Carbon taxes thus join a long line of policy options that face formidable political obstacles due to their imposition of significant and demonstrable losses while
any benefits that they entail may be difficult to recognize.[11] Various strategies have
been proposed for reallocating revenues generated by such a tax, but none are
guaranteed to significantly remove the sting from such a direct form of loss imposition. Indeed, one may use the experience of the U.S. states as a laboratory of
sorts for the political viability of carbon taxes as well as other climate policy tools.
As noted in other chapters in this volume, states have proven themselves to be
unexpectedly active players in climate policy, putting virtually every kind of policy with some capacity to reduce greenhouse gas emissions into operation. The
list of state policy experiments is essentially endless, reaching into areas such as
renewable fuels, energy efficiency and conservation, agricultural and forestry
reforms, and much else.

One might anticipate that the intellectual consensus behind carbon taxation,
the need in many states for additional revenue, and the growing saliency of the
climate change issue in many states would generate a groundswell of support for
some form of carbon taxation. But not a single state has decided to make carbon
taxes a central plank of its climate protection strategy, opting instead for various
mixes of regulatory policies and, increasingly, some versions of a cap-and-trade
arrangement. Carbon taxes have been considered initially in some statewide
reviews of climate and energy policy options, and they also gained new standing
in 2008 and 2009 in California, which confronted daunting fiscal problems and
mounting difficulties in funding implementation of its existing climate policies.
Nonetheless, carbon taxes thus far have tended to quickly drop from serious consideration, presumably due to the political baggage that they carry.

Even existing state energy taxes have not changed much during recent years,
most notably the gasoline excise tax, at the very time that climate change has
climbed high on many state government agendas. Between 2003 and 2010,
twenty-nine states made no changes in their gasoline taxes, while New Mexico
and the District of Columbia decreased their taxes slightly. Even climate-
conscious California held its tax constant at 18 cents per gallon during that
period. The mean tax rate for the fifty states and the District of Columbia
climbed only slightly during this period, from 21 cents a gallon in 2005 to
22.3 cents a gallon in 2010 (see figure 6-2).[12] As tax policy analyst John Peterson
has noted, "Gasoline taxes at all levels of government are kept low and do not
reflect the overall costs of driving, which are estimated at twice what we now pay
in gas taxes. The combined state and federal gas tax per gallon is only 70 percent
in price-deflated terms of what it was 30 years ago."[13]

These patterns on state gasoline taxes are further reinforced by findings from
the National Survey of American Public Opinion on Climate Change. As
Christopher Borick notes in chapter 2, the survey questions exploring whether
"state governments should increase taxes on gasoline in order to reduce con-

Figure 6-2. *Seven-Year Change in State Gasoline Tax Rates, 2003–10*

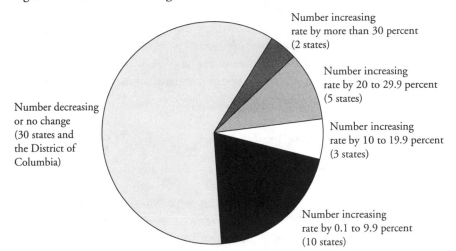

Number increasing
rate by more than 30 percent
(2 states)

Number increasing
rate by 20 to 29.9 percent
(5 states)

Number decreasing
or no change
(30 states and
the District of
Columbia)

Number increasing
rate by 10 to 19.9 percent
(3 states)

Number increasing
rate by 0.1 to 9.9 percent
(10 states)

Source: Tax Policy Center, "Motor Fuel Rates, 2000–2008, 2010" (Washington: Urban Institute and Brookings Institution, March 2010).

sumption" received the lowest rate of support and the highest rate of opposition among the twelve policy options offered to survey respondents. Opposition was fairly consistent and strong in virtually every demographic category (see table 2-30), although it should be noted that the question was posed near the all-time peak in current gasoline prices. Proposed tax increases on all fossil fuels also faced considerable opposition in the survey, although it was less intense than for specific gasoline tax increases.

Further evidence of the political difficulty of moving a serious carbon tax proposal forward was provided by the 110th Congress. Representative John Dingell (D-Michigan), then chairman of the powerful Energy and Commerce Committee, easily overshadowed the ill-fated Stark and Larson bills with a September 2007 proposal of his own to establish a $50 per ton carbon tax that would be phased in over five years and then indexed for inflation. His proposal never took the form of an actual bill but remained a widely publicized "discussion draft" that was commonly viewed as an effort to draw enough negative attention to the idea of a carbon tax to effectively kill the idea. Indeed, Dingell packaged his carbon tax with a proposal to phase out the highly popular mortgage deduction for homes larger than 3,000 square feet, making it even more of a loss-imposition strategy. In turn, Dingell gave little indication of how the revenue derived from the tax might be reallocated, other than to make a brief comment on ways to distribute it across a number of very diverse areas, including the earned income tax credit, Medicare and Social Security, universal health care, conservation, and the low-income home energy assistance program, among others.[14] Dingell never actively supported his proposal and used it instead to advance the case for policy alternatives that were more modest in scope and less direct in terms of cost imposition. In April 2008, he formally withdrew his discussion draft from further consideration, noting that "the reality is that this proposal is off the table for now. I simply cannot support these policies at a time when families in my district are dealing with record gas prices, high levels of unemployment, a home foreclosure crisis, and rising food costs."[15]

When Carbon Taxes Are Implemented

The political impediments to carbon taxes are clearly high but there is some evidence from abroad that they are not necessarily insurmountable. Many members of the European Union have established a range of carbon taxes, some of which cut across fuel sources while others concentrate on specific sources, such as gasoline. A good number were put into place well before climate change became a central concern, driven by other factors, such as the need to reduce air contaminants that pose human health risks (which already are regulated by federal legislation), the desire to reduce reliance on imported sources of fossil fuels, and a preference for taxing consumption rather than labor. That early round of taxes has served as a base for subsequent efforts more closely linked to climate change. As explored by Selin and VanDeveer in chapter 14, the taxes collectively offer some concrete examples of how they operate in practice and even how they fit with other evolving climate tools, used either across the continent or in particular member states. In turn, the U.S. federal and state reluctance to adopt large-scale carbon taxes may not be the end of the story on this matter. A series of more specialized taxes and fees related to the use of fossil fuels have indeed begun to emerge in various state and local governments, as well as a pair of Canadian provinces, primarily in the last few years. The following section reviews the collective experience, summarizing the current set of policies in operation in the EU and in North America while offering some sense of the performance to date.

Lessons from Europe

The underpinnings of the EU odyssey into carbon taxes can be linked to a long-standing commitment across most member states to establish high levels of gasoline taxation. Current EU gasoline tax levels are approximately five to six times the combined federal and state levies in place in the United States, with the EU average between 2002 and 2008 at about $2.40 to $3.10 per gallon. As explored more fully in chapter 7 in this volume, all available studies suggest that those taxes have contributed mightily to far more efficient use of gasoline in Europe in recent decades and is a decisive factor in comparatively lower emissions per capita from the transportation sector in Europe than in North America. Cultural and infrastructure differences also come into play, but it is instructive to note that average

EU fuel economy for new vehicles purchased in 2006 was approximately 38 miles per gallon, far superior to the United States average. As a 2008 Congressional Budget Office analysis concluded, "Europe's higher fuel economy is due primarily to its much higher fuel taxes; the European Union has no mandatory standards for fuel economy."[16] The long-standing European penchant for voluntary fuel economy appears to have changed through a new set of regulations that were introduced in 2008, although implementation is likely to be delayed until at least 2016. It remains ironic that the extended U.S. commitment to mandatory fuel economy standards has produced such modest results in terms of actual fuel efficiency when compared with the taxation route taken in Europe, particularly since the Obama administration focused so heavily on fuel economy standards in its early stage.

European experimentation with carbon taxation goes well beyond conventional levies for gasoline. As highlighted by VanDeveer and Selin in chapter 13, in the early 1990s several EU member states adopted taxes that applied carbon tax principles across multiple sources of fossil fuel, central components in their efforts to respond to climate change well before the negotiations in Kyoto. Scandinavian and Northern European nations such as Sweden, Finland, Norway, Denmark, and the Netherlands were most active in this area, as has remained the case in more recent years. In Sweden, for example, the idea of a carbon tax emerged from the nation's earlier gasoline tax and a 1989 "sulfur tax" that has been applied to coal, heavy fuel oils, and peat.[17]

Whereas the United States moved in the same period toward a cap-and-trade regime for sulfur dioxide (SO_2), the Swedes instead applied a steep tax on SO_2 emissions that is credited with achieving a 30 percent emission reduction between 1989 and 1995.[18] In turn, Sweden has enacted other energy-focused taxes, including a "nitrogen oxides charge" and, in 1990, a cross-cutting carbon tax set at a level of approximately $100 per ton of carbon that rapidly produced a 10 percent decline in national emissions after it went into effect. In 2007, Sweden increased the tax to a level that approximates $150 per ton.[19] Sweden has continually ranked among the most successful EU member states in steadily reducing its emissions while also experiencing considerable economic growth until very recently.[20]

Germany and the United Kingdom also had considerable early experience with energy and gasoline taxes. They were clearly able to take significant steps toward reaching their very ambitious Kyoto reduction targets through unique developments, namely the decline in emissions attributable to the collapse of the manufacturing sector in the former East Germany and the United Kingdom's shift from coal to natural gas facilitated by North Sea discoveries of the latter. Nonetheless, according to political scientist Loren Cass, both nations "used their Kyoto commitments to justify controversial domestic policy changes. In particular, both countries launched new energy taxes to fund reductions in taxes on labor."[21] Neither of those efforts was as bold or as cross-cutting as those developed by some of their neighbors, but they still had the effect of increasing tax levels across multiple fossil fuel sources. These tax policies—seen as a central mechanism for achieving mandated emission reductions that are not covered under the EU-wide cap-and-trade regime and are therefore at the discretion of each member state—continue to be a central point of debate in many European capitals.

Differential Treatment

Substantial evidence exists to demonstrate the ability of such taxes to reduce fossil fuel use and carbon emissions, particularly in cases in which steep taxes are imposed. But one other lesson to emerge from the EU experience in carbon taxation is that use of this tool is not as simple or straightforward in practice as suggested by many of its proponents. In particular, there are numerous exemptions and exceptions woven through many of the tax mechanisms, suggesting a less level playing field for imposing a tax burden than in the classic accounts of how a carbon tax might work. The Organization for Economic Cooperation and Development (OECD) reported 845 separate exemptions for fossil fuel taxes among its member nations in 2008.[22] In some cases, there is an environmental rationale for these changes, such as the accommodation of biofuels when there is debate over actual carbon content or implicit support for diesel fuel given its potential to achieve better fuel efficiency than gasoline. But clearly much of this willingness to reopen and modify taxes is a direct response to organized political pressure rather than any effort to maintain fair treatment by degree of environmental insult. That raises serious questions of equity and transparency in both launching and sustaining such taxes and potentially threatens the efficacy of the instrument, even in instances when political opposition can be overcome.[23]

In Sweden, for example, no sooner was the ink dry on its 1991 national carbon tax than adjustments began to be made due to political pressure. In particular, Stockholm made more generous accommodations under the tax regime for intensive users of fossil fuels, such as major manufacturers as well as the paper production, mining, and horticulture sectors. That has served to shift much more of the burden to those constituencies that are unable to gain exempt status or at least some favored treatment and has been a source of considerable political conflict. These issues have remained prominent in continuing efforts to adjust the carbon tax and related levies in Sweden during the 1990s and the first decade of the twenty-first century. The latest round of reforms was enacted in 2007, resulting in the elimination of taxes on ethanol, increased tax deductions for work-related trips, and a reduced tax on vehicles using diesel fuel. The tax was also adjusted to increase the burden on hydropower and nuclear energy to adjust for their greater profit margins since continental emissions trading under the EU's Emission Trading System (ETS) is expected to produce greater costs for electricity from coal and other fossil fuel sources.

Many other EU members that have pursued some form of carbon taxation have faced somewhat similar experiences. In the United Kingdom, both the Tony

Blair and Gordon Brown governments faced considerable difficulty in navigating toward an equitable tax arrangement given the competing demands of various industrial sectors and fossil fuel sources. Such attempts have often resulted in a dizzying array of exemptions, rebates, and subsidies and likely have undermined the potential impact of the taxes both on emissions and as a revenue source. Germany has faced similar challenges under both the Gerhard Schroeder and Angela Merkel governments in recent decades, with ongoing tax squabbles interwoven with questions of providing subsidies for numerous forms of energy containing widely different amounts of carbon.[24]

The European experience thus presents a picture of carbon taxes that is somewhat at variance with conventional thinking. There is indeed significant evidence that such increases can have the intended effect of reducing fossil fuel use and emissions. But three additional lessons also emerge. First, implementation is not as simple or straightforward as many proponents suggest, reflected in the ongoing political battles for favored status under new carbon tax regimes after their enactment. That is a sobering reminder that no climate policy strategy is pure or self-implementing and that important attention needs to be paid to enacting policy that is viable and sustainable. Second, multiple cases from the European Union suggest that it is politically feasible to garner support for the carbon tax approach. Although the political contexts in which European nations and the U.S. states operate are obviously different, a fairly diverse mix of political parties in Northern Europe have demonstrated willingness to support or extend the life of carbon taxes. Third, the EU experience demonstrates how rapidly various climate policy tools can gain and lose political favor.

Ironically, the EU initially was vehemently opposed to a cap-and-trade program for carbon, which was pushed aggressively by the United States in the negotiations leading up to Kyoto. More than a decade later, the EU has embraced the emissions trading concept on a continental basis and now promotes it as the best international policy option, supplemented by individual member state strategies that frequently rely significantly on carbon taxes. In contrast, efforts to establish an EU-wide carbon tax have foundered, despite earlier promise and support from a number of Northern European member states.[25] That poses an interesting question regarding potential U.S. adaptability on climate policy tools, leading us to consider whether cap and trade and a mix of regulatory programs are the only serious options or whether the federal and state governments might gravitate toward carbon taxes under certain circumstances.

Slouching toward Carbon Taxes: Revisiting the States

While many U.S. states have emulated European nations in their development of climate policy tools, none have followed the model of many EU members and established carbon taxes as a central plank in their climate strategies. However, a growing number of states and municipal governments alike have begun to turn to various methods of taxation of fossil fuels, even if they put a different label on the policy. Most taxes are set at a relatively low level and are unlikely to have sufficient impact on cost to have much influence on energy consumption. But they outline some possible directions for establishing an energy tax mechanism in the U.S. political context and also offer some lessons about ways in which the revenues can be used to secure political support. A pair of Canadian provinces that recently enacted broad carbon taxes also are included in the discussion below.

Public Benefit Funds and Energy

Just as states possess and apply their powers to levy gasoline taxes, they also reserve the authority to tax electricity. Most states with a general sales tax have long applied it to electricity bills. But twenty-two states have gone a step further, creating specialized taxes related to electricity that are publicly described as "public benefit funds" or "social benefit charges." These programs operate in multiple states of every region of the nation except the Southeast. Indeed, none of the states involved use the word "tax" to describe the charges, which are generally applied to the distribution service portion of electricity bills and function in essence like a tax. These states establish a charge of between 0.03 to 3 mills per kilowatt hour, with one mill equivalent to one-tenth of a cent.[26] In Oregon, for example, that translates into a 3 percent fee that is assessed on all electricity bills. Other states such as California, Connecticut, and New Jersey also tend to set relatively high rates, whereas a number of other states have set rates that are considerably lower.

Regardless of the rate, however, one common feature of the programs is that virtually all of them channel all of their revenues into specific renewable energy or energy efficiency projects. Many states that levy the charges have set up new institutions (or expanded existing ones) to pursue intrastate energy projects, and some anticipate receiving additional revenue from other sources, such as proceeds from carbon cap-and-trade auctions in states participating in RGGI. Oregon's funds, for example, are transferred directly into the Oregon Energy Trust, which supports a wide range of energy efficiency and renewable energy programs. Some states have established multiple programs to receive various portions of the public benefit funds, some of which distinguish energy efficiency from renewable energy while others concentrate on specific technologies.[27] There is also a national nonprofit organization, the Clean Energy States Alliance, which attempts to share information about these programs with its twelve participating states and to pursue cross-state collaboration where possible.

Revisiting the Gas Tax

It is indeed tempting to review the flat nature of federal and most state gasoline taxes over the past decade and assume that revisiting this issue is a nonstarter. That is particularly understandable given the vivid memories of the 1993 BTU tax debacle, discussed above. But that may not be the end of the story, particularly given two different developments in recent years that suggest a certain resiliency to this tax and possible ways to consider increases.

First, one important energy vignette from the 2008 presidential campaign involved a perceived political bonus to the one candidate who actively opposed a proposal to suspend the federal gas tax entirely during the summer months in response to rapid increases in the price of gasoline. Then presidential candidate Obama argued in April and May that the "tax holiday" proposed by both Senators Hillary Clinton (D-New York) and John McCain (R-Arizona) was a "gimmick." He suggested that the tax suspension would produce little benefit for consumers, would weaken the trust fund for transportation infrastructure that depends on gas tax revenues, and would send the wrong signals concerning U.S. commitment to pursue greater energy independence. Obama received considerable support for this "profile in courage" position in many media accounts; some analysts and pollsters contend that his stance may have contributed somewhat to his lopsided primary victory over Clinton in North Carolina and better-than-anticipated performance in Indiana.[28]

Second, the state gasoline tax was increased in twenty states between 2003 and 2010. One-half of the increases have been fairly modest, between 0.1 and 9.9 percent, as reflected in figure 6-2. But other states were more aggressive, although they were driven primarily by the need for transportation infrastructure revenue, not by a desire to deter consumption. Gas tax rates rose between 20 and 29.9 percent during this period in Kentucky, Maine, North Carolina, Ohio, and West Virginia. Still larger increases were registered in Georgia (from 7.5 cents per gallon in 2003 to 18.5 cents per gallon in 2010) and Washington state (from 23 cents per gallon in 2003 to 37.5 cents per gallon seven years later). That gave Washington the highest gasoline tax of any state, with Alaska at the other end of the continuum, with an 8 cent per gallon tax that has not changed since its third year of statehood (see figure 6-3).

Direct Democracy

Most state and local governments retain authority to enact legislation through ballot propositions, which can provide important insight into public receptivity to various policy options.[29] Taxation commonly emerges as a prominent issue in various forms of direct democracy, although frequently in relation to efforts to reduce or repeal existing taxes rather than create new ones. Consequently, ballot propositions would hardly seem an auspicious place to find support for new taxes that would address climate concerns. But at least two forms of local ballot propositions in very recent years illustrate the existence of such support, at least in certain settings and for select issues, serving to further reopen the question of the potential political viability of carbon taxes in the United States.

Perhaps the most prominent example of using direct democracy to enact climate-related policy has involved publicly approved renewable portfolio standards

Figure 6-3. *2008 State Gasoline Tax Rates*

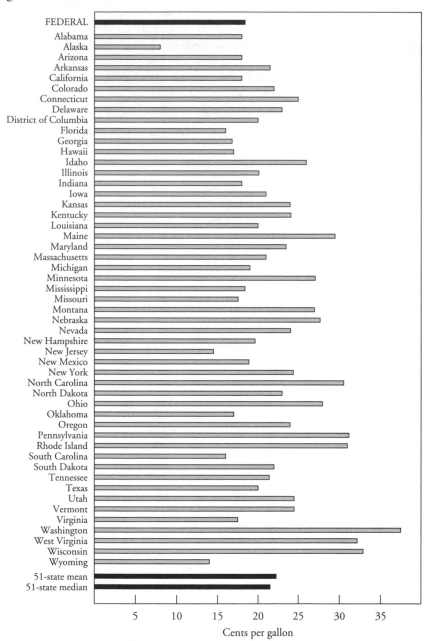

Cents per gallon

Source: Tax Policy Center, "Motor Fuel Rates, 2000–2008, 2010" (Washington: Urban Institute and Brookings Institution, March 2010).

in Colorado (2004), Washington (2007), and Missouri (2008). But ballot propositions also were used to gain strong voter support for the first policy to be explicitly labeled a carbon tax in the United States.[30] In November 2006, voters in Boulder, Colorado, approved by a decisive margin the creation of a $7 per ton carbon tax that is estimated to cost the average household $16 per year and the average business $46 per year. It is expected that the tax, which went into effect in April 2007, will generate about $1 million per year and cover all of the programs operated by the city's Office of Environmental Affairs. That includes all components of the Boulder Climate Action Plan, which is designed to reach Kyoto-like emission reduction targets.

The Boulder levy actually operates more like a public benefit fund than a pure carbon tax, as it focuses primarily on electricity and collects revenues through electricity charges. Consumers who use renewable energy sources receive a discount on their fees. Perhaps most significant, supporters chose to find one source to directly fund climate change mitigation programs and did not shy away from the carbon tax label. According to Mayor Mark Ruzzin, "we were looking for a moniker that would attract people's attention" and quickly gravitated to the idea of a carbon tax as opposed to some other depiction. "It's not a punitive measure intended to penalize residents for buying fossil energy," noted Ruzzin. "That would have turned off some voters. Taxes have always been enough of a challenge, even in Boulder."[31]

Boulder is hardly a typical American city, and its action has not diffused to other municipalities. But it is one concrete example of presenting a modest carbon tax to an electorate and securing approval. In turn, the November 2008 elections also featured an unusually large number of ballot propositions at both the state and local levels that called for increased expenditures for expanding mass transit, one direct proxy measure of public willingness to pay more for a form of transportation that produces lower rates of greenhouse gases per trip than private vehicular travel. Whereas the national average approval rate for such ballot propositions is about 35 percent, in 2008 the approval rate soared to 74 percent. At least fourteen of the approved proposals involved voter support for increases in state or local sales taxes, with many of them concentrated in such Western states as California, Colorado, Nevada, and New Mexico, whereas other initiatives involved bond authorization or use of property tax revenues.[32] All of the expanded activity occurred prior to the gaping fiscal deficits that emerged in many states and localities because of the severe national recession, triggering discussion of alternative ways to address long-term fiscal needs and possibly opening the door to consideration of expanded energy taxation.

Other localities such as San Francisco, New York, and Portland, have moved forward with their own unique variations on the carbon tax, although they used more traditional policymaking channels. In May 2008, the Bay Area Air Quality Management District voted 15-1 to impose a 4.4 cent fee per metric ton of carbon dioxide released by thousands of businesses, ranging from oil refineries and power plants to bakeries and restaurants. In New York, Mayor Bloomberg's ambitious climate change plans included a number of options for applying fees based on climate impact, ranging from electricity surcharges that resemble state public benefit funds to congestion fees placed on vehicles that enter high-density areas at certain peak driving periods.[33] In Portland, the state conducted a pilot experiment in 2006, using sophisticated technology to tax driving on the basis of number of miles driven as opposed to traditional gasoline taxes.[34]

Enter California

California has laid claim to national and even global leadership on climate change through a vast array of policies that touch virtually every sector that generates greenhouse gases.[35] As noted previously, the lone exception to its remarkable breadth of engagement has been carbon taxation. However, there was growing evidence in 2008 that this may be beginning to change, given California's commitment to finding effective ways to meet its ambitious emissions reduction targets and its increased need for revenue to do so amid profound state fiscal problems. Perhaps most notably, the 2006 Global Warming Solutions Act (AB 32) delegates to the California Air Resources Board (CARB) considerable latitude to consider various policy alternatives that will achieve reduction targets. Since that legislation was enacted, the state has encountered serious stumbling blocks, including considerable difficulty in developing its own cap-and-trade program and trying to expand it into a regional network with neighboring states and Canadian provinces through the Western Climate Initiative.

Indeed, cap-and-trade design is not spelled out in California's 2006 legislation, and efforts to develop a strategy have faced sharp criticism from some Democratic legislative leaders who favor a set of more immediate and regulatory steps, some environmentalists concerned about program effectiveness and equity, and many industry leaders concerned about potential compliance costs. Other regulatory programs are struggling to reach their early milestones, as seen, for example, in their failure to add renewable electricity at a rate mandated by the state's renewable portfolio standard. Consequently, California appears increasingly unlikely to reach its widely publicized statewide emissions reduction targets and also faces the growing challenge of funding its programs given its mounting fiscal problems.

In response, CARB has turned increasingly to the possibility of levying various fees that could deter greenhouse gas generation and also provide revenue for program implementation. In its October 2008 "Scoping Plan," the board set forth a stunning range of options that would generally comport with the idea of carbon taxation as opposed to other regulatory mechanisms. The options included an upstream carbon fee on fossil fuels; special fees for methane and other greenhouse gases that have higher "global warming potential" per unit than carbon dioxide; a water "public goods charge" to support greater efficiency in the use of water and of energy in treating and distributing water; congestion pricing; new charges on the purchase of high-emission vehicles; and a modification of state auto insurance to evolve into a "pay-as-you-go" system that increases insurance premiums as driving mileage increases. California's first climate fee was established by CARB in September 2009 through a "cost-of-implementation fee rule" that places a "broad-based, economy-wide" fee on gasoline, coal, natural gas, and diesel fuel in order to cover the administrative costs of AB 32. The fee is expected to generate more than $50 million per year, sufficient to cover the operational costs of AB 32 and repay loans from the state's beverage container recycling funds, which were used to cover costs of early implementation.

One substantial political attraction of these various mechanisms is that under California law they might be classifiable as "fees" and thereby within the jurisdiction of the appropriate boards and agencies to approve or disapprove through interpretation of existing statutes. But in the event that they are deemed "taxes," California's supermajority rules guiding creation of any new tax or an increase in any existing one come into play. Although this fee-versus-tax issue has already come to the forefront in Sacramento, the sheer range of cost-imposition strategies being considered for greenhouse gas sources both expands the classic definition of carbon taxes and suggests possibly greater traction for them at the state level than is generally assumed.

California also established a fourteen-member Commission on the 21st Century Economy through a February 2009 executive order to examine a range of taxation options that could enable Sacramento to develop a viable long-term fiscal strategy. Taxes on energy use and carbon emissions emerged as options, including a "petroleum fuel pollution tax" that would initially add 18 cents per gallon to the cost of transportation fuel and would be adjusted in subsequent years by 7 cents per gallon plus inflation. Such an option was endorsed by the California government employees' union, which contended that "it would simultaneously lay the foundation for a new green economy that could create millions of new jobs and revenue sources, while reestablishing California as a leader in the movement to stem global warming."[36] The commission dropped that option in late 2009, but variations on this approach continued to resurface as California confronted fiscal challenges and also struggled to implement its array of climate policies. Among 2010 candidates for statewide office, Republican Tom Campbell, a business school dean and former member of Congress, has formally embraced the idea of expanded energy taxation as a central plank in future state fiscal reform.

Across the 49th Parallel

Canada occupies a unique position in international climate change circles, having ratified the Kyoto Protocol in 2002 but having enacted virtually no significant policies to reduce its emissions thereafter. Indeed, Canadian emissions have grown since 1990 at a considerably greater rate than in the United States.

Even though Canada's government is highly decentralized and delegates substantial authority in environmental protection, energy, and taxation to its provinces and territories, they have generally proven far less engaged on climate change than their U.S. state counterparts.[37] The rejection of a national carbon tax proposal by the Liberal Party in the 2008 elections was widely seen as further distancing Canada from taking any decisive step on this issue.

Two provinces, however, have begun to follow their U.S. counterparts in expanding their involvement in climate policy but through use of direct cost imposition in the form of carbon taxes. Both Quebec and British Columbia established forms of explicit carbon taxes that have thus far been difficult to advance in the United States. Quebec moved first, with the enactment in October 2007 of a tax set at $3 (Canadian) per ton of carbon dioxide. That translates to an approximate tax of 3.1 cents per gallon of gasoline and 3.6 cents per gallon of diesel fuel (converting from liters and set at March 2008 exchange rates). The tax also applies to coal and natural gas, although it will not fall heavily on the electricity sector given Quebec's heavy reliance on hydroelectric power. The province acknowledges that this relatively low rate is unlikely to substantially alter consumption but emphasizes its symbolic value and its capacity to generate sufficient revenue to cover all anticipated costs of Quebec's Climate Change Action Plan.[38]

Quebec's actions, however, did set the stage for bolder action in the western part of the country, namely through British Columbia's 2007 approval of a consumption-based carbon tax that began at $10 per ton of carbon dioxide in July 2008 and will rise steadily at a rate of $5 per year to a level of $30 per ton by 2012. It did not replace any existing energy tax, such as the motor fuel tax. Applied to gasoline, it began at a rate of approximately 9 cents per gallon and will reach 27 cents per gallon by 2012. At that point, the tax will reach approximately $1.50 per gigajoule of natural gas, $53 per ton of low-heat-value coal, $63 per ton of high-heat-value coal, $75 per ton of coke, and $31 per ton of peat. As in Quebec, however, the impact will likely be modest in the electricity sector, as British Columbia derives more than 90 percent of its supply from large-scale hydroelectric plants, thereby concentrating its impact on other sectors that use fossil fuels.[39]

British Columbia's Carbon Tax Act (Bill 37) is expected to account for approximately 7.5 percent of the province's pledged emission reductions by 2020, which are scheduled to reach 10 percent below 1990 levels by 2020 (or approximately one-third below 2008 levels). The tax is projected to generate approximately $880 million per year by 2010 and 2011. But unlike most of the other fund-generating mechanisms discussed thus far, the British Columbia carbon tax is designed to "recycle" these revenues to firms and individuals through commensurate levels of income tax reduction, with low-income households eligible for a "climate action tax credit." This recycling process was preceded by an initial "climate action dividend" of $100 per person drawn from the provincial surplus.[40] In a somewhat unusual twist, any failure by the British Columbia finance minister to implement those fiscal transfers will result in a 15 percent reduction in the official's salary.

British Columbia's initiative was endorsed by a wide swath of economists and commentators in the provinces and across Canada, just as those groups supported such measures in the United States. But the driving force was Premier Gordon Campbell, who championed the idea and pushed it through the provincial legislature.[41] "We decided it was better to have price certainty," explained provincial climate secretary Graham Whitmarsh in discussing the decision to emphasize a carbon tax over other regulatory tools.[42] Campbell viewed that as a central component of a strategy to make British Columbia a national leader on climate change, along with setting bold emission reduction targets and establishing a Climate Change Secretariat to lead implementation on all climate policies and pressure existing ministries to work cooperatively.

Some early polling suggested that the tax was unpopular, but Campbell and his Liberal Party won reelection in May 2009, outflanking opposition that came primarily from the left-of-center New Democratic Party. At the same time, British Columbia forged ahead on other climate policy fronts, including in its role as the most active of four provinces that are negotiating a cross-border cap-and-trade arrangement with California and other states under the auspices of the Western Climate Initiative.

Whither the Carbon Tax?

This smattering of recent state, local, and provincial experiments with various forms of carbon taxes suggests that the political door is not totally closed on this matter, perhaps even at the federal level. This kind of direct cost imposition is never easy in the U.S. context, whether it entails increases in existing taxes or creation of entirely new levies, so it is important not to underestimate the likely political hurdles. As William Galston and Pietro Nivola have noted, "the public may not welcome the pain that a genuine energy conservation plan inflicts—a stiffer excise tax on gasoline, say—but policymakers do society a disservice if they perennially 'chicken out.' It may well be that intensely partisan politics throw up additional roadblocks to certain unpopular measures that a responsible government ought to take for the sake of the public good in the long run."[43]

Despite that important cautionary reminder, it is important to note that there have been a number of instances in the past three decades in which the "politically impossible" occurred, namely the triumph of a policy idea that was compelling but was seemingly a nonstarter due to the intense opposition expected from the parties that would bear the costs. These instances include a series of deregulatory efforts for specific industries, far-reaching Social Security reforms in 1983 that increased taxes and reduced benefits over time, comprehensive tax reform legislation in 1986 that eliminated a host of special tax preferences in exchange for a general reduction of rates, and 1990 clean air legislation. As scholars who have closely examined these kinds of episodes have noted, they suggest that it is indeed possible to trump the conventional wisdom and enact policy that advances a broad public interest even in the face of intense opposition.[44]

There is no single clear route that leads to such legislative steps and, indeed, many of the examples noted above took place two decades ago or more.[45] It remains unclear whether the 111th Congress will prove more receptive than its predecessors to such legislation, a subject addressed in greater length in chapter 11. In general, however, these policies have followed a pattern consistent with political scientist John Kingdon's classic model of policy formation. Kingdon readily acknowledged the role of political forces, including interest groups.[46] But he also emphasized the role of promising policy ideas, particularly if they could be framed in a way that proved appealing to a fairly diverse set of policymakers. In turn, he saw an essential role for policy entrepreneurs, either elected officials or well-positioned bureaucrats and advocates who occupied unique positions and were able to advance ideas, broker support, and cobble together supportive coalitions, some of which might quickly dissolve after enactment. Political scientists David Beam and Timothy Conlan acknowledge that there are multiple "pathways to power" and that the most common and familiar are those that emphasize pluralistic horse trading among competing interests, narrow partisan advances that rely on tight majority party unity, or largely symbolic measures. But they also note one path that emphasizes an "entrepreneurial-ideational" approach. That can entail expert-driven legislation, such as the 1986 tax reform legislation that they use as a primary case that ultimately garnered political support capable of cutting across traditional partisan and ideological divides.[47]

One sees signs of this very pattern in cases of carbon tax development in member states of the European Union as well as subnational governments in North America. In the United States and Canada, many modest carbon tax initiatives were nurtured by policy entrepreneurs embedded in agencies and ministries, often backed by various think tanks or climate change commissions. A range of influential officials, ranging from Premier Campbell in British Columbia to Mayor Bloomberg in New York City, often played vital roles. Collectively, those cases indicate that classic interest group interpretations of policymaking often are limited, suggesting that the unexpected can occur and that unusual coalitions can coalesce under the right circumstances. That finding has been emerging in a good deal of the latest literature on interest groups, including important analyses of the environmental and energy policy arenas, which show that these groups occasionally produce surprising but potent alliances.[48]

Any serious proposal for a U.S. carbon tax, either as a centerpiece of federal climate policy or as a component alongside other policies, must begin with a very strong base of policy analysts who can embrace and shape a credible proposal. That might include groups such as the nonprofit Carbon Tax Center, which periodically has gathered scholarship and think pieces on the topic and attempted to position itself as a significant advocate on the national stage for such an approach. In concert with the unusually diverse range of scholars, analysts, and even occasionally politicians who are enamored of such policy, such strong advocacy could represent the beginning of an "entrepreneurial-ideational" carbon tax pathway.

Carbon tax proposals often divide interests rather than secure uniform opposition, as is evident in jurisdictions where they are now employed. Even among firms that produce fossil fuels or use them to generate electricity, one sees very different responses to carbon tax proposals among constituencies that depend on coal, gasoline, oil, or natural gas, reflecting the very different burdens that they would face under such a tax. In turn, proponents of non–fossil fuel energy sources, including nuclear energy and hydropower and emerging renewable technologies, are likely to find considerable appeal in such a tax. At the same time, the collection of revenue leads to the inevitable question of how the money will be used and whether it might generate further support.

None of this should be interpreted as a suggestion that a major U.S. carbon tax regime is around the corner. But it encourages consideration of recent experiences in which carbon taxes have been enacted and reconsideration of frequent dismissals that such a step is, politically speaking, a metaphysical impossibility. It also allows for a challenge to much conventional wisdom that concludes that a pure cap-and-trade approach is the premier option, in large part because it "hides" the real costs. A few general lessons from the carbon tax experience to date and thoughts on possible next steps follow below.

Issue Framing

One of the greatest challenges in advancing a carbon tax proposal or any other legislative initiative involves framing, namely the way in which the proposal is described and presented to other policymakers and the general citizenry. Framing is more than a matter of public relations hype and reflects a growing body of work in the social sciences that finds it to be a crucial element of strategic policymaking, particularly in instances where conflict is likely to be considerable.[49] One key element of framing is the question of the links between various issues and interests. Climate policy cannot be hermetically sealed in a legislative or administrative box labeled "environmental protection." It is clearly integrated with other salient matters such as long-term strategies for U.S. energy policy and the viability of the manufacturing sector, including transportation and the major U.S.-based vehicle manufacturers. Interwoven with these issues are questions of infrastructure, such as the capacity of the electricity grid to effectively move power in what promises to be a more decentralized generation system in future decades, as well as the capacity of means of transportation such as highways and mass transit. Overarching all of this, of course, is the evolving national economic crisis and the question of how federal and state governments can raise sufficient revenue to

Table 6-1. *Degree of Support for Increasing Taxes on Gasoline
by Amount Individual Is Willing to Pay Each Year to Produce
More Renewable Energy, in Percent*

Amount willing to pay	Strongly support (10)	Somewhat support (13)	Somewhat oppose (13)	Strongly oppose (60)	Not sure (4)
Nothing	14	11	14	28	4
$1–$50	13	9	24	16	14
$50–$100	18	25	14	17	12
$100–$250	14	19	15	11	14
$250–500	15	15	9	8	11
Over $500	15	8	9	5	14
Not sure	11	14	15	15	32

Source: National Survey of American Public Opinion on Climate Change, 2009.

respond to the many demands for expanded spending at the very time that revenues from their existing tax sources plummet.

Findings from the National Survey of American Public Opinion on Climate Change (NSAPOCC) offer some indication that different framing of tax options can produce some variation in public response. While both a gasoline tax and more general fossil fuel tax faced majority opposition in the sample, the latter clearly had somewhat greater support (see chapter 2). But public sentiment on taxation looks more evenly divided when it is correlated with findings on respondents' willingness to pay extra money per year in order to produce more renewable energy. As tables 6-1 and 6-2 demonstrate, opposition declines steadily as willingness to pay increases. That introduces the question of ways in which public leaders might best frame various forms of carbon taxes and whether certain links between issues and interests might produce greater public support than generally anticipated.

Additional survey analysis suggests that explicitly including anticipated costs when weighing competing policy options can largely eliminate significant differences in the degree of support for carbon cap and trade versus carbon taxes. In the 2009 version of the NSAPOCC, the exploration of these tools was expanded, as reflected in table 6-3. Cap and trade retained greater popularity than carbon taxation when no mention was made of possible fiscal consequences. But those differences essentially disappeared when costs of either $15 or $50 a month per person were added to both policy options, with the former serving as a rough proxy measure of Congressional Budget Office cost estimates of the American Clean Energy and Security Act, which passed the House in June 2009. In turn, a December 2009 survey by Hart Research Associates that was commissioned by the nonprofit U.S. Climate Task Force demonstrated that removing any costs from carbon taxes while adding explicit costs under cap and trade can produce far greater support for the former than the latter. That survey has been used by some

Table 6-2. *Degree of Support for Increasing Taxes on All Fossil Fuels by Amount Individual Is Willing to Pay Each Year to Produce More Renewable Energy, in Percent*

Amount willing to pay	Strongly support (18)	Somewhat support (19)	Somewhat oppose (17)	Strongly oppose (40)	Not sure (6)
Nothing	11	8	16	36	22
$1–$50	22	12	18	15	14
$50–$100	17	24	21	14	8
$100–$250	16	19	17	9	7
$250–500	9	12	11	8	7
Over $500	14	7	8	5	7
Not sure	12	18	9	5	37

Source: National Survey of American Public Opinion on Climate Change, 2009.

carbon tax proponents to exaggerate public support for carbon taxation, as public statements have tended to overlook the imbalanced comparison of costs. But the survey further serves to underscore the importance of framing and ways in which carbon taxation might be made more politically palatable.

Many states have acquired considerable experience in creatively linking issue areas to frame policies and thereby build support for various climate strategies over the past decade, and that has been an essential element in their success in attracting support.[50] One important consideration in building support for any future carbon tax proposal involves the use of revenue that might be generated from such a tax. On one hand, many carbon tax proponents have endorsed some form of revenue neutrality that would entail some commensurate reduction of payroll taxes or issuance of dividend checks. British Columbia has used a combination of those strategies. But it is not at all clear that this is politically the wisest course to take. There was a considerable uproar in British Columbia about the carbon tax, at least initially, with the short-term dividend derided in some circles as a political gimmick and uncertainty expressed as to whether citizens even noticed the reductions in other taxes that are harder to detect. Indeed, this very issue has emerged in the challenge of sustaining key elements of the 1986 Tax Reform Act, as it is highly uncertain that most Americans realized that they were slated for some level of tax reduction in exchange for concentrated losses imposed through elimination of popular deductions.[51]

An alternative approach to the use of revenues involves allotting funds from carbon taxes to further promote climate protection and other social needs such as electricity grid modernization or research and development of alternative energy sources. This approach builds in part on the recent experience with public benefit funds in the United States, the Quebec carbon tax, and some recent levies enacted in the EU as well as the initial use of revenues generated by cap-and-trade

Table 6-3. *Public Support for Cap-and-Trade and Carbon Tax Policy Options, in Percent*

Degree of support	Cap-and-trade without a specified financial cost to the individual	Cap-and-trade with a $15 a month cost to the individual	Cap-and-trade with a $50 a month cost to the individual
Strongly support	17	14	7
Somewhat support	36	28	15
Somewhat oppose	14	22	18
Strongly oppose	20	29	54
Not sure	12	8	6
Degree of support	Carbon tax without a specified financial cost to the individual	Carbon tax with a $15 a month cost to the individual	Carbon tax with a $50 a month cost to the individual
Strongly support	11	14	7
Somewhat support	25	30	13
Somewhat oppose	20	20	19
Strongly oppose	35	30	56
Not sure	9	6	5

Source: National Survey of American Public Opinion on Climate Change, 2009.

auctions in the ten states that make up RGGI. During 2009, numerous proposals illustrating potential links surfaced, including a recommendation from the United Mine Workers to place a fee on electricity to cover the costs of developing carbon capture and storage programs and a proposal from the American Highway Users Alliances (consisting primarily of road construction firms) to enact a carbon tax and direct the proceeds to the federal Highway Trust Fund.[52] Tellingly, a May 2008 survey in Canada found that respondents overwhelmingly preferred using any carbon tax revenues for purposes such as renewable energy and energy efficiency rather than for income tax reductions.[53]

One further link would connect a carbon tax with so-called "sin taxes," excise taxes imposed on goods such as cigarettes and alcohol. Part of the broad political support to increase these taxes in states around the nation in recent decades stems not only from the opportunity to generate revenue but also to deter consumption on public health grounds, particularly for groups such as teenagers who might be especially sensitive to price increases. As economists Alice Rivlin and Isabel Sawhill have noted, "activities that create pollution also impose costs on society" and so could indeed be added to the category of "sin taxes."[54] William Nordhaus creates a similar link when he contends that "allowing people to emit CO_2 into the atmosphere for free is similar to allowing people to smoke in a crowded room or dump trash in a national park."[55] Indeed, if one advanced the case that the sin tax umbrella could extend to fossil fuels, given their climate impacts and other environmental damage, one might compare the different tax levels currently imposed per gallon of gasoline, per gallon of beer and other alcoholic beverages, or per pack of cigarettes, raising possible equity considerations (see figure 6-1). Cigarette taxation presents an especially interesting case, given the steep increase in federal and state excise taxes on cigarettes in recent years. Federal taxes increased 321 percent between 1995 and 2009, and the average state excise tax increased 267 percent during this same period. Indeed, the largest single federal cigarette tax in history went into effect in April 2009, a 62 cent-per-pack increase designed as both a continued deterrent to tobacco use and a funding vehicle for expansion of the State Children's Health Insurance Program.[56]

One final link involves the possible combination of a carbon tax along with a cap-and-trade system. There has been limited discussion of such a "cap-and-tax" approach that would take advantage of the ability to implement a tax provision far more rapidly than a cap-and-trade regime. But the tax could remain in place over time, perhaps serving as a floor beneath which carbon prices would not fall. As Nordhaus has asked, "is there a compromise where the strengths of the carbon-tax regime can be crossed with cap-and-trade to get a hardy hybrid?"[57]

Such a compromise might closely follow the example in British Columbia, which has rapidly moved to implement its carbon tax while entering into longer-term negotiations that could lead to a cap-and-trade regime either within Canada or with states participating in the Western Climate Initiative. A number of EU member states also have done so, including, most recently, France. Remaining active in the ETS system, France announced in September 2009 that it would establish a tax of 17 euros (equivalent at the time to US$24.74) per metric ton of such fossil fuels as coal, gasoline, heating oil, and natural gas. "We cannot keep on taxing labor, taxing capital, and ignore taxes on pollution," explained President Nicolas Sarkozy in endorsing the tax proposal. France would return revenue through tax rebates to households subject to income tax and send refund checks to those exempt from income tax.[58]

Thus far, a good deal of debate over climate change policy options divides parties into rival camps, pitting cap-and-trade proponents against carbon tax supporters. Prior experience in developing policies that serve a broad public interest suggests that careful integration of competing ideas can serve to expand political support and ultimately produce more effective policy. In this instance, consideration of the integration of these tools might be a useful next step.

Notes

1. Michael R. Bloomberg, "Accelerating Local Leadership," keynote address at the United States Conference of Mayors Climate Protection Summit, November 2, 2007 (copy on file with author). Also see "Local Leadership," *Carbon Control News* (http://carboncontrolnews. com/ [November 5, 2007]).

2. William Nordhaus, *A Question of Balance: Weighing the Options on Global Warming Policies* (Yale University Press, 2008), p. 149.

3. Al Gore, "A Generational Challenge to Repower America," speech delivered at Constitution Hall, Washington, D.C., July 17, 2008. Also see Bill Bradley, *The New American Story* (Random House, 2007).

4. Christopher J. Dodd, "The New American Prosperity: Innovation and Energy Independence in the 21st Century," remarks at the Center for National Policy, April 19, 2007.

5. Copps also noted that "Dion, ever the professor, approached the campaign with the rigour he learned in the classroom. Inform and educate and they will come. Unfortunately for him, the classroom and the campaign are worlds apart." Sheila Copps, "Dion's Political Luck Runs Out," *The Hill Times* (October 20, 2008), p. 9.

6. Quoted from the House floor debate in "Taxing Words," *Carbon Control News*, May 2, 2007 (http://carboncontrolnews.com/).

7. Barry G. Rabe, "Regionalism and Global Climate Change Policy: Revisiting Multistate Collaboration as an Intergovernmental Management Tool," in *Intergovernmental Management for the 21st Century*, edited by Timothy J. Conlan and Paul L. Posner (Brookings, 2008), pp. 176–208.

8. Ibid.

9. Reuven S. Avi-Yonah and David M. Uhlmann, "Combating Global Climate Change: Why a Carbon Tax Is a Better Response to Global Warming than Cap and Trade," *Stanford Environmental Law Journal* 28, no. 3 (2009), pp. 3–50.

10. Charles Davis, "Key House Democrat Sees Building Momentum for National Carbon Tax," *Carbon Control News,* December 10, 2008 (http://carboncontrolnews.com/).

11. For a broader discussion of this type of issue and a range of examples outside the environmental arena, see Leslie A. Pal and R. Kent Weaver, *The Government Taketh Away: The Politics of Pain in the United States and Canada* (Georgetown University Press, 2003).

12. Tax Policy Center, "Motor Fuel Tax Rates, 2000–2008, 2010" (Washington: Tax Policy Center, Urban Institute and Brookings Institution, March 2010).

13. John E. Peterson, "Fueling a Tax," *Governing,* March 2007, p. 66.

14. John D. Dingell, "Summary of Draft Carbon Tax Legislation," released September 12, 2007 (on file with author).

15. Quoted in "Dingell Withdraws Carbon Tax Plan, Citing Current Economic Slump," *Carbon Control News,* April 16, 2008 (http://carboncontrolnews.com/).

16. David Austin, *Climate-Change Policy and CO_2 Emissions from Passenger Vehicles* (Congressional Budget Office, October 6, 2008), p. 5.

17. Bengt Johansson, "Economic Instruments in Practice I: Carbon Tax in Sweden," Swedish Environmental Protection Agency (www.oecd.org/dataoecd/25/0/2108273.pdf).

18. Swedish Environmental Protection Agency, *Environmental Taxes in Sweden: Economic Instruments of Environmental Policy*, Report 4745 (Swedish Environmental Protection Agency, 1997).

19. Evan Weber, "Swedish Climate Policy: A Blueprint for World Sustainability," unpublished paper, University of Michigan, 2008; paper on file with author.

20. European Environmental Agency, "Greenhouse Gas Emission Trends and Projections in Europe 2009," EEA Report 9 (2009).

21. Loren R. Cass, *The Failures of American and European Climate Policy* (State University of New York Press, 2006), p. 164.

22. "Economics Climate," *OECD Observer* (May–June 2008), pp. 39–40. Also see Erick Lachapelle, "Interests, Institutions, and Ideas: Explaining Cross-National Differences in the

Implicit Price of Carbon," paper presented at the 2009 Annual Meeting of the American Political Science Association, September 3–6, Toronto, Ontario.

23. In the United States, Fred Krupp of the Environmental Defense Fund argues that any U.S. attempt to enact a carbon tax would bog down in special favors and complexity. Fred Krupp, "Carbon Caps Are the Best Policy," *Wall Street Journal,* March 24, 2009, p. A15.

24. Cass, *The Failures of American and European Climate Policy,* chapter 6. Also see Christina E. Ciocirlan and Bruce Yandle, "The Political Economy of Green Taxation in OECD Countries," *European Journal of Law and Economics* 15, no. 3 (2003), pp. 203–18.

25. Jorgen Wettestad, "The Making of the 2003 Emissions Trading Directive: An Ultra-Quick Process due to Entrepreneurial Proficiency?" *Global Environmental Politics* 5, no. 1 (2005), pp. 1–23.

26. John Dernbach and others, "Stabilizing and Then Reducing U.S. Energy Consumption: Legal Policy Tools for Efficiency and Conservation," *Environmental Law Reporter* (January 2007), pp. 10003–31. This kind of labeling practice for energy taxes is not confined to U.S. states. In Japan, for example, Daniel Aldrich has described "submerged" taxes on electricity that are "all but invisible" and are used to promote nuclear energy. Daniel Aldrich, *Site Fights: Divisive Facilities and Civil Society in Japan and the West* (Cornell University Press, 2008), p. 55.

27. For details on the renewable energy provisions of these state policies, consult the extensive data available through the Interstate Renewable Energy Council (www.dsireusa.org).

28. "Primary Winner: Carbon Tax," *Carbon Control News,* May 7, 2008 (http://carbon controlnews.com/).

29. For an excellent analysis of direct democracy in environmental policy, see Deborah Lynn Guber, *The Grassroots of a Green Revolution: Polling America on the Environment* (MIT Press, 2003), particularly chapter 7.

30. Michele Betsill and Barry G. Rabe, "Climate Change and Multilevel Governance: The Evolving State and Local Roles," in *Toward Sustainable Communities,* rev. ed., edited by Daniel A. Mazmanian and Michael E. Kraft (MIT Press, 2009), p. 210.

31. Tom Arrandale, "A Bolder Boulder," *Governing,* February 2007, p. 56; Katie Kelley, "City Approves 'Carbon Tax' in Effort to Reduce Gas Emissions," *New York Times,* November 18, 2006.

32. Christopher Conkey and Paul Glader, "Mass-Transit Projects Fared Surprisingly Well as Voters Preferred New Taxes to High Gas Prices," *Wall Street Journal,* November 12, 2008, p. A6; Christopher Swope, "Urban Notebook," *Governing,* December 2008, p. 13.

33. Betsill and Rabe, "Climate Change and Multilevel Governance," in *Toward Sustainable Communities,* edited by Mazmanian and Kraft, pp. 201–26.

34. Kathleen Hunter, "The Long and Taxing Road," *Governing,* July 2007, pp. 48–50.

35. Barry G. Rabe, "Governing the Climate from Sacramento," in *Unlocking the Power of Networks,* edited by Stephen Goldsmith and Donald F. Kettl (Brookings, 2009).

36. "Carbon Tax as Budget Fixer?" *Carbon Control News,* December 15, 2008 (http:// carbon controlnews.com/).

37. Barry G. Rabe, "Beyond Kyoto: Climate Change Policy in Multilevel Governance Systems," *Governance* 20, no. 3 (July 2007), pp. 423–44.

38. Jean-Thomas Bernard and Jean-Yves Duclos, *Quebec's Green Future: The Lowest-Cost Route to Greenhouse Gas Reduction* (Toronto: C.D. Howe Institute, October 2009).

39. Karl Froschauer, *White Gold: Hydroelectric Power in Canada* (University of British Columbia Press, 1999).

40. David G. Duff, "Carbon Taxation in British Columbia," *Vermont Journal of Environmental Law* 10, no. 1 (2009), pp. 87–107.

156   BARRY G. RABE

41. For a thorough review of the British Columbia carbon tax case and some of the factors that may have contributed to Campbell's decision to take an active, entrepreneurial role, see Kathryn Harrison, "A Tale of Two Taxes: The Fate of Environmental Tax Reform in Canada and the Province of British Columbia," paper presented at the 2009 Annual Meeting of the American Political Science Association, September 3–6, Toronto, Ontario.

42. Tom Arrandale, "Taxing Times: A Levy on Carbon Goes Live North of the Border," *Governing*, September 2008, p. 30.

43. William A. Galston and Pietro S. Nivola, "Delineating the Problem," in *Red and Blue Nation?* vol. 1, edited by Pietro S. Nivola and David W. Brady (Brookings, 2006), p. 29.

44. Some of the leading contributions to this area include Gary Mucciaroni, *Reversals of Fortune: Public Policy and Private Interests* (Brookings, 1995), and Martha Derthick and Paul J. Quirk, *The Politics of Deregulation* (Brookings, 1985).

45. David Brady and colleagues note that "nothing of a similar nature has occurred in these policy areas since 1990, and several factors lead us to suspect that such actions are less likely today." David Brady, John Ferejohn, and Lauren Harbridge, "Polarization and Public Policy," in *Red and Blue Nation?* vol. 2, Pietro S. Nivola and David W. Brady (Brookings Institution Press, 2008), p. 203.

46. John Kingdon, *Agendas, Alternatives, and Public Policies*, 2nd ed. (New York: Harper Collins, 1995).

47. David R. Beam and Timothy J. Conlan, "Four Pathways to Power: Probing the Political Dynamics of Federal Tax Policy in the Turbulent 1980s and 1990s," in *Seeking the Center: Politics and Policymaking at the New Century*, edited by Martin A. Levin, Marc K. Landy, and Martin Shapiro (Georgetown University Press, 2001), pp. 81–110.

48 Sheldon Kamieniecki, *Corporate America and Environmental Policy: How Often Does Business Get Its Way?* (Stanford University Press, 2006); Michael E. Kraft and Sheldon Kamieniecki, *Business and Environmental Policy: Corporate Interests in the American Political System* (MIT Press, 2007). More generally, see Mark A. Smith, *American Business and Political Power: Public Opinion, Elections, and Democracy* (University of Chicago Press, 2000).

49. According to political scientist Loren Cass, "actors attempt to 'frame' normative ideas in a way that resonates with existing norms and with the interests of the target audience [and] utilize frames to persuade a target audience of the appropriateness of a proposed normative response." Cass, *The Failures of American and European Climate Policy*, p. 6. For a creative application of framing options in the area of energy conservation, see Richard H. Thaler and Cass R. Sunstein, *Nudge: Improving Decisions about Health, Wealth, and Happiness* (Yale University Press, 2008), pp. 36–37. Also see Daniel Kahneman and Amos Tversky, *Choices, Values, and Frames* (Cambridge University Press, 2000).

50. On earlier state experiments with framing in various areas of climate policy, see Barry G. Rabe, *Statehouse and Greenhouse: The Emerging Politics of American Climate Change Policy* (Brookings, 2004).

51. Eric M. Patashnik, *Reforms at Risk: What Happens after Major Policy Changes Are Enacted* (Princeton University Press, 2008), pp. 47–49.

52. Such proposals have grown exponentially in recent years. One increasingly popular option advanced by some utilities is a tax on electricity that would be used to fund research and development of alternative energy, although those most supportive tend to be utilities with relatively small reliance on coal and considerable commitment to renewable energy, whether due to internal decisions or state renewable portfolio standards.

53. Mike DeSouza, "Carbon Tax Gaining Support across Canada: Poll," *Canwest News Service,* May 25, 2008. Cited in Duff, "Carbon Taxation in British Columbia," p. 16.

54. Alice M. Rivlin and Isabel Sawhill, *Restoring Fiscal Sanity: How to Balance the Budget* (Brookings, 2004), p. 118.

55. Nordhaus, *A Question of Balance*, p. 26.

56. U.S. Centers for Disease Control, "Federal and State Cigarette Excise Taxes—United States, 1995–2009," May 2009.

57. Ibid., p. 163.

58. David Gauthier-Villars, "France Moves to Levy Carbon Tax on Fossil Fuels," *Wall Street Journal* (September 10, 2009), p. A10; "Taxing the Carbonivores," *The Economist,* September 19, 2009, pp. 62–63. A December 2009 decision by the Constitutional Council of France put the future of the tax in jeopardy because of concerns about its fairness, given its numerous exemptions, and Sarkozy backed away from fighting the decision in March 2010.

7

The Long and Winding Road: Automotive Fuel Economy and American Politics

PIETRO S. NIVOLA

For more than thirty years, the government of the United States has been trying to reduce the nation's voracious consumption of petroleum by regulating the fuel economy of motor vehicles. The project has not been a notable success. As of 2007, the average fuel economy of brand-new passenger vehicles in the country was, for all practical purposes, about the same as it had been twenty years earlier—under 27 miles per gallon. Counting *all* passenger vehicles on the road, old as well as new, the average miles traveled per gallon of fuel stood at just 20.4.[1] That fact, combined with a relentless increase in the amount of driving, meant that three decades after Congress initiated the automotive energy conservation program, we were actually consuming more fuel per capita than we had averaged when driving around in the gas guzzlers of 1975.[2]

In 2007, lawmakers congratulated themselves for finally facing up to that disappointing performance: they enacted legislation requiring new cars and light trucks to attain a combined level of efficiency of 35 miles per gallon (mpg) by the year 2020. The legislators claimed that the change would not only advance (somehow) "energy independence and security" but also substantially curb the heat-trapping gases that are warming the earth's atmosphere. Then, in May 2009, President Barack Obama announced his intention to nudge Congress's mandate a bit further, proposing to reach a target of 35.5 mpg by 2016.

For all the kudos bestowed on these recent initiatives, they ought to be placed in proper perspective. Thirty-five mpg (or Obama's 35.5 mpg) may seem like a great stride compared with today's 27.5 mpg, but it pales in contrast with the efficiency standards set by the European Union and Japan. The EU's vehicular fleet is scheduled to average around *50 mpg within the next two years* (2012).[3]

Why does the U.S. effort to moderate the use of oil in automotive transportation continue to fall so short? The following chapter tackles this question, proceeding in six segments. First, it outlines in a bit more detail the particular energy-saving regulatory regime on which our politicians have fastened for more than a third of a century. Second, it describes that system's failures—including the fact that its impact on greenhouse gas emissions has been perforce minimal. Third, the chapter shows how other advanced nations have achieved far better fuel economy and hence are able to aim much higher in their prospective efficiency standards. Fourth, it discusses the political reasons for the U.S. lag and for Europe's big lead and, fifth, segues to some basic reflections about what animates our regulatory politics. Finally, the framework for a more enlightened U.S. policy mix is proposed.

The CAFE Conundrum

In the aftermath of the 1974 oil crisis, Congress enacted the so-called Energy Policy and Conservation Act of 1975. "Conservation act" was largely a misnomer. By imposing price controls on all domestically produced crude oil, the immediate effect of the legislation was to induce demand for energy, not conserve it.[4] At the time, however, one portion of the law did appear to offer at least some prospect of lowering the use of fuel: as of 1978, automobile companies would be required, through a mélange of legislated directives and Department of Transportation (DOT) rulemakings, to upgrade the overall average miles per gallon traveled by the passenger vehicles that the firms manufactured.

The resulting corporate average fuel economy (CAFE) standards, as they were called, established separate trajectories for different classes of vehicles, with higher standards set for ordinary cars than for light trucks (sport utility vehicles, vans, and pickups below a certain weight). The standard for new cars became an average of 18 mpg, rising to 27.5 by 1990. The light-truck standard moved from 17.2 mpg (in 1979) to 20.7 mpg by 1991. Two Bush administration rulemakings during 2003 and 2006 sought to raise the light-truck target to 24 mpg for 2011, but the second was overturned by the Ninth Circuit Court of Appeals.[5] Further improvements for the two varieties of vehicles were not ordered until 2007 and, barring further delays in the courts, they will be implemented according to DOT rules issued in the spring of 2008 and subsequently amended to follow the Obama administration's accelerated timetable.[6]

For reasons to be explained shortly, the old differentiation between cars and "trucks" would eventually prove to be one of the program's fatal flaws, but in fairness,

Congress did not foresee its implications, since sport utility vehicles (SUVs) and similar vehicles made up barely 2 percent of the market in 1975.[7] As a general notion, promoting better vehicular miles-per-gallon standards made sense: in the United States, the transportation sector accounts for most of the oil that the economy burns, and motor vehicles are the dominant users within that sector.

At first blush, the results of the CAFE program looked promising. Average passenger car fuel efficiency for the model years 1978 through 1982, for instance, increased by almost 7 mpg (see figure 7-1). From 1982 to 1988, the average climbed at a much slower rate. Still, new vehicles at the end of that six-year span added another 2 mpg to their average.

But there the good news, such as it was, ended. Afterward, the efficiency of new automobiles showed no increase at all until 2002—when average mpg inched to 29 from 28.8, the high point in 1988. Not only had the fuel efficiency of cars essentially flat-lined over fifteen years; cars no longer claimed the dominant market share. With sales of SUVs and vans rising at a rapid rate and subject to a lower standard, the average fuel efficiency of the *overall* fleet of passenger vehicles (cars and these light trucks) had actually declined as of 2006. In 2007, the fleet's average finally topped—albeit by a paltry 0.4 mpg—the level attained twenty years earlier. Even that progression is deceptive. The definition of "light truck" had become arbitrary; it excluded pickups, vans, and SUVs with a so-called gross vehicle weight above 8,500 but under 10,000 pounds. Amid relatively soft gasoline prices, sales of such vehicles had increased (in 1999, for example, more than 521,000 were sold), so by the end of the century about 5.8 million of them were in use.[8] Since these behemoths were not required to meet any mileage standards at all, the true passenger fleet trend—including them—would have looked sorrier still.

That inauspicious record was just one part of the picture—the part pertaining to new vehicles. Because new vehicles represent a small fraction of the on-road stock each year, it takes roughly a decade to turn over the entire inventory.[9] Because CAFE standards govern only new models, their effects inevitably sink in at a snail's pace. After almost three decades of regulation, average miles per gallon for all the vehicles that Americans were driving remained far below the efficiency ratings to which the 1975 legislation had implicitly aspired.

How much did the CAFE apparatus, since its inception, reduce U.S. demand for petroleum, and how much impact did it thereby have on the emission of greenhouse gases? To date, the most authoritative study of this question is a report issued by the National Research Council (NRC) in 2002. It concluded that, without the change in miles traveled per gallon after 1978, the country would have used 2.8 million more barrels of oil per day.[10] What that and every other study of the subject could not pinpoint, however, was how much of the savings could be imputed to the CAFE policy alone, apart from other forces—most notably, rising energy prices during various intervals. The sharp price increases in the 1970s and

Figure 7-1. *New and On-Road Vehicle Fuel Economy, United States*

Miles per gallon

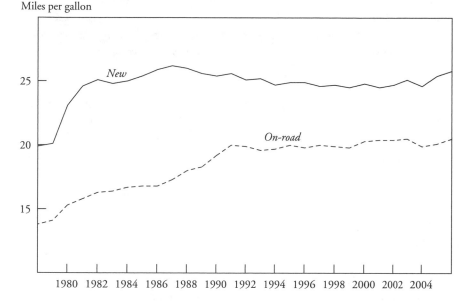

Sources: New fuel economy data drawn from National Highway Traffic Safety Administration, U.S. Department of Transportation, "Revised Summary of Fuel Economy Performance," January 15, 2008 (www.nhtsa.dot.gov/portal/ste/nhtsa/memuitem.43ac99aefa80569eea57529cdba046a0). Other data drawn from Federal Highway Administration, "Highway Statistics Summary to 1995," table VM-201A, and Highway Statistics, 1996–2006, annual editions, table VM-1 for each year.

early 1980s, for example, may well have done more to boost fuel economy during those years than any regulatory strictures did. Similarly, the upturn in miles per gallon that finally began in 2007 almost certainly had more to do with soaring gasoline prices than with the belated congressional action raising standards through 2020.[11]

A more compelling case for CAFE's effectiveness is that, by setting a floor for fuel economy when energy prices sagged between 1983 and 1988, the program probably helped prop up the mpg numbers during that period. That limited stretch of reasonably unambiguous impact, however, would not seem to offer a sufficient basis for crediting CAFE mandates per se with the full 2.8 million barrels of oil a day that were said to have been conserved over the course of the program's existence. As the NRC itself conceded, it remains "difficult to say what fuel consumption would have been had there been no CAFE standards."[12]

Even if, straining credulity, we assume that the fuel economy regulations somehow accounted for *all* of the estimated fuel savings, how much difference have they made in meeting the most important challenge of energy policy: the battle against climate change? Our light-duty vehicles are responsible for only a fifth of U.S. carbon emissions. Lowering the combustion of gasoline by 2.8 million barrels a day

diminished the CO_2 level by approximately 367 million metric tons a year, infer-
ring from the NRC report.[13] But at the time of the NRC's estimate, the United
States was shoveling more than a total of 5,670 million metric tons of CO_2 into
the air annually.[14] A more current figure, of course, would be considerably worse.
Thus, at the very best, the thirty-year regulatory exercise might be said to have
reduced that annual torrent of pollution by less than 7 percent—an amount more
than offset by China's CO_2 output *every month*.[15]

The meagerness of this result has been no secret to framers of environmental
policy, particularly those in active state governments such as California's. In 2002,
California launched a program to cut tailpipe emissions of greenhouse gases
(GHG) to levels far below those projected for the United States as a whole. The
California initiative and those of other states moving to emulate it reflected in
part keen awareness that the U.S. effort (CAFE standards) had accomplished too
little.

Now that it looks as if all legal challenges to the California program have
finally come to an end and as it continues to gain traction, the long-standing deficiencies of the federal fuel-economy struggle may become less relevant. In effect,
the tailpipe standards of California and twelve other states that followed its lead
will supersede Washington's past policies, and CAFE could gradually fade, literally, to a sideshow.

The substitution of California's standards unquestionably received a major
boost with the arrival of President Obama. His administration essentially plans to
spread California's vehicle emissions restraints nationwide. Before, neither the
Supreme Court's verdict in *Massachusetts* v. *EPA*, affirming the regulation of CO_2
under the Clean Air Act (CAA), nor a federal court decision in California uphold-
ing the state's GHG-based substitute, had deterred the U.S. Environmental Protection Agency (EPA) from preempting state law.[16] By turning down Sacramento's
request for a CAA waiver, the EPA had effectively denied the state permission to
go ahead with its plan.[17] Obama changed all that. Within days of taking office,
he directed the EPA to reconsider its position.

Still, it remains far from clear that the White House's new enthusiasm for—
indeed, appropriation of—state-level GHG abatement schemes, even if modeled
on the most aggressive ones like California's, will soon add up to a national lid on
automotive carbon emissions comparable to the limits anticipated in Europe and
Japan.[18] For there, a rather different, more powerful set of policy instruments is
at work.

The divergence, moreover, goes well beyond the telling fact that the EU has
established (however imperfectly) a carbon-trading system, whereas the U.S.
Congress has repeatedly flirted with cap-and-trade proposals but has proven
unable to adopt one. All that Congress managed to enact in 2009 was a "cash for
clunkers" bill, designed to spur consumers to trade in older, inefficient vehicles
for new, greener ones. As one of a series of measures to help stimulate the slump-

Figure 7-2. *Vehicle Miles Traveled (VMT) for Light-Duty Vehicles, United States*

VMT, trillions

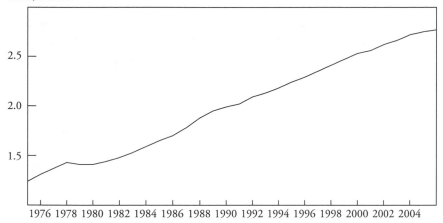

Sources: Federal Highway Administration, "Highway Statistics Summary to 1995," table VM-201, and Highway Statistics, 1996–2006, annual editions, table VM-1 for each year (www.fhwa.dot.gov/policy/ohpi/hss/hsspubs.htm).

ing economy, cash-for-clunkers appears to have served a worthwhile function, by encouraging new-car buyers to move up their purchases amid a deep recession.[19] That the provision also netted notable savings of gasoline, however, is more debatable, for the following simple reasons.

Consumers eyeing new cars would eventually buy them anyway, if not sooner, then somewhat later.[20] Many, perhaps most, of the trade-ins, moreover, tended to be remnant vehicles (literally clunkers) that households already used less frequently, whereas the newly purchased, better-performing replacements naturally get driven more. The swap, therefore, yielded less of a net reduction of fuel use than is widely supposed. According to one estimate, the first $1 billion in federal rebates for the trade-ins actually reduced fuel use by an amount so marginal that it may have totaled no more than a couple of hours' worth of national consumption.[21]

All of which brings us back, for now, to the CAFE framework and its most abiding defect: while mandating vehicular fuel economy may (slowly) alter the composition of fleets, what, if anything, can it do about the driving habits of motorists?[22] Vehicle miles traveled (VMT) by the U.S. light-duty fleet have continued to soar at a pace much faster than the growth of the population throughout the life of the regulatory program (see figure 7-2). When drivers make the equivalent of almost 12 million trips to the moon—and rising—every year, the energy-conserving effect of CAFE is undercut. Indeed, if anything, the CAFE program has *induced* some of the unremitting increase in VMT: inasmuch as mandated fuel economy lowers the marginal cost of driving during periods of flat or declining gasoline prices, people drive their thrifty cars *more*. Estimates of this boomerang, or rebound, effect vary, but even if the consensus is that the magnitude is modest, it presents yet another reason for skepticism that a daily savings of 2.8 million barrels of oil can be imputed to CAFE requirements.

As discussed later, nations that have been more successful in constraining demand for motor fuel—and thus lowering GHG effluents in their transportation sectors—have done so by improving the efficiency of vehicles *and* encouraging people to drive less. What has helped make that two-pronged approach work is not the imposition of fuel economy standards but a longer history of steep prices.[23] The United States, too, could have achieved much greater conservation over the years simply if the price of gasoline had been set consistently higher. Instead, U.S. policymakers have clung to CAFE, which, to paraphrase one wag, has been a little like trying to battle obesity by requiring tailors to make only tight-fitting clothes.[24]

What Other Countries Do

In 2005, per capita consumption of motor fuel in the United States was nearly 620 gallons a year (see figure 7-3). Compare that figure to the figures for the United Kingdom (224 gallons), France (222), Germany (208), and Japan (195). It is tempting, as a first approximation, to just invoke variations in living standards, geography, transportation systems, and the stringency of European and Japanese regulatory activities, to explain away these striking differences in energy intensity.

The United States is a wealthy country. Recessionary interludes notwithstanding, most American households have continued to enjoy rising levels of real compensation decade after decade.[25] Vehicle ownership is more widespread than anywhere else. America is also a vast country, over which people journey long distances, inevitably piling up more vehicle miles traveled. U.S. cities are less dense than European and Japanese urban centers, so naturally more Americans commute by car and fewer use alternative modes of urban transportation.[26] Ridership in the transit systems and trains of Europe and Japan is higher than in the United States, where those alternatives are less well developed. Finally, the United States is not the only country that regulates vehicular fuel efficiency. The EU and Japan have imposed tougher targets than ours, either in the form of direct standards for kilometers per liter (Japan) or through tailpipe-emission regulations to reduce GHG output (the EU).

Most of these propositions hold at least a kernel of truth (in some cases, considerable merit), but all told, they do not suffice. The standard of living (GDP per capita) is roughly comparable among industrial countries, and the rate of automobile ownership in Europe now is no longer a distant second. (Europe's rate is converging on 600 vehicles per 1,000 persons; the U.S. rate is closer to 700 per 1,000 persons.)[27] Distances are indeed great in the United States, but 90 percent of automotive trips here are fewer than 10 miles long, and the average length of

Figure 7-3. *Per Capita Consumption of Motor Fuel, 2005*

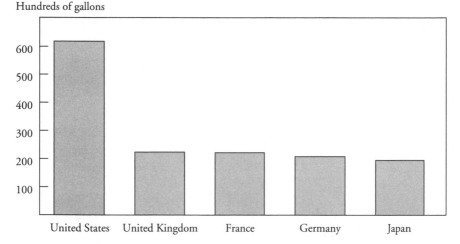

Sources: Consumption data drawn from International Energy Agency, *Oil Information 2007* (http://miranda.sourceoecd.org/vl=11522702/cl=17/nw=1/rpsv/~6673/v2007n17/s1/p1l). Population data drawn from Organization for Economic Cooperation and Development, "Country Statistical Profiles, 2008" (http://stats.oecd.org/wbos/Index.aspx?DatasetCode=CSP2008).

the trips appears to be not much longer than in, for example, the United Kingdom.[28] More than two-thirds of vehicle miles racked up by U.S. passenger vehicles, moreover, take place in urban areas, not the vast expanse of rural hinterlands.[29] Granted, our cities tend to be more spread out than those overseas; hence taking public transit, bicycling, or walking to jobs and services is often impractical. Yet, far more than we like to admit, Americans tend to decline those options even when they are available and feasible. Case in point: An overwhelming percentage of people opt to commute by car in Washington, D.C., a city with one of the world's most modern and elegant transit systems.[30] Yes, our Amtrak often does feel like a third-world passenger rail system in comparison with the rapid trains of Japan and Europe. But, with the exception of a few major corridors, Americans rely not on trains but more extensively on a faster, high-volume mode—airplanes—for long-distance travel.

As for the oft-asserted thesis that the Japanese and Europeans are tougher regulators who therefore get better results, it is simply incorrect. In fact, as noted earlier, neither the EU nor Japan had set mandatory fuel economy or CO_2 targets for motor vehicles until quite recently. (Japan's mandated program began in 1999. The EU's Council of Environment Ministers did not get around to setting mandatory standards until June 2007, though the EU had experimented with a series of voluntary agreements with automobile manufacturers a decade ago.)[31] True, the European target now is exemplary: the equivalent of a vehicular average approaching 50 miles per gallon within the next two years. The explanation for

Figure 7-4. *Unleaded Gasoline Prices and Taxes, First Quarter, 2008*[a]

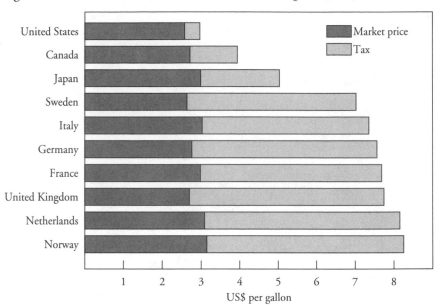

Source: International Energy Agency, *Energy Prices and Taxes, First Quarter, 2008*. Figure 8, p. xxxiv (http://lysander.sourceoecd.org/vl=4338568/cl=19/nw=1/rpsv/~3804/v2008n1/s1/p1l).
    a. Or latest available data.

so remarkable a goal, however, is not that the EU is a uniquely fierce regulator; rather, it is that European automotive fleets were already within striking distance of the goal, thanks to their preexisting efficiency. And that long-standing efficiency, in turn, had little to do with energy mandates (there were no binding ones until three years ago) but a lot to do with the price of fuel.

It is hard to escape the conclusion that price differentials are the single most telling factor explaining the fuel intensity of automotive transportation in the United States. Figures 7-4 and 7-5 display differences among nations in the price of fuel at the pump in early 2008. Even when Americans lamented that the average price of gasoline had topped $4 a gallon, motorists throughout Western Europe were paying the equivalent of more than twice that amount.

These pricing patterns are inversely correlated with vehicle kilometers traveled per capita and with average on-road fuel efficiency of vehicles. Figures 7-6 and 7-7 show the relationships unmistakably: where prices are high, people drive less, and when they drive, they tend to do so in more economical vehicles. Over time, the greatest impact of consistently steep fuel prices is on the kinds of vehicles that consumers chose. The price elasticity of demand for fuel-economic vehicles appears to be as high as -0.7, meaning that, say, a 10 percent rise in fuel prices eventually yields as much as a 7 percent decline in vehicular fuel intensity.[32]

Figure 7-5. *Automotive Diesel Prices and Taxes, First Quarter, 2008*[a]

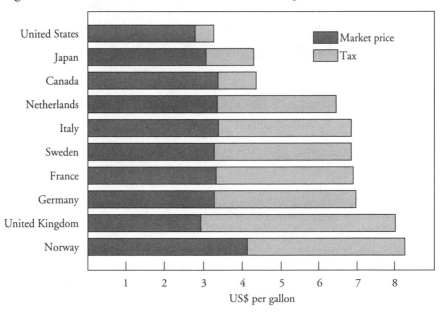

Sources: International Energy Agency, *Energy Prices and Taxes, First Quarter, 2008*. Figure 9, p. xxv (http://lysander.sourceoecd.org/vl-4338568/cl-19/nw-1/rpsv/-3804/v2008n1/s1/p1l). Canadian price data from Natural Resources Canada (http://fuelfocus.nrcan.gc.ca/prices_bycity_e.cfm?PriceYear=0& ProductID=5&LocationID=66,8,39,17#PriceGraph).

a. Or latest available data.

The price elasticity of demand for the *use* of vehicles—that is, the amount of driving—is said to be considerably lower: in the range of –0.2 to –0.3.[33] There is reason, however, to question the low end of that estimate. For one thing, it is likely that the demand response to movements in price is not linear. Rather, it works in quantum steps; when tipping points are crossed, a game change occurs. The sudden spikes in energy prices in 1974 and 1979, for example, quickly shifted not only the mix of vehicles purchased but the extent and form of travel. More recently, the critical break point for U.S. consumers and producers seems to have been the $4 mark for gasoline: when that threshold was crossed, sales of SUVs promptly plunged; smaller cars gained market share; and, for the first time since 1979, VMT fell off sharply.[34] For example, the 4.3 percent—or 11 billion mile—drop in VMT in March 2007, compared with VMT the same time a year earlier, suggests a price elasticity of demand appreciably greater than the –0.2, or even the –0.3, cited above.)

Further, the customary view that demand for automotive travel is relatively price-inelastic in the United States is largely predicated on the fact that Americans, more than other people, are compelled to commute to work by car.[35] Be that

Figure 7-6. *Fuel Price and Vehicle Kilometers Traveled per Capita*[a]

Vehicle kilometers traveled per capita, thousands

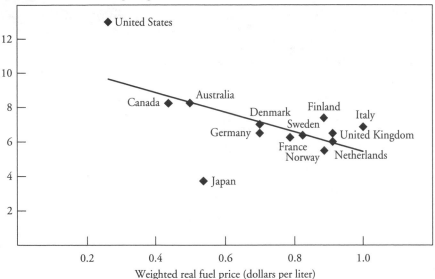

Source: Figure is derived from graph in Lee Schipper, "Automobile Fuel Economy and CO_2 Emissions in Industrialized Countries: Troubling Trends through 2005/6" (EMBARQ/World Resources Institute, 2007), p. 13.

a. The slope of the line through the data approximates the relationship between fuel prices and kilometers traveled per capita.

as it may, an elasticity regularly as low as –0.2 presupposes, implausibly, that almost all of our driving is an immutable necessity, insensitive to relative prices. But motorists in this country take approximately twice as many vehicular trips per capita as the Europeans.[36] Necessary travel such as commuting trips alone cannot account for so wide a chasm. A good deal of driving in the United States, like everywhere else, is discretionary, and consumers can—and do—alter their behavior by making a variety of adjustments: carpooling, changing their mode of travel, combining trips (what transportation economists call trip chaining), or even occasionally renouncing some driving.

If, as is likely, price incentives exert a powerful influence on how motorists consume fuel, two questions ensue: Why are motor fuel prices so much higher abroad? How are other countries able to add that premium? The answer to the first is straightforward: as you can tell by glancing again at figure 7-4, most of the disparity in retail rates reflects a far lower excise tax in the United States. The answer to the second query is more complicated: the politics of energy taxation in Europe and America are worlds apart, and complex historical and systemic reasons are involved.

Figure 7-7. *Fuel Price and Vehicle Fuel Intensity*[a]

Fleet average vehicle fuel intensity (liters per 100 vehicle kilometers traveled)

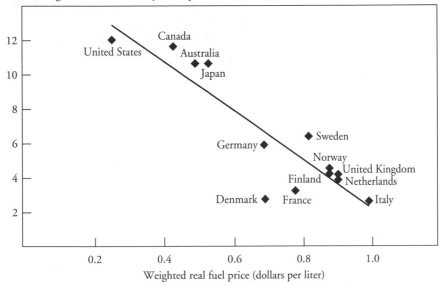

Weighted real fuel price (dollars per liter)

Source: Figure is derived from graph in Lee Schipper, "Automobile Fuel Economy and CO_2 Emissions in Industrialized Countries: Troubling Trends through 2005/6" (EMBARQ/World Resources Institute, 2007), p. 13.

a. The slope of the line through the data approximates the relationship between fuel prices and vehicle fuel intensity.

Comparative Governance

A society's relative disposition to tax the consumption of energy rather than try to regulate it in roundabout ways is to an important extent path-dependent. Nine-teenth-century imperial powers such as Britain and France had long financed their extensive central governments by levying sales taxes on everything from salt, tea, and tobacco to various forms of fuel, including eventually motor "spirits." Taxation of automotive fuel in the United States got a slower start and began at a different level. The state of Oregon initiated the practice in 1919, and most other state governments gradually followed over the next couple of decades.

State preemption delayed and constrained national policy. Congress eventually tapped into the new source of revenue, but the states had staked a larger, prior claim to it. Frequently, the dissent of state governors and legislators to proposed federal fuel taxes was to become an obstacle when tax bills were debated in Wash-ington. The first federal excise tax, masterminded by President Herbert Hoover and limited to 1 cent per gallon, was not adopted until 1932, many years after the first national fuel excise tax in Britain.

Federal gasoline taxation made its debut under inauspicious circumstances. The Great Depression, as Franklin D. Roosevelt came to see, was a bad time to impose new taxes of any kind. Thus, the 1-cent rate remained unchanged until 1940, when revenue needed for military preparations resulted in a half-cent increase. Strict administrative rationing of gasoline during World War II stalled further adjustments, though a 2-cent hike finally occurred in the postwar period with the outbreak of the Korean conflict.

By the mid-1950s, however, it was already too late to turn the rate of federal fuel taxation into a fiscal instrument comparable to those in other western countries. Explosive suburban growth in U.S. metropolitan areas was well on its way to establishing an exceptionally "autocentric" society—one intensely resistant to any measures that would raise the operating costs of automobiles.

Dedicated versus General Purpose Revenue

In addition, the 1956 legislation that authorized construction of the interstate highway system included what would quickly become an additional constraint: mimicking the road financing methods of most states, Congress embraced the principle of dedicating the revenue to a highway trust fund. Gas-tax dollars fed into the fund soon gave rise to a classic iron triangle of construction contractors and users, congressional public works committees, and federal and state transportation agencies whose common interest was plain: to pay for an extensive infrastructure with, in effect, a toll that would remain low enough to maintain robust demand but sufficient to keep replenishing the funding source. Thus, when the U.S. government has succeeded in boosting its gasoline tax, the periodic increases have been, at best, held to a nickel ante—4 cents in 1959, 5 cents in 1982, 5 cents in 1990, 4.3 cents in 1993. Those increments were typically justified as surcharges to shore up the nation's roads, bridges, and, late in the game, some transit systems.[37]

Notice the importance, and distinctiveness, of the U.S. practice of dedicating fuel tax revenues. Few other nations earmark such revenue in the U.S. fashion. The norm of tax policy in most European countries is that the proceeds of all imposts, whether on consumption or incomes, are commingled as general revenue for public purposes of many kinds. To be sure, there have been occasional restrictions. In Britain, for example, Lloyd George, chancellor of the exchequer in 1909, had sought to "hypothecate" money for a special "road fund." However, subsequent treasury ministers repeatedly raided the fund, dismissing as "preposterous" any notion that highway users "are entitled to make binding terms with Parliament as to the application of the taxes levied for them."[38]

Similarly, in France, a separate highway fund existed on paper as of 1952: *le Fonds special d'investissement routier.* But the Ministry of Finance was in the habit of poaching the funds and routinely diverted them to other priorities.[39] What these practices have meant in places like France and the United Kingdom is that revenues from fuel taxes tend to be distributed among multiple claimants. The use of levies on motorists to cross-subsidize additional stakeholders (not just municipal public transit operators but railroads and airlines, for instance) widens the array of vested interests in much steeper tax rates.

Other Budgetary Contrasts

The comparatively constrained applications of fuel levies in the United States, hence their small scale, also reflect a broader systemic difference in fiscal policy-making. In Britain, for instance, the budget-making process is centralized in the treasury, which decides how and what to tax and spend. The budget—each year's program of taxes and expenditures—is prepared discreetly by the Exchequer with limited give-and-take in the cabinet, to say nothing of participation by back-benchers. It is eventually presented to the House of Commons but typically as an indivisible package to be briefly debated and then approved up or down. Parliamentary rejection of any portion, an extreme rarity, can be tantamount to a vote of no confidence and grounds for a full-blown government crisis. An obvious implication of this modus operandi is that "the government," if it so desires, ordinarily can raise taxes on petrol more or less at will.

The French government has been known to operate with even fewer checks. There, the Finance Ministry frequently has had carte blanche simply to decree a percentage ad valorem hike in a national excise tax. With elected representatives in parliament mostly sidelined, public opposition, if simmering, often has no effective outlet.

Compare such norms to those in the United States. The U.S. Constitution vests the power of the purse squarely in the legislative branch. There, responsibilities are divided at least eight ways—among the upper and lower chambers' tax writing, authorizing, appropriations, and budget committees, each of which jealously guards its prerogatives and can upend what the executive proposes. Indeed, the objections of even just a handful of members in a pivotal committee (Senate Finance, for instance) can suffice to obstruct or alter beyond recognition items in a president's budget.

That's pretty much what happened, for example, to President Clinton's proposal for a substantial energy tax in 1993. Clinton presided over clear Democratic majorities in both houses. Nonetheless, by the time a few senators in his own party had finished grinding down the administration's bill, what finally emerged was an entirely different sausage—a gasoline tax hike of only 4.3 cents.[40]

Party Politics

Republican politicians in the United States have been reluctant to decouple the excise on gasoline from its lockbox—the highway trust, which limits the only U.S. national energy tax to a mild user fee. To invite a wider clientele for gas-tax revenue—and thus stir appetites for higher rates—would be to violate party orthodoxy about "new taxes."

Democratic politicians are equally wary, but for a different reason: they deem taxation of motor fuel to be regressive and therefore to be minimized. Sometimes leading Republicans take this populist tack, too. Senator John McCain and Senator Hillary Clinton adopted identical positions during the 2008 presidential campaign: both championed a gas-tax holiday on the grounds that the beleaguered American consumer needed "a break"—never mind that the U.S tax is minimal by international standards.[41] With both sides so entrenched, it is no wonder that legislative efforts to increase the tax, even by a few pennies, fail more often than succeed, frequently by margins greater than 4 to 1 in the House of Representatives.[42]

To appreciate the uniqueness of this bipartisan roadblock, gaze again at the political scene in the United Kingdom or France. On the right in Britain, thanks to party discipline in Parliament and less dispersion of fiscal authority, a Tory government like that of Margaret Thatcher had little to fear from the lucrative proceeds of steep consumption taxes. In fact, such taxes rose repeatedly under Thatcher amid extensive privatization, government downsizing, and austerity measures—in short, with little risk of feeding the equivalent of a congressional spending spree. The perpetual tax revolt of supply-siders in the United States reflects at least in part a conviction that a conservative public sector can be achieved only by "starving the beast."

Meanwhile, liberals in the United States ritually refer to increases in the cost of gasoline as "unfair," "discriminatory," and "unaffordable." Seldom does one hear this rhetoric on the European left. When the socialist government of François Mitterand came to power in 1981, the tax on regular gasoline in France stood at 54 percent of the retail price. By the spring of 1991, the bite was 77 percent.[43] Across the Channel, the British Labour Party has not hesitated to jack up taxes on petrol, either. In the elections of 1992, for example, it was the two parties of the left, Labour and the Liberal Democrats, that attached to their respective "programmes" the boldest proposals for higher tolls on roads and fuel.[44]

Why are the socialists of Europe evidently resigned to tax rates like those shown in figure 7-4 while "progressives" in the United States call the relative bargain here "backbreaking"?[45] Perhaps our left is less confident that the safety nets of the U.S. welfare state can cushion the impact of any added burden on the poor and the middle class. Perhaps, too, officials across the entire U.S. political spectrum are simply less insulated from public opinion. Routinely and overwhelmingly, polls in Europe as well as in the United States indicate that consumers hate higher fuel prices.[46] In a regime such as ours, however, which exposes its politicians to extraordinarily frequent elections and perpetual campaigning, pandering (or sensitivity, take your pick) to voters about energy prices is a perennial spectacle.

The Politics of Regulation

Yet, when crises occur, the same politicians hear a second message: "Don't just stand there; do something!" In the immediate aftermath of the Arab oil embargo in 1973 and the ensuing price shock, pressure mounted to "do something" about the energy crunch. But the one thing no U.S. elected official could do, without self-immolating politically, was to address the problem by flatly telling voters to live with higher fuel prices. Nowhere was this straitjacket more conspicuous than in the big 1975 energy bill which, in the guise of sparing consumers, went out of its way to avoid any tax on energy use and authorized instead a convoluted way to regulate automobile manufactures (CAFE). The populist approach persists. Nearly a third of a century later, amid renewed demands for action on the energy problem, Congress's answer has been similar: Under the 2007 energy act the consumer got another pass: the auto industry would be further regulated.

If one wishes to put the best face on this formula, it could be regarded as a second-best solution, constrained by political realities. CAFE, the argument goes, was genuinely intended to prod short-sighted automakers, not their hapless customers, and it does save at least some fuel. A less charitable interpretation is that the architects of this edifice sought to have things both ways: yes, to obtain some "conservation," but in an oblique fashion, so as to get no flak from motorists. Indeed, the CAFE framers designed a system replete with safety valves, arguably to minimize the political heat from the regulated industry and its workers as well. By legislating miles-per-gallon standards for some classes of vehicles but not others, delegating to DOT the power to make downward adjustments, permitting companies to bank "credits," pulling the purse strings on regulatory budgets, and preempting proactive state governments, Congress put in place elaborate arrangements for avoiding blame.

Thus, in 1980, when it appeared that the costs of CAFE might become onerous to manufacturers struggling to save jobs in the teeth of competition from Japanese imports, President Carter signed legislation empowering the secretary of transportation to lower mileage requirements for four-wheel drive vehicles and light trucks if a manufacturer could demonstrate that it would incur economic difficulties meeting extant standards.[47] (Purveyors of pickups and vans already had a free ride for vehicles that weighed in at more than 8,500 pounds.) The car companies also won a reprieve for entire fleets that failed to meet standards in a given period, provided that they exceeded standards in a subsequent period, thereby gaining "credits" to apply retroactively. Later in the same decade, amid plunging gasoline prices and fewer takers for small, fuel-efficient cars, the companies prevailed on the Reagan administration to lower standards again. Then, between 1996 and 2001, further CAFE pressure on the auto industry more or less came to a complete halt. Congress simply banned the use of DOT-appropriated funds for purposes of new rulemakings entirely, thereby freezing the mpg requirement for light trucks at 20.7 gallons. Only in 2009 did California, as well as other states following California's lead, begin to overcome a federal prohibition on state GHG restrictions that might be stiffer—and hence costlier to industry—than the CAFE equivalent.

In sum, the regulatory process has resembled an intricate *pas de deux*, often moving one step forward and one step back. That is not to suggest that every stage of the exercise has resembled nothing more than dancing in place, or that society hasn't gained anything at all from it. On balance, as the National Resource Council concluded, the world is slightly better off for our having tried to regulate automotive fuel economy—in terms of diminished concentration of greenhouse gases—than if we had done nothing. There is, however, one important sense in which CAFE's marginal net benefit should be further discounted: so politicized a regulatory intervention perhaps made it easier for elected officials to get off the hook. Behind the veneer of an energy policy—which is what the porous and largely symbolic CAFE program amounted to, at least before President Obama gave it more bite—political leaders could more easily evade their responsibility to craft a meaningful agenda. It is to this latter challenge that the final section of this chapter now turns.

An Immodest Alternative

Implausible as it is, let us assume for the sake of argument that public attitudes changed and political leaders suppressed a tendency to campaign for a seemingly free lunch. The first step policymakers would have to take is to ask a fundamental question: what, precisely, is the point of improving the fuel economy of motor vehicles?

The "Energy Independence" Mirage

To reflexively invoke the slogans "energy independence" and "security" (as did the 2007 legislation that bolstered CAFE) is not an intellectually satisfying answer.[48] Oil is sold in a global market, and American consumers will continue to pay the world's price whether or not they are led to consume a little less. With the rest of the world using more oil, thanks in large part to intense demand from gigantic new economies such as China and India, even increasingly stringent efforts to curb consumption in the United States will gain little long-range relief or "independence" from the overall trend in prices.

The same goes for "security." To begin with, the United States purchases only a relatively small share of the oil that it needs from insecure or unstable producers. Nearly 90 percent of the U.S. demand for oil is met by domestic wells and those of suppliers outside the Middle East—and note that the United States imports *no* oil from Iran. Both of the NAFTA trading partners supply more oil than Saudi Arabia does, and both supply more than Hugo Chávez's Venezuela.

True, the disagreeable producers would reap fewer petrodollars if the United States were less profligate—but not a lot fewer and not for long, since other huge customers such as China would soon snap up the quantities of oil that the United States would forfeit. By selling to China, Japan, and Europe, the likes of Iran, for example, will enrich themselves whether or not Americans choose to purchase any of their oil, and they will enjoy only a bit less oil wealth if Americans become more abstemious overall.

What's more, if market perturbations arise from sources such as Iran, the U.S. economy—along with every other industrial economy—will not escape them, because, again, oil is priced in a worldwide marketplace. Recall what happened in the wake of the Iranian Revolution in 1979: oil prices doubled everywhere, including within the United States. The bottom line is that the United States cannot stop the world and get off. Enthusiasts of remedies such as CAFE regulations would do well to begin by conceding that basic constraint. Their policies, after a great deal of huffing and puffing, might mildly enhance "security," but not by much.

A better argument for regulating the use of hydrocarbon-based automotive fuels is that burning them spews CO_2, along with other pollutants, into the atmosphere and contributes to global warming. But that rationale raises a second basic question: if climate change is the core challenge for a rational energy policy, does it make sense to have, as the policy's centerpiece, a regulatory program that takes aim only at gasoline (one petroleum refined product) but not the combustion of *all* fossil fuels and derivatives that contribute to climate change? As everyone knows, U.S. coal-fired electric plants, not just Chinese ones, pump more CO_2 into the air than motor vehicles do. To "crack down" on the cars but not the power stations is a little like trying to save a burning house with buckets of water rather than a fire hose.

Tax Carbon Instead

A meaningful energy policy—that is to say, one confronting the specter of climate change—ought to shed weak reeds like CAFE and move toward a comprehensive carbon tax. A backdoor alternative to such a tax is a vigorous cap-and-trade system with auctioned emission permits. Either way, a stiff tax or its emissions-trading equivalent could reduce gasoline consumption more effectively than has the troubled automotive regulatory regime and, more important, would curtail greenhouses gases from other, more damaging sources (see chapters 5 and 6 for a detailed analysis of both market-based options).

Parenthetically, for reasons suggested in other chapters in this volume, the tax approach is conceptually the simplest and most transparent solution.[49] Cap-and-trade legislation, by contrast, seems tailor made for gaming and dilution, even as it has proven no easier to enact. The loophole-riddled Waxman-Markey Climate and Energy Security Act, for instance, was anticipated to have a modest impact;

it would have priced carbon dioxide at approximately $20 per ton, according to reliable estimates.[50] Even though Waxman-Markey's implicit carbon "price" and that of the Senate's counterpart fell far short of the $50 per ton that is widely regarded as the minimum for a transformative effect, the legislation failed to clear Congress in 2009. If there is any silver lining in the collapse of this clumsy edifice, it would be that Congress might one day revisit the carbon-pricing issue through a more straightforward tax instead.

The burden of any serious effort to tax carbon, of course, would not be light. Indeed, its costs would be felt by all fossil-fuel producers and users—that is, by practically everybody, not least average households facing higher energy bills. As reflected in the findings presented in chapter 2, it is no wonder that, when surveys ask Americans whether they are willing to countenance "increased taxes on electricity so people use less of it," majorities approaching 80 percent object.[51] To offset the adverse economic impact and regressive effect and possibly to soften some of the public's stiff opposition, the tax should be revenue neutral, or close to it, and ought to be substituted for other kinds of levies that are even more harmful to the nation's long-term growth and fiscal equity. Displacing the payroll tax is an obvious candidate.

Adoption of a substantial carbon tax could be a key component of a broader overhaul of the nation's skewed tax system, with its lopsided emphasis on punishing activities that society should reward—like earning, saving, and investing—instead of activities that it should discourage, like polluting and overleveraged consuming. Deficits of historic proportions loom, and new sources of revenues will almost certainly be needed to help trim them. Policymakers should think long and hard before continuing to rely exclusively on higher income and payroll taxes rather than beginning to shift more of the onus onto consumption, as a carbon tax would.

How utopian *is* this proposal? Its odds of becoming politically palatable are long—but maybe not so poor as to be completely out of the question, as Rabe discusses further in chapter 6. In Congress, at least before the Great Recession temporarily muted nearly all talk of new taxes, there had been encouraging signs that senior lawmakers were beginning to take the idea of taxing carbon seriously. In recent years, for instance, the second-most-senior member of the House Ways and Means Committee, California Democrat Fortney ("Pete") Stark, cosponsored a carbon-tax bill with ten-term congressman Jim McDermot, a Democrat of Washington. Another bill, authored by the veteran John Dingell (D-Michigan), chairman emeritus of the House Energy and Commerce Committee, would have phased in a similar tax. A third measure, proposed by Representative John B. Larson, a five-term Democrat from Connecticut and vice chair of the House Democratic Caucus, was perhaps the most interesting, for it would have applied carbon-tax revenue to help ease the payroll tax burden on working households.

The Larson bill sought to do that through a partial rebate mechanism that was complicated and possibly inadequate. (As with almost every energy-related bill in Congress, this one also would have diverted a share of revenues to boost research and development in "clean energy technologies" as well as extend adjustment assistance to "negatively affected" industries.) Nevertheless, Congressman Larson, and his colleagues, were to be commended. Their legislative proposals represented a start. In time, trial balloons like these just might begin to steer Washington's otherwise largely repetitious and sterile energy debate in a promising new direction.

Notes

1. Federal Highway Administration, *Highway Statistics*, table VM-1. Figure is for 2006, the most recent year for which data were available at the time this chapter was written.

2. U.S. Census Bureau, *Statistical Abstract* 2008, tables 2 and 1070. These figures apply to the U.S. population as a whole and only to fuel in cars and light trucks.

3. The EU's target for 2012 is the equivalent of 47 mpg for automobiles with gasoline engines, 52 mpg for diesel engines. *Environment for Europeans: Magazine of the Directorate-General for the Environment* (http://ec.europea.eu/environment/news/efe/24/print_ article_ 4119_wn.htm).

4. For a wider assessment of the Energy Policy and Conservation Act of 1975, see Pietro S. Nivola, *The Politics of Energy Conservation* (Brookings, 1986), chapter 2.

5. *Center for Biological Diversity* v. *National Highway Traffic Safety Administration*, 508 F. 3d 508 (9th Cir. 2007)

6. It remains somewhat unclear exactly how much of an improvement will actually occur under the new rules that DOT's National Highway Traffic Safety Administration (NHTSA) promulgated in April 2008. The new rules allow standards to vary by vehicle size or "footprint." Hence, the bar appears to be lower for a manufacturer that produces more large cars or trucks than for a manufacturer that makes smaller vehicles. Declining oil prices could re-introduce an incentive favoring the former, so overall fuel efficiency for the vehicular fleet could slip again as the product mix shifts.

7. Environmental Protection Agency, *Light-Duty Automotive Technology and Fuel Economy Trends: 1975 through 2008* (September 2008), p. 17.

8. National Highway Traffic Safety Administration, "Frequently Asked Questions: CAFE Overview" (www.nhtsa.dot.gov/).

9. This is a conservative time frame. Schipper, for example, suggests that the actual rate of turnover is somewhere between ten and twenty years. Improvements in the quality and durability of vehicles have lengthened their operational life span. Lee Schipper, "Automobile Fuel Economy and CO_2 Emissions in Industrialized Countries: Troubling Trends through 2005–6," *World Resources Institute*, p. 6 (www.embarq.wri.org).

10. National Research Council, *Effectiveness and Impact of Corporate Average Fuel Economy (CAFE) Standards* (Washington: National Academy Press, 2002), p. 20.

11. To the Bush administration's credit, it is possible that the 2003 and 2006 rulemakings may have had a slight positive effect by 2007 by, at long last, requiring better performance from light trucks. Since the new rules were to have a long lead time (2011), it is highly unlikely that they had more impact than simply the increase in oil prices, which began zooming up again in

2003. Also, since the courts eventually remanded the second of the new rules, it is unlikely that they were a primary incentive for manufacturers.

12. National Research Council, *Effectiveness and Impact of Corporate Average Fuel Economy (CAFE) Standards*, p. 19.

13. Curiously, the NRC report does not describe the carbon footprint in the standard fashion, as million metric tons of carbon dioxide. The estimate of 367 million metric tons of CO_2 used here equates to the NRC's figure of 100 million metric tons of carbon.

14. Energy Information Administration, *Annual Energy Review 2006*, table 12.1, "Emissions of Greenhouse Gases, 1980–2005," p. 341.

15. China's carbon dioxide emissions were estimated to exceed 5,653 million metric tons in 1999: Energy Information Administration, *Annual Energy Review 2005*. Since then, Chinese emissions have soared, surpassing U.S. figures in 2007.

16. *Central Valley Chrysler-Jeep Inc.* v. *Goldstone*, 529 F. Supp. 2d 1151 (E.D. Cal. 2007).

17. *State of California* v. *United States Environmental Protection Agency*, U.S. Court of Appeals, 9th Cir., No. 08-70011.

18. As of 2008, twelve states and the District of Columbia had embraced the California standard, and six others were considering it. Important though that is, together all these states would cover less than half of the market for new cars in the country. By, in essence, appropriating and extending the California system, the Obama administration will fill that gap.

19. The measure was formally titled "Consumer Assistance to Recycle and Save Program," and it passed as part of the Supplemental Appropriations Act of 2009.

20. Although the program helped sell an estimated 700,000 new cars in less than five weeks, by one estimate only about 200,000 of them were additional sales that would not have occurred otherwise. Bill Vlasic, "Brief Relief, but No Cure for Carmakers from Clunker Plan," *New York Times,* August 22, 2009.

21. See Mathew L. Wald, "Doing the 'Clunker' Calculus," *New York Times,* August 8, 2009, p. B3.

22. Cash-for-clunkers schemes, of course, suffer from a similar limitation: they may speed up the displacement of "clunkers" but force no reduction whatsoever in VMTs.

23. For a little over a decade, the European Union has pursued the functional equivalent of fuel efficiency goals in the form of voluntary agreements with automobile manufacturers to reduce tailpipe emissions. Only in 2007 did the EU initiate a mandatory effort. Likewise, Canada's fuel economy program, though modeled more closely on the U.S. program and initiated in 1976, also was voluntary, as has been Australia's. Before 2007, Japan and China were the only other big countries to have imposed mandatory fuel efficiency standards, Japan in 1999 and China in 2005. The nature and vintage of most of these foreign projects suggests that they were of relatively limited consequence for the mpg ranking of their auto fleets over the full lifespan of the U.S. CAFE experiment. In some places—the EU and China, for instance— recent tightening of the regulatory screws, however, could prove consequential in the years ahead. For a summary of the various regulatory regimes, see Feng An and others, *Passenger Vehicle Greenhouse Gas and Fuel Economy Standards: A Global Update* (International Council on Clean Transportation, July 2007).

24. Bob Lutz, *Autoline Detroit,* May 6, 2007.

25. A widely held view in recent years is that the income growth of "middle class" Americans has stagnated. But as Robert Z. Lawrence has persuasively demonstrated, properly measured, significant real gains have been chalked up over the past twenty years, even for blue-collar workers. See Robert Z. Lawrence, *Blue-Collar Blues: Is Trade to Blame for Rising U.S. Income Inequality?* (Washington: Peterson Institute for International Economics, 2008), chapter 2.

26. Pietro S. Nivola, *Laws of the Landscape: How Policies Shape Cities in Europe and America* (Brookings, 1999).

27. See Schipper, "Automobile Fuel Economy and CO_2 Emissions in Industrialized Countries," p. 16.

28. Lee Schipper and others, *Fuel Prices, Automobile Fuel Economy, and Fuel Use for Land Travel: Preliminary Findings from an International Comparison* (Berkeley, Calif.: Lawrence Berkeley Laboratory, 1992), p. 9; U.S. Department of Transportation, *Summary of Travel Trends: 2001 National Household Travel Survey*, p. 16 (http://nhts.ornl.gov/2001/pub/STT.pdf); Department for Transport, *Driving Force: Four-Fifths of Annual Distance Travelled Is by Car*, April 8, 2008 (www. statistics.gov.uk/cci/nugget_print.asp?ID=24).

29. Federal Highway Administration, *Highway Statistics*, table VM-1.

30. A *Washington Post* survey in 2005 found fully 86 percent of Washington area commuters commuting by car (www.washingtonpost.com/wp-srv/polls/2005027/q5/index.html).

31. An and others, *Passenger Vehicle Greenhouse Gas and Fuel Economy Standards*, pp. 11–13.

32. See O. Johansson and Lee Schipper, "Measuring the Long-Run Fuel Demand of Cars," *Journal of Transport Economics and Policy* (September 1997).

33. Ibid.

34. Steven Mufson and David Cho, "Fuel Prices Challenge Cars' Reign," *Washington Post,* June 10, 2008, pp. A1–A19. Vehicle manufacturers were quick to react. In 2008 Ford Motor Company, for example, slashed its production of pickups and SUVs by 90,000 for the second half of the year. Nick Bunkley, "Ford Delays New Pickup and Reduces Production," *New York Times,* June 21, 2008, p. B3.

35. Journalistic discussion of motor-fuel price elasticity sometimes seems to view European consumption habits, like American, as seemingly indifferent to high prices, evidence to the contrary. For example, a piece in the *New York Times* in 2008 raised "questions as to how effective high prices by themselves can be in achieving the ambitious targets for reducing carbon dioxide emissions that European leaders have committed themselves to meeting." Yet, in the very next paragraph of the very same article, it was noted that as gas prices hit the equivalent of $10 a gallon, "purchases in Italy dropped 10 percent compared with the year before." See Elisabeth Rosenthal, "Memo from Europe: A Hard Habit to Break, Even with Gas at $10 a Gallon," *New York Times,* August 29, 2008, p. A7.

36. Schipper, "Automotive Fuel Economy and CO_2 Emissions in Industrialized Countries," p. 15.

37. The Surface Transportation Assistance Act of 1982 began for the first time releasing a small share of new gas-tax receipts for mass transit improvements. The 1991 reauthorization finally gave states much wider discretion to apportion trust fund disbursements to transit.

38. Quoted in William Plowden, *The Motor Car and Politics, 1896–1970* (London: Bodley Head, 1971), pp. 190–91.

39. James A. Dunn Jr., "The Politics of Motor Fuel Taxes and Infrastructure in France and the United States," *Policy Studies Journal* 21 (Summer 1993), pp. 271–84.

40. In the Senate Finance Committee, Senator David L. Boren of Oklahoma and Senator John B. Breaux of Louisiana were able to gut the president's so-called "Btu tax," shrinking it instead to a 7.3-cent increase in the federal excise on transportation fuels. Even that paltry result did not satisfy two other Democratic senators. In the end, the committee settled on 4.3 cents.

41. Michael D. Shear, "As Prices Soar, McCain Returns to Gas Tax Holiday Proposal" (http://blog.washingtonpost.com/the-trail/2008/06/as_prices_soar_mccain-returns.html).

42. Minimal tax increases were defeated, usually in a lopsided manner, on at least five different occasions during the extended "energy debates" of the 1970s.

43. Comité professionnel de pétrole, *Pétrole 90: Éléments Statistique* (Rueil-Malmaison, France: 1991), p. D14.

44. Peter Hughes, "Is Transportation Policy Going to Head Left, Right, or Center?" *Local Transport Today,* April 2, 1992, p. 11.

45. Bill Clinton and Al Gore, *Putting People First: How We Can All Change America* (Times Books, 1992), p. 91.

46. On this point and much of the preceding discussion, see in general Pietro S. Nivola and Robert W. Crandall, *The Extra Mile: Rethinking Energy Policy for Automotive Transportation* (Brookings, 1995), especially pp. 63–64. As is well known, U.S. public opinion is overwhelmingly opposed to higher federal gasoline taxes. An ABC/*Washington Post* poll in April 2007, for example, found 67 percent opposed to increasing "taxes on gasoline so people either drive less, or buy cars that use less gas." Only 32 percent favored this simple and effective idea. See also chapter 2 and chapter 6, this volume, for further discussion on public support of taxes on gasoline.

47. *Congressional Quarterly Almanac* (Washington: Congressional Quarterly, 1980), p. 488.

48. The 2007 legislation is titled Energy Independence and Security Act. Two years later, when the Obama administration announced that it would accelerate the act's timetable, enthusiasts wheeled out similar assertions: "This move will slash our dependence on oil and make us more energy independent," proclaimed one leading advocate. Steven Mufson, "Vehicle Emission Rules to Tighten," *Washington Post,* May 19, 2009, p. 14.

49. See William D. Nordhaus, "Economic Issues in Designing a Global Agreement on Global Warming," keynote address, International Meeting on Climate Change: Global Risks, Challenges, and Decisions, Copenhagen, March 2009.

50. See, for example, Robert Shapiro, "Waxman-Markey: Politics-as-Usual Meets Climate Change" (www.carbontaxcenter.org).

51. See, for instance, the ABC/*Washington Post* poll of April 2007. Seventy-nine percent of respondents opposed such a tax, 20 percent favored it, and 1 percent were unsure. Also see chapter 2, this volume, for further discussion of public opinion regarding electricity taxes as a means to reduce climate change.

8

Encouraging Renewable Electricity to Promote Climate Change Mitigation

IAN H. ROWLANDS

Traditionally, electricity has served to advance diverse development goals for countless societies around the world. Increases in the extent to which communities have been "electrified" have been closely correlated with increases in the values of a range of economic indicators, including gross domestic product and employment level.[1] Indeed, it is understandable that as the world community has developed strategies to advance human welfare through mechanisms such as the United Nations Millennium Development Goals, ensuring "reliable electricity supply to households, businesses, public institutions, commercial establishments, and industry" has been part of the dialogue.[2]

More recently, however, it has been increasingly recognized that the dominant means by which industrialized (and industrializing) societies have delivered electricity services have deleterious consequences associated with them. Significant among these are the impacts of electricity systems on global climate change. Two-thirds of the world's electricity is generated by combusting fossil fuels;[3] indeed, the power sector is estimated to be responsible for 26 percent of all global carbon dioxide emissions.[4]

Fossil fuels dominate in the electricity systems of the United States, as they do in the systems of many other nations worldwide. In 2006, for example, they generated nearly three-quarters of the electricity produced in the United States.[5] Thirty-nine percent of total U.S. carbon dioxide emissions come from the generation of electricity.[6] Given the fact that the United States is a substantial producer and consumer of electricity—indeed, it has been ranked first in terms of world-wide national production[7]—any comprehensive consideration of climate governance in the United States must necessarily include an examination of the country's system for generating, transmitting, and distributing electricity.

Considering the development and sustainability issues associated with the traditional means of generating electricity, a prime focus of this chapter will be to investigate how efforts to increase the use of renewable electricity sources are proceeding in the United States. Particular attention will be paid to the governance issues associated with those efforts: ways in which different levels of government within the federal system are making decisions that are mutually supportive and/or counterproductive. Prospects for increasing the provision of renewable electricity in the country's future climate change policies will be considered, along with alternative courses of action for accomplishing that goal.

Existing Policies

To date, various approaches have been undertaken in the United States at both the federal and state levels in an attempt to focus more strongly on the development of renewable electricity sources. Although not all approaches are considered, this section highlights two policies that have played a significant role in working toward that goal: the production tax credit (PTC) at the national level and the renewable portfolio standard (RPS) at the state level. After reviewing the national and state-level historical experiences with each approach, I consider the arguments of supporters and detractors of the PTC and the RPS to highlight the potential benefits and drawbacks inherent in renewable electricity policy efforts. Those arguments pave the way for a subsequent exploration of emerging approaches in the current renewable electricity debate at both levels of the federal system.[8]

Federal Experience: The Production Tax Credit

As part of the Energy Policy Act of 1992, the U.S. federal government introduced an income tax credit for the production of renewable electricity for qualifying facilities.[9] This policy, which was originally set to expire in 1999, established a ten-year production tax credit of 1.5 cents per kilowatt hour for both privately and investor-owned wind projects and biomass plants using crops grown specifically for energy provision (dedicated or closed-loop crops).[10] Over the years, the PTC has expired on three separate occasions and has been extended five times.[11] The most recent extension was in October 2008 as part of HR 1424, otherwise known as the Emergency Economic Stabilization Act of 2008. Division B of the enactment, the Energy Improvement and Extension Act, made important adjustments to the PTC. First, it extended the in-service deadlines for all existing qualifying renewable technologies to either December 31, 2009 (for wind), or December 31, 2010 (for all other technologies). In other words, a facility must have been or must be in

Figure 8-1. *U.S. Wind Power Capacity, Annual and Cumulative*

Megawatts

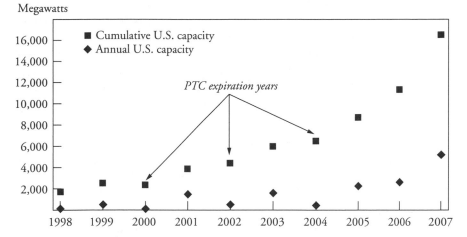

Source: Adapted from Ryan Wiser, "Wind Power and the Production Tax Credit: An Overview of Research Results," testimony prepared for Clean Energy: From the Margins to the Mainstream: Hearing before the Senate Finance Committee, March 29, 2007 LBNL/PUB-971 (http://eetd.lbl.gov/EA/EMP/reports/wiser-senate-test-4-07.pdf), with data from U.S. Department of Energy, Energy Information Administration, Electric Power Annual 2007, DOE/EIA-0348, p. 11.

service by those dates in order to qualify for the tax credit, which varies between 1.0 cents per kilowatt hour and 2.0 cents per kilowatt hour and which is inflation-adjusted over time. Second, the legislation expanded the list of qualifying resources to include marine and hydrokinetic resources, such as wave, tidal, current, and ocean thermal sources of energy.[12] In addition, the legislation also made changes to the definitions of several qualifying resources and facilities.[13]

Over the years, the PTC has drawn much attention from both supporters and critics of its policies. Proponents of the PTC have argued that it has served to help to spur investment in the renewable electricity industry, particularly in the large-scale wind industry. Indeed, the American Wind Energy Association (AWEA) highlights what it perceives to be a direct correlation between the continued presence of the credit and the level of new wind development in the country. Figure 8-1 reveals that the years in which the PTC lapsed were followed by years in which there were significant drops in the level of wind power investment. The corollary also appears to hold true: for instance, the uninterrupted commitment to the PTC between 2005 and 2007 gave a "steady base to build upon, enabling three straight years of growth. The most impressive expansion of the wind industry was seen in 2007, when a record 5,249 megawatts of new wind power capacity were added."[14]

As is often the case in discussions about renewable electricity, supporters of the PTC also contend that its continued existence will lead to significant job creation and local economic development. For instance, in the lead-up to the debate about the most recent extension of the PTC, Navigant Consulting issued a study (commissioned by AWEA and the Solar Energy Research and Education Foundation) that found that failure to extend the credit could result in the loss of 116,000 jobs and $19 billion in investment.[15] The study went on to argue that with greater certainty in the PTC's investment environment—that is, federal commitment to a longer "time-horizon"—the aforementioned benefits could be even larger. They would be generated by more renewable energy installations, more rational transmission planning, greater reductions in installed cost, enhanced private research and development, fewer siting and permitting conflicts, and reductions in operation and maintenance costs.[16]

Opponents of the PTC, however, have also contributed to the policy debate. Some, for instance, highlight the fact that because it is a subsidy, the PTC can make renewable energy developers overdependent on governmental financial contributions and thus discourage innovation. Another point of contention has been the total amount of financial resources channeled through the PTC. During discussions in 2004 about potential PTC extension, one critic, referring to the PTC as a "special-interest handout," argued that it "would cost $3 billion over ten years (2004–2013)."[17] Conversely, of course, many draw attention to the subsidies given to conventional forms of energy—either directly in terms of financial transfers[18] or indirectly in terms of their ability to externalize some of their costs, for instance, the costs of air pollution.[19]

The practical experience garnered through the PTC has also highlighted a number of challenges. For instance, the "stop/start" nature of the PTC has served to create an uncertain investment environment that leads to inefficiencies. AWEA, for one, notes that as "the PTC nears expiration, developers rush to complete projects before the deadline, leading to smaller projects and added costs, which result in higher electricity prices."[20] Others also note that given the stop/start pattern, wind companies are hesitant to set up manufacturing facilities in the United States.[21] Moreover, the tax credit has done little to assist smaller renewable energy facilities, which, some say, is where support should be directed as society aims to transform its centralized electricity system to one that is distributed. Lastly, PTC resources have tended to be largely directed to wind technology, whereas the preferred system for many would include a greater diversity of technologies.[22]

State Experience: The Renewable Portfolio Standard

At the state level, the renewable portfolio standard traditionally has been, and continues to be, the most widely used means of advancing renewable electricity in the United States. This policy serves to reserve a portion of the broader electricity market for renewable resources by obliging market participants to ensure that a predetermined share of their total electricity supply is provided by renewable electricity facilities; that share usually increases over time. Fulfillment of that obligation—on the part of all electricity generators within the market—may often be facilitated by the use of some kind of "tradable renewable energy certificates."[23]

The United States has been identified as the birthplace of the RPS; the term itself was introduced in discussions in California during the mid-1990s.[24] Indeed, the concept, if not the specific phrase, predates that by at least a decade, with an Iowa initiative dating from the early 1980s.[25] It has only been during the past decade, however, that the renewable portfolio standard has become more widely applied[26]—so much so that as of 2009, twenty-nine states and the District of Columbia had implemented mandatory RPS policies that involve markets that, collectively, account for more than half of nationwide retail electricity sales.[27]

As with the PTC, the supporters and opponents of the RPS underscore the potential advantages and drawbacks that it poses as a policy program. Supporters highlight a number of benefits associated with its implementation. For one, it serves to deliver a particular energy policy goal; more specifically, it virtually assures the development of a predetermined quantity of renewable electricity.[28] For example, if a community wants 1,000 gigawatt hours (GWh) of renewable electricity in its system of 100,000 GWh, then a 1 percent RPS will achieve that goal. As a result, it has the potential to be especially effective in reaching public policy goals related to energy and, by association, the environment.

In addition, by virtue of relying on market mechanisms to determine which renewable electricity facilities are constructed and operated, an RPS encourages cost reductions among competing energy producers. Each will be catalyzed to innovate, in order to lower costs, so that it will have a better chance of securing access to the renewable electricity market in its particular jurisdiction. Indeed, while renewable electricity is often cited as being more expensive,[29] a recent review found that the "median bill impact [of a renewable portfolio standard on a typical residential customer] . . . is an increase of only $0.38 per month."[30] Moreover, it is left to the same producers to determine how costs should be reduced; thus, an RPS approach helps to give private market participants greater flexibility in their decisionmaking.

Critics, however, maintain that RPS has several limitations. First, notwithstanding the fact that competition among potential producers can drive the price of a product down, the price under an RPS is not known in advance. Accordingly, the financial impact of the introduction of an RPS system (which may be borne by all ratepayers or all taxpayers or some combination of the two) is discovered only after introduction and implementation of the policy. The uncertainty about the current and future price of renewable electricity can "increase the financial risks faced by [renewable energy technology] developers and [reduce] their incentives to invest" in such technologies.[31] Price uncertainty also holds potential problems for others. Should the cost of renewable electricity rise, at least in the short term "(when installed renewable generating capacity is not adequate to meet government-set demand) . . . electric utilities and, eventually, consumers" would face increased risks.[32]

Second, the financial impacts of RPS strategies may well be distributed unevenly, mirroring the distribution of renewable resources within a particular jurisdiction. Imagine, following the standard approach for an RPS, that a particular target has been implemented in a given area. It will be those parts of the area that have a good (low-cost) endowment of renewable resources that will host the facilities and therefore accrue many of the associated broader benefits, such as job creation, cleaner air, and local economic development. Critics argue that such windfall benefits could lead to, and/or exacerbate, development imbalances within that area.

Third, following the introduction of an RPS there could very well be not only a geographic concentration of activity but also a technological concentration of activity. It may be that the "lowest-cost renewable" is the one that has already had the most technological development, especially given resource availability across different media, such as sun, wind, water, and biomass. As a result, participants in the electricity system will flock toward that particular technology in order to meet their RPS obligations.[33] That, in turn, will serve to increase demand for that technology and could, given increased production of the same, lead to further reductions in its cost. While market proponents would maintain that that is a testament to the effectiveness of the system, others might decry the lack of diversity in the electricity supply portfolio. Indeed, the result may be that "less technologically mature, but potentially promising [renewable energy technologies], such as [solar-photovoltaics] may not receive a sufficient share of support to meet policymakers' development goals. The result can be greater inefficiency and higher costs in the long term."[34]

That result is reflected in the U.S. experience to date, for RPS policies have served primarily to stimulate developments in wind energy: between 1998 and 2007, 93 percent of increases in non-hydropower renewable capacity in states with RPS programs came from wind.[35] In response, some states have attempted to diversify their renewable electricity portfolios by setting aside a portion of their RPS for solar energy and/or distributed generation.[36] That, of course, serves to mitigate some of the advantages of an RPS that supporters cite, particularly with respect to overall costs. Indeed, it is also more "technology specifying" than RPS is in the first place. However, some object to that. Apt, Lave, and Pattanariyankool, for example, maintain that laws "ought to specify requirements that generation technologies must meet, such as low pollution, affordability, power quality, and domestic power sources, and leave the means of realizing the goals to technologists and the market. . . . Specifying the goals rather than the technologies will lead to a technology race that will serve society."[37] Hence, the debate surrounding the desirability of RPS as a policy strategy continues.

Emerging Approaches

A number of additional policy options are emerging in the renewable electricity debate at both the federal and state levels in the United States. Paradoxically, the emerging theme at the federal level is the approach that has recently dominated the state discussions—renewable portfolio standards—and the emerging theme at the state level is a variation on the approach that has recently dominated the federal discussions—the feed-in tariff (FIT), building on tax credits.[38] Thus, a review of recent federal developments provides context for a discussion of new policies at the state level, which first assesses the considerable experiences of feed-in tariffs within Europe. The discussion then turns to the arguments of supporters and detractors of the FIT, which serve to highlight the potential practical advantages and disadvantages of the approach, and sets the stage for consideration of implementation issues surrounding these approaches within a multilevel governance system.

Emerging Themes at the Federal Level

Despite the current significance of the PTC at the federal level, discussions regarding an RPS at the federal level have taken place for more than a decade. Ralls notes that "from July 1996 to August 2005, some twenty-five or more bills were introduced containing some form of renewable standard;"[39] similarly, Sovacool and Cooper observe that "federal legislation to establish a national renewable portfolio standard has failed no less than 17 times in the past 10 years."[40] Indeed, during the "107th, 108th, and 109th Congresses, the Senate passed an RPS, but it did not survive conference committee action."[41] That was turned on its head in August 2007, when "the House of Representatives passed a Federal RPS for the first time, as an amendment to a larger energy bill, by a 220-190 vote. The U.S. Senate, however, was unable to break a filibuster to include the RPS in the final energy bill."[42] Moreover, as highlighted throughout this volume, appetite at the executive level for climate governance was not high during the presidency of George W. Bush.

The political landscape changed in November 2008. With the election of President Barack Obama, coupled with the emergence of a Democrat-controlled Senate and House of Representatives, the prospects for climate governance at the federal level improved dramatically. Indeed, the new president entered the White House with a promise to pursue the Obama-Biden energy plan, entitled "New Energy for America," which called for the establishment of a 10 percent federal RPS by 2012 and also committed to an extension of the federal PTC for five years.[43]

The 111th Congress also saw new legislative developments. Central to discussions of climate governance, of course, is the landmark Waxman-Markey Climate and Energy Security Act. Initially intending to include a requirement for all electricity suppliers to generate 6 percent of their energy from clean sources by 2012, gradually increasing to 25 percent by 2025, the version that was passed in the House on June 26, 2009, established targets of 6 percent in 2010, 9.5 percent in 2014, 13 percent in 2016, 16.5 percent in 2018, and 20 percent in 2021–2030; provisions to meet part of the targets with energy efficiency were also part of the legislation.[44]

A noteworthy effect of the act, aside from its content, has been the renewed interest that it has helped foster at both the federal and state levels. When combined with a new administration also interested in climate governance and the already active involvement of the states in the issue, renewed interest in multilevel climate change governance has begun to take hold.

Emerging Approaches at the State Level

Within the context of renewed attention and interest in climate change governance at the national level, a new approach, traditionally associated with European efforts to advance renewable electricity, likewise seems to be gaining traction within the states.[45] While the RPS has traditionally predominated at the state level, the feed-in tariff has been gaining attention in parts of North America in recent years. In its most basic form, it is a payment (usually at a premium to the market price for conventional electricity) to renewable electricity facilities for every unit of electricity generated, and it is guaranteed for a number of years by a contract between the generator and some public and/or utility authority. Payment levels may be differentiated by technology or even by facility location.[46] For example, Germany's FIT—one of the most cited in discussions of this policy tool—obliged German grid operators to "pay for the feed-in of electricity generated from hydro, landfill gas, sewage treatment and mine gas, biomass, geothermal, wind, and solar sources."[47] In 2005, the minimum payments (which were differentiated by energy source, by size of the facility, and, in the case of wind, by location) ranged from "5.39 euro cents/kWh (kilowatt-hour) for electricity from wind energy as a basic payment and 6.65 euro cents/kWh for electricity from hydropower to 59.53 euro cents/kWh for solar electricity from small façade systems."[48]

FITs have been applied in a number of locations besides Germany. "By the end of 2007, 46 countries and federal states worldwide had introduced feed-in systems as their major instrument to incentivize deployment of renewable electricity—18 out of 27 EU member states are using [feed-in tariffs]."[49]

Like supporters and skeptics of other approaches, those of the FIT concept have identified a number of advantages and disadvantages to the approach. Firstly, proponents argue that FITs have led to an increase in renewable energy facilities. In the earlier days of the European debate—during, in particular, debates surrounding the preferred approach for a harmonized strategy[50]—comparisons often were made between those countries that had traditionally adopted FITs (Denmark, Germany, and Spain) and those that had adopted a variation of an RPS, in particular a "bidding system" (Ireland, Italy, and the United Kingdom). It was maintained that FITs were "superior to other methods that have been tried in the EU."[51] More recent studies reinforce that position. Nicholas Stern, for example, notes that "[c]omparisons between deployment support through tradable quotas and feed-in tariff price support suggest that feed-in mechanisms achieve larger deployment at lower costs."[52]

In addition, the International Energy Agency released a report in which it observed that the "group of countries with the highest effectiveness (Germany, Spain, Denmark and, more recently, Portugal) used feed-in tariffs to encourage wind power deployment."[53] Finally, comparing the two main types of support schemes, namely quota obligations (yet another variation on the RPS approach) and feed-in tariffs, the Commission of the European Communities observed that experience from EU member states suggests that the latter "achieve greater renewable energy penetration at lower costs for consumers."[54] Moreover, the certainty that investors receive with regard to their financial future has often been cited as a reason why feed-in tariffs have led to a significant amount of renewable electricity deployment. For instance, Stern maintained that "the assurance of long-term price guarantees" was central to the success experienced by FITs to date.[55]

As a final advantage, feed-in tariffs also encourage diversity across both space and technologies—a potential benefit in political terms. By distributing policy benefits across different locations in a jurisdiction (including those areas that have less formidable renewable energy resource endowments) and different sectors in the renewable energy industry (including those technologies that are not currently cost effective), FITs can generate support for the FIT approach itself and for renewable electricity in general across a broader range of constituencies.[56] In addition, distributed geographical settings and technological platforms can also serve to improve performance of renewable energy systems through potential resource complementarities.

Critics of feed-in tariffs, however, often focus on their perceived costs. A World Bank study found that electricity prices are lower in markets with competitive policy regimes than in those with feed-in policies.[57] The higher costs are said to follow from the requirement that policymakers set the level of payments for different technologies in advance of their widespread deployment.[58] There are, of course, incentives on the part of renewable energy entrepreneurs—who, in fact, know the cost profile the best—to overestimate the cost. That leads some to conclude that "payment amounts for individual technologies (e.g., wind, solar, geothermal), payment structures (e.g., fixed or declining), and payment duration . . . can require significant 'guesswork' on the part of policymakers as to future market conditions and rates of technological improvements. Essentially, traditional [feed-in tariff] designs require government policymakers to substitute their judgment for that of markets in the selection of long-term, technological 'winners and losers.'"[59]

Just a few years ago, not even one U.S. state had introduced FIT legislation. By May 2008, however, reports of FIT (or FIT-like) legislation were emerging. At that time, one study observed that "six states have introduced feed-in tariff bills, and another eight states have considered, or are considering, similar legislation."[60] California was one of the first to do so, and Michigan's legislation has been one of the most influential.[61] To that list, Gipe would add Washington state, which, he notes, enacted a solar feed-in tariff in 2005, the first of its kind in North America.[62] Indeed, another thirteen states could be added to the list, particularly if the definition of feed-in tariffs is interpreted broadly enough to include production incentives—"cash payments based on the number of kilowatt-hours a renewable energy system generates."[63] Keeping the definition of FIT to the "purest" form— the one based on the original European model—many analysts argue that the program implemented by the municipal utility in Gainesville, Florida, is, indeed, unique in the United States.[64] In any case, it is clear that interest in such an approach at the state level is growing.

Promoting Renewable Electricity in a Multilevel Governance System

The issues surrounding the implementation of some of the most significant existing and emerging policies in the development of renewable electricity sources at both the federal and state levels of government are an important facet of the debate. A major focus of the following discussion surrounds the unique challenges posed by the need to develop policy to meet the often conflicting requirements of jurisdictions regulated by multiple levels of government (see also chapter 14 in this volume). Differing views surrounding the most appropriate geographical reach of policy are explored—namely, whether either "higher" or "lower" jurisdictional areas should be regulated. Here, jurisdictional "levels" are defined only in terms of their geographic reach; a "higher" level has a larger and more physically diverse territory, while a "lower" level has a smaller and less diverse territory. Questions also arise with regard to how policies at both levels would coexist. While the course of future legislation cannot be known unequivocally, there are certainly clear signs that the prospects favoring, for example, some kind of federal RPS are unprecedented. That has encouraged an extraordinary amount of speculation about how this new regulatory requirement would interact with the existing patchwork of state-level activities.

The Traditional Scope of Electricity Systems

Electricity systems historically have been of a relatively restricted geographic scope—at lower geographic levels—for two important reasons. First, electricity must be consumed when it is produced, because electricity is relatively expensive to store, whether by batteries or other means; second, electricity is relatively costly to transport once produced. While transmission systems can serve to move electricity over long distances, not only is it costly to construct high-voltage transmission lines, but energy is lost when moved from generating facility to load center. That means that power stations traditionally have been constructed close to where electricity is in demand. It is true that fuel for power stations (for example, coal and uranium) can be transported over long distances, but in the case of renewable electricity, the "fuel" (for example, solar energy and moving water) cannot be transported in the same way. That constitutes an important underlying concern because it creates a possible limitation to the feasibility of certain proposals for the distribution of electrical energy sources.

Despite historical trends, there are three key reasons why consideration at the "higher" level could serve to catalyze increased use of renewable resources in the electricity supply. First, there would be a larger market for renewable energy technologies, and any individual technology might be able to reduce costs through economies of scale more quickly than would otherwise be the case. Conversely, lack of consideration of technologies at "higher" levels might result in the development of disparate strategies in a variety of lower-level jurisdictions. If that were the case, a renewable energy entrepreneur could very well have to develop slightly different products for different jurisdictions—for example, to meet different siting requirements and/or public participation obligations. The result could easily be "a renewable energy market that deters investment, complicates compliance, discourages interstate cooperation, and encourages tedious and expensive litigation."[65]

Some speculate that in the United States the lack of a single regulatory structure may be serving to slow the pace of development of renewable electricity. Certainly the increase in renewable electricity capacity has, in fact, been quite modest, notwithstanding the considerable attention given to state RPS policies. If large-scale hydropower is excluded, then the figure for the relative share of renewable electricity in the total electricity supply—about 2 percent—is the same today as it was ten years ago. "Even when all state RPSs are included in projections, [the Energy Information Administration] estimates that the contribution of renewable resources is unlikely to exceed 3 percent of total electricity supply by 2017 or 4 percent by 2030."[66]

The absence of a higher-level lead may also be hindering nationwide learning on the issue. While Rabe acknowledges that the predominant state-level RPS approach has fostered some cross-border learning, he concludes that on balance, it has been rather limited: "Much of this cross-state interaction . . . occurs only sporadically and state officials across the continent acknowledge that they lack resources to carefully evaluate other programs and draw important lessons. Review of legislative testimony in all of the states examined as case studies suggests only occasional and often imprecise reference to the experience of other states."[67]

Second, where there is a larger geographical area, there is greater potential for reducing the variability of supply from renewable resources because there would be, by definition, a wider range of resources available. For example, the expansion of geographic scope may provide access to an ocean, which might allow for use of tidal power to complement existing wind power. Sometimes, different renewables act in a complementary fashion—one intermittent resource may produce when another does not. Solar and wind power, for example, have been identified as suitable partners in some North American jurisdictions.[68] In addition, there would be a wider range of the same resource available in the area. It has often been argued, for instance, that wind farms in different "climate/weather" zones can similarly complement each other.[69] As the *Economist* succinctly put it: "The question of where the wind is blowing [in Europe] would no longer matter because it is almost always blowing somewhere."[70] The dispatch of renewable electricity thereby becomes more reliable and the value of its contribution to the electricity grid increases. That reliability can be facilitated by a coordinated approach over a larger geographic area.

Third, activity at the higher level could help to avoid a downward spiral to the so-called "brown" definition of "green":

> This could conceivably happen if competing jurisdictions were trying to attract new investment by loosening their respective definitions of "green." For example, one community might lessen the emission standards for landfill gas–fueled electricity facilities in order to attract the development of a new project (and the associated employment benefits, for instance). Mirroring larger debates about international environmental and social standards, the argument is simply that regulators might be willing to relax their respective standards for "green electricity" if it meant that energy developers would be willing to invest in their economy. A continent-wide standard could prevent this.[71]

Some observers suggest that the activities of individual states already are revealing their interest in using specific definitions to advance their own goals. While they are not, as the quotation above suggests, necessarily motivated by a desire to attract new investment, the particular instances often referenced highlight the ways in which a state has privileged its unique resource endowment—sometimes thought to be on the "browner" scale of green—in fulfilling its renewable electricity obligations. Doran, for example, argues that states "have crafted their RPS policies to meet their respective and often idiosyncratic policy objectives, renewable resource capabilities, and electricity market characteristics."[72] Examples include Pennsylvania, which has a number of coal-based products (including waste coal, coal gasification, and coal mine methane) among the technologies eligible for support under its RPS,[73] and Maryland, which includes poultry-litter incineration as part of its RPS, thus utilizing a by-product from a long-standing state-based industry.[74] In addition to limitations on which technologies are eligible, some states have in-state and/or in-region location requirements: to be eligible, renewable energy must be generated either within the state or within the surrounding region.[75] The "economic development driver" behind many RPSs—and thus the fact that they are being tailored to local conditions—may explain why they have developed relatively independent of each other.[76] Attention at the higher level could serve to preempt this issue.

In addition to the arguments that call for more attention at the higher level, there are three key arguments that support the position that lower levels should play a leading independent role in determining how best to proceed with the development of renewable electricity policy. First, studies have revealed that support for renewable electricity increases when the projects are perceived to be "local" in terms of location, ownership, and process.[77] That relates to the concept of "subsidiarity," the belief that actions should be taken at the lowest level possible—for example, at the local rather than the national level—and also allows for the contribution of "local voices" in promoting sustainability. Indeed, "the argument is simply that those who live in a particular area are best able to judge what approaches are most sustainable."[78] The potential merits of lower-level administration pertaining to renewable electricity are suggested below, as both a theoretical and practical concept:

> Regional consortiums, states, local municipalities, and individual utilities are best positioned to evaluate the panoply of renewable data, in conjunction with their policy objectives, to establish programs that work for their citizens and consumers. At the end of the day, the goal of any renewable program should be to provide cleaner, reasonably priced and reliable electric service. Mandates such as a federal RPS will not achieve these goals.[79]

In addition, it is important to remember that electricity is a local commodity that cannot be easily transported. Therefore the "bar," or the point at which what qualifies for policy support is divided from what does not, may well vary in different locations. Following examples from "eco-labeling" programs, many argue that the best 20 percent of resources should be supported in order to reward a sufficient number of activities while still giving the majority an incentive to perform better. Given the local nature of renewable electricity, communities themselves should be able to define what constitutes the "best 20 percent"; different communities, of course, may arrive at different conclusions.[80]

From a nationwide perspective, because wind energy is often identified as being one of the most cost effective of the renewable electricity technologies—and even more so in areas that have more wind because more electricity can be generated with the same wind turbine—those in the Southeast in particular have argued that they would end up paying a lot of money to those in "windier" parts of the country for renewable energy credits. Moreover, they contend, because the renewable energy activity would be elsewhere, they would not accrue the local benefits often associated with policies to support the promotion of renewable electricity.[81] As it now stands, it is the states in the center of the country—especially the Plains states of North Dakota, Texas, Kansas, South Dakota, and Montana—that would gain from a federal RPS that did not privilege particular technologies, thus encouraging wind power in particular.[82]

Last, in areas that are new and complex, it is advantageous to try as many different policy approaches as possible, so that, to adapt a phrase, "many flowers can bloom." The argument is that the challenges of transforming domestic electricity systems are so great that different strategies must be tried in order to learn what is and is not successful under various conditions. According to this argument, learning can occur only through a process of trial and error, hopefully resulting in ultimately successful outcomes. Suppositions of this kind are often heard in discussions regarding U.S. environmental policy:

> The states are generally believed to act as classic "laboratories of democracy," a concept Supreme Court Justice Louis Brandeis promulgated in a dissenting opinion 75 years ago. State policymakers have access to knowledge of local problems and conditions and are often more accountable to their constituents. Because they are closer to environmental problems and the regulated community, the states can devise more manageable and appropriate policies capable of catering to individual needs and exploiting opportunities peculiar to regions. State action can provide opportunities for experimentation in designing policy, as the existence of many states acting at once promotes diversification and innovation.[83]

With respect to renewable electricity policy, there are fears that higher-level action could serve to water down the best of state-level initiatives and thereby lead to some kind of "lowest common denominator." Such views cut across ideological and geographic lines, reflecting, in the words of one official, "a deep state-based desire that . . . 'the feds not come in and mess up all the good stuff we've been trying to do.'"[84] Indeed, those states that have invested heavily in RPS—in terms of both financial resources and human resources—may well feel unfairly treated if a new federal-level initiative were implemented to change the course that they have taken.

Moving Forward: Summary and Conclusions

This chapter focuses on the efforts being made to increase the use of renewable electricity within the United States, with particular emphasis on the governance issues arising from those endeavors at both the federal and state levels. One issue concerns the means to facilitate increased use of renewable electricity. Notably, the traditional reliance on tax credits at the federal level and renewable portfolio standards at the state level is being supplemented by consideration of an RPS at the federal level along with feed-in tariffs in the states, which build on such tax credits as currently exist at the national level. Arguments have been made in favor of both higher and lower levels of geographical reach in renewable electricity policy—a key consideration in any future climate policy.

Many other important considerations emerge from this discussion. For instance, while different sources of renewable electricity offer a promising way forward, the current and potential roles that other power sector strategies play in climate governance—such as carbon capture and sequestration, energy efficiency and use of low-carbon energy, and nonrenewable options (such as nuclear power)—all continue to warrant significant attention. It also should be recognized that the United States has a highly diverse portfolio of production methods and resources. Indeed, certain states' electricity supply portfolios are dominated by coal (for example, that of West Virginia, where 98 percent of all electricity is generated by this resource), natural gas (Rhode Island, 97 percent), nuclear power (Vermont, 72 percent), hydropower (Washington state, 76 percent), and petroleum products (Hawaii, 78 percent).[85] Those figures underscore the diversity with which policymaking must contend in a system of multilevel governance, and more specifically, the diversity that it must take into account to develop and implement sound solutions regarding renewable electricity.

Last, efforts to promote the increased use of renewable electricity are not always driven primarily by concerns about climate change. As seen with the RPSs currently in place in the U.S. states, for example, economic development often is a major motivator for the increase in attention to electricity from solar, wind, small-scale hydropower, biomass, and other sources.[86] Nevertheless, increased use of renewable sources of electricity is an important part of the broader set of options that needs to be examined and ultimately pursued in order to address the challenge of global climate change.[87]

At a potential turning point in U.S. politics such as the present, it is fitting to conclude this chapter with a focus on the future by exploring the most effective way forward. While much of the discussion presented might suggest that a strategy must ultimately be implemented at either the state or federal level, an optimal approach may consist of a combination of the two. That would serve not only to circumvent the constitutional conflicts that seem to be lurking in the wings[88] but potentially to accentuate the benefits of an approach based on each level.

In practice, that would mean that the work of those advocating state-level strategies to promote renewable electricity should be supported to a greater extent; moreover, increased effort should be made to ensure that evaluation of different strategies is undertaken.[89] A federal strategy to encourage at least some degree of activity and innovation across the country—which would provide a baseline from which individual states (and cities[90]) could operate—also is desirable. Sovacool and Berkenbus, for example, maintain that

jurisdictional overlap is not only possible, but may even be preferable. . . . Federal preemption would not be permitted to snuff out these
"laboratories of democracy" that wish to go forward with bold, aggressive,
and experimental programs. If these state programs are successful over time,
one would expect to see their results gradually incorporated into the federal
program.[91]

Similarly, Kammen argues that "the pursuit and steady increase of renewable
energy portfolio standards as a baseline, and in the cities, states, and regions with
[a] mandate to pursue more aggressive policies, the addition of feed-in laws to
diversify and expand the number and type of clean energy producers" should be
seriously considered.[92]

As highlighted throughout part 4 of this volume, the experience in the European Union also is worth reflection, as the EU also operates under a multilevel
system in which there has been much discussion about the relative desirability of
action by individual member states or by the European Commission as a whole.
In 2001, when the Commission's Directive on Renewable Electricity was introduced, it was anticipated that it was only a matter of time before a harmonized,
EU-wide strategy would be in place.[93] What gradually emerged, however, was
recognition that such a singular approach may not be the best way forward. In its
2005 report, the Commission reported that "harmonisation of support schemes
would be premature, as the internal electricity market is not functioning properly,
greater interconnector capacity is needed, national support to conventional electricity producers continues to distort the market, and there has not been sufficient
experience accumulated to determine the best choice of support scheme."[94] Many
of those points appear equally germane with respect to U.S. policy. Thus, it may
well be that the conclusion reached by the Commission—that the "national
experiments" should continue—might transfer across the Atlantic.

Notwithstanding the fact that strategies at different levels continue to coexist
in Europe, some degree of coordination also appears to be emerging, built on the
respective strengths of the various approaches. In Europe, it is recognized that
even if there eventually is agreement on what instrument is most desirable at
higher levels, that instrument is not likely to be sufficient to catalyze a full range
of renewable electricity investments. Therefore, some activity at the lower levels
is virtually inevitable.[95] That lesson might apply equally to the United States,
where a strategy that is true to a broader notion of "balanced federalism" may
include federal decrees that set "floors" for minimum levels of activity, while individual states would still have the latitude to take the initiative and to respond to
particular, local circumstances.

The EU experience also is instructive with regard to integration across different policy strategies—particularly in the "RPS versus FIT" debate. In Europe,

many support schemes, for example, have been "reformed to introduce market signals through the incorporation of market prices using premiums rather than feed-in tariffs, thus improving the compatibility of the support with internal market rules and adjustments of tariffs to reflect decreasing production costs."[96] In that way, a higher-level preference for an RPS-type approach is made consistent with a lower-level preference for a FIT-type approach. The same conversation is taking place in the United States, where it has been argued that "the two can be structured to work together—and can even do so synergistically."[97] The challenge is, of course, to determine how they can be coupled so that their respective advantages can be realized.

Finally, another debate involves the issue of whether climate governance should concern itself with particular sectors or adopt a broader approach. An example of the former is, of course, the subject of this chapter—namely, strategies for decarbonizing electricity supply systems. An approach that was true to the latter would focus across all climate-relevant sectors; a tangible example of this is the provision for cap and trade within the Waxman-Markey Climate and Energy Security Act. Some argue that just as the FIT strategy is problematic because it "picks favorites"—that is, because it identifies particular renewable electricity technologies for support—any renewable electricity policy is equally problematic for the same reason: by "picking" a specific sector (in this case, electricity) for carbon reductions and thus privileging politicians' judgment over that of the market, the policy is inevitably inefficient. By contrast, they continue, a price on carbon should be established, which would let entrepreneurs find the best strategy for climate change mitigation. That may involve substantial decarbonization of electricity supply systems, or it may not; the market would decide.

In any case, it is clear that the United States is in a position not only to build on the experience that it has accrued at the national and state levels but also to learn from others in pursuing governance strategies for achieving effective energy policies. The United States also is well-poised to exercise leadership in a world that is still searching for sustainable strategies that recognize the need to reduce and eventually to eliminate carbon dioxide and other greenhouse gas emissions.

Notes

1. S. H. Yoo, "The Causal Relationship between Electricity Consumption and Economic Growth in the ASEAN Countries," *Energy Policy* 34, no. 18 (December 2006), pp. 3573–82.

2. Vijay Modi, Susan McDade, and Dominique Lallement, *Energy Services for the Millennium Development Goals* (Washington and New York: International Bank for Reconstruction and Development and United Nations Development Programme, 2005) (www.energyandenvironment.undp.org/undp/indexAction.cfm?module=Library&action=GetFile&Document AttachmentID=1643).

3. International Energy Agency, *Key World Energy Statistics 2008* (Paris: 2008).

4. David Wheeler and Kevin Ummel, "Calculating CARMA: Global Estimation of CO_2 Emissions from the Power Sector" (Washington: Center for Global Development, 2008), p. 1 (www.cgdev.org/files/16101_file_Calculating_CARMA_FINAL.pdf). Note that not only do electricity systems have consequences for global climate change, but so too global climate change has a significant impact on electricity systems: the levels of hydropower reservoirs (and thus their ability to generate electricity) are affected by changing temperature and precipitation patterns. See S. R. Bull and others, "Effects of Climate Change on Energy Production and Distribution in the United States," in *Effects of Climate Change on Energy Production and Use in the United States* (U.S. Climate Change Science Program and the Subcommittee on Global Change Research, 2008) (http://www.climatescience.gov/Library/sap/sap4-5/final-report/sap4-5-final-all.pdf).

5. Energy Information Administration, *Electric Power Annual* (2007), table 1.1, with data for 2006.

6. Energy Information Administration, *Emissions of Greenhouse Gases in the United States 2006* (November 2007), p. 4.

7. International Energy Agency, *Key World Energy Statistics 2008*, p. 27.

8. See, for example, Database of State Incentives for Renewables and Efficiency (2009) (www.dsireusa.org).

9. Coupled with this was the introduction of a "Renewable Energy Production Incentive (REPI)," which conditionally provided an incentive of 1.5 cents per kilowatt hour to publicly owned entities. Further information may be found at Department of Energy, "Renewable Energy Production Incentive," 2009 (apps1.eere.energy.gov/repi/about.cfm [January 5, 2009]).

10. For more information, see, for example, Database of State Incentives for Renewables and Efficiency (www.dsireusa.org/library/includes/incentive2.cfm?Incentive_Code=US13F&State=Federal%C2%A4tpageid=1).

11. Ryan Wiser, "Wind Power and the Production Tax Credit: An Overview of Research Results," testimony prepared for *Clean Energy: From the Margins to the Mainstream: Hearing before the Senate Finance Committee,* March 29, 2007 (eetd.lbl.gov/EA/EMP/reports/wiser-senate-test-4-07.pdf).

12. This continues a trend that has developed over time—the general expansion of the definition of qualifying facilities, though different resources receive different levels of credit. Database of State Incentives for Renewables and Efficiency (2009), (www.dsireusa.org/library/includes/incentive 2.cfm?Incentive_Code=US13F&State=federal&currentpageid=1&ee=1&re=1).

13. Ibid.

14. American Wind Energy Association, "Legislative Affairs" (Washington: 2008) (www.awea.org/legislative/).

15. Navigant Consulting, *Economic Impacts of the Tax Credit Expiration* (Burlington, Mass.: 2008), prepared for the American Wind Energy Association and the Solar Energy Research and Education Foundation (www.awea.org/newsroom/pdf/Tax_Credit_Impact.pdf).

16. Wiser, "Wind Power and the Production Tax Credit."

17. Charli E. Coon, "The Energy Bill Returns: Still a Missed Opportunity" (Washington: Heritage Foundation, June 15, 2004) (www.heritage.org/Research/EnergyandEnvironment/wm521.cfm). For an overview of perspectives, see, for example, Fred Sissine, "Renewable Energy: Background and Issues for the 110th Congress" (Washington: Congressional Research Service, October 5, 2007).

18. Energy Information Administration, *Federal Financial Interventions and Subsidies in Energy Markets 2007,* Report SR/CNEAF/2008-01 (Washington: 2008).

19. V. M. Fthenakis and H. C. Kim, "Greenhouse-Gas Emissions from Solar Electric and Nuclear Power: A Life-Cycle Study," *Energy Policy* 35, no. 4 (April 2007), pp. 2549–57.

20. American Wind Energy Association, "Wind Energy Production Tax Credit (PTC)" (www.awea.org/pubs/factsheets/ptc_fact_sheet.pdf).

21. Wiser, "Wind Power and the Production Tax Credit."

22. Carolyn Elefant, *Show Me the Money: Federal and State Public Funding, Benefits, and Subsidy Programs for Ocean Marine Renewables,* Hydrovision Conference, Sacramento, California, July 18, 2008 (www.slideshare.net/carolynelefant/show-me-the-money-benefits-for-marine-renewables-presentation?type=powerpoint).

23. REN21, "Renewables 2007 Global Status Report" (Paris: REN21 Secretariat, and Washington: Worldwatch Institute, 2008), p. 25 (www.ren21.net/pdf/RE2007_Global_Status_Report.pdf).

24. Nancy A. Rader and Richard B. Norgaard, "Efficiency and Sustainability in Restructured Electricity Markets: The Renewables Portfolio Standard," *Electricity Journal* 9, no. 6 (July 1996), pp. 37–49.

25. Nathan E. Endrud, "State Renewable Portfolio Standards: Their Continued Validity and Relevance in Light of the Dormant Commerce Clause, the Supremacy Clause, and Possible Federal Legislation," *Harvard Journal on Legislation* 45 (2008), p. 262. In contrast, Benjamin K. Sovacool and Jack N. Barkenbus, "Necessary but Insufficient: State Renewable Portfolio Standards and Climate Change Policies," *Environment* 49, no. 6 (July-August 2007), p. 23, reports that the Iowa law dates from 1985 and that it was followed by the introduction of a Minnesota law in 1994.

26. Cliff Chen, Ryan Wiser, and Mark Bolinger, "Weighing the Costs and Benefits of State Renewable Portfolio Standards: A Comparative Analysis of State-Level Policy Impact Projections," LBNL-61580 (Berkeley, Calif.: Lawrence Berkeley National Laboratory, March 2007) (http://eetd.lbl.gov/ea/ems/reports/61580.pdf).

27. Ryan Wiser and Galen Barbose, "Renewable Portfolio Standards in the United States: A Status Report with Data through 2007," LBNL-154E, revised April 25, 2008 (Berkeley, Calif.: Lawrence Berkeley National Laboratory), p. 1.

28. For additional examples of the benefits of the renewable portfolio standard, see, for example, Ryan Wiser, "Renewable Portfolio Standards: What Are We Learning?" NARUC Winter Conference, Washington, March 9, 2004 (eetd.lbl.gov/ea/EMP/reports/Renewable_Std.pdf).

29. Renewable energy proponents maintain that this is because of the subsidies given to conventional electricity, as well as the willingness of society to allow conventional sources to "externalize" some of their costs. See, for example, the work of New Energy Externalities Development for Sustainability 2009 (www.needs-project.org/).

30. Chen, Wiser, and Bolinger, "Weighing the Costs and Benefits of State Renewables Portfolio Standards," p. i. There are, of course, challenges to this assertion. In Massachusetts, for example, "a lack of long-term contracts to support new renewable development (coupled with high demand for RECs and difficulties in siting and permitting) has resulted in ratepayer costs that are substantially higher than anticipated" (Chen, Wiser, and Bolinger, p. vii). More specifically, more than one-quarter of the RPS was met by means of an "alternative compliance payment," set at $55.13/MWh in 2006. Massachusetts, Division of Energy Resources, "Massachusetts Renewable Energy Portfolio Standard: Annual RPS Compliance Report for 2006," February 15, 2008, p. 4 (www.mass.gov/ Eoeea/docs/doer/rps/rps-2006annual-rpt.pdf).

31. Jonathan A. Lesser and Xuejuan Su, "Design of an Economically Efficient Feed-In Tariff Structure for Renewable Energy Development," *Energy Policy* 36 (2008), p. 983.

32. Ibid.

33. As the authors reviewed the future impact of RPS activities, they found that "wind is expected to be the dominant technology, representing in aggregate 62% of incremental state

RPS generation across all of these studies combined." Chen, Wiser, and Bolinger, "Weighing the Costs and Benefits of State Renewables Portfolio Standards," p. ii.

34. Lesser and Su, "Design of an Economically Efficient Feed-In Tariff Structure for Renewable Energy Development."

35. Wiser and Barbose, "Renewable Portfolio Standards in the United States," p. 1. "Big wind" brings with it challenges associated with siting, transmission corridor planning, and development and so on. See Jay Apt, Lester B. Lave, and Sompop Pattanariyankool, "A National Renewable Portfolio Standard? Not Practical." *Issues in Science and Technology* (Fall 2008).

36. Wiser and Barbose, "Renewable Portfolio Standards in the United States," p. 1.

37. Apt, Lave, and Pattanariyankool, "A National Renewable Portfolio Standard? Not Practical." Interestingly, however, recent initiatives have introduced "energy efficiency" into RPS legislation. That would serve, at least to some extent, to counter this trend. See Wiser and Barbose, "Renewable Portfolio Standards in the United States," p. 1.

38. An early example of federal support, somewhat akin to though more modest than the "feed-in tariffs," was the Public Utilities Regulatory Policies Act of 1978. For more on this, see, for example, Richard F. Hirsh, "PURPA: The Spur to Competition and Utility Restructuring," *Electricity Journal* 12, no. 7 (August–September 1999), pp. 60–72.

39. Mary Ann Ralls, "Congress Got It Right: There's No Need to Mandate Renewable Portfolio Standards," *Energy Law Journal* 27, no. 2 (2006), p. 452.

40. Benjamin K. Sovacool and Christopher Cooper, "Big *Is* Beautiful: The Case for Federal Leadership on a National Renewable Portfolio Standard," *Electricity Journal* 20, no. 4 (May 2007), p. 48.

41. Fred Sissine, "Renewable Energy Portfolio Standard (RPS): Background and Debate over National Requirements," CRS Report for Congress (Washington: Congressional Research Service, December 5, 2007).

42. Wiser and Barbose, "Renewable Portfolio Standards in the United States," p. 34.

43. "Barack Obama and Joe Biden: New Energy for America," 2008 (www.barackobama.com/pdf/factsheet_energy_speech_080308.pdf).

44. It is important to recognize that a range of questions regarding the details of any RPS remains. They involve not only the target numbers and dates but also the inclusion or exclusion of specific technologies, the share that should be met by "new" renewables (and how "new" should be defined), and the share that should be met by energy efficiency.

45. Ian H. Rowlands, "Envisaging Feed-in Tariffs for Photovoltaic Electricity: European Lessons for Canada," *Renewable and Sustainable Energy Reviews* 9, no. 1 (February 2005), pp. 51–68.

46. REN21, "Renewables 2007 Global Status Report."

47. International Energy Agency, "Renewable Energy Sources Act (Erneuerbare-Energien-Gesetz EEG) 2004," 2009 (www.iea.org/textbase/pm/?mode=re&id=1969&action=detail).

48. Ibid.

49. Rainer Hinrichs-Rahlwes, "A Harmonized Feed-in System for the EU: Are We Ready to Seize the Opportunity?" *Renewable Energy World*, June 2, 2008 (www.renewableenergyworld.com/rea/news/reinsider/story?id=52505).

50. Ian H. Rowlands, "The European Directive on Renewable Electricity: Conflicts and Compromises," *Energy Policy* 33, no. 8 (May 2005), pp. 965–74.

51. N. I. Meyer, "European Schemes for Promoting Renewables in Liberalised Markets," *Energy Policy* 31 (2003), p. 668. See also International Energy Agency, *Energy Policies of IEA Countries 2002 Review* (Paris: 2002), p. 91, and V. Lauber, "REFIT and RPS Options for a Harmonised Community Framework," *Energy Policy* 32, no.12 (August 2004), pp. 1405–14.

52. Nicholas Stern, "Stern Review Report on the Economics of Climate Change" (London: H.M. Treasury, 2007), p. 366 (www.hm-treasury.gov.uk/sternreview_index.htm).

53. International Energy Agency, *Deploying Renewables: Principles for Effective Policies* (Paris: 2008), p. 17 (www.iea.org/Textbase/npsum/DeployRenew2008SUM.pdf); see also Wilson Rickerson and Robert C. Grace, "The Debate over Fixed Price Incentives for Renewable Electricity in Europe and the United States: Fallout and Future Directions," a white paper prepared for the Heinrich Böll Foundation, February 2007, pp. 9–10 (http://www.boell.org/downloads/Rickerson_Grace_FINAL.pdf).

54. Commission of the European Communities, "The Support of Electricity from Renewable Energy Sources: Accompanying Document to the Proposal for a Directive of the European Parliament and of the Council on the Promotion of the Use of Energy from Renewable Sources," Brussels, January 23, 2008, p. 8 (http://ec.europa.eu/energy/climate_actions/doc/2008_res_working_document_en.pdf).

55. Stern, "Stern Review Report on the Economics of Climate Change," p. 366.

56. For example, Lauber, "REFIT and RPS Options for a Harmonised Community Framework."

57. World Bank, *Statistical Analysis of Wind Farm Costs and Policy Regimes, Asia Alternative Energy Programme*, Working Report 31869 (2000). See also P. Menanteau, D. Finon, and M. Lamy, "Prices versus Quantities: Choosing Policies for Promoting the Development of Renewable Energy," *Energy Policy* 31, no. 8 (2003), pp. 799–812, and T. Ackermann, G. Andersson, and L. Söder, "Overview of Government and Market-Driven Programs for the Promotion of Renewable Power Generation," *Renewable Energy* 22 (2001), pp. 197–204. Of course, the counterargument has already been presented above. Moreover, Rickerson and Grace, "The Debate over Fixed Price Incentives for Renewable Electricity in Europe and the United States," p. 10, maintains that the "feed-in tariff therefore places pressure on technology manufacturers to supply low-cost, reliable systems to project developers."

58. Madlener and Stagl, "Promoting Renewable Electricity Generation through Guaranteed Feed-in Tariffs vs. Tradeable Certificates."

59. Lesser and Su, "Design of an Economically Efficient Feed-In Tariff Structure for Renewable Energy Development," p. 982.

60. Wilson Rickerson, Florian Bennhold, and James Bradbury, "Feed-in Tariffs and Renewable Energy in the USA: A Policy Update" (Washington: Heinrich Böll Foundation, May 2008), p. 3.

61. Ibid., pp. 5–8.

62. Paul Gipe, "Renewable Tariffs and Standard Offer Contracts in the USA," October 28, 2008 (www.wind-works.org/FeedLaws/USA/USAList.html).

63. Database of State Incentives for Renewables and Efficiency, 2009 (www.dsireusa.org/glossary/glossary.cfm?CurrentPageID=8#prod).

64. Karlynn Cory, Toby Couture, and Claire Kreycik, "Feed-in Tariff Policy: Design, Implementation, and RPS Policy Interactions," Technical Report NREL/TP-6A2-45549 (Golden, Colo.: National Renewable Energy Laboratory, March 2009), p. 9.

65. Sovacool and Barkenbus, "Necessary but Insufficient: State Renewable Portfolio Standards and Climate Change Policies," p. 24.

66. Ibid., p. 25.

67. Barry G. Rabe, *Race to the Top: The Expanding Role of U.S. State Renewable Portfolio Standards* (Washington: Pew Center on Global Climate Change, June 2006), p. 24.

68. Kari Larsen, "Load Balancing: PSE Installs Wind with PV," *Renewable Energy Focus* (September–October 2008), pp. 38–41.

69. Ian H. Rowlands and Carey Jernigan, "Wind Power in Ontario: Its Contribution to the Electricity Grid," *Bulletin of Science, Technology, and Society* 28, no. 6 (December 2008), pp. 436–53.

70. "Where the Wind Blows," *The Economist,* July 26, 2007, p. 81.

71. Ian H. Rowlands and Mary Jane Patterson, "A North American Definition for 'Green Electricity': Implications for Sustainability," *International Journal of Environment and Sustainable Development* 1, no. 3 (2002), p. 258.

72. Kevin L. Doran, "Can the U.S. Achieve a Sustainable Energy Economy from the Bottom-Up? An Assessment of State Sustainable Energy Initiatives," *Vermont Journal of Environmental Law* 7 (2006), p. 109.

73. Ibid.

74. Ralls, "Congress Got It Right," p. 468.

75. Endrud, "State Renewable Portfolio Standards: Their Continued Validity and Relevance," p. 264.

76. Barry G. Rabe, Mikael Roman, and Arthur N. Dobelis, "State Competition as a Source Driving Climate Change Mitigation," *New York University Environmental Law Journal* 14, no. 1 (2005), pp. 1–53.

77. E. Heiskanen and others, *Factors Influencing the Societal Acceptance of New Energy Technologies: Meta-Analysis of Recent European Projects* (Energy Research Centre of the Netherlands, 2008) (www.ecn.nl/docs/library/report/2007/e07058.pdf).

78. Rowlands and Patterson, "A North American Definition for 'Green Electricity,'" p. 260.

79. Ralls, "Congress Got It Right," p. 472.

80. Rowlands and Patterson, "A North American Definition for 'Green Electricity,'" p. 259.

81. Sissine, "Renewable Energy Portfolio Standard (RPS): Background and Debate over National Requirements," p. 8.

82. American Wind Energy Association, "Wind Energy: An Untapped Resource."

83. Sovacool and Barkenbus, "Necessary but Insufficient: State Renewable Portfolio Standards and Climate Change Policies," p. 23. See also Daniel Kammen, "It's (Long Past) Time to Plan a U.S. National Energy Strategy," *ClimateBiz,* August 31, 2007 (www.climatebiz.com/blog/2007/08/31/its-long-past-time-plan-a-us-national-energy-strategy).

84. Rabe, *Race to the Top*, p. 26.

85. Energy Information Administration, *Electric Power Annual* (2007), with data for 2006.

86. Barry G. Rabe, "Second-Generation Climate Policies in the American States: Proliferation, Diffusion, and Regionalization," *Issues in Governance Studies* 6 (August 2006) (Brookings).

87. R. E. H. Sims and others, "Energy Supply," in *Climate Change 2007: Mitigation*, edited by B. Metz and others, contribution of Working Group III to the Fourth Assessment Report of the Intergovernmental Panel on Climate Change (Cambridge University Press, 2007).

88. More specifically, the commerce clause of the Constitution permits the federal government to regulate commerce among the states (Article 1, section 8, clause 3). Therefore, should a state RPS policy be deemed an impediment to interstate commerce, a challenge could be launched. In addition, many feel that any "requirement that the renewable energy used to meet a state's RPS obligation be generated within the state itself . . . would almost certainly be struck down." Moreover, this issue is all the more salient "given the recent departure from the Supreme Court of Justices William Rehnquist and Sandra Day O'Connor, who held strong views on the power of states in relation to the federal government." Rabe, *Race to the Top*, p. 25. See also chapter 10, this volume. For additional reflection on potential consistency between new federal legislation and state legislation, see, for example, Endrud, "State Renewable Portfolio Standards: Their Continued Validity and Relevance," and Joshua P. Fershee, "Changing Resources,

Changing Market: The Impact of a National Renewable Portfolio Standard on the U.S. Energy Industry," *Energy Law Journal* 29, no. 1 (2008), pp. 49–77.

89. Edward A. Holt, *Increasing Harmonization among State RPS Programs*, prepared for the Clean Energy States Alliance and the Northeast and Mid-Atlantic RPS Collaborative (Harpswell, Maine: Ed Holt and Associates, August 2008) (www.cleanenergystates.org/JointProjects/RPS/Holt_CESA_RPS_Harmonization_d2_080819.pdf). See, as well, the work of the State-Federal RPS Collaborative at www.cleanenergystates.org/JointProjects/State-Federal-RPS.htm.

90. Cities—though not focused on in this chapter—have played and could continue to play important roles. See Charles W. Thurston, "More State, County, City Governments Expected to Offer Residential Financing," *Renewable Energy World*, October 17, 2008.

91. Sovacool and Barkenbus, "Necessary but Insufficient: State Renewable Portfolio Standards and Climate Change Policies," pp. 27, 29.

92. Kammen, "It's (Long Past) Time to Plan a US National Energy Strategy"; Rickerson, Bennhold, and Bradbury, "Feed-in Tariffs and Renewable Energy in the USA," pp. 14–15. Also note that there is nothing inherently "mutually exclusive" in the different kinds of politics being developed, specifically RPS and feed-in tariffs.

93. Rowlands, "The European Directive on Renewable Electricity."

94. Commission of the European Communities, "The Support of Electricity from Renewable Energy Sources," p. 13.

95. Ibid., p. 6.

96. Ibid., p. 14.

97. Cory, Couture, and Kreycik, "Feed-in Tariff Policy," p. 8.

9

Adapting to Climate Change: Problems and Prospects

MARC LANDY

Much of life, and more of public policy, involves a choice between cure and treatment, between removing the causes and adapting to the effects of trouble. Should I try to force my upstairs neighbor—who's six and a half feet tall and has a black belt in karate—to stop playing the drums at 2 o'clock in the morning, thereby rooting out the cause, or should I buy a pair of good earplugs to adapt to the effects of the noise? Should a state deal with the effects of crime by building more prisons to get more criminals off the street, or should it invest in efforts to get at the root causes of crime—drugs, illegitimacy, and unemployment?

The simple truth is that people and governments choose between cure and treatment options on a cost-benefit basis. But that simple statement, while true, fails to elucidate just how intractable root causes tend to be. They penetrate so deeply into the workings of society as a whole and are so deeply intertwined with cherished values and outcomes that they are extremely painful, difficult, and damaging to remove. Not only would eliminating the root causes of crime be extremely expensive but the governmental intrusiveness involved in *really* eliminating drug use, child abuse, and illegitimacy would dangerously undermine the privacy rights so cherished by a liberal society. And so we don't do it. A prime example of this is the trade-off between medical care and public health. A great deal of medical care expenditure goes to treat illness brought on by lifestyle choices: obesity, cigarette smoking, and drug addiction. Although some effort and funds are spent to discourage those choices—through, for example, anti-smoking campaigns and prosecution of drug dealers—far more is spent on treating their effects. In a free society it is simply too intrusive to force people to eat well or to prosecute drug users.

As we are currently witnessing, the seemingly insatiable greed that drives finance capitalism is capable of ruining lives and bringing the world economy virtually to a halt. And yet there is very little talk of getting at the "root cause" of the current financial collapse, greed. All the serious talk is of adaptation, which in the context of contemporary political economy means regulation. We live with the greedy beast that is the world capital market because it is so integral to providing the level of wealth on which our civilization depends. When the beast rattles its cage too aggressively we do not seek to change its nature. We strengthen the bars.

Until recently, the climate change debate has been dominated by discussion of cure, in the form of reductions in fossil fuel emissions. Cure occupied the moral high ground, seeking to rid civilization of a damaging activity, whereas adaptation to the effects of that activity has been made to seem ethically inferior because it connotes acquiescence. However, as in so many other policy disputes, the moral superiority of cure over treatment is highly contestable. To treat carbon use per se as a moral evil caricatures the role of fossil fuel in modern life. Fossil fuels pollute but they are also intrinsic to the way the people communicate, cultivate, manufacture, transport, heat, cool, educate, and entertain. They provide the energy underpinning everyday life much as markets provide the economic underpinning of much of what is laudable—as well as much that is deplorable—about contemporary civilization.

The current anomalous status of the climate change issue is in large measure due to the gap between the political rhetoric pervading it and an unstated acceptance of the benefits of carbon consumption. On the one hand, climate change has become a very popular political cause because it proffers a powerful apocalyptic message—each one of us is responsible for the coming global environmental cataclysm. Yet despite its great political resonance, the cause of CO_2 reduction has achieved very little practical success. Fossil fuels continue to constitute the overwhelmingly dominant mode of energy production. Petroleum, natural gas, and coal consumption have been far more responsive to changes in price than to exhortations to reduce our carbon footprints. Political leaders have proven unwilling to match their rhetorical condemnations of carbon use with serious practical policies to reduce it because they understand that their constituents simply will not abide the loss of the good life that fossil fuels provide (see, for example, chapter 2 of this volume on the relationship between public policy and public opinion relating to climate change).

Of late, a major shift in the strategy and tactics of organizations concerned with climate change has taken place. The United Nations Development Program now devotes considerable resources to funding adaptation activities in less developed countries.[1] The Heinz Center has issued a major survey of adaptation planning.[2] The Pew Center added a report on adaptation to its influential Climate Change 101 series.[3] Business consultant Alan Atkinson described a recent climate adaptation seminar in the following terms:

> Not long ago, a seminar on climate change adaptation here would have been a lower-profile event. It might have drawn a few dozen people, most of them academics, activists, and development workers. Even the topic would have been seen as controversial, even taboo: "Don't talk about adaptation," went the argument, "because that will signal that we've given up on stopping global warming." But as the evidence mounts that climate change is here, and that adaptation is imperative, that taboo has finally begun to crumble away. And today, there was a room full of officials, business execs, and consultants like me crammed into a rather small auditorium to hear about "Climate Change Adaptation—Finding the Business Opportunities." There was not a whiff of taboo in the room. In its place was the whiff of entrepreneurship—driven in part, I sensed, by a healthy dose of genuine fear.[4]

This chapter attempts to understand the various obstacles that confront climate change adaptation and ends with a call for some modest reforms to address at least some of the obstacles considered.

Markets, Risk, and Uncertainty

Market forces can and will drive a considerable amount of adaptation to climate change. Such voluntary adjustments are perhaps easiest to appreciate when climate change creates benefits. Farmers will cheerfully increase their purchases of seed, fertilizer, and machinery to take advantage of the longer growing seasons that some regions will enjoy if warming occurs. Likewise, shippers and freighter owners will readily adjust their business practices when the Great Lakes remain unfrozen for more of the year. If shorter winters reduce deaths from exposure and damage and injuries from skidding automobiles and from pedestrians slipping on the ice, emergency rooms, ambulance companies, and orthopedic surgery units will readily adjust their schedules accordingly and insurance companies can reduce their premiums. However, negative climate change can also drive voluntary adjustments. Fishermen whose catch is declining can cruise to different fishing grounds farther afield. Faced with water shortages, farmers can shift to more drought-resistant crops. Sweltering homeowners can purchase additional air conditioners (perhaps with money saved from reduced winter heating bills).

The examples cited above pertain to adaptation *after the fact*. Therefore they do not raise all the issues that climate-related spending decisions will pose, the related problems of information and uncertainty. In order to determine whether and how much to invest in adaptation *before the fact,* an investor needs to be able to make a reasoned assessment of how significant the climate-related threat is and how different amounts of investment correlate with different levels of damage prevention. Lack of information and uncertainty are fully in evidence regarding the massive infrastructure investments whose fate might well hinge on changes in climate. Undersea pipelines and oil and gas platforms may face added rigors imposed by more frequent strong hurricanes. Since power plants often are sited along the coast, they may require added protection against the threat of sea level rise. Roads, dams, water and sewer pipes, rail beds, power transmission lines, canals, and seaways may all be subjected to greater stresses due to increased heat, wind, and changes in precipitation patterns. But from the point of view of an investor, regardless of whether it is a government or a firm, the word *may* is simply inadequate.

Of course, investments are never made on the basis of perfect knowledge of the future. But infrastructure investments are especially problematic in this regard because they require long lead times and enormous sums of money. If the risks are underestimated, catastrophe may ensue. If the risks are overestimated, a great deal of extra money will be spent on unwarranted excess protection. Powerful political biases press in the direction of underinvestment. Cash-strapped state and local governments are notorious for underinvesting in low-visibility and long-term undertakings such as upgrading and rehabilitating infrastructure. A great deal of spending on infrastructure also is done by industries that are heavily regulated, most notably the electric utilities. However, they will underinvest in climate change adaptation if state regulators deny them the ability to pass on the cost of those investments to ratepayers.

Insurance

The same investment uncertainty problem, albeit on a smaller scale, affects the individual homeowner. Buying or building a home is the single largest investment that most people make, yet they must make that decision in the face of great uncertainty regarding the degree to which climate change will increase the likelihood that hurricanes, sea level rise, drought, or wildfires will damage or even destroy their property. Insurance provides a mechanism for coping with such uncertainties, but for a variety of reasons, both psychological and political, insurance has not succeeded as an adaptive tool.

Too many homeowners do not think about insurance as the economist thinks they ought to. They treat it as an investment, not as a risk hedge, and therefore they view it as a satisfactory purchase only when they make a claim and it is paid.[5] Hence the popularity of life insurance, since it is the only form of insurance that is almost guaranteed to pay off. Life insurance is not *really* an investment since, statistically speaking, people would be richer if they did not buy life insurance but invested their premiums in the capital markets. It is as much a risk hedge as other forms of insurance. Because of this misconception, homeowners underinvest in property insurance and have been very reluctant to buy insurance against low-probability but highly damaging events like floods.

To increase flood insurance purchases, in 1968 the federal government established the National Flood Insurance Program (NFIP), which offered highly subsidized rates in order to entice more at-risk homeowners to buy.[6] The subsidies extend only to existing structures; premiums for new structures built in high-hazard zones are intended to be actuarially sound. Therefore, the percentage of subsidized policies has declined over time, but 25 percent of all insured properties still pay subsidized rates. Until 2005, despite the subsidies, NFIP premiums were sufficient to pay off outstanding claims. In that year, however, Hurricanes Katrina, Rita, and Wilma combined to incur $21.9 billion in NFIP-insured losses, leaving it $17.5 billion in debt. The program had to borrow extensively from the U.S. Treasury in order to meet its obligations.[7]

Since 2005, Congress has been wrestling with how to both make the NFIP financially viable and improve its ability to perform as an adaptive tool. Both the House and Senate passed reform measures, but as of mid-April 2010, they had been unable to reconcile their differences. The House bill would have extended insurance protection to wind as well as flood damage. Because wind is covered by private insurance, insurers have a powerful incentive to try to prove that storm-related damage was caused by water and not wind. The bill also would phase out subsidies on premiums for businesses and second homes. The Senate version included the second home phase-out but did not extend coverage to wind. It forgave the NFIP's $17.5 billion debt to the Treasury, which the House version did not do.[8]

Private insurance also has proven itself of limited adaptive use. In the wake of Katrina, insurance rates soared. The price of catastrophe reinsurance in the United States increased significantly, rising 76 percent between July 1, 2005, and June 30, 2006, and 150 percent for Florida-only insurers over the same period.[9] Perhaps such steep increases reflect a realistic assessment by insurers about future hurricane risk. If so, they constitute an appropriate adaptive response by providing a disincentive to own or acquire property in disaster-prone areas. But the public has not been willing to abide by such increases, in no small measure because some insurers proved so reluctant and obstructive in paying past claims. The furor that arose in Mississippi led its leading home insurance underwriter, State Farm, to cease writing new policies. Several insurers have stopped writing policies for coastal Florida. Both Allstate and Nationwide Mutual no long write new policies for the eastern half of Long Island.[10] Insurance cannot perform its appropriate risk management role if it is unavailable. In response to the public outcry about soaring rates, Florida has opted to subsidize insurance rates, thereby depriving them of their value as an adaptation incentive.

In 1993, following Hurricane Andrew, Florida established the Florida Hurricane Catastrophe Fund (FHCF), which offers reinsurance for privately issued property insurance at a rate well below the market price. Thus insurance companies were able offer cheaper rates to property owners because the insurance that they must buy to cover their risks is subsidized. The law creating the FHCF stipulates that if reinsurance premiums are insufficient to pay outstanding claims, then it will issue revenue bonds to cover those costs and it may also, on an emergency basis, levy an assessment on all property and casualty policies issued in the state.[11] Both methods of fundraising shift costs away from storm victims to either state taxpayers as a whole or state property and casualty insurance policy holders as a whole. In either case, coastal residents are relieved of the burden of paying the full cost of insuring against the risks that they are incurring by choosing to reside in storm-prone areas. Consequently, insurance is deprived of its role as a market-driven adaptive mechanism.

Obstacles to Adaptation

As is true of most environmental problems, market-driven adaptation to climate change is hampered by externalities. Firms and individuals create environmental harms that they do not have to pay for. As discussed in more detail later, coral reefs suffer from such externalities, as they are degraded by onshore chemical and biological waste that rainwater runoff carries into the streams and that rivers empty into the ocean. No one pays for such wastes, and hence there is nothing to prevent them from harming the coral.

However, adaptation is impeded not only by technical barriers to market operation such as uncertainty, imperfect information, and externalities. Those difficulties are compounded by political objections often grounded on ethical principles. The problem posed by both the NFIP and the Florida insurance examples was not that the insurance market *would not* work, but that the state and national legislatures determined that it *should not* work. So far at least, Congress and the Florida legislature are behaving as if coastal residents should not bear the full risk of their choice of residence if the cost of so doing is viewed as prohibitive. In a related vein, many billions of dollars were spent enabling victims of Katrina to rebuild the towns and cities that the dreadful storm destroyed even though it would have been far cheaper to subsidize them to relocate to areas less prone to flood and wind damage. Similarly, the public is also willing to build water projects to irrigate drought-plagued farms and supplement diminishing water sources for Sunbelt cities rather than to press farmers and city dwellers alike to move to wetter places.

Impediments also arise when existing property rights regimes cannot account for climate-induced change, regardless of whether the change is, on the whole, beneficial. If current trends continue, melting Arctic ice will open up new polar shipping lanes, creating great new opportunities to cut shipping costs and increase trade.[12] The current law of the seas does not adequately address the question of which nations can claim control of shipping lanes that do not currently exist. This commercial bonanza could easily become a serious cause of international conflict.

Other effects of climate change on such issues are already being noticed. For instance, ocean warming is causing pollock to migrate from Alaskan to Russian waters.[13] Because a nation is permitted to exclude others from its territorial waters, this migration is threatening the livelihood of American fishermen. In much of the West, including the most drought-prone regions, water rights were established historically. Ranchers and farmers own the rights to specific quantities of water. The current property rights system makes no allowance for changes in the capacity of the rivers and streams to supply that water.[14] The problem is that a static principle of allocation is being applied to the dynamic reality of fluctuating supply. If the available supply decreases, each possessor of water rights owns a larger fraction of it, leaving little or no water left over for other claimants.

These legal and ethical questions pose the thorniest problems where, even in the absence of climate change, patterns of human settlement and resource exploitation have created very fragile ecosystems. Roads built in most places in the United States are not damaged by warmer temperatures, but Arctic roads are built on permafrost. This very brittle surface is subject to crack when the temperature rises above freezing.[15] Wildfires perform important ecological functions in the Rocky Mountain West; they become a problem only because homes have been built in highly fire-prone areas.[16] The damage from Katrina would have been orders of magnitude less if so many houses along the Mississippi Gulf Coast were not built right along the shoreline and if so much of New Orleans did not sit below sea level. Droughts in the West would not threaten drinking water supplies if the number of people living in low-precipitation areas had not grown so large. The most serious adaptation issues have emerged where human activity has created such ecological vulnerabilities.

The concept of ecological vulnerability also helps to explain why data indicating positive aggregate climatic effects can mask severe negative consequences. For example, some models predict that climate change will increase aggregate precipitation in the United States, thus giving the superficial impression that water will be more readily available for drinking and crops.[17] But in the Mountain West, the availability of water during the long, dry summers depends not on how much precipitation falls but on how and where it falls. Fall and spring rains hardly count. To have water when and where it is needed, Rocky Mountain homes and farms depend on the creation of a sufficient snowpack on the mountaintops and on the slow melting of that snowpack. If there is too little snow or if it melts too quickly, streams and aquifers will dry up during the course of the summer.[18] As these examples demonstrate, what appears to be a good situation nationwide bodes tremendous danger for particular vulnerable ecosystems.

Likewise, general circulation models (GCM) predict that the overall longer growing seasons resulting from global warming will increase aggregate crop yields.[19] However, peach and cherry farmers in Michigan can expect diminished crops because warmer temperatures earlier in the spring will encourage their trees to bud prematurely only to be destroyed by intermittent colder temperatures later in the spring.[20] For frost-vulnerable fruit trees what counts is not average temperature but the *timing* of temperature change. Warming followed by even a brief spell of cold bodes disaster.

Regulatory Failure

Thus adaptation to climate change is mostly a problem created by the coincidence of legal, economic, and ethical impediments to adaptation *and* the human-caused vulnerability of ecosystems. Unfortunately, the particular places where the two factors coincide have also proven to be highly resistant to the forms of regulation and planning that would offer the best hope of fostering successful adaptation. National environmental policy does not deal with ecosystems, except in very particular places like the national parks and national seashores. The landmark statutes that constitute environmental policy deal instead with particular media, such as air and water; particular practices, like surface mining, logging, and grazing on public lands; and the well-being of specific species of animals, including endangered species and marine mammals. Attempts have been made to integrate these various and often conflicting legal strictures into integrated location-based programs such as those that address the Great Lakes and Chesapeake Bay, but those efforts are the exception and their lack of strong statutory underpinning limits their effectiveness.

Despite the mass migration of people to the hurricane- and erosion-prone Atlantic and Gulf seacoasts and to the arid Southwest, there exists no special set of national policies aimed at minimizing the environmental strains that those mass migrations have caused. As of 2003 the population of U.S. coastal counties had grown to 153 million, a 28 percent increase since 1980. Those counties comprise 53 percent of the total U.S. population, but they constitute only 17 percent of its landmass.[21] Still, the United States has not developed anything resembling a coastal land use policy. It has similarly avoided setting restrictions on the settlement and use of dry lands. Indeed, there are few national regulations of any kind regarding where people may settle, or where roads, factories, and public facilities can be sited.[22]

Most states, with the notable exceptions of Oregon and Vermont, have been equally reluctant to make use of powerful but politically unpopular land use policies. Such policies as do exist are mostly a local creation that takes the form of zoning. With some exceptions, localities have not viewed zoning as an environmental tool to be used for the purpose of reducing ecosystem vulnerability; rather, zoning has served for the most part as a means of preventing commercial and industrial facilities from encroaching on residential neighborhoods.

When communities do use zoning as a means of preventing development, the effort has not necessarily been clearly related to the actual *environmental* vulnerability of the excluded land. Instead it has been an effort to maintain low density and preserve open spaces to maintain a particular quality of life regardless of the relative robustness of the ecosystem in the excluded areas.

Land use control and other exclusionary regulations, such as commercial fishing catch limits, aim to protect vulnerable ecosystems by decreasing the demands placed on them. An alternative to demand reduction is engineering. Instead of keeping homes and businesses out of flood-prone areas, human ingenuity and modern technology can be applied to divert rivers, build flood control dams, and install floodgates. Rather than limiting population growth or agriculture in drought-prone areas, it is possible to build additional reservoirs and to make them deeper in order to minimize evaporation losses. But not only are these engineering alternatives very costly in dollar terms, they also involve painful environmental trade-offs. Over the past several decades large numbers of dams have been destroyed in order to enable rivers to flow freely and wetlands to recover. Therefore, a call to build larger and deeper reservoirs—and the dams necessary to create them—will be greeted with deep hostility and powerful political opposition on the part of those who champion dam destruction. Likewise, the imposition of floodgates and other flood control structures have numerous and hard-to-anticipate impacts on aquatic ecosystems and are therefore anathema to those seeking to conserve those systems.

Each of the following three sections looks at an important and illustrative climate-related problem—Gulf Coast hurricanes, coral reef destruction, and drought in the Rocky Mountain West—and the difficulties encountered in devising adaptation policies to cope with them. It should be noted that all of these examples are about *water,* not temperature per se. For practical purposes the most serious climate change issues affecting the United States involve water—more of it, less of it, or alterations in its chemistry.

The Gulf Coast

Hurricane Katrina provides an example of the issues and difficulties involved in climate change adaptation. The U.S. Gulf Coast has always been hurricane prone, but recent research indicates that climate change is likely to cause an increase in either the number or the severity of hurricanes, or both.[23] Patterns of settlement and infrastructure development have greatly exacerbated the damage to life and property that such severe storms are likely to cause. Katrina was not among the most severe storms ever to strike the coast, but it did wreak by far the most property damage. Katrina proved so devastating because the Louisiana and Mississippi Gulf coasts had been developed so as to put a vast amount of valuable, poorly protected assets in the path of the storm.

It is no coincidence that the oldest parts of New Orleans were largely spared by Katrina. The early French, Spanish, and American settlers had the wit to build on the limited amount of high ground available. As the city spread, whole neighborhoods were built below sea level, some protected by levees but others not. The storm surge that Katrina produced breached and cracked several levees as well as flooded neighborhoods, such as the Lower Ninth Ward, that were not protected by levees in all directions. Along the Mississippi Coast, Katrina destroyed the bulk of the houses built along the immediate coast, which were completely exposed to the storm's winds and to the storm surge.[24]

On three separate occasions, one before the storm and two since, attempts to improve New Orleans's capacity to adapt to flooding have been rebuffed. In 1965 Congress authorized an Army Corps of Engineers plan to dramatically improve the city's flood defenses. The central feature of the Lake Pontchartrain and Vicinity Hurricane Protection Project was a proposal to build floodgates across the passes from the Gulf to Lake Pontchartrain to prevent storm surges from entering the lake. Barrier-dampened hurricane surges would then be contained by the existing local levees along the three outfall canals that penetrated into metro New Orleans from Lake Pontchartrain.[25]

The project, however, was never completed. By 1971 cost estimates had risen to almost $200 million, nearly three times the 1965 figure. Local opposition was growing based on both environmental fears and the increase in the local share of the cost of the project.[26] The major New Orleans newspaper, the *Times-Picayune*, editorialized against the project, claiming that it lacked public support and demanding that the Corps prove that the project would have no adverse environmental impact on the lake.[27] Although work on the project had already begun, the National Environmental Protection Act of 1969 was invoked retroactively to require that it be subject to an environmental impact statement (EIS), which the Corps filed. A local environmental organization, Save Our Wetlands, brought suit to halt construction, claiming that the EIS was inadequate. A key argument made by the plaintiffs was that the floodgates would interfere with the migration of fish and shellfish between the lake and the Gulf. That argument was adopted by federal judge Charles Schwartz, who enjoined the Corps from engaging in further floodgate construction pending the submission of a revised EIS.[28]

Schwartz's decision effectively ended the effort to build floodgates. The heightened levels of environmentalist and media opposition to the plan, combined with the added costs of conducting a more elaborate EIS and of meeting the more stringent environmental standards that such a revision would inevitably entail, forced the Corps to determine that the project was no longer politically or financially feasible.[29]

With respect to adaptation to climate change, what is most noteworthy about the controversy over the project is not the actual decision but how little the debate centered on the likelihood that the plan would work and how much it focused on arguments about cost and shellfish. Storm surge was the source of Katrina's destructive energy. Failure to build floodgates would inevitably, *someday*, place drastic surge pressure on the levees protecting the lakeshore and the outflow canals. Since the floodgates that the Corps proposed were never built, one cannot know for sure whether they would have blocked the storm surge sufficiently to sap Katrina's destructive energy. But if further study showed them to be inadequate or excessively environmentally destructive, one might have expected the city of New Orleans and the state of Louisiana to press the Corps to develop better and less destructive plans. Instead, the media and the political class appeared content to simply allow the project to die. Despite some further Corps efforts to build higher levees, the city was left vulnerable to the storm surges that the Corps had warned it about.

Since Katrina, recovery policy and policy debate have continued to show insufficient concerned about adaptation. At two key junctures adaptive concerns were broached and then summarily dismissed. The original recovery plan submitted to New Orleans mayor Ray Nagin by the Urban Land Institute called for reducing the city's footprint to enable it to protect itself better from future flood threats.[30] Nagin seemed to be on the verge of endorsing the plan but then abruptly repudiated it in the wake of the widespread public protest that it elicited.[31] The city never again gave serious consideration to whether to rebuild its most flood-prone neighborhoods.

The only serious congressional effort to introduce adaptive principles into the Katrina recovery plan was likewise unsuccessful. Known as the Baker Bill in honor of its sponsor, Richard Baker (R-Louisiana), the proposal would establish a public corporation, the Louisiana Recovery Corporation, with the authority to issue $80 billion in bonds to pay off lenders, restore public works, and, most important, purchase destroyed properties. It would buy destroyed homes at a minimum of 60 percent of pre-Katrina equity. Armed with that significant amount of equity, in addition to the payouts from flood and homeowners' insurance, homeowners could afford to buy homes on higher ground. And, because of the corporation's capacity to acquire and assemble large parcels of devastated land, whole neighborhoods could be recontoured and redeveloped on the basis of flood-resistant landscape design and architectural principles that could not be applied in rehabilitating single-family houses built within preexisting plot lines.[32] But the Bush administration sealed the Baker Bill's demise by opposing it, calling it a "needless layer of bureaucracy."[33] The administration offered no substitute proposal.

The Baker Bill was the last attempt to use federal monies as a mechanism for encouraging reduction of Louisiana's flood risk by encouraging resettlement and altering land use. Instead, Congress enabled the state to use community development block grant (CDBG) funds to establish a housing rebuilding program called the Road Home. The Road Home provided a maximum of $150,000 to Katrina-ravaged homeowners to use either to rebuild their homes or to purchase homes elsewhere in the state. The percentage of the grant that they received depended on the percentage of damage done to their home. All other forms of compensation—including other federal and state grants as well as flood and homeowners' insurance—were deducted from the Road Home grant. That meant that those receiving more than $150,000 from insurance were not eligible and that $150,000 was an absolute cap on total compensation for anyone receiving Road Home assistance.[34]

As the name implies, the purpose of the program was to bring people back to Louisiana, not to encourage climate change adaptation. If homeowners chose to use the money to purchase a home outside the state, they received 40 percent less than if they chose one of the two other options. And an unintended consequence of the $150,000 cap meant that the flexibility of home siting would be further limited by lack of sufficient funds to buy or build homes in less flood-prone areas of the city or state. That amount simply was not enough to rebuild anywhere other than the site of the damage, and the fractional basis for calculating the grant meant that many would actually receive far less than $150,000. The Road Home thus provided a powerful incentive for homeowners to refurbish their existing properties on the existing footprint—a highly counterproductive result from the standpoint of climate adaptation.

Although major opportunities for adaptation were missed in the wake of Katrina, some positive adaptive steps were taken. Perhaps the most significant involved the imposition of elevation requirements. If one lives in a floodplain, one must buy flood insurance to qualify for a mortgage. To qualify for flood insurance, one must promise to meet FEMA elevation requirements. After Katrina, FEMA redrew the maps that specified what elevation was required in each floodplain, and the new maps often required much higher elevations. That means that new and rebuilt houses most be built higher off the ground, perhaps by as much as 16 or 18 feet, thus enabling flood waters to rush below the house, presumably causing little damage.[35]

Louisiana and Mississippi both adopted state uniform building codes that set as a minimum the standards specified by the International Building Code (IBC) and the International Residential Code (IRC).[36] Those codes mandate uniform design, construction, and inspection standards for both residential and commercial buildings, including standards for mechanical and electrical equipment, plumbing, gas appliances, and fire prevention. The standards set for construction of commercial buildings are far more stringent than those previously imposed along the Mississippi and Louisiana Gulf Coast and should therefore significantly improve the capacity of buildings to resist the impact of wind and floods.

Finally, the state of Mississippi did undertake a significant effort to encourage resettlement in less flood-prone locations. The vast bulk of the flood damage caused by Katrina occurred on the more heavily populated south side of interstate 10, which runs east to west across southern Mississippi. Land north of I-10 is far less flood prone, but it did not yet contain the infrastructure necessary for development to take place there. HUD granted Mississippi's request for $641,075,000 in CDBG monies to build water, wastewater, and stormwater infrastructure in the six affected coastal counties, the bulk of which was to be spent north of I-10.[37] Thus the state made a significant investment in providing the necessary preconditions for settlement on higher ground.

Coral Reefs

Coral reefs occur close to the junction of land, sea, and atmosphere; therefore they are vulnerable to both the terrestrial and the maritime influences of human activity and climate change. Climate-induced rises in ocean temperatures increase coral bleaching and reduce carbon calcification. Bleaching occurs when corals suffer loss of the symbiotic algae that provide the colorful pigments that corals normally display, bleaching them white. The loss of symbiotic algae deprives the corals of the nutrients that they need to survive, grow, and reproduce.[38] Sixteen percent of corals worldwide were extensively damaged in 1997–98 by coral bleaching. Higher CO_2 concentrations in the atmosphere have led to greater levels of dissolved CO_2 on the ocean surface, raising ocean acidity and thereby lowering the concentration of carbonate. Corals and other marine organisms depend on this substance, in the form of calcium carbonate, to build their skeletons.[39]

The impact of climate change has been greatly exacerbated by a wide variety of human-induced stresses on highly vulnerable coral reef ecosystems. By 1998, an estimated 11 percent of the world's reefs had been destroyed by human activities, the most destructive of which include runoff of excessive nutrients and contaminants from agricultural land, sedimentation, and overfishing. Excessive nutrients—which are added to the coral reef environment primarily by the runoff of nitrogen- and phosphorus-rich fertilizer from farmland into rivers and then into the sea[40]—endanger reefs by fostering the growth of phytoplankton, which reduces water clarity and light availability. Contaminants include heavy metals, pesticides, herbicides, and solvents.

Sediment deposits interfere with coral growth and force the coral colony to expend energy to attempt to remove them.[41] Sediment also deprives coral colonies of the hard, stable surfaces that they need to establish new colonies, and it limits light penetration and increases water turbidity. Sediment is deposited by runoff from the land and by the stirring up of seafloor sediment due to dredging, mining, land reclamation, and other marine construction activities. Commercial and recreational fishing endanger reefs by removing fish and other organisms, such as giant clams and sea cucumbers, which are vital to the survival of the coral reef ecosystem. Fishing vessels also damage reef structure by indiscriminate casting of nets and boat anchors.[42]

In 1972 the United States launched one of its most ambitious place-based environmental initiatives, the National Marine Sanctuaries Act (NMSA). It was designed to provide fragile and significant marine environments, such as coral reefs, with a level of protection similar to that which the national parks provide to comparable land masses. The NMSA gives the secretary of commerce the authority to designate sanctuaries and to issue regulations to govern them; that authority has been delegated to the National Oceanic and Atmospheric Administration (NOAA). One of the first marine regions to qualify for sanctuary status was Key Largo, in the Florida Keys. The Florida Keys constitute North America's only living coral barrier reef and the world's third-largest barrier reef system. In 1981, the waters adjacent to Key Looe were also designated a marine sanctuary, and in 1990 the two sanctuaries were combined to form the Florida Keys National Marine Sanctuary (FKNMS). In 2001, NOAA created the Tortugas Ecological Reserve and made it part of the Florida Keys National Marine Sanctuary, which then became the largest U.S. marine sanctuary.[43]

The NMSA gives FKNMS impressive powers to protect the coral barrier reef against threats to its viability. FKNMS rules prohibit removing or injuring coral; discharging trash or other pollutants; dredging or drilling the seabed; anchoring a vessel on live coral in water less than 40 feet deep; releasing exotic species; and taking protected wildlife. To discourage the use of anchors, the sanctuary has placed mooring buoys at heavily visited reef sites. To maximize the number of boats using the buoys, small boats are encouraged to tie up to one another with only one boat tied directly to the mooring buoy.[44]

In order to protect especially critical, at-risk populations and habitats more fully, the sanctuary has established four types of special zones that impose more stringent regulations. Twenty-three of the zones are labeled "no-take," meaning that they fully prohibit fishing, lobstering, tropical fish collecting, or any other consumptive activity. Although they make up less than 1 percent of the sanctuary in total area, they protect 65 percent of shallow coral reef. Ecological reserves, which encompass a variety of large, contiguous habitats, are designed to preserve biodiversity; provide spawning, nursery, and residence areas for marine life; protect habitats and species not covered by existing fishery management regulations; and allow areas to remain in or to return to a natural state. Sanctuary preservation areas (SPAs) are smaller zones situated along heavily used areas of the reef tract. These zones separate conflicting uses and prevent further resource degradation. Special use/research-only areas are set aside for scientific research and educational purposes. Entry into these areas is restricted, allowing scientists to monitor the effects of no-diving and no-take regulations on the existing environment.[45] Other bird nesting, resting, and feeding areas and turtle nesting beaches are zoned as wildlife management areas. Public use and taking is not prohibited, but it is restricted by no-access buffer zones, no-motor zones, idle speed only/no wake zones, and closed zones. Twenty of the twenty-seven such areas are under the management of the U.S. Fish and Wildlife Service.[46] The stringent measures taken by the FKNMS have undoubtedly slowed the rate of coral destruction along the Florida Keys barrier reef. Nonetheless, coral deterioration continues.[47]

The limitation of the marine sanctuary approach is that it can regulate only activities that occur within its boundaries, whereas many of the causes of coral destruction originate elsewhere. For example, a study conducted in 2002 showed an accumulation of microorganisms associated with human feces on Florida Keys coral, the result of sewage pouring into the ocean from sewage pipes located well outside the sanctuary boundaries.[48] That is just one example of the impact on reefs of so-called "non-point" sources of water pollution: fertilizer and pesticide runoff from farms, runoff of soil and building materials from construction sites, sediment unearthed by dredging and mining, and human sewage and animal feces. Although the Clean Water Act aims to regulate such sources, its record of success is quite poor, especially when compared to its ability to regulate "point" sites such as pulp mills and power plants, in which cases the discharge comes from discrete pipes that are easy to locate and to monitor.

Coral reefs are not self-contained systems. Many species of reef animals, including the spiny lobster, experience their larval phase far upstream of the Keys at far distant points in the Caribbean; ocean currents bring them to the Keys.[49] Thus the health of the Keys' coral reef ecosystem depends on the health of the ecosystems where the larvae are spawned as well as the health of the ocean spans that they travel on their journey to the Keys. As both the human feces and the larvae examples demonstrate, there can be only limited value in treating any particular coral reef in isolation.

Rocky Mountain West

The Rocky Mountain West is an arid region even in the best of times, and climate change threatens to worsen the drought conditions that threaten farms and forests there. As stated earlier, the threat comes not simply from less precipitation but from a decline in the quantity and duration of the snowpack. If the mountains cannot retain enough snow for a sufficiently long period of time, then there will be less snowmelt to feed the streams that in turn supply the water sources for trees, animals, crops, and people. Even if enough snow falls, should the melt begin too early, the moisture will dissipate too fast and the streams will run dry too soon. In most parts of the Western snowmelt region, a greater percentage of annual precipitation has been falling as rain than as snow, and in addition, the snow cover has been diminishing earlier in the year.[50]

Not only do such conditions threaten drinking water supplies, but they also greatly exacerbate the threat of wildfire. A drier land surface allows more fires to ignite, and desiccated vegetation allows fire to spread more quickly. Since 1980 average area burned in the United States each year has almost doubled. Forested area burned between 1987 and 2003 was 6.7 times the area burned between 1970 and 1986, and a higher fraction of the 1987–2003 total occurred at higher elevations.[51] Warmer, drier weather leads to drier soil, which in turn creates drier vegetation, which makes fire ignition easier and speeds up the growth of a fire. Particularly in the Northwest, where most wildfires occur in the summer, the wildfire increases correlate with warmer summer temperatures, longer growing seasons, and diminished snowmelt.[52]

Wildfires have long played a role in Western ecosystems. They become problematic when homes and farms are built in fire-prone areas. Land use control is the most effective policy for minimizing their destructiveness and also for dealing with inadequate water supplies, but that approach flies in the face of the political and economic pressures for real estate development and population growth that continue to prevail. Small water impoundments that can be made to mimic snowmelt through controlled release can reduce the problems caused by reduced snowpack. Larger and deeper reservoirs can also provide reserve water supplies, as depth reduces evaporation. But as mentioned earlier, environmentalists deeply oppose the damming of rivers because of the myriad ecological disturbances that dams and reservoirs cause.

Current Developments

The Obama administration came into office deeply committed to addressing global climate change, including through more aggressive action to cope with adaptation issues. With its active encouragement, representatives Henry Waxman (D-California) and Edward Markey (D-Massachusetts) introduced the Waxman-Markey Climate and Energy Security Act, passed by the House of Representatives, which includes a subtitle devoted to adaptation.[53] The subtitle is divided into two parts: domestic and international. The domestic part is further divided into three sections. One is devoted to adaptation in general, one to public health, and one to natural resources, and each is controlled by a different agency—NOAA, Health and Human Services, and Council on Environmental Quality (CEQ), respectively. NOAA is tasked with chairing a national council to serve as a forum for interagency consultation regarding adaptation. The council will be composed of the directors of all relevant federal agencies.[54]

NOAA also is required to develop and publish adaptation vulnerability assessments that examine the impacts of climate change on human health, natural systems, resources, infrastructure, and social and economic sectors. The assessments are both national and regional in scope. At the regional level they are intended to establish priorities among vulnerable systems and anticipate the costs of climate impacts on those systems. Within one year of the national assessment, each federal agency on the national council must submit to the president and Congress an agency adaptation plan describing the current and anticipated future climate adaptation impacts that fall within the agency's purview along with a set of prioritized actions to cope with those impacts. The bill also requires NOAA to create a National Climate Service to provide state, local, and tribal governments with adaptation-related data, and it also authorizes the Department of the Treasury to provide climate adaptation aid to them.[55]

The act sets up a parallel organizational structure for dealing specifically with climate change effects on natural resources. It designates a lead agency, CEQ, and establishes another interagency coordinating mechanism, the Natural Resources Climate Change Adaptation Panel, chaired by CEQ, to coordinate federal agency strategies, plans, and programs related to natural resource effects.[56] As it did in the earlier section on adaptation, it requires each of the relevant federal agencies to develop and promulgate plans detailing their current and projected efforts to address the impacts of climate change, but the scope of the plans is confined to natural resource impacts. It also mandates the Treasury Department to create a fund to provide federal natural resource agencies and the states with funds to implement adaptation programs.[57] The public health section of the act resembles the other two in that it too establishes a lead agency (in this case HHS), requires that agency to create a national strategy for addressing climate change impacts, and authorizes federal funds to be spent to implement its strategy.[58]

To address adaptation issues overseas, the act puts USAID in charge of its International Climate Change Adaptation Program. Approximately half of the program's funds are to be given to the international agencies and programs established by the United Nations Framework Convention on Climate Change (UNFCCC). The rest will be spent on programs and grants to assist vulnerable nations to plan and implement adaptation activities.[59]

These proposals are impressive in that they delegate environmental responsibilities to all national agencies, as well as provide aid to states, international agencies, and other nations.

Although they create several different frameworks for action, they do not specify what any action will consist of, nor do they provide any sense of how much federal funding will be made available to support national, regional, state, or international adaptation initiatives. Therefore, the adaptation subtitle of the Waxman-Markey Climate and Energy Security Act should be read as an effort by key congressional leaders, with the active support of the Obama administration, to stimulate federal agencies and departments to demonstrate a greater interest in and concern for adaptation questions, as well as to provide frameworks for interagency deliberation and coordination. The proposals provide no guidance as to how those questions should be posed or what specific policies should be adopted to address them. In the following, concluding sections, this chapter provides a more substantive set of recommendations to address some of those issues.

Conclusion: Proposals for Reform

This chapter highlights an array of obstacles to adaptation, ranging from excessive population densities to overextraction of resources and counterproductive property law. Some of the obstacles, especially coercive and draconian land use planning and reallocation of water rights, are so unpalatable to property owners and legislators that there is virtually no chance of their being adopted in the foreseeable future. Therefore, despite my own conviction that preventing further settlement of many coastal areas and fire-prone mountain areas is desirable and that the current water rights regime is based on an anachronistic concept of water supply availability, I do not propose reform of either land use planning or water rights laws. Rather, this chapter concludes by looking at three areas of policy where reform is feasible, although politically challenging. Each area is directly associated with one of the three specific adaptation problems highlighted in this chapter—hurricane-induced flooding, drought, and deterioration of coral reefs—in the belief that they may well have the potential to prove useful regarding other adaptive problems.

Insurance

This chapter discusses the disincentives to adaptation that current state and federal insurance regulations and subsidies create. Because no devastating hurricanes have occurred since 2005 and public sympathy for hurricane victims is no longer at its apogee, it would be politically possible for Congress to reform the Flood Insurance Program to make it actuarially sound, meaning that premiums would rise significantly for many policy holders and thus the costs of recovery from future storms would not be borne so heavily by the taxpayer at large.

Kunreuther and his associates have also proposed new forms of insurance that offer promise as a means for encouraging adaptive behavior. He urges insurance companies to create an all-hazards form of insurance rather than write specific flood, fire, and earthquake policies. Such a practice would benefit the companies in that it would better protect them against a sudden spate of unexpected disasters of a particular type in a particular region. It is sufficiently unlikely that there would simultaneously appear an outbreak of floods in the Gulf Coast, wildfires in the Rockies, and earthquakes in California, for instance. The all-hazards approach is simply an expansion and a refinement of the ongoing effort of insurance underwriters to spread their risks.[60]

The all-hazards approach would be especially promising if it took the form of long-term insurance (LTI). Traditionally, natural disaster insurance policies have been written as annual contracts, renewable at the option of the insurer. This practice burdens property owners who find themselves subject to unforeseen rises in premium prices, not to mention outright cancellation. Insurers incur high administrative costs due to the necessity of performing yearly reevaluations of policies and coping with irate and contentious holders of canceled policies. LTI significantly lowers administrative costs because policies are not reviewed and reevaluated so often, and it also benefits consumers because it removes the threat of cancellation. It is valuable as an adaptive device because, due to the fact that it is long-term, it can be coupled with long-term loans to the insured to engage in mitigation efforts. Such efforts would no longer appear prohibitively costly; indeed, they would save the premium holder money, if the reductions in annual premiums resulting from mitigation efforts were greater than the annual cost of paying off the loan. This policy reform has the remarkable quality of making all parties—insurers, banks, and consumers—better off. Even if it is not possible to ensure that the mitigation loan interest rate is lower than the cost of long-term insurance, tying the two together remains a promising adaption avenue as long as building codes mandate state-of-the-art mitigation materials and techniques. Any benefits of improvements in the form of lower insurance rates will serve to lessen the cost of the improvements.[61]

Engineering and Construction

Since the 1950s, engineered approaches to environmental problems have been viewed with increasing skepticism. Dams that used to be viewed as essential means of providing electricity, preventing floods, and creating new sources of water supply have come to be seen as destroyers of free-flowing rivers and menaces to the survival of aquatic plants and animals. As the story of the Lake Pontchartrain and Vicinity Hurricane Protection Project illustrates, building floodgates and other efforts to engineer flood prevention have also been thwarted on environmental grounds. I do not claim that they should have been built; rather, the discussion should have been about how to protect New Orleans adequately while minimizing environmental damage and cost rather than presenting a simple demonstration of environmental damage and cost.

The challenge of climate change adaptation should stimulate a reconsideration of the anti-engineering bias. The proper way to think about any environmental intrusion is on a comparative risk basis. As the likelihood of catastrophic storms increases and the costs that they entail grow, the risks associated with various forms of flood barriers may no longer be seen as more severe than the risk of floods. Likewise, the need to dam streams and rivers needed to create greater reservoir capacity may come to outweigh the risks that such water impoundments create. In the absence of land use authority to keep people from locating in flood-prone or water-deprived places or other excessively fragile ecosystems, the next best approach may be to engineer forms of protection against the elements and systems to create additional water supply.

Low-Impact Development Techniques

Marine sanctuaries cannot protect coral reefs from the toxins and wastes that reach them from shore. Because such pollution is largely the result of runoff from many different agricultural, manufacturing, and residential sources, it has proven very difficult to regulate and control. Stormwater drains do not typically channel water to treatment facilities but carry runoff directly into streams, rivers, and lakes, which, in turn, carry it to the ocean. Fortunately, new low-impact development techniques (LIDs) are being developed that seek to eliminate the toxins and other polluting substances from rainwater before they enter waterways. LIDs enable natural infiltration to occur as close as possible to the original area of rainfall:

> By engineering terrain, vegetation, and soil features to perform this function, costly conveyance systems can be avoided, and the landscape can retain more of its natural hydrological function. This is usually best accomplished by creating a series of smaller retention/detention areas that allow localized filtration.[62]

Among the techniques for retaining and filtering runoff are grass buffers, sand beds, and holding ponds. Swales planted with grass and other vegetation that captures and filters runoff can substitute for curbs and gutters along residential streets. Driveways, roads, and parking lots can be constructed of permeable pavement surfaces that allow water to flow through into the soil below.[63] The various professions and firms involved in residential and infrastructure design and construction cannot be expected to master and implement such novel techniques too quickly. But if they are incorporated into building codes, the curricula of architectural and engineering schools, and seminars at trade shows and professional meetings, their inherent economic and environmental advantages should enable them to be adopted incrementally over time.

These approaches are hardly a panacea. But one can hope that they will slow the rate of climate-related property and ecological damage sufficiently to enable citizens to fully engage in the broader discussions about property rights and land use that a more comprehensive and effective adaptation to climate change demands.

Notes

1. United Nations Development Program, "Adaptation to Climate Change" (www.undp.org/climatechange/adapt/).

2. John Heinz III Center for Science, Economics, and the Environment, "A Survey of Climate Change Adaptation Planning" (Washington: n.d.) (www.heinzctr.org/publications/PDF/Adaptation_Report_October_10_2007.pdf).

3. Pew Center for the Climate, "Climate Change 101: Adaptation" (www.pewclimate.org/docUploads/Adaptation_0.pdf).

4. Alan Atkisson, "Climate Change Adaptation: From Big Taboo to Business Opportunity," January 16, 2009 (www.worldchanging.com/archives/009316.html).

5. Dwight Jaffee, Howard Kunreuther, and Erwann Michel-Kerjan, "Long-Term Insurance (LTI) for Addressing Catastrophe Risk," Working Paper 2008-06-05 (Working Risk Management and Decision Processes Center, Wharton School of the University of Pennsylvania, August 2008), p. 4. Hereafter referred to as "Long-Term Insurance."

6. The NFIP is administered by FEMA. A full description of the program appears on the FEMA website (www.fema.gov/about/programs/nfip/index.shtm). See also *Climate Change and Insurance: An Agenda for Action in the United States,* Allianz Group and the World Wildlife Fund, October 2006, p. 29 (www.pewclimate.org/docUploads/Allianz%20WWF%20report.pdf). Hereafter referred to as *Climate Change and Insurance.*

7. Benton Ives, "2007 Legislative Summary: Regulatory Policy: Flood Insurance Reauthorization," *CQ Weekly Online,* January 7, 2008, p. 55 (http://library.cqpress.com/cqweekly/weeklyreport110-000002652081).

8. Erin McNeill, "House Passes Bill to Phase Out Federal Flood Insurance Subsidies," *CQ Weekly Online,* January 28, 2008, p. 268 (http://library.cqpress.com/cqweekly/weeklyreport 110-000002661167); Erin McNeill, "'Strong' Flood Bill Passes in Senate, Could Face Problems with Offsets," *CQ Weekly Online,* May 19, 2008, p. 1353 (http://library.cqpress.com/cq weekly/weeklyreport110-000002877950).

9. "Long-Term Insurance," p. 2.

10. Ibid., p. 3; also *Climate Change and Insurance*, p. 31.

11. Florida Office of Insurance Regulation, "Overview of the Florida Hurricane Catastrophe Fund (FHCF)" (www.floir.com/FHCF.aspx); see also Brent Winans, "Florida Flirting with Hurricane Insurance Disaster," *IRMI Insights,* August 2008, pp. 1–6 (http://www.irmi.com/Insights/Articles/2008/Winans-Citizens-Hurricane-CAT-Fund.pdf); "Florida's Hurricane Insurance Woes Mount," *Orlando Sentinel,* June 16, 2008 (http://blogs.orlandosentinel.com/news_politics/2008/06/floridas-hurric.html).

12. Scott G. Borgerson, "Arctic Meltdown: The Economic and Security Implications of Global Warming," *Foreign Affairs,* March–April 2008.

13. Kenneth R. Weiss, "Migrating Alaskan Pollock Are Creating the Potential for a New Dispute with Russia," *Los Angeles Times,* October 19, 2008 (www.latimes.com/news/science/environment/la-na-pollock19-2008oct19,0,6362925.story).

14. Terry L. Anderson and P. J. Hill, "Evolution of Property Rights: A Study of the American West," *The TL Anderson, PJ Hill - Journal of Law and Economics* 18, no. 1 (1975), p. 163.

15. U.S. Arctic Research Commission, *Climate Change, Permafrost, and Impacts on Civil Infrastructure*, Permafrost Task Force Report, Special Report 01-03, Executive Summary, December 2003 (www.arctic.gov/files/PermafrostForWeb.pdf).

16. T. Schoennagel, T. T. Veblen, and W. H. Romme, "The Interaction of Fire, Fuels, and Climate across Rocky Mountain Forests," *BioScience* 54 (2004), pp. 661–76.

17. R. M. Adams, and D. E. Peck, "Effects of Climate Change on Water Resources," *Choices* 23 (2008), pp. 12–14.

18. P. Mote and others, "Declining Mountain Snowpack in Western North America," *Bulletin of the American Meteorological Society* 86, no. 1 (January 2005).

19. John Reilly and others, "U.S. Agriculture and Climate Change: New Results," *Climatic Change* 57 (2003), pp. 43–69.

20. *Great Lakes Restoration and the Threat of Global Warming* (Healing Our Waters–Great Lakes Coalition, May 2008), p. 32 (http://online.nwf.org/site/DocServer/Great_Lakes_Report.pdf?docID=3901).

21. Kristen M. Crossett and others, *Population Trends along the Coastal United States: 1980–2008*, U.S. Department of Commerce, National Oceanic and Atmospheric Administration, National Ocean Service, September 2004, p. 3 (http://oceanservice.noaa.gov/programs/mb/dfs/coastal_pop_trends_complete.pdf).

22. Richard Nixon was the last president to make a serious effort to formulate and pass land use legislation. Initially his administration and Senator Henry Jackson (D-Washington) each

wrote separate land use bills, but then they joined forces behind a common bill that adopted the administration's approach. The bill ultimately died in Congress; after giving it due consideration, President Ford chose not to reintroduce it. See John C. Whitaker, *Striking a Balance: Environment and Natural Resource Policy in the Nixon-Ford Years* (Washington: American Enterprise Institute, 1976).

23. Kerry Emanuel, "Increasing Destructiveness of Tropical Cyclones over the Past 30 Years," *Nature* 436, August 2005, p. 686.

24. A good account of the storm and its aftermath can be found in Christopher Cooper and others, *Disaster: Hurricane Katrina and the Failure of Homeland Security* (New York: Times Books, 2006).

25. Leonard Shabman and Douglas Woolley, *Decisionmaking Chronology for the Lake Pontchartrain and Vicinity Hurricane Protection Project*, Final Report for the Headquarters, U.S. Army Corps of Engineers, March 2008, Executive Summary, p. 6. Hereafter referred to as ACE Report.

26. Ibid., pp. 2–37.

27. "Hold Off on Barriers," *Times-Picayune*, July 14, 1977, p. 22.

28. *Save Our Wetlands et al.* v. *Early J. Rush et al.*, U.S. District Court, Eastern Louisiana, March 1978. (www.iwr.usace.army.mil/inside/products/pub/hpdc/docs/19771230_SOWLv Rush_injunction_order.pdf).

29. ACE Report, pp. 2–42.

30. Bring New Orleans Back Commission, *Rebuilding New Orleans*, March 20, 2006 (www.nolaplans.com/plans/BNOB/Mayors%20Rebuilding%20Plan%20Final.pdf).

31. "Timeline of the Planning Process in New Orleans," NOLA Plans, New Orleans Plan Database (www.nolaplans.com/timeline/).

32. Alyson Klein, "House Bill Sets Up Corporation for Katrina Redevelopment," *Congress-Daily* (December 16, 2005) (www.govexec.com/dailyfed/1205/121605cdam2.htm); Adam Nossiter, "A Big Government Fix-It Plan for New Orleans," *New York Times*, January 5, 2006 (www.nytimes.com/2006/01/05/national/nationalspecial/05buyout.html?pagewanted=1&_r=2).

33. Martin H. Bosworth, "Controversy Swirls around Louisiana Reconstruction Plan," *ConsumerAffairs.com*, January 29, 2006 (www.consumeraffairs.com/news04/2006/01/nola_reconstruction.html).

34. Louisiana Recovery Authority, "The Road Home Housing Programs Action Plan Amendment for Disaster Recovery Funds," Louisiana Office of Community Development, Division of Administration (www.hud.gov/content/releases/pr06-058.pdf).

35. "FEMA Requires Residents Adhere to Elevation Requirements from ABFEs," *Claims Journal*, February 2005 (www.claimsjournal.com/news/national/2006/02/07/65135.htm).

36. "Louisiana Speaks: Tools for Successful Implementation" (www.louisianaspeaks.org/cache/documents/27/2787.pdf); "Mississippi Adopts International Building Code," *Bookmark Inc.* (www.bookmarki.com/Mississippi-Adopts-International-Building-Code-s/242.htm).

37. Mississippi Development Authority, *Gulf Coast Regional Infrastructure Program, Disaster Recovery*, 2008, p. 114 (www.mississippi.org/content.aspx?url=/page/actionplan&#GCRIP).

38. Robert W. Buddemeier, Joan A. Kleypas, and Richard B. Aronson, *Coral Reefs and Global Climate Change: Potential Contributions of Climate Change to Stresses on Coral Reef Ecosystems*, Pew Center on Global Climate Change, February 2004, pp. ii, 15 (www.pewclimate.org/docUploads/Coral_Reefs.pdf). Hereafter referred to as Coral Reef Report.

39. C. Wilkinson, *Status of Coral Reefs of the World: 2002* (Townsville, Queensland, Australia: Global Coral Reef Monitoring Network and Australian Institute of Marine Science).

40. Coral Reef Report, p. 9.

41. B. Riegl and G. M. Branch, "Effects of Sediment on the Energy Budgets of Four Scleractinian (Bourne 1900) and Five Alcyonacean (Lamouroux 1816) Corals," *Journal of Experimental Marine Biology and Ecology* 186 (1995), pp. 259–75.

42. Coral Reef Report, pp. 10, 12; J. Cortes, "A Reef under Siltation Stress: A Decade of Degradation," in *Proceedings of the Colloquium on Global Aspects of Coral Reefs: Health, Hazards, and History*, edited by R. N. Ginsburg (University of Miami, 1993), pp. 240–46.

43. "National Marine Sanctuary History Timeline," National Marine Sanctuaries, NOAA (http://sanctuaries.noaa.gov/about/history/welcome.html).

44. Florida Keys National Marine Sanctuary, "Marine Resource Protection" (http://florida keys.noaa.gov/resource_protection/welcome.html).

45. International Coral Reef Initiative, "The Use of Marine Zoning in the Florida Keys National Marine Sanctuary (Florida, U.S.A.)" (www.icriforum.org/secretariat/florida.html).

46. Florida Keys National Marine Sanctuary, "The Zoning Action Plan" (http://florida keys.noaa.gov/regs/zoning.html).

47. Marine Protected Areas of the United States, "Case Studies Florida Keys Marine Sanctuary" (http://mpa.gov/helpful_resources/florida_keys.html).

48. "Preliminary Evidence for Human Fecal Contamination in Corals of the Florida Keys, USA," *Marine Pollution Bulletin* 44, no. 7 (July 2002), pp. 666–70.

49. John C. Ogden, "Marine Managers Look Upstream for Connections," *Science* 278, no. 5342 (November 21, 1997), pp. 1414–15.

50. Mote and others, "Declining Mountain Snowpack in Western North America."

51. *Climate Change and Insurance.*

52. A. L. Westerling and others, "Warming in the Earlier Spring Increases Western U.S. Forest Fire Activity," *Science*, August 18, 2006, pp. 940–43.

53. 111th Congress, 1st session, HR 2454, Subtitle E—*Adapting to Climate Change*. As of mid April 2010, the bill had passed and was awaiting action by the Senate (http://frwebgate. access.gpo.gov/cgi-bin/getdoc.cgi?dbname=111_cong_bills&docid=f:h2454ih.txt.pdf).

54. Ibid., section 462. They include NOAA, EPA, USDA, the Department of Commerce, DOD, DOE, HHS, DHS, HUD, DOI, DOT, ACOE, CDC, FEMA, NASA, and USGS.

55. Ibid., sections 463–467.

56. Ibid., sections 484–485.

57. Ibid., sections 486–490.

58. Ibid., sections 472–73.

59. Ibid., sections 493–95.

60. Howard Kunreuther, "Has the Time Come for Comprehensive Natural Disaster Insurance?" in *On Risk and Disaster*, edited by Robert Daniels, Donald Kettl, and Howard Kunreuther (University of Pennsylvania Press, 2006), pp. 175–202.

61. "Long-Term Insurance."

62. "Low-Impact Development Practices for Storm Water Management," *Toolbase Services* (www.toolbase.org/Technology-Inventory/Sitework/low-impact-development).

63. Ibid.

PART III

Are Federal Institutions up to the Challenge of Climate Change?

10

Courts and Climate Policy: Now and in the Future

KIRSTEN H. ENGEL

Since the beginning of the environmental movement in the early 1970s, environmental advocates have made litigation a cornerstone of their strategy to improve environmental quality. With respect to just about every environmental issue to surface—mining on federal lands, air and water pollution, hazardous and nuclear waste disposal, lead poisoning, endangered species—advocates have turned to the courts to compel regulators to impose new or more stringent regulations or to delay or stop construction projects, mining, logging, and other activities that advocates deem harmful to the environment.[1] While never an exclusive strategy, litigation has figured prominently, along with lobbying and organizing, in the environmentalists' toolbox.

Therefore it should come as no surprise that many advocates of action on climate change are turning to the courts. Indeed, climate litigation has blossomed, with a proliferation of cases in the last several years.[2] Since 2005, the number of climate change cases filed annually has jumped from just five to more than thirty-five in

The author would like to thank the Law College Association of the College of Law for its contribution to this research through a summer research grant and to the participants at the National Conference on Climate Governance at the Miller Center of Public Affairs, University of Virginia, December 11–12, 2008. The author would also like to thank Barry Rabe, Timothy Lytton, J. B. Ruhl, and Don Kettl for their insightful comments on earlier drafts and Sarah Gotshall and Julia Jolley for their excellent research assistance. The final product and its flaws, however, are solely the responsibility of the author.

2008 and just under twenty-five in 2009.[3] Among others, cases have been filed to compel the Environmental Protection Agency to regulate greenhouse gas emissions from motor vehicles under the Clean Air Act,[4] to force federal agencies to assess the impacts of their activities on climate change pursuant to the National Environmental Policy Act,[5] to require industrial emitters to cut their greenhouse gas emissions to avoid contributing to the perceived public nuisance of global warming,[6] and to encourage the United States to regulate climate change so as not to run afoul of international human rights law.[7] While current climate change litigation differs in significant respects from the environmental litigation of the past few decades— an important difference is that state governments are among the parties that sue most frequently—there is a similar reliance on the judicial branch to step in and deliver when little action is forthcoming from the other branches of government.

Commentators are deeply divided on whether the litigation strategy has benefited the environment. On one hand, Gerald Rosenberg argues that environmentalists' use of the courts has been mostly misplaced. In his view, their efforts would have been better spent in the political arena: "Litigators substituted legal principles for lobbying, writs of *mandamus* for political mobilization, and brief-writing for button-holing."[8] On the other hand, Gordon Silverstein argues that strong reliance on the courts has resulted in the "juridification" of environmental policy—a transition from a more open-ended approach to government decisionmaking to a more formalized process with its attendant delays and vulnerability to changing judicial attitudes toward deferring to administrative agencies.[9] But still others point to the benefits of environmental litigation—to the many instances in which litigation has triggered the establishment of entire regulatory programs and citizen suits have resulted in fines and penalties for violators that previously were overlooked or outright ignored by state and federal enforcement authorities.[10]

Not surprisingly, use of litigation to compel government action on climate change already has its own defenders[11] and critics.[12] Much of the scholarly attention in this area has been devoted to a critique of the legal merits of the claims in the cases being filed, with particular emphasis on the doctrinal weaknesses in a small subset of the cases filed: those alleging liability for a common law nuisance.[13]

In terms of substantive outcomes, litigation cannot claim to have reduced greenhouse gas emissions by any significant amount, at least not yet. Nevertheless, there is little question that the courts can influence—and indeed already have influenced—current climate policy through the exercise of their unique authority on matters of statutory interpretation, their power to compel agencies to act, and their capacity to impose common law liability. Their influence may be modest and may demonstrate deep divisions within the judiciary over the proper scope of the courts' role in matters of hard-fought public policy, but the courts have clearly made their mark on current climate policy.

Focusing on the number of tons of greenhouse gas emissions reduced by legal order or even on the legal merits of the cases filed is unlikely to shed much light on the true extent of the courts' impact on climate policy. To the extent that a case filed for the purpose of reducing climate change triggers regulation to reduce greenhouse gases, it will have succeeded in its primary objective, even if the plaintiffs lose the lawsuit or leave the courtroom with a smaller package of relief than they originally sought. Litigation can influence policy generation and reform in important ways, from framing issues to generating policy relevant information.[14] The strength of the legal claims being made therefore is not the only factor that is important in evaluating the contribution of litigation to addressing climate change.

Climate-related litigation has the capacity to affect public opinion on climate change through the manner in which it addresses the issue of climate science, climate "victims," and legal disputes over efforts to regulate the sources of greenhouse gases. Specifically, judicial treatment of climate change can

—depoliticize climate change by filtering issues, such as climate science, that have become highly contentious in the public debate through the supposedly "neutral" system of the courts

—identify real and highly sympathetic victims of climate change, thus translating the rather unspecific, uncertain, and futuristic impacts predicted by scientists into real and immediate losses of great significance

—highlight the fit, or lack thereof, between the existing framework of federal and state environmental laws and the problem of climate change, thereby providing a baseline against which the costs and benefits of a new regulatory scheme may be compared

—provide feedback on the magnitude of the liability risk to private industries that contribute to greenhouse gas concentrations, thus giving such industries and politicians a sense of the value of the preemption of such liability in a future regulatory scheme.

While the courts' treatment of climate issues obviously has implications for the likelihood and shape of future climate legislation, characterizing the trend of the courts' influence is difficult, if not impossible, to do at this time. It also must be recognized that the nature of the current framework of climate regulation is shaping the current role of the courts in climate policy. Should federal climate legislation be adopted, Congress's choice of regulatory approaches will control the magnitude and nature of the courts' future role in addressing climate change. As highlighted by several other chapters in this volume (see those in part 1 in particular), the two most frequently discussed options for the structure of federal legislation are a cap-and-trade program similar in nature to the acid rain program under the 1990 amendments to the Clean Air Act and a cooperative federalism scheme similar to that which applies to conventional air pollutants under Title I of the Clean Air Act. While the acid rain trading program has not been a significant source of litigation, a carbon cap-and-trade program would likely be larger and more complex and hence generate a larger number of disputes. Regardless of which is ultimately enacted (or indeed, whether some wholly different scheme wins approval), federal climate legislation is likely to bring with it a significant uptick in climate change litigation.

The Influence of the Courts on the Development of Climate Policy

Litigation is being pursued both by those seeking greater regulation of climate change (environmental organizations for the most part and states) and those seeking to hold such regulation at bay (primarily industry litigants). The pro-regulation litigants currently have the upper hand, having filed 85 percent of the climate change cases docketed to date.[15] Lawsuits filed by the anti-regulation litigants consist of challenges to state vehicle standards for greenhouse gases, challenges to EPA's determination that greenhouse gas emissions cause or contribute to conditions that endanger public health or welfare, and challenges to state and local greenhouse gas regulations. Because the number of "anti" climate regulation cases pales in comparison to the number of "pro" cases and because the focus of this chapter is on what litigation contributes to pro–climate regulation efforts, the remainder of the chapter concentrates on the lawsuits brought by groups seeking to use the law to decrease climate change.

A review of climate change litigation filed thus far reveals plaintiffs' use of three basic litigation strategies.[16] The first is to compel federal agencies to regulate greenhouse gas emissions under existing statutory authorities. A second is to compel federal agencies to take climate change impacts into account in government decisionmaking, such as in the decision to permit a new coal-fired power plant. And a third is to hold large industrial emitters liable for their greenhouse gas emissions under the common law. While the third category of cases has received most of the attention in the media and in academic journals, cases in the first two categories are far more numerous.

The largest number of cases in the first category, those compelling federal agencies to regulate, have been filed by environmental organizations. While that is what might be expected, more surprising is that a good number have been filed by states. The states appearing most frequently as plaintiffs are California, Massachusetts, New York, New Jersey, Connecticut, and Oregon—the same states that are among the most active in terms of adopting state climate change policies. These states often appear as plaintiffs alongside prominent environmental organizations, such as the Natural Resources Defense Council, the Sierra Club, and the Center for Biological Diversity.

Many of the cases in which the plaintiffs are seeking to trigger federal regulation concern judicial review of EPA's failure to grant a petition seeking a rule regulating greenhouse gases under an existing environmental statute.[17] That was the posture of *Massachusetts* v. *EPA,* the only climate change case to reach the Supreme Court.[18] The case grew out of the decision by Massachusetts and other states and environmental organizations to contest EPA's rejection of a petition, filed by the

International Center for Technology Assessment, to regulate greenhouse gases from new motor vehicle emissions under the Clean Air Act. Potential litigants are continuing to follow the same strategy, filing rulemaking petitions with the agency that, if rejected, will form the basis for a lawsuit. California, in particular, has filed several rulemaking petitions under the Clean Air Act, including requests that EPA regulate greenhouse gas emissions from ocean-going vessels,[19] airplanes,[20] and nonroad vehicles and engines, which would include a large variety of outdoor power equipment, recreational vehicles, farm and construction machinery, and logging and mining equipment. [21] Such petitions are not limited to requesting regulation under the Clean Air Act. The Center for Biological Diversity petitioned to list several species as endangered under the Endangered Species Act due to the impacts of climate change on their habitat.[22]

The "rulemaking petition to litigation strategy" was given a boost in *Massachusetts* v. *EPA*. In that decision, the Court not only held that an agency's refusal to regulate is subject to judicial review—a previously unsettled issue—but also that an agency's refusal to apply a statutory standard that exists as a threshold to the agency's authority to regulate will be subject to exacting scrutiny. The Court distinguished between that and an agency's refusal to bring an enforcement case, a matter Court precedent leaves presumptively to agency discretion. Although both involve the courts in the allocation of an agency's scarce resources, the Court held that the latter is more suitable to judicial review.[23] The Court furthermore held that an agency decision not to regulate could be based only on factors that the statute makes relevant, and not, crucially, on political considerations.[24]

The second type of lawsuit, those seeking to compel federal agencies to take climate change impacts into account in government decisionmaking, are for the most part being filed by various environmental organizations under the National Environmental Policy Act. For example, an environmental group sued the U.S. Forest Service for failing to prepare an environmental impact statement on the global warming potential of the methane that would be released by certain coal mining activities.[25] Another example is a Center for Biological Diversity suit challenging the failure of the Fish and Wildlife Service to consider the stresses on polar bears and walrus resulting from global warming in regulations permitting the incidental killing of polar bears and Pacific walrus during oil exploration and production activities.[26]

The third litigation strategy seeks to hold large industrial greenhouse gas emitters liable for their emissions under the common law. As with the first category of actions, those seeking to compel federal regulation, states and local governments are the lead plaintiffs in several of these cases: a group of plaintiffs made up primarily of northeastern states seeks to hold liable major owners of coal-fired power plants in the Midwest and Southeast;[27] California pursued an action against six major automobile manufacturers;[28] and a native village in Alaska sought an action for damages against seventeen major oil and gas companies.[29] One of the few common law cases that does not fit the mold of state versus large greenhouse gas emitter is that of *Comer* v. *Murphy Oil,* in which a class of Mississippi Gulf Coast property owners has sued insurance, oil, coal, and chemical companies, seeking relief from property damages caused by Hurricane Katrina.[30] In each of the common law actions, the plaintiffs allege that the defendants' contribution to global warming through their greenhouse gas emissions render them liable for injunctive relief[31] or, in the case of the auto manufacturers and the oil, gas, coal, and insurance companies, monetary damages.[32]

The Capacity of the Courts to Influence Climate Change Policy

Development of regulatory controls on domestic greenhouse gas emissions and international negotiations on global targets are quintessential duties and prerogatives of the political branches. The failure of Congress to enact comprehensive climate legislation or of the executive branch to put in place a scheme under existing laws to regulate greenhouse gases deprives the courts of their easiest, most clear-cut role: enforcement of the law. Nevertheless, by virtue of their authority on matters of statutory interpretation, their power to compel agency action, and their control of common law liability determinations, the courts have some capacity to further climate regulation, even in the absence of clear mandates from the political branches. Exercise of those authorities is mostly discretionary, however, and requires courts to surmount considerable doctrinal impediments. As a result, judges differ widely in the degree to which they exploit the full force of their authority in the absence of more definitive action by the executive or Congress. Climate change litigation reveals the contrasting views of the courts themselves regarding their capacity to go out ahead of the political branches. In addition, external limits exist on the efficacy of court action on climate change.

The Unique Role of the Courts

POWER OF THE COURTS TO IMPOSE COMMON LAW LIABILITY

Since the early nineteenth century, courts have imposed common law liability on parties that cause environmental harm. Private and public nuisance cases constitute the nation's oldest "environmental regulation" and once served as models for later-enacted smoke ordinances, some of the nation's first environmental laws.[33] During the early twentieth century, the Supreme Court adjudicated complex public nuisance cases brought by states against neighboring states and the sources of pollution within those states.[34] Only with the enactment of modern pollution control statutes, which began in the 1970s, has the Court held that such statutes displace the authority of courts to redress environmental harms through common law liability judgments. Judges' liability determinations have thereby been replaced with preventive regulations derived from legislation drafted by democratically elected legislators and administrative regulations developed by expert administrative agencies through participatory public procedures.[35] Thus common law liability standards functioned as the default regulatory standards prior to the development of statutory and regulatory law and even afterward as a source of gap-filling authority.

Because of their role in applying the common law, courts hold the key to tort law, an entire body of law and precedent that could have a profound impact—provided that the doctrinal kinks can be worked out—on industry's response to climate change in the absence of a positive regulatory program from Congress or the executive. Tort lawsuits filed against major greenhouse gas emitters seeking injunctive relief or damages provide the courts with an opportunity to shape the private industry response to climate change.

The Power to "Say What the Law Is"

The 1803 case of *Marbury* v. *Madison* established that it is the courts' role, in the U.S. system of separated powers, to "say what the law is."[36] It is therefore the privilege and the burden of the courts to act as a check on unconstitutional or unlawful legislative or executive action by giving the final word on what the Constitution and federal statutes mean. The federal courts are therefore in the cat's seat in terms of interpreting the degree to which existing federal laws may already address climate change. Furthermore, when combined with the Administrative Procedure Act, which provides for judicial review of agency action (including an agency's failure to act), *Marbury* means that, barring congressional repeal of the law in question, the courts have the final say with regard to whether the executive is in compliance with existing laws construed to address climate change and if not, to compel them to come into compliance.

The power of the federal courts to say what the law is gives them a pivotal role in determining the applicability of existing environmental statutes to climate change. Not surprisingly, that power was very much on display in *Massachusetts* v. *EPA*, when the Supreme Court was faced with the question of whether the Clean Air Act (1970), one of the nation's oldest environmental laws, applied to greenhouse gas emissions. The Court held that it did, under the act's capacious definition of pollutants, which, according to the Court, "embraces all airborne compounds of whatever stripe."[37] Accordingly, the Court ruled that EPA had to determine whether emissions of greenhouse gases from motor vehicles endangered public health or welfare, the decisional precursor to regulation of such emissions under the act (in 2009, EPA issued its determination that they did). Indeed, interpretation of the jurisdictional scope of the Clean Air Act provides the basis for EPA's potential regulation of most large industrial sources of greenhouse gases.

The Power of the Courts to Determine Which Plaintiffs Have Standing to Sue

Under Article III of the Constitution, the federal courts are limited to adjudicating "cases and controversies." The Court has interpreted that phrase to mean suits brought by a plaintiff who can demonstrate an injury in fact that is fairly trace-able to a defendant's action (or inaction) and that can be redressed by a court.[38] Standing has developed into a potentially difficult hurdle in cases in which climate change is the basis of the plaintiff's alleged injuries. Because greenhouse gases emit-ted by natural and human activities the world over mix together in the stratosphere and are responsible, collectively, for certain impacts, it is impossible to pin the blame for any particular impact—sea level rise, for instance—on a particular defendant's action in emitting greenhouse gases or failing to prevent the emission of greenhouse gases. Thus, to find standing based on alleged injury due to climate change impacts, courts must somehow reconcile the fairly exacting causation and redressability requirements in judicial precedents on standing with the attenuated relationships that exist in the case of climate change. As discussed further below, the question of standing has been foremost in the cases brought against EPA for failure to address climate change under the Clean Air Act and those brought against private sources of greenhouse gas emissions alleging common law liability (see also chapter 12 in this volume on EPA's effectiveness in greenhouse gas regulation).

The issue of standing is of supreme importance; if no party can allege an injury from greenhouse gas emissions that can be remedied by a court, then the issue of climate change mitigation is reserved exclusively to the political branches. If, on the other hand, at least some parties have standing, the courts are "in the game" and exist as an alternative route to compel action where the political branches are resistant to act. The courts' determination of *who* has standing has impacts on policy as well, as different potential plaintiffs will have different levels of resources for litigation and will be motivated to seek court action under different sets of cir-cumstances. For example, a holding that recreational organizations have standing to sue industrial facilities for having contributed to global warming that is linked to the extinction of certain wildlife species would all but eliminate standing as a barrier to climate change litigation and open the decisions of government regula-tors and private entities to oversight by the courts to the extent allowed by sub-stantive law. On the other hand, a holding that only states have standing due to their quasi-sovereign authority over lands within their borders would give the courts a significant, but comparatively limited, role.

Thus far the courts have avoided any definitive ruling on the question of the scope of standing over climate change and hence who can and cannot sue for adverse climate change impacts. Standing was a major issue in *Massachusetts* v. *EPA*; because both states and environmental organizations were plaintiffs, the Court finessed the standing inquiry by ruling that the plaintiffs had standing under a more relaxed standard applicable only to states. The Court also held that the posture of the lawsuit—which exploited a statutory provision specifically allowing for judicial review—warranted a more relaxed approach to the standing inquiry.

Accordingly, the Court held that Massachusetts, the lead plaintiff, had alleged a sufficient injury as a result of uncontested testimony that climate change will cause sea levels to rise, swallowing the Massachusetts coastline. It rejected the EPA's argument that such injury was insufficient for standing purposes since that and other climate impacts are "widely shared" by government and the public at large. Thus, because the presence of the states in the case enabled the Court to rule on the narrower ground of whether the injury was sufficient to support state standing, the answer to the more interesting question with much more far-reaching implications—the injury necessary to support the standing of the environmentally concerned citizen—has yet to be answered.

An important point is that the Court's ruling on the redressability prong of the standing inquiry could have implications for the standing of the environmentally concerned citizen. EPA had argued that the plaintiffs failed to demonstrate redressability in the case, as even a court order compelling EPA to regulate the greenhouse gas emissions of new motor vehicles under the Clean Air Act would result in the reduction of just a tiny fraction of the global total of greenhouse gas emissions responsible for climate change. Hence, the court order could guarantee little to no reduction in the climate change impacts of which Massachusetts and the other plaintiffs complained. The Court rejected that argument, holding that the plaintiff need not demonstrate that the sought-after court remedy alone would remediate the plaintiff's injury but that it was sufficient that the remedy would contribute to mitigating the plaintiff's harms by reducing emissions that would otherwise occur. This significant ruling on the remedial prong of the standing inquiry does not depend on Massachusetts' status as a sovereign state and hence would seem to support the standing of an environmentally concerned citizen who sues to abate at least a comparably large amount of emissions through an action against a government or a private party.

The common law tort actions that have addressed the standing inquiry indicate that a private plaintiff who alleges injury to his or her property will be held to have standing to sue over climate change damages. Thus in *Connecticut* v. *American Electric Power,* the Second Circuit Court of Appeals held that land trusts, by virtue of the scope and extent of the land-related damage that they will sustain under climate change, satisfy the standard for injury-in-fact under the standing inquiry.[39] A panel of the Fifth Circuit Court of Appeals, in *Comer* v. *Murphy Oil USA*, similarly held that private owners of land harmed by Hurricane Katrina had standing to sue against greenhouse gas emitters in actions for trespass, negligence, and nuisance.[40] However, that decision was recently (and controversially) dismissed by the Fifth Circuit when the court, having voted that all of the judges of the Fifth Circuit must rehear the case (an action that, according to the court's rules, vacates the panel's decision), failed to muster a quorum of unrecused judges to actually re-decide the case.[41]

Institutional Impediments to a More Expansive Judicial Role

SAYING WHAT THE LAW IS DOESN'T MAKE IT SO

The courts may give the final word on "what the law is," but when it comes to acting on that interpretation, they are largely powerless. Courts are limited in the degree to which they can single-handedly effectuate policy. Where an action to implement the law must be taken by the executive branch, the courts are generally powerless to effectuate even a litigation victory won against a federal agency. In cases in which the agency is in disagreement with the court order, agencies have proven quite capable of delaying their compliance and the courts are loath to intervene in the agency's internal business to compel them to act.[42] Furthermore, agencies are adept at obtaining congressional action to overturn a decision with which they disagree.[43]

EPA's delay in responding to the Supreme Court's remand order in *Massachusetts* v. *EPA* is an excellent case in point. On the merits, the Court had rendered the plaintiffs the greatest victory possible given the posture of the case: a determination that greenhouse gases were indeed pollutants covered by the act and a remand, back to the EPA, ordering the agency to determine whether the emission of greenhouse gases from motor vehicles met the statutory standard of "causing or contributing" to air pollution that "endangers public health or welfare" based only on the public health criteria mentioned in the statute.[44]

In the two years after the Supreme Court's decision, however, EPA failed to determine whether greenhouse gas emissions from cars met the Clean Air Act's endangerment criteria or to promulgate greenhouse gas emission standards for motor vehicles. Instead, EPA initially responded by issuing a 588-page "Advanced Notice of Proposed Rulemaking," stating its disagreement with the regulation of greenhouse gases under the Clean Air Act and requesting comment on literally dozens of issues related to the practicality and feasibility of regulating greenhouse gas emissions under a laundry list of Clean Air Act provisions that the EPA had determined "may be applicable to regulate [greenhouse gases]."[45]

At times, only a change in administrations can reverse an agency's recalcitrance in complying with a court order. The plaintiffs were unsuccessful when they filed suit to compel the agency to publish its determination a year after the Supreme Court handed down its decision that EPA had to determine whether motor vehicle emissions of greenhouse gases met the Clean Air Act trigger for regulation— that they "endanger human health or welfare."[46] EPA did in fact issue such an endangerment determination, but not until two years later, several months into President Barack Obama's administration.[47] It also seems to be the change in administration that has triggered the agency's willingness to regulate greenhouse gas emissions from mobile sources and to begin the process of regulating stationary sources under the existing Clean Air Act, authority that the Supreme Court told the agency that it had in the *Massachusetts* v. *EPA* decision.[48]

The *Massachusetts* v. *EPA* example notwithstanding, an important caveat is in order. Even in the absence of a change of administration, the doctrine of judicial precedent means that the decision of a higher court can alter policy in other cases even if an agency succeeds in eluding the court's mandate in the particular litigation at issue. For example, while the EPA took its time in responding to the Court's remand order in *Massachusetts* v. *EPA,* states and advocacy groups wasted no time using the Court's holding that greenhouse gases are "air pollutants" under the Clean Air Act to halt the construction of new coal-fired power plants. In one such case, a Georgia county court judge enjoined the construction of a 1,200-megawatt coal-fired power plant based in part on the plant owners' failure to comply with Clean Air Act requirements for the plant's air pollutant emissions, including, the court ruled—directly following *Massachusetts* v. *EPA*—the air pollutant of carbon dioxide.[49] Earlier, in a less explicit reliance on the High Court's decision, Kansas rejected a permit for a pair of new coal-fired electric plants (1,400 megawatts total), citing the contribution of such plants to global warming.[50] Finally, in an interesting twist, environmental advocates sought to use the EPA's own adjudicatory body, the Environmental Appeals Board, to implement the *Massachusetts* v. *EPA* decision. Environmental advocates challenged the EPA's failure to regulate carbon dioxide emissions from a new waste coal-fired electric power plant in Utah.[51] In its decision, the Environmental Appeals Board held that the EPA has permitting authority to impose a technology-based limit for carbon dioxide emissions and its reason for not doing so, based solely on its historical interpretation, is erroneous.[52] Consequently, the board remanded the permit to reconsider imposing a technology-based limit.[53] That successful challenge serves as a precedent for EPA permit decisions affecting industrial plants throughout the country.

Not all of the judicial outcomes discussed above have "stuck"; appeals courts can reverse climate change regulatory victories in the lower courts and politicians can amend laws held to require that climate change be taken into account. Thus, for instance, the Georgia appeals court reversed the county court decision that had enjoined the construction of the coal-fired power plant mentioned above, disagreeing with the lower court's application of *Massachusetts* v. *EPA*.[54] Similarly, a bill was introduced in the Republican-led Kansas legislature to overturn the state's denial of air permits to the two new coal-fired plants mentioned above. The bill was vetoed by the state's Democratic governor, and an effort to override her veto was narrowly defeated in the legislature.[55] Nevertheless, the multiple ways in which an issue may arise before an adjudicatory body at the federal, state, or local level provide opportunities for a precedent to have a legal effect even if stymied in one or more courts.

JUDICIAL RELUCTANCE TO GO AHEAD OF THE POLITICAL BRANCHES IN ALLOCATING RESPONSIBILITY FOR CLIMATE CHANGE

While still in their infancy, the common law liability actions that have been filed against large sources of greenhouse gas emissions have revealed intensely differing views of the appropriateness of courts going ahead of the political branches to assign legal and financial responsibility for climate change. The three federal district court opinions dismissing the common law liability lawsuits filed against industrial greenhouse gas emitters are a case in point. In each, the court dismissed the suit on the basis that it presented a nonjusticiable political question.[56] The trial courts in *Connecticut* v. *American Electric Power*, a public nuisance action against the nation's largest electricity producers; *California* v. *General Motors,* a public nuisance suit against several of the nation's largest automobile manufacturers; and *Native Village of Kivalina* v. *ExxonMobil Corp.*, a tort law action against twenty-four oil, energy, and utility companies, ruled that they lacked the ability to determine when the defendants' conduct was unreasonable in the absence of a an initial determination by the political branches.[57] The courts found that the adjudication of the case would require them to balance the competing interests of reducing emissions, on one hand, and preserving economic and industrial development on the other.

For instance, the *American Electric Power* court determined that, in order to provide the plaintiffs their requested relief—a cap on the defendants' carbon emissions and an order compelling the defendants to reduce their emissions on an annual basis by an unspecified percentage—the court would first have to make several essentially political determinations. Those would include such questions as whether the societal costs of reducing such emissions should be borne by just a segment of the electricity-generating industry and their industrial and other consumers, whether those costs should be spread across the entire electricity-generating industry (including utilities in the plaintiff states) or to other industries, and what the implications of those choices would be for the nation's economy and energy independence—and, by extension, for national security.[58]

Nevertheless, the 2009 appeals court decision soundly reversing the *American Electric Power* trial court demonstrates the lack of consensus on the capability of courts to allocate responsibility for climate change in the absence of a prior determination by the political branches. Unlike the district court, the appeals court framed the case as an ordinary tort action well within the competence of the courts. The court rejected the defendants' characterization of the case as a complex action requiring the court to establish national or international policy on climate change and instead emphasized that the plaintiffs seek "[a] decision by a single federal court concerning a common law of nuisance cause of action [in a case] brought by domestic plaintiffs against domestic companies for domestic conduct."[59] The court held that the plaintiffs' characterization was furthermore undercut by the fact that federal courts have successfully adjudicated complex common law nuisance cases for more than a century.

Perhaps the reluctance of some courts to adjudicate the global warming nuisance cases should not be so surprising. The plaintiffs in these lawsuits are seeking none other than a court order imposing potentially significant costs on parties whose greenhouse gas emissions contribute a small proportion of the total greenhouse gas emissions that cause global climate change. Moreover, few if any scientists would attribute actual climate impacts to the emissions of one or only a few defendants. In these cases, the court has little basis for justifying why the particular emitters before it are being asked to pay and not others, apart from the unlucky circumstance that they happened to have been sued. In such a situation, the court's authority is at its lowest ebb.

How Climate Litigation Can Affect the Public Debate over Federal Climate Legislation

Climate litigation is unlikely to be effective in reducing greenhouse gases without support from the legislative and executive branches. Nevertheless, climate litigation filters issues relevant to regulation and in doing so, affects the public debate on regulation.

DEPOLITICIZING CLIMATE SCIENCE

Gordon Silverstein writes that the fundamental attraction or "allure" of the courts is the widespread perception that, unlike politics, the judicial process is neutral and objective.[60] Fear of the abuse of political power and concern about corruption, he argues, fuel demands for increasingly legalistic solutions to social problems.[61] The neutral aura provided by judicial institutions can help depoliticize issues that reach the courts. To the extent that partisanship can stand in the way of efforts to form a consensus on the need for government action, this depoliticizing function can help pave the way for regulation.

A major barrier to climate change regulation in the United States has been the success of efforts to undermine the credibility of climate science. The science at issue is that relied on to demonstrate that climate change is occurring and that human-induced emissions of greenhouse gases are a major cause of the change. Climate change is a physical phenomenon; how it occurs and what its impacts will be are understandable only through the tools of science. By questioning the science, critics of regulation have been successful in keeping climate change off the regulatory agenda. Climate change litigation, however, and specifically the Supreme Court's opinion in *Massachusetts* v. *EPA,* showed respect for the science underlying projections of climate change. In this important case, the Supreme Court signaled its acceptance of scientific conclusions as part of its ruling and in doing so refused to allow disagreements over scientific aspects of climate change to delay addressing the legal issues. Because of the respect that attends the pronouncements of courts, especially that of the Supreme Court,[62] such an endorsement is important.

For much of its time on the public agenda, the question of whether human-induced greenhouse gas emissions are causing climate change has been cast as a matter of great uncertainty. That viewpoint has persisted, despite rigorous evidence that a strong consensus on this issue has existed within the scientific community since at least the mid-1990s.[63] Indeed, as recently as 2003, the Bush administration used scientific uncertainty as a rationale for not regulating greenhouse gas emissions from motor vehicles.[64]

Characterizing as uncertain the climate science on the link between global warming and the greenhouse gas emissions of factories and cars is, of course, powerfully advantageous for the opponents of climate change regulation. The oil industry pushed the characterization of the science as uncertain in its advertising campaigns,[65] and while not all of those who espoused that view were politically motivated to do so, media and government reports document the length to which high-ranking Bush administration officials went—at times editing government-funded scientific reports—to play up the uncertainties surrounding the human role in climate change.[66] How could anyone support the costly regulation of industry when it was possible that neither the problem nor the human connection to it was real?

The *Massachusetts* v. *EPA* litigation provided an opportunity for the judiciary to depoliticize the science surrounding the issue of global warming. In that case, the EPA had refused to regulate greenhouse gas emissions from motor vehicles under the Clean Air Act, a position that it defended on statutory grounds, arguing that the act did not cover greenhouse gases. It also based its position on policy grounds, offering the argument, among others, that even if the act did cover greenhouse gases, uncertainties in climate science regarding the contribution of human activities to global warming justified delaying action.[67] In the opening lines of its opinion, the Court used its bully pulpit to undercut the argument of scientific uncertainty by showing respect for the work and conclusions of climate scientists. Writing for a five-justice majority, Justice Stevens stated that a "well-documented" rise in global temperatures has coincided with increases in atmospheric concentrations of carbon dioxide and that "[r]espected scientists believe the two trends are related."[68]

While the Court never voiced its direct disagreement with EPA's characterization of the scientific record, it ruled that the simple invocation of scientific uncertainty was patently insufficient to justify a refusal to regulate.[69] The clear implication is that such breezy characterizations of the science are insufficient; only careful analysis will suffice. Finally, as court rules allow parties to submit amicus briefs, a group of world-renowned climate scientists (many of whom were the authors of the scientific report that EPA characterized as demonstrating the uncertainties of climate science) submitted a brief summarizing the scientific consensus on the issue of causation and explaining the areas of remaining uncertainty.[70]

By rehabilitating the science behind climate change, the Court lent credibility to scientific predictions of the impacts resulting from such change and the greenhouse gas reductions needed to prevent certain types of environmental impacts from occurring. That would seem to support the efforts of those seeking greater climate regulation. Other developments, however, may counter the rehabilitation of climate science effectuated by the courts. The unauthorized publication of climate scientists' e-mails, dubbed "Climategate" in the media, is an example of a development that threatens to undermine the credibility of climate scientists.[71]

IDENTIFYING VICTIMS AND CONCRETE REPERCUSSIONS OF INACTION

To overcome the status quo—inaction—advocates of regulation must be able to generate public support for regulation. To do so, it is critical that they be able to provide compelling examples of the harms that will occur as a result of inaction and, if possible, point to identifiable victims whose health or welfare will be compromised or sacrificed by the government's failure to act. While the seminal reports of the Intergovernmental Panel on Climate Change (IPCC) provide an assessment of the predicted impacts of climate change, much of the discussion is abstract and presented at the global scale.[72] Certainly nothing in the IPCC reports enables the reader to understand the impacts of global climate change at the state level or to identify particular persons affected and learn how their lives may radically change as a result of climate change.[73] Instead, climate litigation is doing just that: providing regulators with not only the most detailed accounts of predicted impacts that the science will support but also with a growing list of sympathetic victims, both human and animal.

Two legal actions, both concerning native peoples, shed light on the social costs of climate change and demonstrate that climate change is affecting real people—the 399 residents of a traditional Inupiat village—in fundamental and irreversible ways. In the case of *Kivalina* v. *ExxonMobil*, information about specific effects on individuals makes the story personal. Kivalina is located at the tip of a six-mile long barrier reef between the Chukchi Sea and the Kivalina and Wulik Rivers in Northern Alaska. The public learns that, due to global warming, the sea ice that once formed a protective cocoon around Kivalina is much thinner, leaving the village to be battered by waves. The damage is now so extensive that Kivalina is becoming uninhabitable and the entire community must be relocated, at the cost of millions of dollars.[74]

Similarly, in the petition of the Inuit peoples before the Inter-American Court of Human Rights, the public learns exactly what can happen to native traditions when sea ice gets thinner due to global warming.[75] The case also revealed that more people and equipment fell through the ice, that people died while pulling a whale up on top of thin ice, and that many families went hungry if they failed to hunt earlier in the season before the ice melted. It is also explained that because the snow is no longer the deep dense kind that the villagers traditionally used to build igloos, young people have died for lack of shelter.[76]

While the *Kivalina* v. *Exxon Mobil* case and the Inuit petition give the impacts of climate change a human face, the many petitions filed under the Endangered Species Act give the costs of climate change an "animal face." The most sympathetic of these is that filed to list the polar bear as an endangered species due to dwindling sea ice.[77] The 170-page petition, complete with stunning pictures of mother polar bears with their cubs, describes the manner in which thinning sea ice threatens the survival of polar bear populations due to a shortened seal hunting season, reduced availability of prey, reduced access to denning areas, increased need to swim and travel greater distances in search of prey, and increased human presence from expanded commercial fishing operations.[78]

Finally, in still other climate change cases, the abstraction of many of the predicted environmental impacts of climate change on a global scale are presented on the much smaller scale of a single subnational region, such as the northeastern United States, or a single state, such as California. Thus, in the complaint filed in *Connecticut* v. *American Electric Power,* it is noted that climate change will accelerate sea level rise, leading to the permanent loss of 5,000 square miles of dry land while water levels in the Great Lakes drop, choking wetlands, reducing the output of hydropower plants, and reducing tourism in forested areas because the display of fall colors is shorter.[79] In *California* v. *General Motors,* California details the millions of dollars that it will have to spend in response to coastal erosion from sea level rise and the substantial sums of money that it is spending to accommodate the earlier snowpack melt.[80]

These and other stories affect the public's understanding of climate change and hence the public debate. Climate litigation demonstrates the ways in which climate change will affect the environment on a scale that is familiar to most people and provides an opportunity for those whose lives are far removed from the impacts of climate change to glimpse how climate change is currently affecting the everyday lives of others. Such stories cannot be found in scientific reports, but they can be found in litigation documents.

Revealing the Inadequacies of Current Law

Public debates over regulation routinely grapple with the alleged adequacy or inadequacy of current regulatory authorities to address the problem at hand. When a government agency is sued for failure to regulate, the adversarial process gives the agency an incentive to supply illustrations of the inapplicability of current laws to escape liability for its failure to use them. Thus the many lawsuits that have been filed against government authorities for failure to regulate climate change are a source of analyses of the current holes in the applicability of existing law in addressing climate change.

The *Massachusetts* v. *EPA* case illustrates the manner in which the adversarial process uncovered aspects of the current regime regulating air pollution that rendered it inadequate for the regulation of climate change. As discussed above, the plaintiffs filed suit against EPA to compel the agency to regulate greenhouse gas emissions from mobile sources. Hence, their lawsuit was premised on the argument that the Clean Air Act constituted a wholly adequate legal basis for compelling reductions in the contribution to global warming made by cars and trucks.

That assumes that the Clean Air Act compels the EPA to regulate "air pollutants" from new motor vehicles and that greenhouse gases are "air pollutants" under the extremely broad definition provided by statute.[81]

Yet as the EPA quickly pointed out in litigation briefs, the plaintiffs' statutory argument potentially proved too much. If carbon dioxide was an "air pollutant" for the purposes of the act's mobile source provisions, it also would appear to be an air pollutant for purposes of the act's other provisions, including Title I, which is the vehicle through which the act limits pollution emissions from stationary sources. Under Title I, the EPA is required to establish national ambient air quality standards for each "air pollutant" listed in order to designate areas as "attainment" or "nonattainment" areas under those standards and to leave to states the job of achieving attainment within their jurisdiction.[82] In its efforts to deflect the plaintiff's claims, the EPA argued that the act did not apply to greenhouse gases because Title I's use of an ambient-based target to achieve air pollution goals made no sense when applied to a greenhouse gas.[83] In doing so, EPA supplied a powerful argument to those seeking new legal authorities to regulate factories and other stationary sources of greenhouse gas emissions.

The common law climate change liability actions filed by state government plaintiffs demonstrate how litigation can signal the inadequacies that exist under current law simply by virtue of the legal theories chosen and the identity of the plaintiffs. The plaintiffs in *Connecticut* v. *American Electric Power* sued the owners and operators of five electric power corporations, five of the largest emitters of carbon dioxide in the United States.[84] Tellingly, the states sued the corporations for injunctive relief (abatement of emissions) under a theory of federal and state public nuisance. This simple choice of legal theory strongly signaled the lack of available statutory authorities by which to compel emission reductions; given the numerous hurdles to establishing liability under common law, only a plaintiff with no other legal option would attempt such a lawsuit.[85]

A second signal provided by the *American Electric Power* case is found in the identities of the plaintiffs and defendants in the suit, which raise concerns about the inadequacy of state regulation and hence the need for a federal regulatory solution. The plaintiffs in the lawsuit were some of the nation's more aggressive state climate regulators, actively pursuing caps on the emissions of power plants within their borders, and the defendants were out-of-state corporations.[86] Reliance on the efforts of even the states that are "leaders" in climate legislation is insufficient when the nation's largest greenhouse gas emitters are located in other states and thus outside the jurisdiction of those leaders.

The final and perhaps definitive signal concerning the adequacy of existing legal authorities is provided by the district court decision in both the *American Electric Power* and the *California* v. *General Motors* cases. In ruling in both cases that the plaintiffs' common law claims presented nonjusticiable political questions, the

courts demonstrated the need for regulatory standards to guide the courts in deciding liability cases.

BLAMING INSTITUTIONS OTHER THAN CONGRESS

Litigation can exert a powerful influence in terms of framing the causes of a
given problem and the persons or institutions that are to blame, potentially over-
powering alternative frames provided by other sources.[87] Litigation necessarily
frames the defendants that are being sued as the culprits and frames the "issue"
along the lines of the legal theory employed in the case.

In the case of climate change, litigation against EPA and other federal agencies
has succeeded in framing the issue as the executive branch's failure to address this
important environmental problem. Litigation against large emitters, such as the
electric power corporations in the *American Electric Power* case or the car manufacturers in *California* v. *GM*, provides a secondary narrative, which frames the
problem as one caused by profligate corporate polluters. This framing is a direct
outcome of the defendants and legal theories available to plaintiffs in the climate
change context.

The important point for the purposes of this discussion, however, is that both
methods avoid placing blame on Congress. Yet critics could point their fingers
directly at Congress. Congressional failure to act can very easily account for the
continued lack of any federal climate regulatory program; it is part and parcel of
Congress's inability to reach consensus on a whole host of pressing issues facing the
nation, which are explored more fully in chapter 11. Similarly, the very need for
climate policy now could be blamed on Congress's failure in the past to develop an
energy policy based on renewable resources instead of fossil fuels, to build a transportation system based on public transportation instead of the automobile, or to
put an end to a whole host of subsidies provided to the oil industry.[88]

TURNING INDUSTRY DEFENDANTS INTO SUPPORTERS
OF FEDERAL CLIMATE LEGISLATION

Litigation can generate support for climate regulation among industries subject to climate lawsuits. For industry, the prospect of long and costly trials focused
on pollution from industrial plants and the prospect of widely varying judgments
establishing emissions standards based on vague standards of unreasonable conduct under public nuisance could render the alternative of legislation attractive.
That may be the case especially if the legislation provides for liability immunity.

The Influence of Climate Policy on the Role of the Courts

The tools that Congress chooses to use in future climate legislation will largely
drive the amount and type of future climate litigation and hence the future role
of the courts in climate policy. Much will depend on two factors: whether Congress itself establishes the terms of the regulatory scheme, as it has when legislat-

ing a cap-and-trade program, or instead delegates a large measure of implementation authority to agency administrators, as it has when regulating according to a cooperative federalism model. Finally, much will depend on whether Congress preempts state climate change regulation or common law liability actions and, if so, the scope of the preemption. For related discussions of these issues in this volume, see chapter 4 relating to preemption and chapter 12 on challenges relating to the administration of climate policy programs.

Recent bills in Congress demonstrate that with respect to these choices, nothing is settled. Most of the major legislative proposals employ a cap-and-trade scheme,[89] including the bill passed by the House during the 111th Congress.[90] But cap and trade is losing favor and competing proposals severely limit the scope of a market trading scheme. The same is true with respect to the issue of taxes (the latest proposals include taxing oil producers rather than including them in a cap-and-trade regime) and various types of government support for nuclear power, offshore oil and gas drilling, and "clean coal" technologies.[91] And whereas a House-based bill adopted an uneasy compromise on the preemption of state climate laws (preempting state and regional cap-and-trade regimes for five years), other proposals being floated (and so far rebuffed) would preempt state and local climate legislation altogether, along with all regulation of greenhouse gases under current environmental laws and all lawsuits claiming that greenhouse gas emissions constitute a common law tort.[92]

A Federal Greenhouse Gas Cap-and-Trade Scheme

In crafting federal climate legislation, Congress must decide whether to employ the more traditional regulatory model, often referred to as "command and control" regulation, under which sources are individually subject to emissions controls based on health, performance, or technology goals, or to employ a market-based tool, such as a carbon tax or an emissions cap-and-trade program. As explored in chapters 5 and 6 in this volume, of the two, a market-based program appears to be the preferred alternative for carbon regulation and, among market-based instruments, a cap-and-trade program appears to be the clear front-runner, despite many economists' preference for a carbon tax. Which model is used will have important implications for future federal climate regulation precisely because the judicial role is likely to differ substantially depending on various elements of regime design.

A review of the litigation record indicates that courts have played only a minor role in shaping the implementation of the acid rain program—which, in fact, has been remarkably impervious to legal challenge. Exceptions include occasional challenges to EPA regulations,[93] infrequent disputes between parties that benefit from the national trading market established under the program, and states that are in some way interfering with that market.[94]

Commentators attribute the comparative lack of litigation under the acid rain program to the minimal role of EPA in implementing the program vis-à-vis the

agency's traditional role in nonmarket-based environmental programs.[95] Under
the Clean Water Act, for instance, EPA must digest a mountain of empirical data
about available pollution control technologies and then impose abatement
requirements on individual polluters based on its judgment of whether a technology meets a broadly worded statutory standard that asks EPA to balance costs
against environmental benefits and energy use. In contrast, EPA's task under the
acid rain program has been relatively easy and discretion-free. Congress itself
established the system of freely tradable sulfur dioxide emission rights ("allowances") as well as the criteria for the allocation of those rights among electric
utility plants, a relatively discrete and homogenous category of emission sources.
It left for EPA the more limited and comparatively straightforward job of setting
up the reporting and accounting system needed to ensure adequate enforcement.

The EPA's lack of involvement in decisionmaking related to the allocation of
allowances, the primary factor in determining utilities' compliance costs, is likely
the key to the dearth of litigation under the acid rain program. Because of EPA's
noninvolvement, firms have exhibited less interest in the administrative process
and there have been fewer disputes with the agency leading to litigation.[96] View-
ing the cap-and-trade program in isolation, the courts' most important function
will be to police the emissions trading market against interference by states seeking to benefit from restricting the market in some manner.[97]

Due to the manifold differences between the scope, complexity, and availability of solutions to the problem of acid rain vis-à-vis climate change, however, it
may be reckless to impute the limited litigation under the acid rain program to a
carbon cap-and-trade regime enacted in the future.[98] First, the emissions reductions needed under a climate change program dwarf those under the acid rain
program; hence the scope, intrusiveness, and stringency of a climate change program will vastly exceed those of the acid rain program. Second, a program to
reduce climate change will involve the regulation of many more industrial sectors
than just electrical power generation. While power plants are responsible for two-
thirds of all sulfur dioxide emissions in the United States, they are responsible for
only one-third of U.S. carbon dioxide emissions. Hence, a carbon cap-and-trade
program must cover many different sectors, increasing the administrative complexity of the program as well as the difficulty of monitoring compliance and
thereby elevating litigation risk.

Third, there is no short list of "quick fixes" for reducing carbon dioxide as there
is for sulfur dioxide. With respect to acid rain, existing utilities were able to rely
more heavily on low-sulfur-emitting plants, to switch from high- to low-sulfur
coal, and to install scrubbers to remove post-combustion emissions. However,
there are no easy ways to reduce carbon dioxide from existing plants in the electricity sector; there is no such thing as a scrubber for carbon dioxide or a "low-
carbon" fuel. Instead, reductions in carbon emissions from the electricity sector

must come from conservation and energy efficiency as well as greater use of renewable resources, an objective that requires a more varied list of strategies, boosting administrative complexity and monitoring costs and hence, litigation.

A final factor worth mention is the comparative international scope of the acid rain versus a climate change cap-and-trade program. The problem of acid rain is primarily a bilateral problem, wherein both U.S. and Canadian emissions (though disproportionately those emanating from the United States) cause the acid rain that affects, for the most part, the two countries involved. Because climate change is truly a global problem, with all countries of the world contributing to the problem as well as being affected by it, there is a greater likelihood that a U.S. domestic regulatory program, such as a cap-and-trade model, will be somehow linked to programs of other countries (see also the chapters in part 4 of this volume on the relationship of U.S. climate change policy to trans-Atlantic and global opportunities in this realm). The integrity of linked trading regimes lies in adequate enforcement and monitoring systems, topics strongly influenced by the courts.[99]

With the prospect of federal climate legislation more real than ever, the scope of potential litigation under the legislation is becoming clearer. All signs point to an active role for the courts under proposed legislation in sorting out the allocation of allowances and the use of offsets.[100] If Congress fails to establish clear directives on how much of the allowances will be distributed for free to regulated parties and how much will be auctioned off, litigation on those points is likely. Furthermore, the clear trend in the draft legislation is to allow firms to satisfy their obligation to reduce emissions through the purchase of "offsets"—emissions mitigation achieved by third parties. Litigation is likely over what qualifies as an offset and whether it constitutes a real and verifiable reduction in the emissions that would otherwise occur.

For example, is a promise by a landowner in Oregon not to cut down the forest on his land a creditable offset? Must the farmer be monitored to ensure that he does not, in fact, cut down the forest? The House-passed bill delegated authority over agricultural offsets (forestry sequestration, changes in land management, and methane capture from farms through the use of biodigesters) to the Department of Agriculture in a move than many environmentalists criticize as undermining future attempts to ensure that offsets represent additional and verifiable reductions in emissions.

Furthermore, any future federal emissions trading program will come into existence against a backdrop of increasingly entrenched climate regulatory programs at the state and regional levels, including one or more greenhouse gas cap-and-trade programs that are actually up and running. In addition to the Regional Greenhouse Gas Initiative (RGGI) in the northeast, California and the Western states, under the auspices of the Western Climate Initiative (WCI), are in the process of establishing their own cap-and-trade programs, as discussed more fully in chapter 5 of this volume. Besides these cap-and-trade programs, states are moving forward with a variety of climate mitigation measures, from California's greenhouse gas emissions standards to renewable portfolio standards and green building codes.

As noted throughout this volume, enactment of a federal cap-and-trade program will pose the sticky legal questions of whether and how much federal climate legislation might preempt any state legislation. Thus far, the preemption debate is focusing on how a federal cap-and-trade program would "mesh" with state programs—specifically, whether a federal program would establish a minimum federal cap (preempting less stringent state caps) but allow states or regions to adopt more ambitious caps or deadlines.[101]

Future battles over the scope of federal preemption under the supremacy clause of the Constitution will wind up in the courts. Much will hinge, of course, on the statutory language enacted. Certainly, the more explicit Congress is with respect to its intention to either preempt or not preempt state climate programs, the fewer the legal challenges. Nevertheless, regardless of the approach adopted by Congress, litigation over the preemption issue is likely to be considerable. That is attributable in no small part to the indeterminateness of the legal tests for preemption and to the inconsistency in preemption case law, as well as the documented proclivity of judges to resolve preemption questions according to the judge's personal ideology.[102]

In future disputes over the scope of federal preemption, all parties—EPA, the states, regulated sources, and environmental organizations—will have strong equitable claims, which is likely to elevate the contentiousness of the issue. EPA will cite the need for an unfettered national emissions trading market to achieve emissions reductions at the least cost. The states will argue from the vantage point of state sovereignty, the benefits of state experimentation, and the minimal nature of the conflicts between federal and state requirements. Regulated sources will likely side with EPA, citing the additional costs and duplication resulting from overlapping federal and state programs. Environmental groups are likely to be split, reflecting a broader lack of consensus within the environmental community on the desirability of emissions trading in general. Beginning in the 1980s, some environmental organizations, especially those with a national focus, such as the Conservation Foundation and Environmental Defense (formerly known as the Environmental Defense Fund), became strong supporters of emissions trading.[103] Others, often ones with more of a grassroots focus, such as the Sierra Club, Environmental Action, and Greenpeace, are less favorably disposed to emissions trading, concerned that it is vulnerable to cheating and might create dangerous pollutant "hotspots" with localized adverse environmental or health effects in particular geographic areas.[104] Based on such equitable concerns, a number of environmental justice organizations in California have come out against implementation of the California carbon cap through an emissions trading scheme.[105]

In sum, given the experience with the acid rain trading program, a federal cap-and-trade program could signal a more modest role for the courts, but that result would be unlikely given the litigation that could be generated over the rules governing the market trading program as well as the question of the scope of federal preemption.

A Cooperative Federalism Framework

Enactment of a carbon cap-and-trade program is not inevitable and, some argue, not necessarily the best policy, either. Some commentators argue that a cooperative federalism framework, modeled on the major pollution statutes, is a better choice.[106] Under this approach, the federal government takes the lead in establishing nationally applicable standards to achieve a particular goal, such as the protection of health or the promotion of cost-effective technology. At the same time, the states are offered the opportunity to apply the standards to individual sources, often through a permit program, and to enforce the standards within their own boundaries. The benefits of a cooperative federalism approach include its capacity to spur innovation; its ability to address emissions from all sectors of society, from industrial to residential;[107] and its ability to leverage the authority and capacities of the states to meet emission reduction targets.[108]

Like a federal cap-and-trade program, a cooperative federalism regime is likely to result in a large role for the federal courts. The reason would not be so much a large number of claims of federal preemption, but the greater role traditionally exercised by EPA in the implementation of cooperative federal programs. That, in turn, generates more opportunities for legal challenge. Shep Melnick and other commentators have documented the types of legal challenges that occur when Congress delegates broad authority to the administration or agency overseeing a particular program. Congress's historical practice of giving EPA and other federal agencies huge or even utopian goals without the resources needed to achieve those goals has been a fertile source of litigation, as environmental groups often seek the assistance of the courts to compel EPA to deliver what the statute appears to call for.[109] However, even when not arguably utopian, the delegation of regulatory authority to an agency can give rise to both procedural and substantive legal challenges to agency action. Groups such as business and environmental organizations can challenge the legality of the procedures used by the agency as inadequate under the governing statute or the Administrative Procedure Act and the agency's substantive decisions as inconsistent with Congress's statutory directive. The less specific the statutory delegation, the greater the opportunities for litigants to claim that the agency's actions are inconsistent with Congress's intent.[110]

If a large number of legal challenges are filed under a cooperative federalism regime, it can lead to the rearranging of EPA's priorities. Matters under litigation become the agency's top priority, while more pressing environmental matters are moved to the bottom of the pile.[111] From the standpoint of administration, researchers have found that a large amount of litigation serves to redistribute budgetary resources within EPA to the litigation "hot spots" and perhaps away from other more pressing budgetary needs.[112] Finally, a large volume of litigation can result in elevating the importance of the agency's legal staff and downgrading the importance of staff whose work is usually unrelated to litigation, such as agency scientists.[113]

Conclusion

This chapter attempts both to assess the current contribution being made by the courts toward climate policymaking and to predict the courts' influence on a future federal climate regime. More than anything else, the analysis reveals the depth and the scope of the degree to which legislators, agency regulators, and courts influence each others' dockets. While the courts' docket of climate litigation is profoundly influenced by the absence of federal climate change legislation, that litigation is in many respects affecting the public debate over the future of climate regulation. Regardless of whether Congress chooses to regulate climate change in the future under a market-based cap-and-trade regime or one more resembling a traditional cooperative federalism regime—or a combination of the two—the program adopted is likely to invite a large role for the courts. That role in turn will shape the policy decisions and administration of the regulatory program.

Notes

1. Mining on federal lands: *Kleppe* v. *Sierra Club*, 427 U.S. 390 (1976); air pollution: *Sierra Club* v. *Ruckelshaus*, 344 F.Supp. 253, *aff'd*, 4 ERC 1815 (D.C. Cir.), aff'd by an equally divided court, 412 U.S. 541 (1973); water pollution: *Natural Resources Defense Council* v. *Costle*, 568 F.2d. 1369 (D.C. Cir. 1977); hazardous and nuclear waste disposal: *Vermont Yankee Nuclear Power Corporation* v. *Natural Resources Defense Council*, 435 U.S. 519 (1978); lead poisoning: see, for example, *Natural Resources Defense Council* v. *Train*, 510 F.2d 692 (D.C. Cir. 1974); endangered species: TVA v. Hill, 437 U.S. 153 (1978).

2. Robert Meltz, *Climate Change Litigation: A Growing Phenomenon*, Report to Congress 1 (2008): "Though the first court decision related to climate change appeared 18 years ago, the quantity of such litigation has mushroomed in recent years: more than two dozen cases pursuing multiple legal theories are now pending."

3. David L. Markell and J. B. Ruhl, "An Empirical Survey on Climate Change Litigation in the United States," Public Law Research Paper 433 (Florida State University College of Law, April 6, 2010) (http://ssrn.com/abstract=1585341).

4. *Massachusetts* v. *EPA*, 549 U.S. 497, 529 (2007).

5. See, for example, *Montana Environmental Information Center* v. *Johanns*, No. 07-CV-01331 (D.D.C. filed July 23, 2007), challenging the Department of Agriculture's Rural Utility Service's use of low-interest loans to help finance the construction of at least eight new coal-fired power plants.

6. *Connecticut* v. *American Electric Power*, 406 F. Supp. 2d 265 (S.D.N.Y. 2005).

7. "Inuit Petition Inter-American Commission on Human Rights to Oppose Climate Change Caused by the United States," December 7, 2005 (www.earthjustice.org/library/legal_docs/petition-to-the-inter-american-commission-on-human-rights-on-behalf-of-the-inuit-circumpolar-conference.pdf).

8. Gerald Rosenberg, *The Hollow Hope: Can Courts Bring About Social Change?* (University of Chicago Press, 1991), p. 292.

9. Gordon Silverstein, *Law's Allure: How Law Shapes, Constrains, Saves, and Kills Politics* (Cambridge University Press, 2009), pp. 1, 127.

10. Lettie McSpadden, "The Courts and Environmental Policy," in *Environmental Politics and Policy: Theories and Evidence*, edited by James P. Lester (Duke University Press, 1995), p. 251.

11. See, for example, David Hunter, "The Implications of Climate Change Litigation for International Environmental Law-Making," in *Adjudicating Climate Control: Sub-National, National, and Supra-National Approaches*, edited by H. Osofsky and W. Burns (Cambridge University Press, 2009); Alice Kaswan, "The Domestic Response to Global Climate Change: What Role for Federal, State, and Litigation Initiatives?" *University of San Francisco Law Review* 42, no. 1 (2007), pp. 99–100; David A. Grossman, "Warming Up to a Not-So-Radical Idea: Tort-Based Climate Change Litigation," *Columbia Journal of Environmental Law* 28, no. 1 (2003), pp. 1–62.

12. Most of the venom against climate change litigation is reserved for common law liability actions. See Theodore J. Boutrous Jr. and Dominic Lanza, "Global Warming Tort Litigation: The Real 'Public Nuisance,'" *Ecology Law Currents* 35 (2008), pp. 80–89; David Dana, "The Mismatch between Public Nuisance Law and Global Warming," Northwestern Law and Economics Research Paper 08-05, May 6, 2008 (http://ssrn.com/abstract=1129838), rejecting a role for common law courts in addressing climate change, arguing instead that the states should be limited to using state legislation to serve the purpose of prodding more meaningful consideration of global warming by the federal political branches; Shi-Ling Hsu, "A Realistic Evaluation of Climate Change Litigation through the Lens of a Hypothetical Lawsuit," *University of Colorado Law Review* 79, no. 3 (2008), pp. 701–66, arguing that litigation can play at most a modest role in bringing about greenhouse gas reductions but not that it is an inappropriate strategy in the absence of legislative action; Thomas W. Merrill, "Global Warming as a Public Nuisance," *Columbia Journal of Environmental Law* 30, no. 2 (2005), pp. 293–334.

13. Merrill, *supra* note 12 ; Shi-Ling Hsu, *supra* note 12; and Grossman, *supra* note 11.

14. Timothy Lytton, "Using Tort Litigation to Enhance Regulatory Policy Making: Evaluating Climate Change Litigation in Light of Lessons from Gun Industry and Clergy Sexual-Abuse Lawsuits," *Texas Law Review* 86, no. 7 (2008), p. 1875; Kaswan, "The Domestic Response to Global Climate Change"; Kirsten H. Engel, "Harmonizing Regulatory and Litigation Approaches to Climate Change," *University of Pennsylvania Law Review* 155, no. 6 (2007), pp. 1563–1604.

15. Markell and Ruhl, *supra* note 3.

16. There are numerous excellent sources for a more detailed discussion of federal climate change litigation developments. A good place to start is with the chart "Climate Change Litigation in the U.S.,"compiled by Michael Gerrard (www.climatecasechart.com/).

17. "Mandamus §1 Definition," *American Jurisprudence,* 2nd ed. (Westgroup, 2000), pp. 268–69, defining mandamus as a civil judicial remedy commanding performance to undertake a particular duty required by law.

18. *Massachusetts* v. *EPA,* 549 U.S. 497 (2007).

19. *California* v. *Johnson,* "Petition for Rulemaking Seeking the Regulation of Greenhouse Gas Emissions from Ocean-Going Vessels," October 3, 2007 (http://ag.ca.gov/cms_pdfs/press/N1474_Petition.pdf).

20. *California* v. *Johnson,* "Petition for Rulemaking Seeking the Regulation of Greenhouse Gas Emissions from Aircraft," November 6, 2007 (http://ag.ca.gov/cms_attachments/press/pdfs/n1501_aircraft_petition_final.pdf).

21. "Petition for Rulemaking Seeking the Regulation of Greenhouse Gas Emissions from Nonroad Vehicles and Engines," January 29, 2008 (http://ag.ca.gov/cms_attachments/press/pdfs/n1522_finaldraftnonroadpetition3.pdf). In this petition, California was joined by the states of Connecticut, Massachusetts, New Jersey, and Oregon.

22. "Before the Secretary of the Interior, Petition to List the Polar Bear (Ursus maritimus) as a Threatened Species under the Endangered Species Act," February 16, 2005; "Petition to List Acropora Palmata (Elkhorn Coral), Acropora Cervicornis (Staghorn Coral), and Acropora prolifera (Fused-Staghorn Coral) as Endangered Species under the Endangered Species Act," March 2004; "Before the Secretary of the Interior, Petition to List the American Pika (Ochotona Princeps) as Threatened or Endangered under the United States Endangered Species Act," October 1, 2007; "Before the Secretary of Commerce, Petition to List the Ribbon Seal (Histriophoca Fasciata) as a Threatened or Endangered Species under the Endangered Species Act," December 20, 2007; "Petition to List the Pacific Walrus as an Endangered Species under the Endangered Species Act," February 2008.

23. *Massachusetts* v. *EPA,* 549 U.S. at 527-28.

24. Ibid. at 533 ("Under the clear terms of the Clean Air Act, EPA can avoid taking further action only if it determines that greenhouse gases do not contribute to climate change or if it provides some reasonable explanation as to why it cannot or will not exercise its discretion to determine whether they do.") See also Jody Freeman and Adrian Vermeule, *"Massachusetts* v. *EPA*: From Politics to Expertise," *Supreme Court Review* 2007 (2007), pp. 96–97.

25. *Wildearth Guardians* v. *United States Forest Service*, No. 09-1089, 2009 U.S. App. LEXIS 16387 (2009).

26. *Center for Biological Diversity* v. *Kempthorne*, No. C-07-0894 EDL (N.D. Cal. 2007). This case was recently transferred to the United States District Court for the District of Alaska. 2007 U.S. Dist. LEXIS 53187 (2007).

27. *Connecticut* v. *American Electric Power Co.*, 406 F.Supp.2d 265 (S.D.N.Y. 2005).

28. *California* v. *General Motors Corp.*, No. C06-05755 MJJ, 2007 WL 2726871 (N.D. Cal. September 17, 2007).

29. *Native Village of Kivalina* v. *ExxonMobil Corp* (N.D. Cal., Complaint filed February 26, 2008).

30. *Comer* v. *Murphy Oil USA*, 585 F.3d 855 (5th Cir. 2009).

31. In *American Electric Power*, the plaintiffs seek a court order mandating a reduction in the facilities' emissions. *Connecticut* v. *American Electric Power Co.*, 406 F.Supp.2d 265, 270 (S.D.N.Y. 2005) (citing State Complaint at ¶ 6 (No. 104CV05669); OSI Complaint at ¶ 10 (No. 104CV05670)).

32. In *California* v. *General Motors*, the state is seeking monetary damages. Second Amended Complaint for Damages and Declaratory Judgment at ¶ 2, 6, *California* v. *General Motors Corp.*, No. C06-05755 EMC (N.D. Cal. Oct. 24, 2006). Similarly, in *Kivalina*, the village is seeking monetary damages to cover, among other expenses, the costs to the village of relocating due to rising sea levels, a cost estimated at between 90 and 400 million dollars. Complaint for Damages at ¶ 6, *Native Village of Kivalina* v. *ExxonMobil Corp.*, No. CV-08-01138 SBA (N.D. Cal. Feb 26, 2008).

33. See Arnold Reitze, "The Legislative History of U.S. Air Pollution Control," *Houston Law Review* 36, no. 3 (1999).

34. See *Georgia* v. *Tennessee Copper Co.*, 206 U.S. 230 (1907), a public nuisance case in which Georgia sued a Tennessee copper smelter for emitting fumes that were destroying forests, crops, and orchards in Georgia; *Missouri* v. *Illinois*, 180 U.S. 208 (1901), a public nuisance case in which Missouri sued to prevent Illinois from discharging sewage waste into the Mississippi River above St. Louis.

35. *City of Milwaukee* v. *Illinois and Michigan*, 451 U.S. 304 (1981), federal common law of public nuisance displaced by the Federal Water Pollution Control Act of 1972.

36. *Marbury* v. *Madison*, 5 U.S. (1 Cranch) 137 (1803).

37. *Massachusetts* v. *EPA*, 549 U.S. 497, 529 (2007).

38. *Lujan* v. *Defenders of Wildlife*, 504 U.S. 555, 560-65 (1992).

39. *Connecticut* v. *American Electric Power Co.*, 582 F.2d at 339–49.

40. *Comer* v. *Murphy Oil USA*, 585 F.3d. 855, at 11–20.

41. *Comer* v. *Murphy Oil USA*, No. 07-60756 (5th Cir., May 28, 2010).

42. Plaintiffs can file suit under the Administrative Procedure Act to ask the courts to use their authority to "compel agency action unlawfully withheld or unreasonably delayed," 5 U.S.C. § 706(1). However, the courts use the factors included in the case of *Telecommunications Research and Action Center* v. *FCC*, 750 F.2d 70 (D.C. Cir. 1984) to decide whether to grant the "extraordinary remedy of mandamus," and those factors are biased against mandamus relief when Congress has failed to establish a deadline for agency action and the agency can claim the issue is complex.

43. Rosenberg, *The Hollow Hope*, pp. 281–82. Although environmentalists won the legal battle to stop the Alaska pipeline, Congress promptly overrode the courts and the pipeline was built; ditto with respect to the TVA's Tellico Dam project.

44. *Massachusetts* v. *EPA,* 127 S.Ct. at 1463.

45. Ibid.

46. The plaintiffs in *Massachusetts* v. *EPA* filed a petition for mandamus, seeking a court order compelling the agency to make the endangerment decision within sixty days. The federal appeals court denied the petition. *Massachusetts* v. *EPA*, No. No. 03-1361 (D.C. Cir., Slip Op. June 26, 2008) (order denying the petition). The one judge on the three-judge panel to write a decision in the case found the lack of a specific congressional deadline and the fact that only a year had passed to be determinative (Tatel, J., concurring in part and dissenting in part from the denial of the petition).

47. EPA, Proposed Endangerment and Cause or Contribute Findings for Greenhouse Gases under Section 202(a) of the Clean Air Act, 64 Fed. Reg. 18886 (April 24, 2009).

48. See EPA, "Notice of Proposed Rulemaking to Establish Light-Duty Vehicle Greenhouse Gas Emission Standards and Corporate Fuel Economy Standards," signed September 15, 2009; EPA, "Final Mandatory Reporting of Greenhouse Gases Rule," September 22, 2009.

49. *Couch* v. *Friends of Chattahoochee, Inc.*, No. 2008CV146398 (Ga. Sup. Ct. June 30, 2008) (order reversing final decision of ALJ), rev'd in part, *Longleaf Energy Assocs., LLC* v. *Friends of Chattahoochee, Inc.*, 681 S.E.2d 203 (Ga. Ct. App. 2009). This is the first judicial ruling that applies *Massachusetts* v. *EPA* outside the transportation sector.

50. Steven Mufson, "Power Plant Rejected over Carbon Dioxide for First Time," *Washington Post*, October 19, 2007, p. A01.

51. *In re Deseret Power Electric Cooperative*, PSD Permit No. OU-000204.00, PSD Appeal No. 07-03 (2008).

52. *In re Deseret Power Electric Cooperative*, PSD Permit No. OU-000204.00, PSD Appeal No. 07-03, *Order Denying Review in Part and Remanding in Part*, at 9 (Decided November 13,

2008) (http://yosemite.epa.gov/oa/EAB_Web_Docket.nsf/Recent-Additions/C8C5985967D
8096E85257500006811A7/$File/Remand...39.pdf).

53. Ibid.

54. *Longleaf Energy Assocs., LLC* v. *Friends of Chattahoochee, Inc.*, 681 S.E.2d 203 (Ga. Ct. App. 2009).

55. "Kansas Governor's Third Coal Plant Veto Sustained," *Environmental News Service,* May 1, 2008 (www.ens-newswire.com/ens/may2008/2008-05-01-094.asp).

56. *Connecticut* v. *American Electric Power*, 406 F.Supp.2d 265 (S.D.N.Y. 2005); *California* v. *General Motors,* No. C06-05755 MJJ, 2007 WL 2726871 (N.D. Cal. September 17, 2007).

57. *Connecticut* v. *American Electric Power*, 406 F.Supp.2d at 272; *California* v. *General Motors,* No. C06-05755 MJJ, 2007 WL 2726871 (N.D.Cal. 2007); *Native Village of Kivalina* v. *ExxonMobil Corp.*, 663 F.Supp.2d 863 (N.D. Cal. 2009).

58. *Connecticut* v. *American Electric Power*, 406 F.Supp.2d at 273.

59. *Connecticut* v. *American Electric Power,* Nos. 05-5104-cv, 05-5119-cv (Slip op. 2d Cir. 2009), at 23.

60. Silverstein, *Law's Allure,* p. 3.

61. Ibid.

62. See Benjamin Whittles, "The Supreme Court's Looming Legitimacy Crisis," *New Republic,* June 25, 2007, reporting on poll results indicating the high public approval ratings received by the Supreme Court in relation to other government institutions though noting figures that may presage a future legitimacy crisis.

63. Naomi Oreskes, "Beyond the Ivory Tower: The Scientific Consensus on Climate Change," *Science* 306, no. 5702 (December 2004), p. 1686 (www.sciencemag.org/cgi/content/full/306/5702/1686).

64. Control of Emissions from New Highway Vehicles and Engines, 68 Fed. Reg. 52,922, 52,930 (September 8, 2003).

65. See allegations contained in the Kivilina Complaint, paragraph 171-212.

66. See House Committee on Oversight and Government Reform, *Allegations of Political Interference with Government Climate Change Science: Hearing before the House Committee on Oversight and Government Reform*, 110 Cong., 1 sess., March 19, 2007. See also Andrew C. Revkin, "Bush Aide Softened Greenhouse Gas Links to Global Warming," *New York Times,* June 8, 2005; Andrew Revkin and Matthew Wald, "Material Shows Weakening of Climate Reports," *New York Times,* March 20, 2007; James V. Grimaldi and Jacqueline Trescott, "Scientists Fault Climate Exhibit Changes; Smithsonian Head Denies Politics Altered Arctic Show Message," *Washington Post,* November 16, 2007, p. A01.

67. Federal Register 68, 52930-31.

68. *Massachusetts* v. *EPA,* 549 U.S. 497 (2007).

69. The Court stated that if the EPA truly believed that the scientific uncertainties were "so profound" that it could not make a judgment concerning whether greenhouse gases from motor vehicles contribute to climate change, then "it must say so." 549 U.S. 497, 534 (2007).

70. Brief of Amici Curiae Climate Scientists David Battisti et al. in support of Petitioners, Massachusetts v. EPA, 127 S. Ct. 1438 (2007) (No. 05-1120) (http://supreme.lp.findlaw.com/Supreme_Court/briefs/05-1120/05-1120.mer.ami.scientists.pdf).

71. Andrew C. Revkin, "Hacked E-Mail Is New Fodder for Climate Dispute," *New York Times,* November 20, 2009 (www.nytimes.com/2009/11/21/science/earth/21climate.html?_r=1&ref=environment).

72. See *IPCC Fourth Assessment Report: Climate Change 2007*, Working Group II Report, "Impacts, Adaptation and Vulnerability" (www.ipcc.ch/ipccreports/assessments-reports.htm).

73. Hunter, "The Implications of Climate Change Litigation," p. 4: "This focus on specific injuries is critical for building political support; such cases link climate change with the lives of ordinary people. Reports of a global increase in temperature of 1 [degree] or even 5 [degrees] have little meaning to most people."

74. *Kivalina* v. *ExxonMobil*, Complaint at paragraph 16-17.

75. "Petition to the Inter American Commission on Human Rights Seeking Relief from Violations Resulting from Global Warming Caused by Acts and Omissions of the United States," December 7, 2005.

76. Ibid., pp. 37–43.

77. "Before the Secretary of the Interior, Petition to List the Polar Bear (Ursus maritimus) as a Threatened Species under the Endangered Species Act," February 16, 2005.

78. Ibid., pp. 41–55.

79. *Connecticut* v. *American Electric Power*, Complaint.

80. *California* v. *General Motors*, Complaint for Damages, and Declaratory Judgment and Demand for Jury Trial, September 20, 2006.

81. See "Brief for Petitioners, *Massachusetts* v. *EPA*," at 8. That definition provides that the term "air pollutant" "includ[es] any physical, chemical . . . substance or matter which is emitted into . . . the ambient air." 42 U.S.C. 7602(g).

82. See Clean Air Act, §§ 108 and 109.

83. *Massachusetts* v. *EPA*, Brief for the Federal Respondent in Opposition at 23-24.

84. *Connecticut* v. *American Electric Power*, Complaint at paragraph 1-2.

85. See Merrill, *supra* note 12; Hsu, *supra* note 12.

86. See Engel, *supra* note 14.

87. See Lytton, "Using Tort Litigation," p. 1845, demonstrating the manner in which litigation against the gun industry framed the problem of gun violence as the fault of the gun industry.

88. See Mona Hymel, "The United States' Experience with Energy-Based Tax Incentives: The Evidence Supporting Tax Incentives for Renewable Energy," *Loyola University Chicago Law Journal* 38, no. 1 (2006), pp. 43–80; Roberta Mann, "Waiting to Exhale?" Global Warming and Tax Policy," *American University Law Review* 51, no. 6 (2002), pp. 1135–222.

89. For a summary of these proposals, see Pew Center on Global Climate Change, *Economy-Wide Cap-and-Trade Proposals in the 110th Congress: Graphical Analysis and Summary of Key Legislation* (www.pewclimate.org/federal/analysis/congress/110/cap-trade-bills). See also Victor B. Flatt, "Taking the Legislative Temperature: Which Federal Climate Change Legislative Proposal Is 'Best'?" *Northwestern University Law Review Colloquy* 102 (2007): 123–150; John C. Dernbach, "Harnessing Individual Behavior to Address Climate Change: Options for Congress," *Virginia Environmental Law Journal* 26, no. 1 (2008): 111–14.

90. On December 6, 2007, the Senate Environment and Public Works Committee voted 11-8 to favorably report S 2191, the Lieberman-Warner Climate Security Act.

91. Juliet Eilperin, "Kerry, Graham, and Lieberman to Unveil Climate Bill," *Washington Post*, April 24, 2010 (www.washingtonpost.com/wp-dyn/content/article/2010/04/23/AR2010042304703.html).

92. Robin Bravender, "Sen. Voinovich Throws Curveball at Senator's Plan to Limit GHG Regs in Bill," *New York Times*, April 22, 2010 (available at: http://www.nytimes.com/cwire/2010/04/22/22climatewire-sen-voinovich-throws-curveball-at-senators-p-32487.html).

93. See, for example, *Texas Municipal Power Agency* v. *EPA*, 89 F.3d 858 (D.C. Cir. 1996) challenging the methodology used by the EPA to initially allocate sulfur dioxide allowances to utilities.

94. This category includes lawsuits filed by New York companies against New York to invalidate a law that restricted the geographic marketability of allowances in an effort to eliminate local acid rain "hot spots" and lawsuits filed by low-sulfur coal interests against the efforts of Illinois and Indiana to provide incentives for utilities to use coal mined within their boundaries. *Clean Air Markets Group* v. *Pataki*, 338 F.2d 82 (2d Cir. 2003), restricting trades by in-state utilities that New York feared would create an acid rain hot spot; *Alliance for Clean Coal* v. *Bayh*, 72 F.3d 556 (7th Cir. 1995), striking down an Indiana statute offering incentives to utilities to use the high-sulfur coal mined in Indiana; *Alliance for Clean Coal* v. *Miller*, 44 F.3d 591 (1994), striking down an Illinois statute encouraging utilities to use high-sulfur coal mined in Illinois.

95. See A. Denny Ellerman, "Are Cap-and-Trade Programs More Environmentally Effective than Conventional Regulation?" Working Paper 03-015 (Massachusetts Institute of Technology, Center for Energy and Environmental Policy Research, October 2003) (http://web.mit.edu/ceepr/www/publications/workingpapers/2003-015.pdf).

96. Ibid. To support his argument that administrative discretion over individual compliance costs breeds litigation in the context of a cap-and-trade program, Ellerman points to the revealing fact that the one area in which EPA has had discretion over allowance allocation—units brought into phase I of the program as substitution and compensation units—has also been the source of the most significant litigation. It should be noted that the benefits of a more detached regulator essentially playing only the role of "banker" has been recently criticized as insufficient to ensure that cap-and-trade programs do not undercut environmental goals in the context of a more heterogeneous population of regulated sources. Leslye McAllister argues that agencies must also analyze and disseminate market performance information, assist regulated entities in designing compliance plans, and formulate a contingency plan in case of program weakness or failure. Leslye K. McAllister, "Beyond Playing 'Banker': The Role of the Regulatory Agency in Emissions Trading," *Administrative Law Review* 59, no. 2 (2007), pp. 269–314. While there are clear benefits to an expanded administrative role in a cap-and-trade regime, such an expansion may increase the litigation filed.

97. See *supra* note 95 citing cases in which Illinois and Indiana disrupted the market for sulfur dioxide allowances by providing incentives for in-state industries to purchase coal mined in state.

98. The following discussion is taken largely from Holly Doremus and W. Michael Hanemann, "Of Babies and Bathwater: Why the Clean Air Act's Cooperative Federalism Framework Is Useful for Addressing Global Warming," *Arizona Law Review* 50, no. 3 (2008), pp. 809–16.

99. See Douglas Kysar and Bernadette A. Meyler, "Like a Nation State," *UCLA Law Review* 55, no. 6 (2008), p. 1635.

100. Waxman-Markey Climate and Energy Security Act of 2009; Clean Energy Jobs and American Power Act (the Kerry-Boxer bill).

101. William L. Andreen, "Federal Climate Legislation and Preemption," *Environmental and Energy Law and Policy* 3, no. 2 (2009), p. 284.

102. See David Spence and Paula Murray, "The Law, Economics, and Politics of Federal Preemption Jurisprudence: A Quantitative Analysis," *California Law Review* 87, no. 5 (1999), pp. 1164–67.

103. Hugh S. Gorman and Barry D. Solomon, "The Origins and Practice of Emissions Trading," *Journal of Policy History* 14 (2002), p. 296.

104. Ibid.

105. See "California Environmental Justice Movement's Declaration on Use of Carbon Trading Schemes to Address Climate Change" (www.ejmatters.org/declaration.html).

106. See Doremus and Hanemann, "Of Babies and Bathwater," pp. 805–06, citing Martin Parry and others, "Squaring Up to Reality," *Nature Reports: Climate Change,* May 29, 2009

(http://www.nature.com/climate/2008/0806/full/climate.2008.50.html). Doremus and Haneman make a three-step argument: radical reductions in greenhouse gas emissions will be required to stabilize global greenhouse gas emissions at levels that scientists believe will be necessary to prevent conditions that will endanger human health and the environment; the absence of an effective technology to control greenhouse gas emissions leaves only two pathways available to reduce emissions: consuming dramatically less fossil fuel or developing novel methods of capturing and sequestering greenhouse gas emissions; and either pathway will require drastic behavioral shifts and radical technological innovation, neither of which, it is claimed, are readily supplied by a carbon market alone. With respect to the latter argument, use of a cap-and-trade mechanism does not guarantee technological innovation and a cap-and-trade program focused on large industrial facilities such as utilities and consumer fuel producers will not reach the large proportion of greenhouse gas emissions that are attributable to individual decisions about lifestyle and consumption—which are estimated to account for nearly one-third of the nation's total emissions.

107. Ibid., p. 814.

108. Ibid., p. 828.

109. R. Shep Melnick, "The Political Roots of the Judicial Dilemma," *Administrative Law Review* 49, no. 3 (1997), pp. 585–98; Rosemary O'Leary, "The Impact of Federal Court Decisions on the Policies and Administration of the U.S. Environmental Protection Agency," *Administrative Law Review* 41, no. 4 (1989), pp. 549–74.

110. Michael J. Mortimer, "The Delegation of Law-Making Authority to the United States Forest Service: Implications in the Struggle for National Forest Management," *Administrative Law Review* 54, no. 3 (2002), pp. 940–41.

111. O'Leary, "The Impact of Federal Court Decisions," pp. 549, 561–62.

112. Ibid., p. 566.

113. Ibid., p. 566–67.

11

Can Congress Govern the Climate?

BARRY G. RABE

The first major step taken by a branch of the federal government on climate change was the Supreme Court's 2007 decision in *Massachusetts et al.* v. *U.S. Environmental Protection Agency et al.* This case pitted a sizable team of state and municipal officials against the executive branch of the federal government on the question of whether greenhouse gases could be defined as air pollutants under federal law. A narrow majority sided with the plaintiffs, but Bush administration resistance to such a definition resulted in additional litigation rather than closure. Virtually every branch and level of the U.S. government was engaged in this case, and the Obama administration has since brought significant changes in the executive branch response to the case as well.

The absence of the legislative branch of the federal government throughout this process, however, has been conspicuous. Ironically, the Supreme Court case was based in large part on an attempt to divine congressional intent nearly two

I am very grateful to Christopher Borick, Christopher Bosso, Marc Gaden, Donald Kettl, Michael Kraft, Erick Lachapelle, Judith Layzer, Paul Light, Sidney Milkis, Pietro Nivola, and Margaret McCarthy for thoughtful comments on earlier versions of this chapter, a much shorter version of which was presented in March 2007 at a congressional briefing in conjunction with the Legislating for the Future project. Funding from the Brademas Center on the Study of Congress at New York University was valuable in launching this work in 2007. I am also very grateful to Sourav Guha and Margaret McCarthy for research assistance on congressional committee involvement.

decades ago. In 1990, Congress enacted its most recent amendments to the Clean Air Act of 1970, which may—or may not—have included sufficient elasticity to allow carbon dioxide to be added to the list of air pollutants as scientific under-standing of its role in climate change has matured. Since that enactment, Con-gress has offered remarkably few formal utterances on climate change, essentially having delegated the lead role in U.S. climate policy development to the Bush administration and to state officials from Sacramento to Augusta. In response, the Obama administration began to develop an "administrative approach" to climate change in 2009, discussed further in chapter 12 of this volume. That approach would require the Environmental Protection Agency (EPA) and related agencies to radically reverse course from that of the prior decade and unilaterally take the lead in developing federal climate policy. The EPA not only defined greenhouse gases as an air pollutant but also launched a rulemaking process in the event of extended congressional inability to address climate change in a coherent manner. That placed the executive branch in a unique bargaining role, essentially daring Congress to get its act together or be rendered a bit player.

In many respects, *Massachusetts* v. *U.S. Environmental Protection Agency* mir-rors a larger pattern in recent decades of congressional inaction on issues of pro-found intergenerational consequence, including entitlement programs such as Social Security and Medicare. Congress also has struggled mightily in recent decades to reach any semblance of consensus on a host of environmental and energy concerns, including many with relevance to climate change. This chapter attempts to examine what Congress has in fact done to date on climate change as well as the challenges that it confronted in the first half of the 111th Congress to undertake any serious effort to craft a more purposive federal role. The discussion emphasizes far-reaching efforts in the House of Representatives to either disguise costs through regulations, compensate for them through generous subsidies, or minimize them by providing so much flexibility with respect to compliance that emerging legislation might have minimal impact in the event that it is enacted.

Climate Disengagement amid Decades of Environmental Disengagement

Climate change provides members of Congress with numerous incentives to pass the legislative buck, whether to other levels and branches of government or to future generations. The most significant anticipated negative impacts of climate change are likely to be realized well after their tenure—and life expectancy—except in the case of very young legislators who anticipate multigenerational congressional careers. Moreover, any congressional effort to curb U.S. emissions unilaterally will invariably be piecemeal in global terms, as the United States currently is responsi-ble for less than one-quarter of annual global emissions, having been eclipsed in recent years by China. As a result, opportunities for members of Congress to claim credit for stabilizing the climate are modest at best, as even significant U.S. reductions could not guarantee any specific level of stabilization. In addition, most conceivable policy tools designed to reduce emissions would likely confront an anguished constituency, whether electric utilities responding to renewable energy mandates or a carbon cap-and-trade regime, vehicle manufacturers contending with mandated carbon emission reductions, or citizens facing higher energy costs through a carbon tax scheme. Many climate policy options begin with concentrated political opposition to the costs imposed, and they may well lack influential policy advocates. All of those factors make it highly attractive to avoid blame by simply maintaining the status quo or by launching an avalanche of subsidies and indirect cost imposition strategies.[1]

In many respects, Congress's difficulty in coming to terms with climate change reflects a generation of legislative inaction on a host of pressing environmental issues. That helps explain the dramatic decline in federal legislation that addresses new environmental challenges or revises earlier statutes when modernization is overdue. According to an index of "major federal laws on the environment" constructed by Norman Vig and Michael Kraft in 2010, thirty-four laws were enacted or revised during the 91st through the 102nd Congress. Subsequent congressional output has declined markedly, with only eight major laws enacted or revised between the 103rd and 110th Congress. In fact, Congress has been stunningly quiescent on a wide range of environmental topics since November 15, 1990, when George H.W. Bush signed into law the very Clean Air Act Amendments that stood at the center of the Supreme Court case. As political scientists Christopher Klyza and David Sousa have noted in a careful analysis of this matter, "Congress has been unable to reauthorize statutes, to adopt new laws to address emerging environmental problems or . . . to give sound statutory grounding to pragmatic experiments."[2]

This prolonged congressional silence coincides with some significant innovations in the design of U.S. environmental policy, including policy related to climate change. Collectively, those innovations suggest that it is indeed possible to move beyond the limitations of earlier "command-and-control" policies with new approaches that offer substantial improvement of environmental quality along with more flexible methods of implementation. They increasingly utilize market-based principles such as emissions credit trading and fees on emissions, surmount traditional medium-based barriers to overall environmental protection, and place greater emphasis on achieving measurable environmental outcomes.[3] In many instances, they are best reflected in a set of ever-expanding state and local government actions on climate change in the United States, producing a patchwork of policy experiments distributed across the nation.

Nonetheless, the most recent congressional environmental policy outputs between 1990 and the end of 2009—and the ones with the greatest likely consequences for greenhouse gas emissions of any federal statute enacted since the early stages of the Clinton administration—run directly contrary to the new approaches and their underlying principles. They tend to focus explicitly on energy, with potentially vast environmental consequences. First, the 2005 Energy Policy Act does demonstrate that it is possible for Congress, after more than four years of deliberation, to achieve a broad consensus that crosses partisan lines, but the law represents a purely distributional approach.[4] Its 551 pages of text are packed with a dizzying array of subsidies, insurance guarantees, and regulatory safeguards for nearly every conceivable existing and potential energy source. As political scientists Thomas Mann and Norman Ornstein have noted, this legislation "manages to distribute generous public subsidies to producers—some large and transparent, others small and privately targeted to beneficiaries—without addressing in any serious way the need to reduce consumption of fossil fuels or expand alternative sources of energy."[5] It remains virtually impossible to discern the economic, energy-related, environmental, or climatic impact of this legislation. If anything, the Energy Policy Act has considerable potential to increase greenhouse gas emissions and complicate the challenge of expanding the use of market-oriented tools in future rounds of policy due to the range of subsidies and protections that it has put in place.

In December 2007, two years after Congress enacted the Energy Policy Act, it passed the Energy Independence and Security Act. By that time, Congress was beginning to give more explicit attention to climate change and numerous proposals for some version of a carbon cap-and-trade program were introduced in both chambers. However, those options never received extended consideration, and they were shelved in favor of another legislative product that was top-heavy with the additional subsidies, incentives, and loan guarantees to disparate energy developers that constitute the bulk of the act's 822 pages. Congress did include a mandate calling for some new energy efficiency commitments; a dramatic expansion in the annual production of biofuels (most notably, corn-based ethanol from domestic farms), from 4.7 billion gallons in 2007 to some 36 billion gallons by 2022; and the first increase in mandatory vehicular fuel efficiency in more than two decades. But no sooner was the legislation signed into law than many states and firms decried the biofuel mandate as unfeasible and a growing scholarly chorus questioned whether such fuel is any better than gasoline in terms of its environmental or greenhouse gas effects. In turn, the federal hike in vehicular efficiency was automatically eclipsed by more ambitious efforts in California that were embraced by fourteen other states and ultimately led to unilateral action by President Obama to raise the federal bar significantly for fuel efficiency. As with the Energy Policy Act, sorting out the greenhouse gas ramifications of the Energy Independence and Security Act remains uncertain at best.

Those bills set the stage for the largest experiment in alternative energy subsidization in U.S. history. Of the $787 billion included in the 2009 American

Recovery and Reinvestment Act, approximately 10 percent will ultimately be directed toward "clean energy." It remains impossible to assess how those dollars will be invested over the long term, given the vague nature of many key provisions in the legislation and the substantial role that states and localities will play in pursuing "shovel-ready" priorities. But this case confirms the congressional appetite to "pass the energy pork" rather than make tough decisions on the climate, including those that might impose visible costs on any constituency. Indeed, the three massive energy bills of the 2000s consistently embrace policy tools that are likely to offer the least cost-effective approach to emissions reduction imaginable. They are desirable primarily as a purely political undertaking that allocates rewards to some stakeholders while hiding actual implementation costs from average citizens.

Challenges for the 111th Congress and Its Successors

The legacy of these subsidy programs made the 111th Congress and its successors uncertain players in any future exploration of policies to address climate change coherently. The uptick in the saliency of climate change in recent years and a frenzy of new legislative proposals introduced in 2009 suggested a strong likelihood of intensified legislative attention. That seemed especially plausible given the 2008 election results, which produced strong Democratic majorities eager to move on a range of domestic issues and a new president far more inclined to embrace federal climate change legislation than his predecessor. But amid the understandable desire shared by some members to cobble together some form of new legislation and push it through the legislative process, Congress needed to step back and reflect on a larger set of challenges that must be addressed to prepare for a constructive long-term role in the development and nurturing of viable policies. As of mid-2010, it was not at all clear that such steps had been taken amid a feverish effort to secure votes for a massive climate bill that in some critical respects resembled a large-scale version of the 2005 and 2007 energy bills.

Deep-seated concerns about congressional capacity not only to "do something" but to produce legislation that is ultimately viewed as effective has not been confined in recent decades to climate change, environmental protection, and energy. Indeed, one can scan a range of relatively recent legislative outputs in such areas as homeland security, prescription drug coverage under Medicare, bankruptcy procedures, efforts in the 1990s to streamline agricultural subsidies, and oversight of elementary and secondary education to emerge with a host of questions about congressional capacity to forge and sustain viable policy. All of this took place before the recent efforts to enact massive rescue operations of financial and vehicle manufacturing firms while raising the question, in the words of political scientist Barbara Sinclair, "Is the 'meat grinder' that is the legislative process now so badly defective that it produces 'spoiled sausages'?"[6]

Indeed, regardless of partisan composition, the list of congressional outputs that stand as models of effectiveness for tackling tough issues with a reasoned mix of cost imposition and benefit distribution is relatively modest. Almost invariably, scholars point to such steps as the 1983 Social Security Act, the 1986 Tax Reform Act, the 1990 Clean Air Act Amendments, and the 1996 Welfare Reform Act as leading examples of congressional "profiles in courage." In such instances, prominent policy entrepreneurs built unique coalitions to devise novel responses to pressing policy problems, often in the face of significant interest group or partisan opposition. But such steps remain rather rare, and not all endure through years of implementation.[7] That is the legacy that the 111th Congress inherited, amid soaring expectations of its ability to take an electoral mandate and deliver landmark legislation in numerous areas of contentious public policy.

Overcoming Partisanship, Polarization, and the Elixir of Unified Government

No area of public policy is immune from partisan divides and the challenges of polarization. Yet the intersection of environmental protection and energy, which is exactly where one finds the issue of climate change, may be uniquely divisive. Political scientists Henry Brady, John Ferejohn, and Lauren Harbridge have compared partisan divides across different areas of public policy, and they conclude that environmental policy and energy policy superbly illustrate areas "where partisan ideological differences are apparent and show signs that polarization matters." Noting the penchant for deadlock in such areas, they conclude that "there is a risk that polarization may limit the ability of the government to address long-range domestic policies, particularly those that require altering the distribution of benefits."[8] Climate change may only exacerbate that tendency, especially when one moves beyond the issue of subsidies and into the thornier questions posed by options such as regulation, carbon cap and trade, and carbon taxes. As Representative John Dingell (D-Michigan) noted prior to his ouster as chair of the House Energy and Commerce Committee, looking back on more than a half-century of service in the House, "This is probably going to be the hardest task that I have had in my career in Congress. I don't think we have any easy components here before us."[9]

There has been enormous pent-up demand in some quarters for congressional movement on climate legislation, and the unified Democratic control of the presidency and both chambers in Congress following the 2008 election left many sanguine about the prospects for rapid action on climate change along with a host of other issues. President Barack Obama quickly endorsed enactment of cap-and-trade legislation that would build closely on the model developed by the Regional Greenhouse Gas Initiative (RGGI), which auctions all of its emission allowances to establish a carbon pricing signal. In turn, many active supporters of federal climate legislation assumed significant leadership roles in the 111th Congress and took steps to "reframe" the issue in order to increase its appeal, by linking it, for example, with popular ideas such as "green jobs" and "home-grown energy development." But as political scientist Richard Nathan noted, there is often an "easy assumption that a new administration will make big and bold changes, that they will be accepted by Congress, and quickly go into effect. The legislative process in Washington is one big hurdle."[10]

Recent history in Washington is littered with moments of great expectation following an election, especially if a unified government emerges. Scholars have long questioned whether unified government enhances the prospects of legislative enactment, and recent experience gives one pause.[11] The Clinton odyssey into national health reform is a prominent example, whereby forceful and extended presidential pressure failed to produce even a vote on legislation on the floor of either the Democrat-controlled House or Senate in 1993 or 1994.[12]

But perhaps more relevant to the climate case, the Clinton-Gore administration entered office in January 1993 with a very ambitious environmental and energy agenda. It contained a flurry of proposals that included a national BTU tax on all energy sources to reduce consumption and raise revenue for deficit reduction; reform of hazardous waste cleanup and drinking water legislation; increased grazing fees on public lands; an overhaul of outdated mining legislation enacted during the Grant administration; and elevation of the EPA to cabinet level. Aside from a modest increase in gasoline taxes, none of the proposals secured approval in the 103rd Congress, which was declared by the League of Conservation Voters to be the least-productive legislative session on environmental matters in a quarter-century.[13]

After this standoff and the election of a Republican Congress in 1994, the Clinton administration turned to more incremental strategies that maximized its latitude through use of executive power. Ironically, the George W. Bush administration experienced a somewhat similar fate on environmental matters, this time in the face of unified Republican Party control of both branches of Congress during much of its tenure. Perhaps most notably, a major Bush initiative to expand emissions trading efforts through its Clear Skies initiative proved very controversial and never won congressional support. Much like its predecessor (and the Obama administration in 2009), the Bush administration turned instead toward administrative strategies to realize as much of its environmental agenda as possible, though it moved in a direction rather different from that of the Clinton administration.[14] What remained unclear in 2010 was whether the 2008 election would be one that would open the door to far-reaching policy change, as was the case following the 1932, 1964, and 1980 elections.

Regardless of the partisan distribution of congressional membership, any climate change strategy more complex than allocating subsidies to disparate energy sources is likely to result in divisions that defy simple partisan or sectoral lines. Electric utilities with substantial volumes of nuclear or hydroelectric power in their portfolio respond differently to various climate policy proposals than those that rely heavily on coal. The transportation sector divides sharply on policy options depending on a vehicle manufacturing firm's current fuel efficiency and likely product development capacity, even before different modes of transportation—such as road vehicles and airplanes, trains, buses, and other forms of mass transit—are taken into account.

Some of the nastiest battles on climate policy at the state level have emerged among generators of competing renewable energy technologies, such as those for wind, solar, and geothermal power, all fighting for favored status under any new plan.[15] Further fault lines include regional variation in the type and volume of energy use and receptivity to expanded use of so-called "carbon offsets" in forestry and agriculture. Such divides may easily trump partisan alliances, making any effort to assemble workable legislative majorities difficult at best. The frequency and intensity of these fissures call into question the capacity of Congress not only to enact some form of climate legislation but also to fashion policy that is reasonably cost effective and that can be implemented effectively over subsequent decades.

Fostering Deliberative Capacity

Although Congress has proven generally incapable of reaching any agreement on climate change policy, it certainly has demonstrated the ability to pass the microphone around at hearings and to talk about the subject. Between September 1975 and December 2006, at least 175 congressional hearings that gave substantial attention to climate change were conducted.[16] Seventeen standing House or Senate committees each sponsored at least one of the hearings, with especially heavy concentrations in the years 1989 (20 hearings), 1998 (15), 1993 (12), and 1992 (11). The hearings addressed a wide range of topics, particularly the scientific understanding of climate change but also policy considerations. A major focus in the late 1990s was the repeated examination of the Kyoto Protocol, even after it became evident that the Senate would never endorse ratification.

The congressional capacity for hearings reached new heights in the 110th Congress, with more than 200 new hearings held in 2007–08. The pace showed no sign of slowing through the first half of the 111th Congress.[17] A far greater percentage of more recent hearings addressed policy issues than ever before and some demonstrated willingness to grapple with fundamental questions in future climate policy design. In contrast, many earlier congressional hearings on climate change clearly entailed a form of political grandstanding, featuring witnesses and formats more suitable to high-decibel talk shows than serious deliberation. One can see in the more recent body of hearings the beginning of some serious discussions.

Discussion is not tantamount to deliberation, however, and many of the hearings suggest a pattern that reinforces larger concerns about a congressional incapacity for serious deliberation that can hinder coherent policy development. As

political scientists Gary Mucciaroni and Paul Quirk have noted, extending opportunities for "informed debate" allows legislators to weigh competing claims and
move toward more constructive policy developments, reflected in select cases such
as the 1995 Senate debate over welfare reform.[18] In contrast, it is not at all clear
that most of the flurry of climate change hearings have approached the bar of
informed debate. Some legislators publicly lamented the frequency of hearings in
2007 and 2008 and the relative paucity of discussion over specific legislative proposals and policy issues, suggesting that the hearings provided an opportunity for
various committee chairs to become visible on the issue without having to take a
stand.

Indeed, the relative absence of deliberation was perhaps best illustrated in the
Senate run-up to an anticipated floor debate over the Boxer-Lieberman-Warner
Climate Security Act, in which Senate Republicans insisted that clerks read the
entire 492-page proposal on the floor. After that incident, neither serious debate
nor a vote on the bill ever took place. Ironically, matters were likely more difficult
in the House, where there was even less evidence of serious climate policy deliberation prior to that chamber's decision in mid-2009 to assemble a massive bill
and push toward a final vote with unusual speed.

Congressional capacity for serious deliberation over climate science and policy
options may have been further impoverished by the 1995 termination of the Congressional Office of Technology Assessment (OTA).[19] OTA was created in 1972 to
provide analysis for Congress on a series of topics related to technology, including
those directly linked to energy, environmental protection, and transportation. Its
1991 report, *Changing by Degrees: Steps to Reduce Greenhouse Gases*, was an early and
unusually comprehensive analysis of technologies and policy options for greenhouse
gas reduction. The report was influential in climate policy development in a number of states and local governments.[20] By mid-decade, given its reputation for independence and ability to draw on a skilled staff and network of researchers from
unusually diverse disciplinary and institutional backgrounds, OTA was uniquely
positioned to be a major source of analytical support to Congress.

OTA, however, became a symbolic pawn in an effort by a new congressional
majority to demonstrate its rapid commitment to shrinking the federal government, and it has not been replaced since 1995. Entities such as the Congressional
Research Service and Congressional Budget Office have produced important
analyses on climate change issues, but those analyses reflect the agencies' narrower
jurisdictions and do not address the sort of issues that once fell to OTA. As a
result, Congress has become far more dependent on briefings and direct guidance
from external constituents, such as prominent industries and environmental
advocacy groups, than it would likely have been had OTA endured, placing it at
a significant disadvantage with legislatures in many states and other nations that
have nurtured their own analytical capacity.

Navigating the Committee Thicket

A further impediment to congressional deliberations on climate change remains the myriad of House and Senate committees that can lay claim to at least some semblance of jurisdiction over the issue, reflected in the numerous committee sponsors of legislative hearings, indicating rival entities competing for input. However, such a sprawling set of committee overseers existed before the current decade. In fact, it was a serious concern as early as the first congressional hearings on climate change, which occurred during the Gerald Ford presidency. "Allocating responsibilities in the vast and pressing topics of energy, natural resources, and environmental policy was the most intricate intellectual and political challenge," wrote Roger Davidson and Walter Oleszek more than three decades ago. "The subjects were broad yet tightly intertwined; potential claimants for the jurisdiction were numerous."[21] That recognition led to serious review of ways to better integrate various committee activities, including proposals for a "super committee" on environment and energy. But all such proposals were defeated, and periodic tinkering with committees and subcommittees in subsequent decades failed to create a supportive context for serious deliberation on most environmental and energy issues, particularly those as complex as climate change policy. Philip Clapp of the National Environmental Trust wrote in 2007 that "the House has struggled to change the country's course on energy on and off for 30 years, largely unsuccessfully, in part because of Balkanized committee jurisdictions and the lack of a central leadership group."

Those issues were especially evident in the 110th Congress as numerous Senate and House committees convened one or more climate change hearings (see figures 11-1 and 11-2), following closely the pattern of broad committee involvement in the formation of the 2005 and 2007 energy bills and posing a significant challenge for the 111th Congress. Some kinds of climate bills, such as those concerning carbon cap-and-trade policies, were likely to further expand the pool of engaged committees given their broad scope and inordinate complexity. These bills addressed familiar sources of emissions, such as electricity generation and major industry, but also considered emissions from aircraft, carbon offsets from agriculture and forestry, metrics for emissions disclosure and mechanisms to verify their accuracy, financial oversight provisions for newly formed carbon markets, and the expansion and reorganization of federal agencies and departments that would see their duties expand dramatically and would have to design ways to share information and work in close collaboration. Indeed, any broad climate bill would result in a labyrinth of engaged committees, as last seen in the construction of a new regime to redefine and oversee homeland security. In 2009, the House—unlike the Senate—took significant steps to streamline decisionmaking in anticipation of this challenge.

Figure 11-1. *Senate Hearings on Climate Change, GHG Emissions, and Renewable Energy*

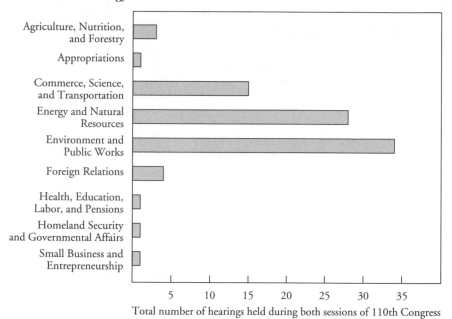

Total number of hearings held during both sessions of 110th Congress

Source: Documents on file with author. For updated listings of climate-related hearings, see http://globalwarming.house.org/legislation/.

House Speaker Nancy Pelosi's January 2007 decision to establish the Select Committee on Energy Independence and Global Warming, chaired by Massachusetts Democrat Edward Markey, was a bold gambit to create a more visible venue for deliberation. Markey used his perch to sponsor forty-six hearings in the 110th Congress, more than any other body in either chamber. Many of them, however, were highly dramatic affairs, reflected in such unusual hearing titles as *What's Cooking with Natural Gas, Shock and Oil,* and *On Thin Ice.* The hearings frequently garnered considerable media attention but hardly approached the standard of serious deliberation and seemed unlikely to influence future legislation. The Select Committee was extended into the 111th Congress, but it remained formally constrained from taking any policy development role and instead epitomized a "show horse" committee that won awards for its dynamic websites but in reality served to shift resources from policy deliberation to climate melodrama.

The November 2008 decision to oust John Dingell in favor of Henry Waxman (D-California) as chair of the House Energy and Commerce Committee was a more significant step, one designed to accelerate the committee's role in forming ambitious climate legislation and giving Waxman the pivotal role in forging deals. The Energy and Commerce Committee has long been a major force in any pol-

Figure 11-2. *House Hearings on Climate Change, GHG Emissions, and Renewable Energy*

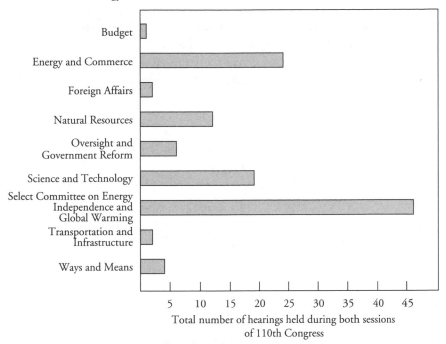

Total number of hearings held during both sessions
of 110th Congress

Source: Documents on file with author. For updated listings of climate-related hearings, see http://globalwarming.house.org/legislation/.

icy dealing with environmental and energy issues. The committee convened twenty-four separate hearings on climate change during the 110th Congress and introduced a 441-page document in late 2008 outlining general principles to guide future climate policy. But it was seen by many Democrats as too timid in moving ahead with serious policy development, and Waxman quickly signaled that he wanted to take a more aggressive posture. That entailed making Energy and Commerce the driving force on climate change in the House but forging a close alliance with Markey to marginalize other committees and propel legislative developments during the first months of the 111th Congress.

The Senate did not follow suit, resulting in ongoing jurisdictional struggles between the Environment and Public Works Committee and the Energy and Natural Resources Committee to become the dominant force in climate change. Both committee chairs, Barbara Boxer of California and Jeff Bingaman of New Mexico respectively, convened a large body of hearings in the 110th Congress, many of which promoted markedly different versions of climate legislation that they cosponsored. These proposals offered significantly different packages of cap-and-trade and related policies, including major differences on the stringency of reduction targets, the continuing role for states that took action in advance of any federal legislation, and the implementation duties of rival entities such as the Environmental Protection Agency and the Department of Energy.

The difficulty of Senate action amid competing committees and members was on full display during 2008, as repeated efforts to advance a carbon cap-and-trade bill never resulted in a single floor vote on any provision. Not only did a demand to read the entire bill aloud delay matters but, in a perhaps ominous sign, sirens blared through the Capitol as the reading took place, indicating that tornadoes threatened Washington. This pattern continued into the 111th Congress, where the divides between Boxer and Bingaman and their respective committees were quickly apparent. Indeed, their differences were only compounded as other major committees, such as Foreign Relations, chaired by John Kerry (D-Massachusetts) and Finance, chaired by Max Baucus (D-Montana) entered the fray in a more extensive manner than ever before.

Engaging the Executive Branch

Along with finding a way to govern itself, Congress also must face the challenge of engaging and overseeing the executive branch under any future federal climate legislation. Congress essentially evaded the question of whether carbon dioxide could be declared an air pollutant when it wrote the Clean Air Act Amendments, ultimately punting the issue to the judicial and executive branches. So, in addition to facing the considerable challenge of forging coherent legislation, the 111th Congress and its successors must also begin to take seriously the challenge of fostering executive branch capacity and discerning ways to provide appropriate oversight.

Climate change is hardly the only area in which Congress has proven unwilling or unable to play a constructive role in relation to the executive branch, having failed to effectively oversee federal agencies responsible for implementing federal environmental laws regardless of partisan control. As the Reform Institute has noted, "Congress has eschewed nearly all serious oversight of agencies and programs."[22] That lack of oversight has been evident in climate policy for more than a decade. During the latter 1990s, a series of legislative amendments—known as Knollenberg riders because they were sponsored by Representative Joseph Knollenberg (R-Michigan)—made it essentially illegal for the EPA and other federal agency officials to spend any time in active discussion of climate change and policy development. That resulted in almost comical events, wherein House staffers would hover in the back of conference rooms, making sure that federal agency officials did not go too far in discussing climate change in public venues.

During the first six years of the George W. Bush presidency, the Republican-led Congress largely avoided oversight duties as presidential appointees imposed tight constraints on policy analysis and pronouncements relevant to the climate by federal agency scientists and staff. Once Democrats returned to power after the

2006 elections, they spent considerable energy in ratcheting up oversight, particularly in challenging key decisions by EPA administrator Stephen Johnson to deny California's request for a waiver to implement its carbon control program for vehicles. Some hearings on the Johnson decisions took on an almost comical tone. In attempting to discern whether senior Bush administration officials had guided Johnson's thinking, committee members first had to resolve the "Where's Stephen?" question, focusing primarily on how to locate the EPA chief and much less on securing an active response from him. Indeed, the Bush administration approach to overseeing federal agencies with some responsibility for climate concerns was a dominant theme in many congressional hearings in the latter half of 2008, after the failure in June to either hold debate or a vote in the Senate over a climate cap-and-trade proposal.

Collectively, there remains little evidence that any recent Congress has given serious thought to the kind of executive agency capacity building that would be necessary to implement any future climate policy successfully, including evidence from 2009 hearings in the push to cobble together a legislative package that could pass the House. The lack of constructive congressional relations with the executive branch and its agencies on environmental and energy governance is longstanding, but it has particular relevance for any future climate change policy. More than four decades after the initial Earth Day, the EPA must work within its original structure—which analysts have long found suspect, fragmented as it is across the environmental media of air, water, and land and along functional and regional lines—when forced to confront the "incoherent regulatory agenda" set for it in piecemeal fashion by various Congresses (see chapter 12 of this volume).

As the National Academy of Public Administration concluded through a series of studies of EPA and environmental governance, the overall congressional role in environmental policy has served to "drive the agency in a dozen directions, discouraging rational priority-setting or a coherent approach to environmental management."[23] The Department of Energy—with a very small core staff and a massive web of contractual agreements with private entities for analysis and service delivery—faces profound issues of its own. Very different Senate and House committees oversee these entities, and there has been no sign of congressional effort to look at constructive ways to build capacity and foster collaboration between them. This is contrary to the experience in a number of U.S. states and European Union member states that have paid far more attention, in managerial terms, to the important relationship between the environment and energy use.

President Obama's decision to designate Carol Browner as the national "climate czar" with close political connections to the Oval Office seems likely to only complicate development of a constructive congressional role in executive branch oversight in the coming years. Browner was one of many czars appointed to high-saliency posts by the president, free from Senate confirmation and largely independent of congressional oversight. Other prominent Obama climate appointees, such as EPA administrator Lisa Jackson and Energy Secretary Steven Chu, regularly appeared before congressional committees and often served as lead witnesses endorsing prominent proposals in high-profile hearings. But the Browner appointment triggered considerable interbranch tension. It further complicated the path toward constructive executive-legislative relations in future climate governance and raised questions about how a czar might preside over the broad interdepartmental collaboration likely to be required if major climate legislation is enacted.

Grafting any new federal climate change policy onto this fragmented management system raises fundamental questions concerning the capacity of federal agencies to work across internal divides as well as to engage the host of other federal departments and entities that must play some role on so complex an issue. Addressing the issue of climate change entails far more than a conventional air pollution issue would. Regardless of the revised definition of the status of carbon dioxide under the Clean Air Act, climate change cannot simply be deposited into the hands of an EPA assistant administrator for air and radiation or the secretary of energy. Other departments—such as the Department of Agriculture, of the Interior, of Transportation, of Homeland Security, and of Health and Human Services—will need to be active and constructive players and partners, working in concert with the EPA and the Department of Energy rather than at cross-purposes.

Any U.S. return to an active international role in climate policy development will necessitate coordination between the Department of State and those units responsible for domestic compliance with international agreements, as was brought into vivid relief by the developments at the 2009 Copenhagen climate summit. As a thoughtful 2008 report from the National Association of Clean Air Agencies noted, "implementation of a national GHG emission reduction program will require sustained integration of programs and skills on a large scale, across multiple agencies and responsibilities."[24]

There is little if any indication that Congress has given serious thought to what steps it must take to prepare federal agencies and departments to implement any future climate change policy. None of the leading federal climate bills introduced in the 110th or the 111th Congress offered anything that resembled a careful plan to foster a viable cross-agency climate management network. Despite the bills' considerable differences, they tended to follow a pattern that spelled out in substantial detail technical provisions such as reduction goals and timetables, offset provisions, and other core elements and then combined these with extensive lists of distributional subsidies. Scant attention was given to fundamental governance questions. Instead, those were often compressed in brief sections that designated one unit (most commonly, the EPA) in the lead role, the assumption being that it would work out the details with counterparts scattered across the federal (and state) bureaucratic landscape.

Further complicating any future implementation is that many of the bills called for the creation of entirely new entities, many of which would take a direct role in establishing a national market for carbon and would be expected to oversee many aspects of future carbon emissions trading and management. Hence, one finds proposals for such entities as a "climate change credit corporation," a "carbon market efficiency board," a "climate technology financing board," and an "office of carbon market oversight" popping up in various legislative plans. None of them were well-defined, and key strategic considerations were largely ignored; it was often unclear whether they would be embedded in an existing agency or department or instead function as a nonprofit organization. Little was said of staffing plans or budgets, much less about how core duties might be carried out or how they might build on best practices from more experienced nations and states.

What was consistent was that elements of these proposals were modeled, in some cases explicitly, on the very federal financial institutions whose performance came under withering scrutiny in 2009 and that hardly appear to constitute role models for effective governance. At the same time, some private entities that were eager to play central roles in the development of a carbon trading system during much of the 110th Congress no longer existed by the middle of the 111th. In September 2008, for example, Lehman Brothers not only declared bankruptcy but closed its international and domestic "carbon desks" in the process. The fundamental reexamination of federal oversight of financial institutions occurred alongside hearings on climate legislation in 2009, but with little linkage between the two.

All of these issues would be an enormous challenge for a highly functional legislative body that had maintained management units with sufficient resources and high morale. But any future legislative strategy to design a workable policy will be compounded by a fragmented history of environmental governance at the federal level that has only become more severe in the past decade. Amid the inertia in Washington, other governments, from Sacramento to London, have seriously begun to deal with the issue of the resources, mix of disciplines, and administrative structures that will be needed to implement newly enacted climate change policies—including the development of specialized areas of expertise, establishment of mechanisms for inter-institutional coordination, and expansion of internal analytical capacity.[25]

Congress has yet to demonstrate any comparable ability to think carefully about such demands, much less begin to advance strategies to address the longer-term challenges of climate governance within the existing tapestry of federal institutions. Even the march toward passage of climate legislation in the House in June 2009 was preoccupied with finding ways to secure a majority vote on some legislative package, in the hope that any serious problems could be addressed at some later time, rather than with any serious discussion of preparing the federal government for implementation if legislation were enacted.

It is striking how frequently the case of the 1990 Clean Air Act Amendments is used to quiet such discussion, guided by the assumption that because Congress "did it once" in assembling Title IV, which ushered in a now-celebrated program for emissions trading in sulfur dioxide, it can do it again. But what is often over-looked in that legislation is that the sulfur dioxide issue was relatively straightfor-ward, given reliable metrics, prior federal and state experience in regulation, and a ready supply of low-sulfur coal as an emission-reducing substitute. The other provisions of that legislation have not been as smoothly implemented, resulting in prolonged battles over other key components. Indeed, almost immediately after George H.W. Bush signed the 1990 legislation into law, notable Democrats in Congress such as Dingell and Waxman aggressively attacked the EPA for per-ceived shortcomings in implementation.[26]

This battle has continued over successive presidencies, and adding carbon to the mix only elevates the challenge for policymaking coherence by the 111th or any future Congress. Indeed, a particular challenge for any Congress keen to "make history" on climate change will be paying attention to details essential to effective implementation of any new policies, unless it is prepared to punt on those matters, referring them instead to the president and a climate czar not subject to Senate confirmation.

Engaging the States

U.S. legislative bodies are not inherently incapable of enacting climate change leg-islation or providing oversight and resources to guide implementation. To date, however, the entities that have done so operate exclusively in state capitals, not Washington, D.C. Well over half of U.S. state legislatures have enacted one or more major policies designed to reduce greenhouse gas emissions, representing clusters of states in every region of the nation. Large states with professional leg-islatures that traditionally take early steps in public policy, such as California and New York, have received the most notoriety for their efforts. But they have no monopoly on this policy domain, with increasingly active engagement among states in the Southwest, the Midwest, and New England. Indeed, the world's first carbon cap-and-trade bill was enacted by the sprawling and decidedly part-time legislature in New Hampshire in 2001. The collective experience suggests signif-icant capacity among elected state legislators to design and oversee steps to reduce greenhouse gas emissions, often with fairly broad support. This dynamic has, of course, yet to transfer to Congress.

The growing body of state policy experience presents Congress with an oppor-tunity to learn from state examples of policy design and political tactics for assem-bling coalitions of interests to secure legislative enactment. But it is not evident that Congress has paid much attention to state practice, much less attempted to learn any lessons from it. Between 1975 and 2006, the multitude of congressional hearings on climate change produced only two hearings with a significant focus on state experience. In 1989, a field hearing of the Senate Environment and Public Works Committee featured some discussion of how evolving Connecticut energy efficiency policy could reduce greenhouse gas emissions. Fifteen years later, a one-day gathering of the Senate Commerce, Science, and Transportation Committee focused largely on climate change impacts on particular states and regions, with one speaker assigned to address state policy developments.

That began to change somewhat during the 110th Congress, with a series of hearings in both chambers that allowed a number of elected state and local officials to comment on their experience. Those sessions, however, tended to follow a fairly common format, whereby each official would outline actions taken to date in his or her jurisdiction, call upon the federal government to acknowledge such early activity, and request federal funding to sustain or expand state or local efforts. There is little evidence to indicate serious deliberation on possible state and federal roles in any future federal regime or careful efforts by members of Congress to draw lessons for future policy design from state experience.[27] A 2008 review of various federal climate proposals concluded that "there is very little discussion in these bills or in Congress about the role that states and localities could play in designing or implementing national GHG regulations."[28] Even the flurry of hearings in 2009 confined the role of state policymakers largely to claiming credit for their actions and maneuvering to retain some continuing role under a federal regime, rather than considering serious lessons from state and regional experience that might offer principles of best practice to guide federal policy development.

That reflects a larger pattern in recent years of deeply strained federal-state relations, perhaps most notably in such arenas as education, health care, homeland security, energy, and elections management. Environmental protection has long suffered from significant federal and state tensions, attributable in part to the lopsided ratio of federal mandates to intergovernmental revenue transfers to states.[29] Tensions have only intensified in recent years, and Congress clearly has not found a way to actively engage states in constructive discussion on future directions in environmental policy, much less on options for collaborative federalism in future climate policy development.

Since the demise of the U.S. Advisory Commission on Intergovernmental Relations in 1995 for reasons similar to those that led to the termination of OTA, there has been no successor to facilitate intergovernmental learning or formal deliberation between legislators at the federal and state levels. As a result, according to Paul Posner, we now lack "institutional opportunities for officials to meet collectively to discuss agreements that cross governmental and sectoral boundaries."[30] Reflecting the missed opportunities within these larger trends, no congressional committees or members have emerged as effective champions of serious intergovernmental deliberations. Consequently, a vast body of state elected and appointed officials literally has greater expertise with climate policy design and implementation than their federal counterparts, yet they remain a resource largely untapped by Congress.[31]

Grinding the Sausage: Securing 219 Votes in the House

The House of Representatives demonstrated in June 2009 that it was possible for at least one chamber of Congress to secure majoritarian support for a far-reaching climate bill. That initiative hinged on the use of the streamlined committee review process to orchestrate tightly scripted hearings and accelerate movement of a bill from committee to floor and considerable entrepreneurial skill in building and sustaining a supportive coalition. It also relied heavily on aggressive use of amendment powers to minimize direct cost imposition and instead promote distributional benefits to select members and constituencies at every turn. That approach tended to dismiss serious policy deliberation, capacity building, and intergovernmental engagement in favor of a desperate search for sufficient votes to pass some version of the bill, with the hope that any attendant problems could be later cleaned up in the Senate, in conference review, or after enactment during implementation.

Despite a packed legislative agenda that was dominated by concerns about economic recovery, in May 2009 the House Energy and Commerce Committee advanced HR 2454, the American Clean Energy and Security Act, with considerable speed, reconciled it rapidly with versions emerging from other committees, and presented it to the full House, where it was approved by a seven-vote margin in June 2009.

It was hardly the first bill to pass through such a process, one that in many respects adhered closely to the classic Bismarck formulation of "sausage making" invoked above by Sinclair. Indeed, the American Clean Energy and Security Act (ACESA) featured many of the trappings of what Theodore Lowi described nearly two generations ago as "interest group liberalism," capable of securing consensus through the sprawling distribution of potential benefits and incentives to key constituencies that provided direct input into the construction of the legislation.[32]

But ACESA in many respects transcended even Lowi's most robust cases of interest group liberalism from earlier periods, through a 1,482-page document that was packed with virtually every policy tool imaginable that might in some way reduce greenhouse gases except those that would impose direct costs on energy consumers to deter consumption. This legislation generously allocated subsidies, incentives, and grants in attempting to suppress energy costs; it was argued that it could thereby foster substantial economic development at little or no cost to the American citizenry. In turn, it embraced regulation only insofar as its costs would be imposed indirectly and it would be difficult to trace to the legislation. The experience demonstrated how climate protection legislation could be advanced politically through the classic process of distributional politics.

Ironically, the House approach was markedly different from the first major climate legislation proposal of 2009, which was introduced by President Obama shortly after his inauguration. Obama endorsed a carbon cap-and-trade system heavily modeled on the experience of the Regional Greenhouse Gas Initiative, one that would employ an auctioning mechanism to impose costs, thereby putting a carbon-pricing mechanism in place and generating government revenue. "The experience of a cap-and-trade system thus far is that if you're giving away carbon permits for free, then basically you're not really pricing the thing and it doesn't work, or people can game the system in so many ways that it's not creating the incentive structures that we're looking for," Obama said in his first statement on climate policy as president. That was followed in short order by the release of the president's first budget. That document made clear what such a strategy would mean in fiscal terms, projecting that auctions for carbon emission allowances would generate an estimated $648 billion for the Treasury during its first decade of operation.

Obama issued his proposal at the peak of his political popularity, yet the idea was almost immediately eclipsed by the House, which was determined to move forward rapidly with a decidedly different approach. It would entail a diverse tapestry of policies that blended varying forms of regulation, a cap-and-trade program, and subsidies, all focused on maximizing efforts to keep direct costs for energy as low as possible, particularly in the near term of the next several election cycles. The proposal was to make it difficult for citizens to link any future price increases that might occur to specific policies, thereby minimizing any political risks to the legislation's proponents.

The House proposal would allow auctioning of only 15 percent of allowances under its cap-and-trade provision during the initial decade or so of operation. Most allowances would be allocated free of charge through a process that could be continually adjusted to reward various constituents and potential swing voters. Provisions such as generous definition and oversight of agricultural and forestry offsets were expanded continuously, to such an extent that no emission reductions might be required for the first eighteen years of the program.[33] In turn, so-called "border adjustments" were included to protect energy-intensive industries from foreign competition. Those features were linked with innumerable other provisions, including a renewable portfolio standard, continued support for a renewable fuel standard, and an extraordinarily detailed set of energy efficiency standards and incentives.

This legislative package was in many respects the brainchild of an advocacy coalition that brought together five leading environmental groups and twenty-six major corporations under the auspices of the U.S. Climate Action Partnership (USCAP). Its formal proposal, the "Blueprint for Legislative Action," outlined national emission reduction targets from 2012 to 2050, a cap-and-trade program with a "robust offsets program," and an allocation system whereby "a significant portion of allowances should be initially distributed free to capped entities and economic sectors particularly disadvantaged by the secondary price efforts of the cap," although over time auctioning of allowances would be increased. It also endorsed major new commitments to carbon capture and storage technology, renewable energy, improved vehicle and fuel performance standards, and major commitments to energy efficiency standards.

The USCAP Blueprint became, in effect, the literal blueprint for what would evolve into ACESA, enabling House leaders to contend that diverse sectors of society had converged on a compromise proposal that could become a focal point in the 111th Congress. The Waxman-Markey climate tag team moved adroitly to use the USCAP report to rebuke any proposal calling for explicit carbon pricing, whether through auctioning or some form of carbon tax; instead they attempted to reframe their package as an economic development alternative. The report was a focal point of a four-day marathon of hearings in early May 2009 that involved nearly fifty invited witnesses and that, although they allowed for some range of debate, were clearly intended to allow USCAP members to dominate the process.

Most of the exchanges focused on the cap-and-trade provisions of the bill, with discussion of other components, such as the renewable portfolio standard and energy efficiency mandates, confined to brief segments during the final day of hearings. A consistent theme emerged from USCAP representatives: they generally stayed on message, repeatedly embraced cap and trade as a proven method based on earlier national experience with sulfur dioxide, predicted that overall costs would be modest, and endorsed offset provisions that would be fairly generous and flexible. Perhaps most important, the hearings served to crush any possibility that direct cost imposition through an auctioning process, much less a carbon tax, had a political future in the 111th Congress. Support for an allocation process that was either totally or substantially free predominated during the hearings.

The hearings and the subsequent revisions of ACESA leading up to a floor vote also demonstrated that free allocation could be used as a distributional policy tool, in essence enabling allowances and related favors to be dangled before potential allies and then distributed in exchange for support for the bill. Under most models of emissions trading, allocations would be based on some baseline level of emissions, which might be the projected emissions for a given year or an average across years. But each subsequent step of the House legislative process increased the complexity of the allocation process. For example, repeated adjustments in the allocation formula were made that appear to have had little to do with emissions but to have been made to create bargaining opportunities in the quest for a supportive majority of House members. Anticipated opposition in late June from approximately three dozen members who represented agricultural districts, for example, was assuaged by offering ever more generous terms on offsets, switching jurisdictional oversight on offsets from the Environmental Protection Agency to the more friendly terrain of the Department of Agriculture, providing more favorable technical assessment of the climate impacts of corn-based ethanol, and giving bonus allocations to rural-based electricity generators. Other key constituents extracted their own benefits, many linked to the allocation process. All the while, the bill swelled from an initial length of 630 pages in early May to more than 1,200 pages by late June, including continuous adjustment of the allocation formula to garner votes for final passage.

That set the stage for the seven hours of floor debate on June 26 that culminated in a final floor vote of 219-212 in favor of the bill, generally along party lines. During the early hours of the morning of the vote, 319 pages of new text were inserted into the bill, all clearly designed to solidify its majority. The ACESA process demonstrated how a market-based tool can be transformed to use its allocation process and related provisions as a form of distributional policy. That not only allowed ACESA proponents to shore up allies who might receive more favored status through allowances but also contributed to a mantra among supporters that the legislation would not cause energy prices to rise (or at least not very much very soon), that overall program costs would be minimal, and that economic development benefits would be tangible and significant.

Indeed, numerous additional sweeteners were added throughout the weeks leading up to the floor vote, all relatively modest in overall budget terms but individually attractive to a particular legislative district or constituent. They included aggressive use of the colloquy process on the floor of the House, whereby members secured specific benefits for their district from Waxman, the chairman, during the televised proceedings, ranging from funding for a hurricane research center in Orlando to credits for early emission reductions registered with a nonprofit clearing house based in Chicago.

ACESA became so massive and complex in the form that passed the full House that it became virtually impossible to conduct a reliable economic analysis of the entire package, leaving each side to gravitate to any published study that supported its views. Indeed, a detailed review by the Congressional Research Service of competing studies on the cap-and-trade provisions of the bill concluded that reliable cost analysis was virtually impossible.[34] That gave the bill's proponents some advantage through sheer uncertainty, reflecting the real possibility that any future cost increases would be indirect and difficult to trace directly to the legislation.

But the extraordinary complexity of the bill and the confusion over its final content also left it vulnerable to reframing by opponents as a stealth-like form of massive cost imposition. The complexity of the legislation also suggested that because it had so many moving pieces and so many loopholes, it might never approach its emission reduction targets. All of these issues became evident as the venue shifted to the Senate, where the House model provided a baseline for consideration, but prolonged delays into mid-2010 left the future of the legislation in considerable doubt.

Conclusion

Climate change poses daunting challenges for any governing body, but they are compounded in the U.S. case because U.S. greenhouse gas emissions are so high and the capacity of federal institutions such as Congress to address the issue is so suspect. More than thirty-five years after the first congressional hearing on climate change, it remains difficult to see any evidence of constructive legislative engagement. That reflects a series of fundamental challenges facing Congress in the modern era, ones that may only be exacerbated by the scope and nature of climate change.

Congressional engagement on such an issue is not a metaphysical impossibility, nor is it inconceivable except in the event of dramatic climatic catastrophes. New environmental policy does tend to emerge after triggering events prompt rapid policy formation.[35] That can become increasingly feasible in the aftermath of a decisive election and amid mobilization for far-reaching legislative initiatives. In turn, there is also the possibility of a legislative product that does move forward through the proverbial sausage-making process and defies predictions of gridlock. But as the experience of the 2009 House climate bill suggests, the emerging bill may be so saturated with distributional favors that it raises serious questions about the likely effectiveness of the legislation if it is enacted into law. Both pork-laden legislation and legislative collapse loomed as distinct possibilities as a new decade and the final stages of the 111th Congress began.

There are, however, some important precedents over the past quarter-century in which Congress has acted to address long-term environmental challenges in the face of stiff interest opposition and did so in a constructive manner. One prominent example entails the very amendments to the 1990 Clean Air Act that nearly two decades later became fodder for the federal courts. Despite the recent controversy over reinterpreting that legislation to include carbon dioxide, it remains widely heralded for its launch of the sulfur dioxide emissions trading system. The legislation also updated a wide range of other regulatory requirements for conventional air pollutants with its sweeping Title V provisions. Perhaps most relevant to the current case, the Clean Air Act was enacted after prolonged legislative gridlock and in the face of formidable opposition from such organized interests as electric utilities, unions representing coal miners, and large manufacturers. Acid rain was indeed a primary driving force, but polling suggested the relatively low saliency of this issue and low standing on a very crowded national agenda by 1990. In turn, even likely allies were divided over whether to support the legislation. There were major differences between leading environmental advocacy groups over the appropriateness of using market-based policy tools instead of traditional command-and-control mechanisms. Even political champions of the legislation, such as President Bush and Senate Majority Leader George Mitchell, received stunningly little political credit for what remains a relatively rare, functional example of "Washington at work."[36]

There remained few signs in the 111th Congress that history might soon repeat itself on climate change legislation. The early push for legislation by a popular new president was followed by a relatively short and intense battle in the House that passed an extraordinarily complex bill by a narrow majority that reflected a partisan divide. The emergence of other issues as agenda priorities served to deter serious exploration of the issue by the Senate, leaving considerable uncertainty over whether any legislation would be enacted before the November 2010 elections. At the same time, a number of promising proposals for next steps were being explored in Congress, although they tended to be overshadowed by the political theatre surrounding the ACESA legislation. Some of those provisions could provide guidelines for more constructive congressional engagement, which will be considered in the concluding chapter of this volume.

Notes

1. Judith A. Layzer, "Deep Freeze: How Business Has Shaped the Global Warming Debate in Congress," in *Business in Environmental Policy: Corporate Interests in the American Political System,* edited by Michael E. Kraft and Sheldon Kamieniecki (MIT Press, 2007), pp. 93–126; Leslie A. Pal and R. Kent Weaver, *The Government Taketh Away: The Politics of Pain in the United States and Canada* (Georgetown University Press, 2003).

2. Christopher McGrory Klyza and David Sousa, *American Environmental Policy, 1990–2006: Beyond Gridlock* (MIT Press, 2008), p. 94.

3. Daniel J. Fiorino, *The New Environmental Regulation* (MIT Press, 2006); Daniel A. Mazmanian and Michael E. Kraft, *Toward Sustainable Communities,* rev. ed. (MIT Press, 2009).

4. P.L. 109-58.

5. Thomas E. Mann and Norman J. Ornstein, *The Broken Branch: How Congress Is Failing America and How to Get It Back on Track* (Oxford University Press, 2006), pp. 217–18.

6. Barbara Sinclair, "Spoiling the Sausages? How a Polarized Congress Deliberates and Legislates," in *Red and Blue Nation? Consequences and Correction of America's Polarized Politics,* vol. 2, edited by Pietro S. Nivola and David W. Brady (Brookings, 2008), p. 56; also see William A. Galston and Pietro S. Nivola, "Delineating the Problem," in *Red and Blue Nation? Consequences and Correction of America's Polarized Politics,* vol. 1, edited by Pietro S. Nivola and David W. Brady (Brookings, 2008), p. 33.

7. On the Social Security case, see Paul Light, *Artful Work: The Politics of Social Security Reform* (Random House, 1985). On the Tax Reform Act, see Timothy J. Conlan, David R. Beam, and Margaret Wrightson, *Taxing Choices: The Politics of Tax Reform* (Washington: CQ Press, 1990). On the clean air case, see Richard Cohen, *Washington at Work: Back Rooms and Clean Air* (Allyn and Bacon, 1995). On the welfare case, see Ron Haskins, *Work over Welfare: The Inside Story of the 1996 Welfare Reform Law* (Brookings, 2006).

8. David W. Brady, John Ferejohn, and Laren Harbridge, "Polarization and Public Policy: A General Assessment," in *Red and Blue Nation? Consequences and Correction of America's Polarized Politics,* vol. 2, edited by Nivola and Brady, pp. 203, 210.

9. John Dingell, "Remarks to Annual Meeting of the National Wildlife Federation," Washington, March 30, 2007.

10. Richard P. Nathan, "From 'Can-Do' to 'Candor' Public Administration: The 1960s and What about the Future?" Nelson A. Rockefeller Lecture delivered to a meeting of the State Academy for Public Administration, Albany, New York, October 7, 2008.

11. A classic contribution to this scholarly debate is David R. Mayhew, *Divided We Govern* (Yale University Press, 1991).

12. Haynes Johnson and David S. Broder, *The System: The American Way of Politics at the Breaking Point* (Little, Brown, and Company, 1996); Theda Skocpol, *Boomerang: Clinton's Health Security Effort and the Turn against Government in U.S. Politics* (New York: Norton, 1996).

13. Klyza and Sousa, *American Environmental Policy, 1990–2006,* p. 52; Richard N. L. Andrews, *Managing the Environment, Managing Ourselves,* 2nd ed. (Yale University Press, 2006), pp. 350–96.

14. Barry G. Rabe, "Environmental Policy and the Bush Era: The Collision between the Administrative Presidency and State Experimentation," *Publius: The Journal of Federalism* 37, no. 3 (Summer 2007), pp. 413–31.

15. Barry G. Rabe and Philip A. Mundo, "Business Influence in State-Level Environmental Policy," in *Business and Environmental Policy: Corporate Interests in the American Political System,* edited by Michael E. Kraft and Sheldon Kamieniecki (MIT Press, 2007), pp. 265–98.

16. Margaret McCarthy, "Congressional Hearings on Climate Change," unpublished 2007 paper on file with author.

17. Sourav Guha, "Congressional Hearings on Climate Change in the 111th Congress," unpublished 2009 paper on file with author.

18. Gary Mucciaroni and Paul J. Quirk, *Deliberative Choices: Debating Public Policy in Congress* (University of Chicago Press, 2006).

19. Bruce Bimber, *The Politics of Expertise in Congress: The Rise and Fall of the Office of Technology Assessment* (State University of New York Press, 1996).

20. Congress of the United States, Office of Technology Assessment, *Changing by Degrees: Steps to Reduce Greenhouse Gases* (OTA, 1991).

21. Roger H. Davidson and Walter J. Oleszek, *Congress against Itself* (Indiana University Press, 1977), p. 173.

22. Reform Institute, *Restoring Order: Practical Solutions to Congressional Dysfunction* (Los Angeles: Reform Institute, 2006), p. 3.

23. National Academy of Public Administration, *Setting Priorities, Getting Results: A New Direction for EPA* (NAPA, 1995), p. 8; NAPA, *Environment.gov: Transforming Environmental Protection for the 21st Century* (NAPA, 2000).

24. National Association of Clean Air Agencies, "Preserving the Rights of States and Localities to Set More Stringent Greenhouse Gas Reduction Requirements than the Federal Program," discussion paper for the conference "Defining the Role of States and Localities in Federal Global Warming Legislation," Arlington, Virginia, February 12–13, 2008, p. 17.

25. Barry G. Rabe, "Governing the Climate from Sacramento," in *Unlocking the Power of Networks,* edited by Stephen Goldsmith and Donald F. Kettl (Brookings, 2009).

26. Cohen, *Washington at Work,* pp. 207–27.

27. In a statement that is highly representative of comments offered by other state or local officials, New Jersey governor Jon Corzine said at a hearing of the Senate Environment and Public Works Committee on March 1, 2008, that "states' actions are the foundation for future federal programs and, as such, the federal government needs to recognize the critical resources states bring to bear on this issue. Federal monies need to be made available now to states who

are leading in the development of policies on this issue, acknowledging the critical role that those states' planning and actions have on development of federal programs. . . . States are currently the leaders in addressing climate change, and will likely continue to push the envelope after federal legislation is enacted. Federal legislation should facilitate the role of states as policy innovators by explicitly preventing federal preemption of state programs that go beyond federal minimum requirements, as well as preventing preemption of state programs outside the scope of federal initiatives."

28. National Association of Clean Air Agencies, "What Role Can States and Localities Play in Implementing a Federal Greenhouse Gas Reduction Program?" discussion paper for the conference "Defining the Role of States and Localities in Federal Global Warming Legislation," Arlington, Virginia, February 12–13, 2008, p. 23.

29. William T. Gormley Jr., "Money and Mandates: The Politics of Intergovernmental Conflict," *Publius: The Journal of Federalism* 36, no. 4 (Fall 2006), pp. 523–40.

30. Paul Posner, "New Intergovernmental Forums Needed to Address 21st Century Challenges," *Management Insights* (www.governing.com, posted June 2006); also see Timothy J. Conlan and Paul L. Posner, *Intergovernmental Management for the 21st Century* (Brookings, 2008).

31. Former senator Pete Domenici (R-New Mexico) was among the first to make this observation, noting in 2006 that "Washington lawmakers don't yet sufficiently realize that there is a growing cadre of experts in many states across the country who do know how to develop climate legislation." Quoted in Michael Northrup and Sassoon, "The Good News from the States," *Environmental Finance,* November 2006, p. 536.

32. Theodore J. Lowi, *The End of Liberalism* (New York: Norton, 1969). I am indebted to Sidney Milkis for raising this parallel shortly after passage of the ACESA legislation in June 2009.

33. Gregory C. Staple, "A House upon a Rock," *Environmental Forum,* September–October 2009, pp. 24–29.

34. Larry Parker and Brent D. Yacobucci, *Climate Change: Costs and Benefits of the Cap-and-Trade Provisions of H.R. 2454* (Washington: Congressional Research Service).

35. Robert Repetto, *Punctuated Equilibrium and the Dynamics of U.S. Environmental Policy* (Yale University Press, 2006).

36. Cohen, *Washington at Work*, pp. 207–27.

12

Greenhouse Regulation: How Capable Is EPA?

WALTER ROSENBAUM

Who wills the end must also will the means.

—After Emanuel Kant, *Grounding for the Metaphysics of Morals*

It is September 2008. David Bookbinder, the Sierra Club's chief climate counsel, is testifying about the feasibility of regulating greenhouse gases before the Senate Committee on Environment and Public Works. His testimony concerns the complexities involved in EPA regulation through the Clean Air Act, and he is finished—almost. As an afterthought, he poses one further consideration. "While it is clear that the Clean Air Act is well-suited to taking on greenhouse gases and climate change, I do not know whether the same is true of the agency itself," he observes. "Given the unique challenges presented by global warming, it would be useful to examine whether EPA's current organizational structure is best suited for dealing with climate issues."[1]

That is a good question, and one that deserves better congressional consideration than it has been given. When the Supreme Court announced its decision in *Massachusetts* v. *Environmental Protection Agency* (2007), it determined that greenhouse gas emissions are eligible for regulation under the Clean Air Act—the "endangerment finding"—and required EPA either to regulate those emissions or to determine that greenhouse gases (GHGs) are not a risk to public health and welfare. The Court's decision unleashed a cascade of 341 new climate warming bills, resolutions, and amendments by the beginning of the 111th Congress, culminating in June 2009 with House approval of the elephantine Waxman-Markey Climate and Energy Security Act (HR 2454), which was destined to falter in a Senate preoccupied with national health and foreign policy issues. Despite its density, HR 2454 resembled all its congressional predecessors and its principal alternative Senate proposal (the Boxer-Kerry bill) in at least two crucial respects.[2] It cast on EPA the strategic responsibility for domestic GHG emissions regulation.[3] And its 1,492 pages were virtually barren of attention to the issues of governance inherent in any consideration of EPA's role in GHG emissions management—as if administration were merely incidental to legislating.

In Search of Governance

Governance concerns EPA's ability to carry out its mission as the major institutional manager of a GHG regulatory regime. Governance is concerned more about the means than the ends of policy, and it focuses on ability to implement rather than legislative intent. It's a matter of agency competence or capacity. Inattention to EPA's governance capacity and the additional resources that it may require to undertake a new GHG regulatory program deeply pervades even the most comprehensive legislative proposals recently considered by Congress.

For example, one essential, if highly contentious, element in a national cap-and-trade regulatory strategy—a strategy that is commonly proposed in GHG legislation—must be apportionment of responsibility between the state and federal governments in setting emission goals and allocating emission rights. This issue involves adequate regulatory authority, which is the essential statutory grounding of any GHG legislation and one of several governance foundations on which EPA's institutional competence to control GHG emissions must rest. However, a review of major GHG regulatory bills in the 110th Congress by the Congressional Research Service indicated that "in every case but one the 'primary entity' is EPA, and there is very little discussion in these bills or in Congress about the role that states and localities could play in designing or implementing national GHG regulations."[4] Virtually the same verdict could be applied to the 111th Congress. Most significant, governance issues are pervasive in both the alternative regulatory pathways most frequently debated within Congress, in the White House, and within the wider policy community.

Two Competing Regulatory Regimes

Of the two regulatory pathways, the one favored by the Obama administration is a comprehensive climate change bill including a cap-and-trade emissions control strategy, the centerpiece of most congressional GHG proposals, together with

other common provisions such as those promoting energy conservation and efficiency, those stimulating energy technology development, those financing a
"smart" national electric grid, and those mandating a renewable energy portfolio
standard for electric utilities.

However, the second pathway, regulation through the Clean Air Act (CAA)
fortified by *Massachusetts* v. *EPA*, would become the default option should Congress and the White House fail to agree on new GHG legislation. While the
Obama administration clearly favors new legislation grounded on cap and trade,
it is preparing to regulate with the CAA if the 111th Congress fails to enact HR
2454 or some alternative cap-and-trade legislation. In September 2009, for example, EPA administrator Lisa P. Jackson announced that when the agency regulates
stationary sources of GHGs under the CAA, it will require large industrial facilities emitting at least 25,000 tons of GHGs annually to obtain construction and
operating permits for those emissions.[5] In December 2009, Jackson announced
the agency's expected "endangerment" finding—that GHGs threaten the public
health and welfare and that on-road vehicle emissions contribute to that threat—
thus complying with its mandate in *Massachusetts* v. *Environmental Protection
Agency.*

Proponents of the CAA option call it a "regulatory jump start." Opponents,
like Representative John Dingell (D-Michigan), dismiss it as a "glorious mess."
The CAA has a plausible but perhaps elusive appeal in seeming to offer an immediately implementable measure of emissions control built on a well-established
federal-state governance structure, while apparently requiring relatively little additional congressional action to initiate. Proponents believe, moreover, that EPA has
the existing authority to regulate directly and to set emission standards for major
GHG emission sources, such as coal-fired power plants, as well as the ability to
enact a national cap-and-trade program to unify state and regional GHG markets.

Congress, of course, cannot anticipate the totality of implementation issues
entailed in a GHG regulatory program. Still, many of the fundamental administrative concerns are obvious, though also contentious enough to invite avoidance.
As these issues multiply, Congress's neglect of them places enormous responsibility on EPA for creating, clarifying, and resolving its foundations for regulatory
governance. Since the legislative compass points relentlessly toward EPA as the
destination for GHG regulation, David Bookbinder's question becomes compelling: Can EPA do the job?

Common Foundations for Regulatory Governance

Good regulatory governance through either policy pathway is grounded on
resources adequate and appropriate for policy implementation.[6] A reasonable
inventory of such essentials for EPA's GHG emissions regulation task would at
least include

—*Sufficient new or existing statutory authority to achieve the necessary substantive goals for GHG emissions regulation.* That implies, among other fundamentals, a clarity and explicitness in the definition of EPA's own authority and in the apportionment of authority between EPA and other government entities participating in regulatory decisionmaking.

—*A transparent, equitable, and accountable process for program development.* A new GHG regulatory regime must entail a process for negotiation and organizational collaboration with other agencies—and within EPA—in crafting an institutional design that embodies Congress's intentions. Procedural transparency, equity, and accountability should characterize such procedures as well as the agency's normal regulatory decisionmaking.

—*Adequate organization and resources.* The bricks and mortar of administrative capacity begins with an organizational design appropriate to the agency's mission. Factors to be considered include funding, personnel, technical competence, and materials, all of which must be compatible with policy goals.

—*Political feasibility.* The most formidable test of governance design can be political durability. The political resilience of a governance structure is compounded from qualities such as effective public and private constituencies, operational compatibility with collaborating institutions, durable legislative support, and politically skillful leadership, among other assets.

The two alternative regulatory pathways exemplify these governance issues in different ways. However, both policy designs pose a common, fundamental, and politically formidable governance issue: whether EPA's current organizational design is adequate to the task. That question is implicit in all discussions of EPA's ability to regulate GHG emissions, yet it is also the issue least likely to be addressed.

A Common Concern: EPA's Media-Centered Organization

EPA has a limited capability to absorb any new GHG regulatory program. The agency's structure, fundamentally unchanged since EPA's creation in 1972, has ossified despite profound changes in the agency's regulatory world. Over the intervening years, numerous studies have recommended major changes in the agency's organizational structure. The fresh administrative tasks posed by GHG legislation will require innovation and exacerbate many of EPA's embedded design anomalies. These tasks involve both agency authority and organizational consequences.

Therefore, the primal EPA governance issue posed by both regulatory pathways and foreign to almost all current discourse about GHG governance capability is whether EPA is designed to regulate GHG emissions competently. Three aspects of EPA's current administrative structure are relevant. First, EPA's budget, regulatory authority, and technical resources have evolved from its inception essentially around the axis of major "media offices" and statutes regulating pollutants according to the media through which they are transported or in which they ultimately accumulate, such as air, water, solid waste, and hazardous waste—what has been called EPA's "stovepipe" design. Moreover, EPA's ten decentralized regional offices are not structured to operate across regional lines or national jurisdictions.

EPA's stovepipe design has been the impetus for numerous reform proposals for three decades because it manifestly inhibits EPA's ability to effectively address pollution issues involving multiple media and cross-regional jurisdictions and to develop holistic approaches to pollution management—the kind of problem posed by GHG emissions.[7] Illustrations of GHG regulation issues abound:

—Potential groundwater contamination from the geological sequestration of CO_2—which might be permitted as a regulatory option—would likely require the air and water media offices to devise a joint implementation strategy.

—The creation of spent sorbent materials from carbon capture technologies would require integrated management of groundwater, hazardous waste, and solid waste programs.

—Regulation of domestic U.S. GHG emissions would require reconciliation with regional and global GHG treaties and accords.

A report to former EPA administrator Stephen L. Johnson by the National Advisory Council for Environmental Policy and Technology highlighted this theme by concluding that "many of the challenges ahead for the EPA and for the nation's environment are multi-media or not even directly connected to the Agency's traditional environmental media approaches." The 2008 report spoke specifically to the dysfunctional impact of stovepipe organization and the need to transcend it in regulating GHGs:

> EPA must achieve better integration and active collaboration between its programs and improve its ability to work in partnership with other federal agencies and with states, tribes and other external stakeholders to understand the problems and to develop and implement solutions . . . it will be important to devise a cross-program tracking system to be able to [monitor] cross-program activities. In fact, success in demonstrating progress toward larger environmental goals (e.g., reduction of GHG emissions) involving actions by two or more program offices could be one of the more valuable procedural outcomes of this entire planning and implementation process.[8]

A plausible, and the most often proposed, remedy for EPA's media-bound structure is congressional enactment of a new organic EPA statute (none currently exists). Such a statute would be intended, in the words of the National Academy of Public Administration, to create "a reorganization of its internal structure to end the current fragmentation among separate media offices. By adopting an integrated, multi-media pollution-control statute that can serve as EPA's organic act, Congress can create a statutory mission for the agency so it can work more efficiently than the single-medium laws now allow."[9] Even a less ambitious statute providing cross-media authority crafted to the specific requirements of GHG regulation would be helpful.

A second organizational challenge is that EPA's regulatory programs are for the most part premised on the assumption that the pollutants to be regulated and their emission sources are local or regional and that regulatory goals, impacts, and feasibility therefore are usually determined within the local or regional context. A third, closely associated issue tied to EPA's media-bound regulatory structure is that thresholds defining when a potential pollutant (in this case, GHGs) requires regulation are usually determined through risk analysis based on human health considerations.

But regulatory standards for GHGs cannot be based purely on local or regional impacts, nor can GHG emission thresholds be adequately characterized though traditional modes of human risk analysis. In fact, GHG emissions are fundamentally different from any of the other regulated pollutants on which the agency's design is premised. Unlike other air pollutants, as EPA has noted,

> GHGs are relatively evenly distributed throughout the global atmosphere. As a result, the geographic location of emission sources and reductions are generally not important to mitigating global climate change. Instead, total GHG emissions in the U.S. and elsewhere in the world over time determine cumulative global GHG concentrations, which in turn determine the extent of climate change. As a result, it will be the total emission reductions achieved by the US and the other countries of the world that will determine the extent of climate change mitigation."[10]

Moreover, GHG emissions do not affect public health directly; instead, they affect global atmospheric conditions, which may affect humans indirectly—for example, through continental temperature changes, which might stimulate the development or proliferation of human pathogens. Such human impacts, evolving over vast temporal and geographic distances, can seldom be characterized by the traditional modes of risk analysis commonly used in environmental regulation. In addition, the impact of domestic U.S. emission reductions will depend on international GHG regulatory programs, since, for purposes of GHG regulation, the earth's atmosphere is a single global "common."

A review of the European Union's efforts to implement the first phase of its Emission Trading System (ETS) or the experience of the more innovative states might provide some practical guidelines—and cautionary tales—to inform Congress and agency leaders about possible approaches to estimating GHG emission reductions and human health risks associated with greenhouse gases (see, in particular, chapter 5 of this volume for further discussion on the ETS and chapter 4 for a discussion of state regulatory initiatives). In both cases, regulators have had to come to terms early with the unique problems posed in setting GHG emissions standards.

The Governance Challenges of Cap and Trade

The most innovative feature of the GHG legislation debated in Congress is the cap-and-trade strategy for emissions control to which it is commonly anchored. This strategy entails a suite of regulatory requirements, including the creation of a national market in tradable GHG emission rights, emission caps, and emission registries and monitoring, with federal support for numerous complementary federal and state programs promoting energy conservation, energy efficiency, and much else. Cap and trade therefore raises closely related issues of authority and organizational design.

Creating Authority: The Challenge of Regulatory Federalism

The governance foundation of the cap-and-trade strategy is presumed to be regulatory federalism. This complex blending of complementary federal and state regulatory authority has evolved over more than three decades of collaboration in implementing existing federal environmental laws such as the Clean Air Act and the Clean Water Act. Although the constructive experience with regulatory federalism is a potentially solid foundation for new GHG emissions regulation, the resilience of this regulatory structure will be severely tested by the governance innovations that cap and trade requires. The regulatory federalism required by most cap-and-trade proposals raises issues of federal and state authority that are unlike those addressed, and often resolved, by prior federal-state collaboration in implementing other federal environmental statutes.

Capitalizing on Regulatory Federalism

The capability of the state and federal governments for collaborative environmental management has evolved from experience with numerous federal laws, including the Clean Air Act, the Clean Water Act, and the Toxic Substances Control Act. The result has been a durable federalized institutional culture in which the EPA's ten regional offices assume a major role in mediating between state, regional, and federal government entities. Numerous resources already exist to facilitate cooperative administration through collaborative planning, including the Government Results and Performance Act, numerous EPA federal-state "performance partnerships," and the information-sharing system involved in pollution monitoring and emission control.[11]

Through such experience, a tradition of consensus building has evolved in reaching regulatory decisions, and it can provide a substantial foundation for a new federal GHG regulatory program. At the same time, cap and trade will thrust enormously enlarged responsibilities on the regional offices to provide states with guidance in such critical tasks as oversight of GHG emissions regulation, for which they are made responsible in most legislative proposals, and for coordination of emission source registration and monitoring. At the least, the states will expect substantial federal financial and technical support mediated regionally for such work.

EPA also has considerable experience with alternative federal-state regulatory roles, which could serve as models for a future GHG regulatory program. The CAA invests the states with primary responsibility for monitoring and enforcing national ambient air quality standards and gives them the latitude to set standards that exceed federal requirements. The National Pollution Discharge Elimination System in the Clean Water Act, however, delegates to the states the authority to establish water quality standards and to monitor and enforce pollution controls, subject to federal guidelines. In contrast, the Toxic Substances Control Act requires EPA to implement virtually all of its provisions.

The institutional culture that has developed between EPA and the states over more than three decades of shared environmental governance has given rise to an important understanding about the responsibilities of each:

> Over the years, the general principle of having environmental decisions made by a qualified authority close to the problem has become widely accepted. Therefore, assuming that the state has the proper authority and makes decisions that are consistent with national policy, delegating national programs to the states is generally viewed as desirable. It is typically assumed that the states know the local environment, local stakeholders, and local political, economic, and social circumstances better than someone in a remote EPA office. EPA, however, is expected to know enough about state decisions made regarding major facilities to ensure that these decisions are consistent with national policy. This requires the good-faith sharing of information.[12]

In short, EPA already has invested considerable administrative and political capital in the development of a successful system of environmental regulation in collaboration with the states. However, adroit negotiation between EPA's national and regional offices will also be required to ease some of the predictable political and administrative dissonance sure to occur under cap and trade.

Dissonant Federal and State Regulatory Jurisdictions

Despite the institutionalized structures already in place to facilitate cap and trade, one fundamental aspect of a new GHG regulatory regime is guaranteed to provoke a collision of conflicting expectations and competing constituencies between EPA, state officials, and state agencies: the allocation and reconciliation of authority between EPA and states over their respective regulatory jurisdictions. The design of regulatory authority will be especially contentious because the states have demonstrated considerable initiative over the last decade in crafting innovative GHG regulatory programs in response to the federal government's inertia. The emissions targets and new regional regulatory jurisdictions inherent in the state programs often sharply conflict with proposed new federal GHG regulations. (Also see part 1 of this volume for further discussion on the relationship between federal and state initiatives.)

By the time the Obama administration was inaugurated, sixteen states had adopted greenhouse gas emission reduction targets, thirty-nine states had joined the multistate Climate Registry, and multistate partnerships had been formed to create at least three major regional cap-and-trade programs: the Regional Greenhouse Gas Initiative, the Western Climate Initiative, and the Midwestern Climate Initiative.[13] In addition, California has enacted a regulatory program for the transportation sector that twelve other states propose to adopt. State officials are unlikely to regard a new, preemptive federal GHG program benignly. Thus, an inherent dissonance between Washington and the states over implementation of a national GHG program becomes a primal reality confronting EPA throughout future GHG regulatory negotiations. "The states will not be happy with EPA," observed a former high official in EPA's Office of Regulatory Compliance, "and EPA will have to re-earn the leadership role it has lost since EPA abandoned the initiative on GHG issues."

Muddled Allocation of Regulatory Oversight and Compliance Authority

Another matter certain to set regulatory federalism on edge is the extent to which federal legislation authorizes EPA, rather than the states, to establish emission caps, allocate emission permits, set long-term emission reduction targets, and otherwise define the essential operational details of a cap-and-trade program. A congressional decision to invest EPA with considerable discretion in establishing emission caps and apportioning emission rights is an invitation to a brawl involving prolonged litigation, exacerbated conflict between and among federal and state governments, and laggardly regulatory impact. Such results, in turn, may generate daunting governance problems, many of which could be avoided with an explicit congressional mandate concerning emission targets, schedules, permit allocations, and related regulatory issues.

California's experience is a cautionary tale about the perils of legislative default on these matters. After legislation was passed leaving decisions about how to implement the cap to the state's Clean Air Regulatory Board (CARB), "interbranch tensions surfaced over agency interpretation of the statute," reports Barry Rabe:

> The governor promptly concluded that cap-and-trade was the appropriate route and used his executive authority to require state officials to begin to assemble such a program. But the response from the legislature has been swift and intense, placing the entire future of the program under considerable uncertainty. Leaders in the California Senate have threatened CARB with

steep funding cuts if they put too much effort into cap-and-trade instead of emphasizing a series of regulatory actions that could be implemented promptly. "The implementation of Assembly Bill 32 is getting bogged down in arcane discussions over intercontinental trading schemes, 'carbon markets,' and free 'credits,'" lamented Senate President Don Perata.[14]

In contrast, a much better precedent for enhancing EPA's governance capacity is the design of Title IV of the Clean Air Act Amendments of 1990, which defined within the legislation, or clearly delegated to EPA, such key elements as emission caps and permit allocations in the mandated SO_2 trading program.

Given the history of regulatory federalism, most states are likely to oppose any federal preemption of state regulatory authority that denies them substantial latitude in implementing a national GHG regulatory program. EPA's governance capability can be enhanced if some fundamental principles are built into both the federal legislation and the resulting administrative regulations and guidance. A short list includes the following:

—*Delegating as much authority as possible to the states for emissions registries, monitoring, and enforcement.* "It is typically assumed that the states know the local environment, local stakeholders, and local political, economic and social circumstances better than someone in a remote EPA office."[15]

—*Involving stakeholders actively and sharing data in the governance structure.* This would include data sharing on discharges and emissions, compliance, and ambient air quality; transparency in the management of data permits; and enforcement.

—*Reserving to the states the authority to regulate GHG emissions through land use planning, transportation and infrastructure development, building codes, and other actions based on traditional state and local authority.*

—*Protecting the ability of states and localities to set standards above and beyond any federal requirements.* The Clean Air Act contains such a reserve provision, and several legislative proposals in the 110th and the 111th Congress included language preserving states' rights to enact more stringent provisions. However, under a cap-and-trade program, a generic savings clause may not be sufficient to ensure that state and local provisions to reduce GHG emissions actually result in reduced overall GHG emissions. States and localities need to have the ability to take allowances off the market if they so choose. Otherwise, sources covered by more stringent state and local reduction requirements could simply sell their "excess" allowances to sources not covered by the more stringent requirements.[16]

The Challenge of Program Development and Process

EPA has created an internal planning entity in anticipation of a transition to a national GHG regulatory regime, which will also require coordination at a much higher level among a multitude of federal entities. A minimal list includes the departments of energy, state, agriculture, commerce, and treasury and independent agencies such as the Federal Energy Regulatory Commission, the National Oceanographic and Atmospheric Administration, and the Federal Trade Commission.

The Obama administration is planning to facilitate energy policymaking at the highest executive level by adding to its burgeoning White House "czaraucracy" a new "energy czar," former EPA administrator Carol Browner. Browner is expected to facilitate federal energy policy through a new White House Office of Energy and Climate Change Policy (and presumably through the agency's transition to GHG regulation as well). Browner is a veteran and a highly respected Washington administrator with formidable skills. Still, the efficacy of this strategy for coordinating the sprawling welter of executive agencies implicated in GHG regulation has yet to be tested.[17] Experience with other executive "czars" reaching back to the Nixon administration suggests its effectiveness is problematic at best.[18]

The transitional planning to national GHG regulation should also continue to incorporate features of process design that have long characterized EPA's relationship with the states, including "building a voice of the regulated" into the process by providing for active stakeholder involvement, maintaining transparency in deliberations, and ensuring an infrastructure of accountability. The National Association of Clean Air Administrators, for example, notes that

> [t]echnologies and knowledge about the types of programs that can effectively reduce GHG emissions are also rapidly evolving. As part of implementing a national GHG program. . . . [a]t the federal level, state and local experts could form an advisory body that provides real-time guidance to the implementing federal agency (likely EPA); such guidance would be used to improve program implementation (including by strengthening the federal program or by considering new ways of achieving the goals of the federal program).[19]

Administrative Resources: Funding, Staffing, and Technical Competence

The transition to a new GHG regulatory program and its subsequent implementation will require EPA to draw on substantial administrative resources that it presently lacks, including the following:

FUNDING

Congress has progressively diminished EPA's annual appropriations in real dollars since the mid-1980s. The agency currently receives approximately 50 percent of its 1980 appropriations despite an enormous expansion of its mission—even without GHG regulation. EPA's science funding in particular has been significantly diminished.[20] Moreover, relatively little congressional attention has been given to the administrative costs and human resources required of a GHG cap-

and-trade program.[21] EPA has a limited capability to reallocate budgetary dollars internally. All estimates of additional administrative costs imposed by cap and trade guarantee the new administrative expense will overwhelm the agency's capacity to adjust within current funding. For example:

—Many cap-and-trade schemes would probably require EPA to establish a new administrative capacity to distribute proceeds from the auction of GHG emission rights and from consumption allowances to state and local governments, private sector firms, and certain individuals. EPA's employee union has asserted that it might require a 300 percent increase in some existing EPA offices.[22]

—EPA may be required to inventory GHG sources not covered by cap and trade, such as landfills, natural gas systems, and small fuel combustion sources.

The Congressional Budget Office (CBO) estimated that the much-debated America's Climate Security Act of 2007 (S 2191, the "Lieberman-Warner Act") introduced in the 110th Congress would have required an increase in discretionary spending of $3.6 billion from 2009 to 2018, mostly for EPA implementation activities.[23] If the estimated additional costs of S 2191 to other agencies had been added, the CBO estimate would have climbed to $8.2 billion for the same period.[24] Such estimates, however, are highly speculative and often exclude mandates for future EPA activities whose cost defies present calculation.

These estimates do not address the contentious issue of federal support for state implementation of a GHG regulatory regime. The states have repeatedly indicated that they expect significant federal assistance.[25] While additional federal spending on the administration of new GHG regulations would be inevitable, the amount and allocation of the funds would have a profound impact on EPA's governance capabilities, but one that is presently difficult to assess.

STAFFING

EPA's organizational design is antique. EPA today deploys its workforce largely on the basis of a model that has not been substantially updated since 1988. Anticipating GHG regulation, EPA's employee union has called on Congress to require a new workforce analysis and strategy, warning that the agency is unprepared to undertake new GHG regulatory duties, even with the additional $3 billion boost in EPA appropriations requested by the Obama administration for FY 2010.[26] For example:

—An especially demanding new workload will probably fall to the agency's Office of Air and Radiation (OAR), which is likely to inherit much of the responsibility for designing the GHG emissions monitoring and reporting system.

—Since litigation is a way of regulatory life, EPA's Office of General Counsel will need a substantially expanded staff to handle the anticipated effusion of new legal issues created by GHG management.

Since much of the actual responsibility for implementing cap-and-trade regulation will fall on the states, EPA can also expect vigorous state pressure to provide financial support for related technical and administrative activities, which presumably must come from the agency's appropriations.

Scientific, Technical, and Economic Capacity

A GHG regulatory program will place heavy demands on EPA's scientific resources, technical capabilities, and economic planning. In many respects, EPA has substantial resources and experience in both the scientific and economic aspects of environmental regulation, as well as experience in managing the cap-and-trade market mandated for SO_2 in Title IV of the Clean Air Act Amendments of 1990. Nonetheless, EPA has no practical experience with GHG emissions control. A prospective CO_2 emissions market would differ in significant ways from the SO_2 emissions market created by Title IV.[27] Moreover, GHG emissions differ fundamentally—in both scientific and economic terms—from most other environmental pollutants regulated by EPA. However, EPA has been preparing for several years to implement a GHG regulatory program and appears to possess a promising scientific and economic foundation to initiate the program—if the agency receives more robust budgetary and administrative support.

EPA differs from other regulatory agencies in having a very large and experienced scientific staff, laboratories, and workshops. A GHG regulatory program would require EPA to have, among other technical capacities, the ability to estimate GHG emissions "upstream" and "downstream" in the energy economy, to determine appropriate ambient air concentrations and caps for CO_2 and related GHGs such as hydrochlorofluorocarbons (HGCs), and to provide scientific and technical support to state and local regulators in implementing a national GHG cap-and-trade regime. Beyond cap and trade, scientific competence would be required in promoting energy efficiency, alternative fuel development, and perhaps in developing transportation emission estimates and control technologies.

Since the early 1990s, EPA's ability to address GHG science issues has expanded. For example, the Office of Atmospheric Programs currently has a staff of approximately 260 and an additional 60 persons representing EPA in domestic and international climate policy discussions. Approximately 150 staff members work on climate change issues. "We have actually increased our science staff and capability," observed an official in EPA's Office of Atmospheric Programs, "and there's lots of opportunity for scientists to work. We're getting ready for climate warming regulation because we know it's coming." Discussions with other EPA officials suggest that EPA's scientific capacity and morale will not be a continuing casualty of the agency's turbulent relationship with the Bush White House, which repeatedly intervened in the agency's scientific deliberations and reports.

Nonetheless, regulating GHG emissions within a cap-and-trade market poses numerous scientific and technical challenges that the agency must address. EPA's prior experience with SO_2 and NOx monitoring under Title IV of the Clean Air

Act Amendments of 1990 can provide at least limited assistance, but important new issues are likely to arise. They include the following:

—*Emissions monitoring.* While equipment exists for monitoring continuous GHG emissions from coal-fired utilities, the technology for complex, multi-stack emission sources such as oil refineries is not yet available. Monitoring of upstream GHG sources—for example, natural gas and petroleum pipelines—would require as yet unproven or unavailable technologies.[28]

—*Emissions control.* GHG emission controls are still experimental. For example, carbon capture and sequestration (CCS), the most frequently proposed control technology, is not yet technically proven or economically practical for use by coal-burning electrical utilities, the major domestic source of GHG emissions.

—*Compliance monitoring.* Monitoring GHG compliance requires a technology different from that currently used to monitor pollution emissions in existing EPA regulatory programs. While preliminary research on GHG technologies has been done, EPA continues to rely primarily on industry self-reporting and site visits as its primary enforcement tools in existing programs.

—*Scientific review and accountability.* While EPA has an established internal process of scientific research, review, and evaluation for its existing programs, scientific modeling and other technical aspects of a new GHG program are sufficiently challenging that a scientific advisory committee may be needed to increase both the program's technical capacities and its credibility with stakeholders and Congress.[29]

—*Registry development.* EPA has limited experience with registry structures.[30] Generally, the states have assumed the lead in the design and implementation of registries.[31] Reconciling a prospective federal emissions registry with existing and planned state and regional registries will be an essential element of any cap-and-trade program. Existing state and regional registries, such as the current regional Climate Registry, may specify criteria for emissions registration that differ from those of a federal registry.[32] States may regulate emission sources that differ from the sources mandated by federal law.

—*Offsets management.* Some provision for emission offsets is an integral component of almost all proposed cap-and-trade programs. Offsets propel EPA into a technical and economic terra incognita, raising significant issues about the scope of EPA's authority to deal with agricultural and foreign offsets, monitoring, accountability structures, and other essential elements of offset management.[33] Title III (A) of the Lieberman-Warner bill, for instance, did not specify how EPA should distribute the pool of offsets to project developers.

Modeling and Market Management

Economic or emissions allocation modeling of alternative GHG regulatory policy options and implementation strategies are essential to the legislative design of a GHG emissions control program, the writing of subsequent regulations and guidelines, and the evaluation of regulation impacts. It is widely understood that economic and allocation models are always constrained by the array of assumptions underlying their creation and by the inevitable limitations inherent in such hypothetical underpinnings.[34] The models are nonetheless valuable because they can suggest the comparative effectiveness and cost-effectiveness of alternative policy designs, create rough bounds on costs and benefits, and help to assess policy administrative and political feasibility, among other important purposes.

EPA has considerable expertise and experience in economic and technical modeling for pollution regulation. The agency's Office of Air and Radiation—and especially its Air Quality Monitoring Group—have provided EPA, Congress, and the states with an enormous volume of modeling information since EPA's creation. OAR's competence in the economic modeling of GHG regulatory policies was demonstrated by its preparation of the *EPA Analysis of the Lieberman-Warner Climate Security Act of 2008,* widely cited during congressional consideration of that legislation.[35] While GHG emissions regulation poses substantial technological challenges for EPA, the ability to accomplish the required economic modeling or technical modeling and related tasks appears to be among EPA's stronger assets and contributes to its regulatory competence.

GHG modeling, however, comes equipped with political barbs. Many assumptions built into the models used to assess technical, economic, and administrative policy options involve politically contested issues. It is important that congressional legislation provide EPA with sufficient guidance on how emissions policy will be implemented—for example, which GHG emissions will be regulated and how emission rates will be calculated—to preclude leaving the agency with too much discretion in resolving politically contentious modeling issues, which would unnecessarily diminish the administrative or political feasibility of the mandated GHG program. For example, the method for calculating or "grandfathering" emissions from existing regulated facilities for purposes of permit allocation is disputed. A calculation based on a facility's output of a service or commodity and one based on its actual production of GHG emissions will yield significantly different emissions estimates for regulatory purposes and involve important cost and distributive equity issues.[36]

Another politically contentious modeling issue is how much consideration should be given to the impact of GHG emissions regulation on the global competitiveness of any industry or facility. "EPA will have to take care of some U.S. industries to preserve their competitiveness," observed a former EPA high planning official. "It is difficult to determine which industries would be affected by competitiveness, although some, like primary metals and chemicals, would be likely." Congress will need to provide EPA with explicit guidance on such prickly allocation issues to facilitate the allocation process.

EPA's capacity to administer a GHG marketing system is another matter. The European Union's experience with its pioneering Emission Trading System, initiated in 2005—the only multistate GHG regulatory regime yet initiated glob-ally—is confronting substantial technical, economic, and political problems. While the ETS cap-and-trade emissions market differs in many respects from most current congressional GHG proposals, it also has become a showcase of several implementation issues likely to confront EPA's own cap-and-trade mar-ket.[37] The most important of those issues include difficulties in creating and monitoring an emissions registry, the steep decline in the trading price of carbon as a result of overallocated emission permits, and increasing pressure from a number of EU states as a result of the widespread European economic recession beginning in 2008 to cut the ambitious ETS target of a 20 percent reduction in EU GHG emissions by 2020. These, among other matters, have been indicted for the failure of the ETS to achieve its initial targets between 2005 and 2008. There has been little evidence that the EU experience has informed congres-sional deliberations on a domestic cap-and-trade program or that EPA has yet addressed some of the implications of the EU experience for its own governance capabilities.

International Issues

A new GHG regulatory regime is likely to require a considerable expansion of EPA's international responsibilities and organizational resources. The scope of international activities will vary according to which version of a legislative GHG regulatory program is considered, but most versions require some minimal agenda of responsibilities and capacities.

The sine qua non of the international "to do" list is a technical and administra-tive capability for negotiation with other international entities to reconcile the domestic GHG cap-and-trade targets and emission levels with existing or prospec-tive national, regional, and international GHG treaties. "Promoting compatibility of a U.S. climate program with programs in other countries is critical for a num-ber of reasons," explains an Aspen Institute study. "In the near-term, establishing at least some links between a U.S. program and other countries' programs could allow firms regulated in the U.S. to take advantage of a global emissions trading market."

Numerous studies suggest global emissions trading would result in dramatic cost savings. In addition, program links could be especially valuable for compa-nies with facilities in many countries; such multinational companies would ben-efit from compatible regulatory frameworks and the ability to shift emission reduction credits among their various entities."[38] The Lieberman-Warner bill, for instance, directs EPA to promulgate rules for registering and issuing offset allowances for emission reduction or sequestration projects in other countries in accordance with the "Clean Development Mechanism" of the United Nations Framework Convention on Climate Change (UNFCCC). It also allows EPA to promulgate regulations, in accordance with the UNFCCC, approving the use in the United States of emission allowances issued by countries with mandatory absolute limits on GHG emissions and a program of comparable stringency.

Technical issues will be challenging. EPA's mandated emission levels, caps, and emission reduction schedules will need to be related to international GHG data and other nations' regulations, and negotiations over future emissions management, particularly in developing nations, will be required. Most congressionally proposed GHG regulatory legislation allows domestic regulated facilities to satisfy a portion of their emission compliance requirements through credits from foreign trading programs, assuming that they meet an EPA-determined standard of stringency comparable to that of the U.S. program.

EPA's Office of International Affairs (OIA) has considerable experience with regional and international collaboration on such transboundary issues as air pollution and toxics regulation, marine pollution, and clean energy technologies. However, discussions with current and past EPA officials suggest that OIA staff and competencies will require significant diversification if EPA is to undertake the international responsibilities implicit in a domestic GHG regulatory program (see also part 4 of this volume, which explores the prospects for the United States in engaging the international community in global climate change efforts).

Regulatory Jump-Start or Misfit? The Clean Air Act

Regulation of greenhouse gas emissions through the Clean Air Act appeals to many proponents of rapid federal action because it is available, on the shelf, and EPA-initiated. EPA has more than three decades' experience with the CAA, the Supreme Court has sanctioned its use as a GHG regulatory instrument, and EPA administrator Jackson is prepared to use its existing authority to initiate immediate GHG emissions regulation if the 111th Congress stalls on omnibus GHG legislation. Opponents consider it impractical if not unworkable, at best a goad to congressional action on a more appropriate GHG regulatory design.

Substantial governance issues are implicit in attempting to assimilate greenhouse gases within the CAA's existing regulatory framework. "Government is an unusual animal," observed a former Reagan White House official. "No matter what it ingests, it has the ability to manufacture antibodies to kill it." Likewise, there are plenty of antibodies available for CAA-based regulation. The route to regulation by the CAA must traverse problematic EPA authority, since regulation requires of EPA a very substantial time commitment, new implementation structures, and scientific resources that currently are constrained. As the previous discussion suggests, many of these governance issues are also inherent in alternative proposals involving cap-and-trade programs such as the Waxman-Markey Climate and Energy Security Act. In the end, it seems doubtful that the CAA path will enable EPA to act with greater initiative—or broader restraint on GHG emissions—than might be achieved through comprehensive new legislation.

EPA Authority

Greenhouse gases do not conform to the character of pollutants that the CAA was intended to regulate. GHGs do not create localized environmental damage, but they do have serious regional and global consequences. It also is impossible to establish an ambient air quality standard for CO_2 regulation, which creates a potential inability to place reasonable limits on emission sources or to protect the most sensitive populations, as required by the CAA. At the least, the CAA will require major congressional amending, which may, in turn, consume considerable time and generate much litigation.

Administrative and Technical Capability

EPA officials have anticipated the need for a substantial increase in staff and funding with GHG regulation under the Clean Air Act, yet the magnitude of such an increase is problematic. The agency has, for instance, initiated a GHG reporting registry and increased staffing to undertake the economic modeling required for establishing GHG emission controls. Still, the additional and often unpredictable responsibilities entailed in CAA-based regulation compound EPA's long recognized, chronic workforce deficiencies.[39] EPA union officials have called for a major new workforce analysis (the last was made in 1989), asserting that GHG regulation through the CAA would require perhaps tripling staff in some offices, such as the Office of Air and Radiation, despite the Obama administration's $3 billion increase in the agency's FY 2010 budget.[40] Business organizations have predicted that the agency's Office of General Counsel will also require a hefty staff increase to handle the expected increase in litigation generated by the new climate rules.

Another major challenge for EPA, as with alternative regulation through an omnibus new GHG bill, concerns identification of desirable GHG emission control technologies under the CAA for motor vehicles and stationary sources. In either case, EPA intends to require the "best available control technology" (BACT) to reduce CO_2. BACT has not yet been determined for CO_2, and its determination is destined to be contentious. The current status of emission controls involves large uncertainties. If EPA decides to regulate motor vehicle GHG emissions, as would seem to be implied by its "endangerment" finding, the agency faces what the National Academy of Science characterized as "huge analytic tasks, including the challenge of cost-benefit analysis of phenomena that are difficult to quantify.[41] Vehicle emission control technologies have at least been experimentally developed and tested. The situation is quite different when it comes to stationary sources, for which control technologies are at a very early stage of development and largely unproven. CAA regulations initially would require perhaps 3,000 major new sources to meet the new permit standards; eventually, an estimated 14,000 stationary sources would be covered by the BACT standard.[42]

An additional concern involves the most commonly proposed new emission control technology, carbon capture and storage (CCS). Essentially, CCS involves capturing CO_2 emissions from large point sources, such as coal-fired utilities, in the form of a mineral carbonate or injecting them into deep geological or ocean formations, where they can be stored—or "sequestered"—indefinitely. CCS involves substantial ecological and economic issues, including the long-term environmental impact of CO_2 storage, the commercial viability of the technology, and the implacable opposition of many major environmental organizations. The first experimental CCS technology in the United States to be commercially tested is being installed at the Mountaineer Power Plant in Mason County, West Virginia.

Finally, many of the issues entailed in offsets management under the Waxman-Markey Climate and Energy Security Act or similar legislation would arise under regulation through the Clean Air Act. EPA has had some experience with the domestic use of offsets in regulating NOx and SO_2 with Title IV of the CAA, but CO_2 emission offsets will launch EPA into agricultural and foreign offset management, with which it has very little experience and for which its current staff capability is inadequate.[43] EPA's authority to deal with agricultural and foreign offsets will have to be clarified, particularly in relation to its impact on the programs of the Department of Agriculture and the Department of State.

Federal-State Program Development

GHG emission standards must be reconciled with existing state and regional GHG emission markets such as the Regional Greenhouse Gas Initiative and the Western Climate Initiative. New partnerships will be needed to determine the relative responsibilities of local, state, and federal agencies in emissions monitoring and registries. The CAA provides no guidance on how this essential process is to evolve. For example, the CAA contains language permitting the states to exceed EPA's national air quality standards, but it is not clear that that provision would also allow states to withdraw federally allocated GHG emission allowances as a strategy to exceed federally mandated GHG emission standards, as many states wish. Both the National Association of Clean Air Agencies (NACAA) and the Environmental Council of the States (ECOS) have suggested the need for specific language in the CAA to allow this option.[44]

From a broader perspective, it appears imperative that EPA—or Congress—initiate action specifically to ensure a collaborative federal-state process in implementing GHG regulation under the CAA. That might involve creation of a federal-state advisory entity to participate actively in planning for regulatory implementation through the CAA. It is especially important to create data standards and arrangements for data sharing between federal and state regulatory agencies through existing entities such as the National Environmental Information Exchange Network (to which all fifty U.S. states now belong) and the Climate Registry, which involves states active in state or regional GHG emissions regulation. Cooperative arrangements such as these also are important for creating openness, transparency, and credibility in the regulation of greenhouse gases under the Clean Air Act.

Political Feasibility

Apart from the challenges involved in organizing to administer a GHG regulatory program competently, EPA seems predestined to confront major political issues that might be mitigated through the planning process. One inevitable problem will be protracted litigation with the regulated sectors under whatever regulatory pathway it eventually chooses. Corporate interests expecting to be regulated under the CAA have generally been outspokenly critical of the prospect of EPA's retaining or allowing highly variable state and regional GHG emission standards, emission caps, and monitoring requirements, as EPA seems prepared to propose with implementation under the CAA. Spokespersons for many large GHG emissions sources, such as the National Petrochemical and Refiners Association, have also expressed concern that EPA's announced intention to discriminate between different GHG emission sources and to regulate initially only the large emitters (more than 25,000 tons annually) under the CAA will invest the agency with too much discretion.[45] The extent to which such a surge of new litigation can be mitigated is problematic, but it must at least be considered, and major stakeholders must be accorded considerable opportunity to participate in the process of program development.

Significant new institutional negotiations will be needed with other federal entities certain to be involved in GHG regulation. Institutional authorities and roles must be clarified for EPA in working with the Department of Energy (DOE), the Department of State, the Department of Agriculture, and a multitude of other federal entities that will be drawn into GHG regulation. The DOE, in particular, is destined to be a major EPA collaborator in such essential regulatory activities as determining offset "equivalence" and "additionality" with respect to emission standards for domestic GHG sources and monitoring sequestration technologies. The appointment of Carol Browner as the Obama administration's new energy czar within the president's cabinet points toward the necessity and contingency of competent interdepartmental coordination in regulating greenhouse gases under the CAA. The extent to which Browner's new office has the authority and political weight necessary for high-level federal coordination of GHG regulation, whether through the CAA or an alternative, will be an important part of the prognosis for the program's effectiveness.

These and other issues of political feasibility related to either major GHG regulatory pathway discussed are always a major and perhaps the most fundamental determinant of the success of GHG regulation.

Conclusions: Looking for the Vital Signs of Governance

Any consideration of the governance implications of domestic GHG regulation is pitched at the edge of imponderables. The Obama White House and Congress have numerous options, including implementation through the Clean Air Act, enactment of new GHG legislation—most likely some variant of the Waxman-Markey Climate and Energy Security Act—or some other permutation of current proposals. As this chapter suggests, an explicit and candid discussion of the embedded governance issues in either pathway appears to be among the most essential—yet neglected—components of Washington's current discourse on GHG regulation.

Notes

1. Testimony of David Bookbinder, chief climate counsel, Sierra Club, before the Senate Committee on Environment and Public Works. *Hearing on Regulation of Greenhouse Gases under the Clean Air Act,* September 23, 2008 (http://sierra club.typepad.com/compass/files/shortened_bookbinder_testimony.doc).

2. Boxer-Kerry (S 1733) is summarized by EPA, "Clean Energy Jobs and American Power Act of 2009, October 23, 2009" (www.epa.gov/climatechange/ economics/economicanalyses.html#cleanenergy); Pew Center on Global Climate Change, "Climate Change Legislation: On to the Senate" (www.pewclimate.org/ blog/roym/climate-change-legislation-senate).

3. The substantial new responsibilities assigned to EPA by HR 2454 are summarized in Columbia Law School, Climate Legislation Resource Center, "Legislative Actions on Climate Change in the 111th Congress of the United States: Agency Mandates" (www.columbia.edu/centers/climatechange/legislation).

4. National Association of Clean Air Agencies, "Conference Materials for 'Defining the Role of States and Localities in Federal Global Warming Legislation'" (Washington: National Association of Clean Air Agencies, February 2008), p. 25 (www.4cleanair.org/documents/GWConferenceMaterials.pdf).

5. These permits must demonstrate the use of best available control technologies (BACT) and energy efficiency measures to minimize GHG emissions when facilities are constructed or significantly modified. BACT has not yet been defined for CO_2.

6. This conceptual approach to governance is suggested by Robert R. Nordhaus and Kyle W. Danish, *Designing a Mandatory Greenhouse Gas Reduction Program for the U.S.* (Arlington, Va.: Pew Center for Global Climate Change, May 2003) (www.pewclimate.org/docUploads/USGas.pdf).

7. See, for example, EPA, Office of the Inspector General, *Studies Addressing EPA's Organizational Structure*, Report 2006-P-00029, August 26, 2006; Governmental Accountability Office, *Major Management Challenges and Program Risks: Environmental Protection Agency*, Report GAO-03-2003, January 2003; National Academy of Public Administration, statement of Dr. Janet L. Norwood before the Subcommittee on Energy Policy, Natural Resources, and Regulatory Affairs, House of Representatives, September 21, 2001 (www.napawash.org/ resources/testimony/testimony 09_21_01.html).

8. National Advisory Council for Environmental Policy and Technology, "NACEPT's Comments on EPA's Draft 2009-2014 Strategic Plan Change Document," December 30, 2008 (www.epa.gov/ocempage/nacept/reports/pdf/2009 _0130_151224607.pdf).

9. National Academy of Public Administration, statement of Dr. Janet L. Norwood.

10. EPA, "Regulatory Greenhouse Gas Emissions under the Clean Air Act," *Advance Notice of Proposed Rulemaking*, April 12, 2008, p. 116.

11. Congress has facilitated federal-state planning in many ways. In addition to passing environmental legislation and appropriating EPA funds, Congress requires EPA to set specific environmental goals (see EPA's strategic plan at www. epa.gov/oefu/plan/plan.htm) and reviews the agency's progress toward those goals. The Government Performance and Results Act of 1993 (GPRA) requires each agency to develop a strategic plan with goals, objectives, and measures of success. GPRA also requires EPA to submit performance reports each year (see www. epa.gov/ocfu/finstatement/2003ar/2003ar.htm). EPA relies on its regional offices and the states to collect the information needed to provide these reports to Congress. Information must be received in a timely fashion and must be in a consistent format.

12. Stanley Laskowski, Richard Morgenstern, and Allen Blackman, *Environmental Decentralization in the United States: Seeking the Proper Balance between National and State Authority*, Discussion Paper 05-42 (Washington: Resources for the Future, October 2005) (www.rff.org/Publications/Pages/PublicationDetails .aspx?PublicationID=17414).

13. Committee on Energy and Commerce, *Climate Change Legislation Design White Paper: Appropriate Roles for Different Levels of Government*, February 2008 (http://energycommerce. house.gov/Climate_Change/white%20paper%20st-lcl% 20roles%20final%202-22.pdf).

14. Barry G. Rabe and Marc Gaden, "Governing the Climate from Sacramento," in *Toward Sustainable Communities*, 2nd ed., edited by Daniel A. Mazmanian and Michael E. Kraft (MIT Press, 2009), p. 28.

15. Laskowski, Morgenstern, and Blackman, *Environmental Decentralization in the United States*.

16. Two options, among others, have been suggested: federal legislation that contains language expressly authorizing states and localities to retire allowances from sources in their jurisdictions; and federal legislation that allocates allowances directly to the states. States would then have discretion in allocating allowances to sources; with control over allowances, states could give fewer allowances to sources, thus forcing greater reductions.

17. There are several other complimentary planning innovations. A high-level coordinating entity, such as an interagency regulatory group, should exist to facilitate planning between EPA, the states, and other relevant federal entities, such as the Department of State and the Department of Energy. This interagency group should develop a strategic plan for the federal implementation of GHG regulation. Concurrently, EPA should initiate similar high-level strategic planning among its national office, its regional offices, and state environmental agencies expected to implement the new program.

18. Randy James, "A Brief History of White House 'Czars'," *Time CNN*, September 23, 2009 (www.time.com/time/politics/article/0,8599,1925564,00.html).

19. National Association of Clean Air Agencies, "Conference Materials for 'Defining the Role of States and Localities in Federal Global Warming Legislation,'" p. 19.

20. Cited in J. Clarence Davies Jr., *Nanotechnology Oversight: An Agenda for the New Administration* (Washington: Woodrow Wilson International Center, 2008), p. 10. See also Robert M. Sussman, "Science and EPA Decisionmaking," *Journal of Law and Policy* 12 (April 2004), pp. 573–87.

21. The Lieberman-Warner bill introduced in the 110th Congress was an exception of sorts. It did make a genuflection in this direction by mandating that proceeds from the auction of emissions rights authorized by the legislation must first be used to fund "EPA and other activities required by S 2191" and to ensure adequate funding for the Bureau of Land

Management (limited to $300 million) and the Forest Service (limited to $300 million) for emergency firefighting activities. Whether the anticipated revenue will be sufficient for EPA's requirements is difficult to determine.

22. Congressional Budget Office, *Cost Estimate: S 2191, America's Climate Security Act of 2007* (Washington: April 10, 2008), p. 1.

23. Ibid.

24. Estimate provided by Julie Rosenberg, EPA Office of Atmospheric Programs; see also Congressional Budget Office, *Cost Estimate: S. 2191*. California, by way of comparison, hired more than 200 new staff, mostly for CalEPA, when the state initiated its GHG regulatory program. The CBO did not distinguish the cost to EPA for implementing the Waxman-Markey Climate and Energy Security Act from other required new discretionary spending, instead estimating that the total discretionary funding required between 2010 and 2019 would be $49.9 billion. See Congressional Budget Office, *Cost Estimates: HR 2454, American Clean Energy and Security Act of 2009* (June 5, 2009), p. 2.

25. See, for example, National Association of Clean Air Agencies, "Conference Materials for 'Defining the Role of States and Localities in Federal Global Warming Legislation.'"

26. The U.S. Chamber of Commerce has estimated the new workforce requirements at between 45,000 and 50,000 new positions.

27. Most legislatively proposed GHG markets, for example, require consideration of international GHG emissions and sources in modeling domestic emissions caps and allocations and provide for both domestic and international emission offsets to emission limits.

28. World Resources Institute, *Responses to Questions on Options for U.S. Climate Policy Design and Implementation: Submission to the U.S. House of Representatives Committee on Energy and Commerce Climate Conference , March 19, 2007* (Washington: World Resources Institute, 2007) (http://pdf.wri.org/wri_house_ energycommerce.pdf).2201

29. World Resources Institute, "Insights from Modeling Analyses of the Lieberman-Warner Climate Security Act (S 2191)," *In Brief: Innovative Policy Solutions to Global Climate Change* (May 2008) (Arlington, Va.: Pew Center for Global Climate Change) (www.pewclimate.org/in-brief/l-w-modeling).

30. U.S. experience to date with voluntary programs to address climate change has been quite valuable. Initiatives such as the Environmental Protection Agency's Climate Leaders program have given participating companies essential knowledge about measuring and tracking their GHG emissions and identifying innovative and cost-effective ways to reduce them. The California Climate Action Registry likewise affords leading companies the opportunity to develop comprehensive GHG inventories and report progress toward lowering their emissions. The Climate Registry, a nascent GHG registry initiative, will allow companies to measure and report progress on reducing emissions in states across the country. World Resources Institute, *Responses to Questions and Options*, p. 32.

31. Congress passed an appropriations bill in December 2007 with $3.5 million in funding for the Environmental Protection Agency to establish a mandatory GHG reporting program in the United States. The legislation requires the EPA to establish a draft rule for this registry within nine months and a final rule within eighteen months. The legislation does not specify which facilities or emissions will be subject to reporting.

32. For example, "A federal registry may turn out to be less rigorous and/or comprehensive— either at the outset or in the future—than desired by states and localities. Also, states may have regulatory or voluntary programs that require the reporting of data elements that differ from federal requirements. The federal registry may be created solely to support specific legislation, such as the Lieberman-Warner Climate Security Act of 2008 (S. 2191). S. 2191 created a

regulatory program to reduce direct emissions of GHGs through a cap-and-trade program. Because the bill currently contains language instructing EPA to create a registry that primarily accounts for the direct emissions resulting from combustion of fossil fuels during energy production (and possibly some mobile source emissions), a registry that is established *solely* in response to this bill would not account for all GHG emissions." National Association of Clean Air Agencies, "Conference Materials for 'Defining the Role of States and Localities in Federal Global Warming Legislation,'" p. 39.

33. Committee on Energy and Commerce, Climate Change Legislation Design White Paper.

34. A brief and useful review of these limitations is provided in Janet Peace and John Weyant, *Insights Not Numbers: The Appropriate Use of Economic Models* (Pew Center for Global Climate Change, April 2008).

35. The CRS report indicates that the most comprehensive analysis was conducted by EPA. The report is entitled *EPA Analysis of the Lieberman-Warner Climate Security Act of 2008: S. 2191 in 110th Congress* (March 14, 2008). The analysis employs a suite of models and base cases, along with some useful sensitivity analyses. The CRS report focuses on three of the models, two base cases, and sensitivity analysis as appropriate.

36. "The method for grandfathering—historical emissions or output-based—was hotly debated by interested parties. Those wanting output-based allocations—i.e., allocations based on a facility's historical output of electricity or other products, rather than its GHG emissions— argued that firms should be rewarded for past investment in efficiency and the use of relatively lower-emitting or zero-emitting technologies (e.g., natural gas, hydroelectric, renewables, or nuclear power). Others believe that the permits should go to firms which will need them most at the outset, so they can afford to cover increased fuel costs and invest in new technologies and fuels." Eileen Claussen and Robert W. Fri, "A Climate Policy Framework: Balancing Policy and Politics," in *A Climate Policy Framework: Policy and Politics,* edited by John A. Riggs (Queenstown, Md.: Aspen Institute, 2004), p. 6.

37. Sally McNamara and Ben Lieberman, "EU's Climate Change Package: Not a Model to Be Copied," *Web Memo 1800,* February 6, 2008 (www.heritage.org/Research/Energyand Environment/wm1800.cfm).

38. Kyle W. Danish, "Linking a U.S. Federal Climate Program with International and Sub-Federal Climate Programs," in *A Climate Policy Framework,* edited by Riggs, p. 73.

39. GAO, *EPA Budget Execution,* GAO-08-1109R (September 26, 2008).

40. "Climate Agenda Spurs Calls for Major New EPA Workforce Analysis" (www. carbon controlnews.com [July 31, 2009]). A Chamber of Commerce official was quoted in the same document as asserting that GHGs will require between 45,000 and 50,000 new employees.

41. "Emerging Needs in Decision Support," *in New Directions in Climate Change Vulnerability, Impacts, and Adaptation Assessment: Summary of a Workshop* (www.nap.edu/ catalog/12545.html).

42. EPA, "Fact Sheet—Proposed Rule: Prevention of Significant Deterioration and Title V Greenhouse Gas Tailoring Rule" (Docket ID No. EPA-HQ-OAR-2009-0517) (www.epa. gov/nsr/fs20090930action.html).

43. A very useful summary of major offset issues can be found in a collaborative publication of six nonprofit member organizations (Climate Trust, Pew Center on Global Climate Change, California Climate Action Registry, Environmental Resources Trust, Greenhouse Gas Management Institute, and Climate Group), *Insuring Offset Quality: Integrating High Quality Greenhouse Gas Offsets into North American Cap-and-Trade Policy* (July 2008) (www.pew climate.org/docUploads/OQI-Ensuring-Offset-Quality-white-paper.pdf).

44. See, for example, Environmental Council of the States, *On the Need for State Level Involvement in Federal Climate Action,* Resolution Number 08-8, Approved April 15, 2008; National Association of Clean Air Agencies, "Conference Materials for 'Defining the Role of States and Localities in Federal Global Warming Legislation.'"

45. John M. Broder, "EPA Moves to Curtail Greenhouse Gas Emissions," *New York Times,* October 1, 2009, p. A1.

PART IV

Reconnecting the United States
with the World

13

Re-engaging International Climate Governance: Challenges and Opportunities for the United States

STACY D. VANDEVEER AND HENRIK SELIN

Climate change is the defining issue of our time.

—Ban Ki-moon, United Nations Secretary General, 2007

Climate change will have wide-ranging implications for U.S. national security interests over the next twenty years.

—Thomas Fingar, deputy director of National Intelligence Analysis and chairman of the National Intelligence Council, June 25, 2008

The best way to advance America's interests in reducing global threats and seizing global opportunities is to design and implement global solutions.

—Senator Hillary Clinton, nominee for U.S. Secretary of State, January 13, 2009

The United States of America—its firms, public sector, nonprofit organizations, and 300 million-plus citizens—each year emits a staggering amount of carbon dioxide and other greenhouse gases (GHGs) into the Earth's atmosphere. Furthermore, that fact—combined with the long-standing U.S. unwillingness to enact serious federal GHG mitigation policies or to engage in international political action in good faith—is viewed as deeply unjust (and dangerous) by nearly every non-American who sits down with U.S. representatives in any

international forum to discuss climate change. The arrival of the Obama administration in early 2009 raised the hopes and expectations of climate-concerned
officials, scientists, and activists around the globe looking for aggressive U.S. climate change policy at home and abroad. Those expectations and the realities of
the U.S. history regarding emissions and policy both pose challenges and offer
opportunities for U.S. policymakers seeking to engage international actors and
various forums on climate change issues.

This chapter explores three general sets of opportunities and avenues for
expanded U.S. involvement in international climate change governance, encompassing multiple sets of options for U.S. climate change policymakers and advocates as they seek to re-engage in international climate change cooperation under
the Obama administration. The three broad opportunities and avenues include
—global forums under United Nations auspices
—North American continental cooperation
—ad hoc multilateral and bilateral cooperation arrangements.

The chapter argues that the United States can choose to engage in international climate change cooperation at various levels, ranging from global policymaking to ad hoc bilateral forms of cooperation. It begins with a brief comparison of U.S. GHG emissions with those of other nations, followed by a discussion
of the UN-affiliated global cooperation regime. The chapter then turns to issues
of North American continental cooperation and next discusses bilateral and multilateral possibilities to address challenges related to climate change. It concludes
by returning to the challenges involved in integrating these three types of international policy approaches with emerging multilevel climate governance in the
United States.

Taking Stock:
The United States in World Emissions

To provide context for the ensuing discussion, the enormous differences in global
national and per capita GHG emissions must first be brought to light, with a
focus on the United States in particular. In 2007, for example, a mere nineteen
countries among the 192 UN members were responsible for more than 70 percent of global carbon dioxide emissions from fossil fuel use and cement production, which is very carbon intensive (see table 13-1).[1] Among nations, China
recently surpassed the United States as the world's largest annual CO_2 emitter, due
to its rapid, fossil fuel–driven industrialization. Yet in per capita emissions, the
United States still ranks much higher than China—19.4 metric tons versus
5.1 metric tons. When the United States is compared with India, also among the
countries that emit the most GHGs annually, the gap in per capita emissions is
even more striking—19.4 versus 1.8. In other words, the average American emits

Table 13-1. *Top Five Estimated Emitters of CO_2 Emissions from Fossil Fuel Use and Cement Production, 2007*

Country/region	Percent share of global emissions	Metric tons per capita
China	24	5.1
United States	21	19.4
EU-15	12	8.6
India	8	1.8
Russia	6	11.8

Source: Netherlands Environmental Assessment Agency, "Global CO_2 Emissions: Increase Continued in 2007," June 13, 2008 (www.mnp.nl/en/publications/2008/GlobalCO2emissionsthrough2007.html).

almost four times more than the average Chinese and almost eleven times more than the average Indian citizen.

The most economically developed countries also manifest large differences in per capita emissions. For example, the per capita emissions of the fifteen EU member states (EU-15) that accepted a collective emissions reduction goal under the Kyoto Protocol are less than half those of the United States. Since the EU-15 and the United States have similar levels of economic development, their divergent per capita GHG emissions levels demonstrate that emissions are not a simple product of a country's level of wealth. Furthermore, EU-15 emissions collectively are now less than they were in 1990, while U.S. emissions have grown at slightly less than 1 percent a year since then. Some EU countries are also actively seeking to reduce their per capita GHG emissions. Swedish policy, for example, seeks to reduce its per capita GHG emissions from just under 8 tons per person (already lower than the EU-15 average) to 4.5 tons.[2]

Another contextual point is worth noting: Many in the international community know that a multitude of U.S. states, cities, civil society organizations, universities, and firms have not been sitting idly by in the wake of federal refusal to enact domestic climate change policy. Public, private, and civil society actors from Europe and elsewhere not only follow initiatives such as the Regional Greenhouse Gas Initiative (RGGI) in the U.S. Northeast and policy developments in California and among the Western states but also actively participate in these policy developments.[3] In other words, as U.S. federal representatives engage in international climate change negotiations, representatives from other states possess a great deal of information about what is already being done—and about what is feasible—within U.S. political and economic contexts. Many subnational climate change policymakers in the United States also cooperate with international actors to put pressure on Washington to act more aggressively to reduce GHG emissions at home and abroad, resulting in pressure on the federal government from all sides.

The Global Forum: UNFCCC, Kyoto, and Beyond

Global climate change law and policy are shaped by a complex mix of changing scientific developments and the material interests and values of actors at the state, nongovernmental organization, and private sector levels. Efforts to mitigate climate change are outlined in two major multilateral treaties: the 1992 United Nations Framework Convention on Climate Change (UNFCCC) and the 1997 Kyoto Protocol. Global policies may also be shaped by international discussions and debates about what kind of cooperative institutions might follow the Kyoto Protocol, including the continuing development of the initiatives that emerged from the 2009 Copenhagen summit. However, as discussed further below, the influence of those discussions and their outcomes remained unclear even after the 2009 summit.

The Global Framework: UNFCCC

The UNFCCC was negotiated between the publication of the first report of the Intergovernmental Panel on Climate Change (IPCC) in 1990 and the 1992 United Nations Conference on Environment and Development in Rio de Janeiro, where it was signed by the representatives of 154 nations and thereby adopted. It entered into force in 1994 (after ratification by 50 countries), and 191 countries and the EU had ratified the treaty by 2010. The United States ratified the UNFCCC in 1992, during the George H. W. Bush administration, thereby accepting the terms of the treaty and incorporating them into U.S. law and policy. As a framework convention, the UNFCCC defines the climate change issue, sets out a broad strategy for addressing climate change, establishes an administrative secretariat to oversee treaty-related activities, and lays out a legal and political framework within which states can cooperate over time.

Like other framework conventions, the UNFCCC includes commitments by states to continue research on particular environmental issues, to track and report their emissions, to periodically report their findings and relevant domestic implementation activities, and to meet regularly to discuss common issues at Conferences of the Parties (COPs). COP-1 was held in Berlin in 1995, and COP-15 took place at the 2009 Copenhagen Climate Change Summit. COPs have repeatedly played host to difficult, often tense, international negotiations on a variety of issues and to many subsequent agreements between parties on rules, procedures, and joint programs. Generally, framework conventions do not include detailed commitments for mitigation or adaptation, which are left to subsequent protocol negotiations to address. Similar framework convention–protocol approaches exist for environmental issues such as the protection of the stratospheric ozone layer, combating acid rain, and related transboundary air pollution problems, and addressing biodiversity loss.

Article 1 of the UNFCCC defines climate change as "a change of climate which is attributed directly or indirectly to human activity that alters the composition of the global atmosphere and which is in addition to natural climate variability observed over comparable time periods." The adverse effects of climate change are identified as "changes in the physical environment or biota . . . which have significant deleterious effects on the composition, resilience or productivity of natural and managed ecosystems or on the operation of socio-economic systems or on human health and welfare." To avoid climate change–induced adverse effects, Article 2 sets the long-term objective of "stabilization of greenhouse gas concentrations in the atmosphere at a level that would prevent dangerous anthropogenic interference with the climate system." While all UNFCCC parties endorsed that objective, the EU has attempted to link it to specific temperature increases (see also chapter 14, this volume). EU policy states that the need to limit global temperature increases to 2 degrees Celsius or less should guide policymaking. President Obama and other major state leaders endorsed that goal in 2009, but few (if any) have enacted any law to achieve that goal.

Article 3 of the UNFCCC establishes the principle of "common but differentiated responsibilities" for countries in addressing climate change. The phrase encapsulates the notion that all countries share an obligation to act but that industrialized countries such as the United States have a special responsibility to take the lead in reducing GHG emissions because of their relative wealth and historical contribution to the problem. The UNFCCC therefore divides countries into two groups, listed in Annex 1: industrialized countries and countries with economies in transition (pertaining in particular to former communist countries), plus the EU. Annex 1 has been modified since the UNFCCC was adopted to include forty countries and the EU. The UNFCCC stipulates that Annex 1 countries should work to reduce their anthropogenic emissions to 1990 levels, but no deadline was set for achieving that target. The UNFCCC did not assign non-Annex 1 countries (that is, developing countries) any mandatory commitment to reduce national GHG emissions.

The UNFCCC preamble recognizes that some countries are "particularly vulnerable" to climate change, including "low-lying and other small island countries, countries with low-lying coastal, arid, and semi-arid areas or areas liable to floods, drought, and desertification, and developing countries with fragile mountainous ecosystems." Many of the most harmful effects of a warming climate will take place in developing countries, which historically have contributed least to global GHG emissions. For example, developing countries with large, densely populated and low-lying coastal areas, such as Bangladesh and India, will experience many of the first impacts of sea level rise and increased storm intensity. Millions of poor, small-scale farmers in Africa and other tropical countries face changes in growing seasons and precipitation patterns. Climate change policy advocates frequently cite the UNFCCC's acknowledgment of dangers faced by many developing counties and the fact that most of those countries have contributed little to global climate change as important justifications for industrialized countries to act more decisively to reduce their emissions and increase various forms of international assistance.

The Kyoto Protocol

In response to mounting scientific evidence about human-induced climate change (much of it presented in the second IPCC report, in 1995) and to growing concern about negative economic and social effects of climate change among environmental advocates and policymakers, between 1995 and 1997 the UNFCCC parties negotiated the Kyoto Protocol. The final stage of the protocol negotiations was extremely contentious on a number of issues—both between countries and within the U.S. negotiating team and federal institutions. In particular, United States and European negotiators differed on both the targets for emissions cuts and the policy mechanisms to be allowed or recommended for parties to reach their targets. Only as a result of last-minute compromises by a number of major countries was agreement achieved on a final treaty, brokered in part by Al Gore, the U.S. vice president.[4]

To enter into force, the Kyoto Protocol had to be ratified by fifty-five countries, including enough Annex 1 countries to account for 55 percent of that group's total GHG emissions. While fifty-five countries quickly ratified, it took much longer to meet the 55 percent criterion. By the early 2000s, most Annex 1 countries had ratified, but either Russian or U.S. ratification was needed to meet the 55 percent requirement, as both are relatively large emitters. Eventually Russia ratified, but only under heavy pressure from EU officials, who made ratification an informal precondition for supporting Russia's application for membership in the World Trade Organization. The treaty entered into force in 2005. Following ratification by Australia in 2008, the United States became the only Annex 1 country that chose not to become a party. By 2009, the Kyoto Protocol had been ratified by 190 countries and the EU.

The Kyoto Protocol regulates six greenhouse gases: CO_2, methane (CH_4), nitrous oxide (N_2O), perfluorocarbons (PFCs), hydrofluorocarbons (HFCs), and sulfur hexafluoride (SF_6). UNFCCC Annex 1 countries committed themselves to collectively reduce their GHG emissions by 5 percent below 1990 levels by 2008–12. To achieve that goal, thirty-eight states set individual reduction targets. Some parties agreed to cut their emissions, while others consented only to slow the growth in their emissions. For example, the EU-15 took on a collective target of an 8 percent reduction while the United States and Canada committed to cuts of 7 percent and 6 percent respectively; Iceland, in contrast, agreed to limit its emissions to 10 percent above 1990 levels. Postcommunist countries such as Russia and those in Central and Eastern Europe agreed to cuts from 1990 levels, but many of those cuts were achieved by the economic restructuring that followed the end of their communist political and economic systems.

The Kyoto Protocol outlines five broad ways in which UNFCCC Annex 1 countries with reduction commitments can meet their targets:

—Develop national policies that lower domestic GHG emissions (the protocol does not restrict or mandate any particular domestic policy).

—Calculate benefits from domestic carbon sinks (for example, forests) that soak up more carbon than they emit and count them toward national emission reductions.

—Participate in transnational emissions trading schemes with other Annex 1 parties (in other words, Annex 1 countries can create markets in which emissions permits can be bought and sold).

—Develop a joint implementation (JI) program with another Annex 1 party and get credit for lowering GHG emissions in that country.

—Design a partnership venture with a non-Annex 1 country through the clean development mechanism (CDM) and get credit for lowering GHG emissions in the partner country.

The latter three options—international allowance trading, JI, and CDM—were pushed by U.S. negotiators to provide flexibility and reduce the costs of complying with the Kyoto commitments by allowing various actors to reduce emissions wherever (and however) it was most efficient, including in other countries. UNFCCC parties and observers hoped that these implementation mechanisms (often called the "Kyoto mechanisms") would help policymakers and private sector actors learn how best to reduce emissions over time in an affordable manner and in ways that would drive international investments between countries at various levels of economic development. The many rules, guidelines, and administrative procedures required to operate these mechanisms have been hammered out in negotiations among the parties to the UNFCCC since the adoption of the Kyoto Protocol. These rules and procedures are confirmed at annual UNFCCC COPs.

In general, the U.S. refusal to ratify the Kyoto Protocol resulted in reduced U.S. influence during the COPs-based negotiations on rules and procedures, particularly after 2001, when the Bush administration officially opposed U.S. ratification and the entry into force of the Kyoto Protocol. Furthermore, because the United States remained outside the protocol, it remained outside the operation of its flexible mechanism schemes. The United States and many domestic actors thus were generally unable to take advantage of the potential efficiency gains under the mechanisms, and both developed and developing countries were deprived of potential U.S. investments within the mechanisms. Nowhere are the implications of that clearer than in Mexico, where interest in GHG reduction on the part of policymakers and firms largely evaporated as a result of the U.S. refusal to ratify Kyoto and participate in the Kyoto mechanisms.[5]

Before and after Copenhagen

The Kyoto Protocol covers parties through 2012, a fact that engendered interest among climate policy advocates in negotiating a follow-up agreement. At COP-13 in Bali in 2007, UNFCCC parties formally launched a political process designed to negotiate a follow-up agreement to the protocol. A tentative location and date for adopting the next agreement was set for Copenhagen in December 2009. At COP-14, in Poznan, Poland, an ambitious schedule of meetings, summits, and consultations was outlined for 2009 in hopes of successfully reaching agreement at COP-15 in Copenhagen. Also in 2007, the IPCC fourth assessment report underscored the growing seriousness of climate change problems and the ever-increasing confidence of scientific researchers in their data, projections, and knowledge. Debates about what should come after Kyoto also became commonplace among scholars, environmental advocacy groups, and private sector actors.[6]

The arrival of the Obama administration in early 2009 raised hopes among climate policy advocates that U.S. leadership might contribute to the finalizing of an important agreement at the Copenhagen summit. Obama administration officials and congressional leaders (some of whom either attended or closely monitored international climate negotiations) faced the daunting prospect of attempting to make international and domestic policy decisions simultaneously. The international post-Kyoto negotiations, before and after Copenhagen, include a host of major issues and challenges, among them the following:[7]

—*Targets and timetables.* Finding GHG reduction targets that are both aggressive enough to make a real difference in atmospheric GHG concentrations and politically, economically, and technically feasible

—*National commitments.* deciding which countries can and should take on mandatory emission reduction commitments and how those commitments should be formulated

—*Joint mitigation mechanisms.* how to further develop international collaboration through, for example, international permit trading, joint implementation, and clean development mechanisms

—*Forest issues.* whether issues of deforestation and sustainable forest management should be linked to climate change mitigation efforts and commitments under the new treaty and how that might be accomplished

—*Addressing adaptation.* what the agreement should say about challenges associated with adapting to environmental and social impacts of climate change and whether it should stipulate specific adaptation commitments

—*Financing and capacity building.* how international efforts should support capacity building and economic and political changes around the world, including financing and technology transfer to developing countries

—Information and assessment. how continuous international cooperation should generate and use data about environmental changes, policy measures, and economic costs and benefits

Because the Copenhagen summit produced no treaty, no promise of a future treaty, and no binding agreement on any issues, the list above is probably best viewed as a set of points in an ongoing debate. Both in terms of its logistics and its substantive accomplishments, the Copenhagen summit demonstrated more of the limitations than the promise of multilateralism. Media outlets around the world reported on the long lines to get into the building where the negotiations were held, which sometimes took five to ten hours, along with the anger and frustration characterizing much of the negotiations. In the end, some areas of consensus were forged among state representatives on several of the issues listed above.[8] While most observers acknowledge that progress was made on some fronts, the resultant Copenhagen Accord is weak and quite vague in terms of states' declared commitments, controversial in terms of its substance and the process by which it was negotiated, and without any legally binding commitments.

The accord was negotiated in closed sessions in the summit's final two days, by a small number of representatives of the world's largest GHG emitters. Delegates could agree only to "take note" of the accord during the COP-15 final plenary session, failing to agree on how it relates to the UNFCCC. The text repeats many of the general principles and broad promises outlined in the UNFCCC (finalized seventeen years earlier), causing many observers to question the assertion that it represented a step forward. In terms of reducing GHG emissions, states endorsing the accord pledged to enact domestic policies and report on those activities—again, not unlike with the UNFCCC. The accord includes mention of a science-based need to cut emissions substantially if the goal of restricting global temperature increase to 2 degrees or less is to be met. Defenders of the accord note that it may yet provide a framework for more meaningful, future climate change cooperation. Critics decried the accord and the summit itself as a nearly complete failure.[9]

A detailed discussion of all seven issues listed above is beyond the scope of this chapter, but a few comments on the status of some major issues by mid-2010 are warranted. On the development of targets and timetables, the distance between the EU position on one hand and outright opposition to climate policy action on the other, as advocated by some large oil exporting states, seems to define the boundaries of the space for negotiation. One exception is the continued advocacy of some small island states (mostly developing countries) and many G-77 countries for more aggressive mitigation schedules (for industrialized countries) than those proposed by the EU. For example, many developing countries called on Annex 1 states to cut emissions by 40 percent of 1990 levels by 2020. There is no evidence that such cuts were ever seriously considered by Annex 1 negotiators. While most states agree that long-term GHG cuts are needed by mid-century, large disagreements among states persisted about how aggressive GHG mitigation targets should be in the near term (five to fifteen years) and medium (fifteen to twenty-five years) term. States also differed substantially on whether reduction commitments should be written into binding treaties or simply pledged in public.

Although many countries argue that because of its years of inaction and comparatively inefficient use of fossil fuels, the United States must make more stringent commitments than it has proposed in international venues or considered in congressional policy debates, Europeans generally are willing to compromise on this point to forge an agreement that the United States will actually join. The accord, which was substantially shaped by President Obama, Secretary of State Clinton, and the large U.S. negotiating team, leaves the United States to define its own mitigation goals. Achieving agreement on near-term GHG reduction goals is most difficult. For example, EU officials pushed for a 20 percent reduction (from 1990 levels) by 2020, while President Obama spoke of returning U.S. emissions to 1990 levels by 2020.

Two of the biggest questions with respect to national commitments concern *which states* will agree to make them (including whether some larger emitters among developing countries will make any sort of mandatory emissions reduction commitment) and *what forms* such commitments might take. While the EU position set the initial agenda, proposing a continuation of developed-country commitments on a national, annual emissions basis, that approach was revisited at the insistence of the United States and other states.[10] The Kyoto Protocol exempted developing countries from mandatory GHG reductions based on the UNFCCC principle of "common but differentiated responsibilities." In recent years, major industrializing countries with substantial and rapidly growing emissions—such as China, Brazil, India, Mexico, South Korea, and Taiwan—have come under increasing political pressure to accept some kind of GHG restrictions beyond 2012.

Questions remain as to what type of restrictions would be appropriate and verifiable. For example, Chinese officials expressed some readiness to commit to improving energy efficiency but were unwilling to allow data on any such improvements to be verified. While industrialized countries and countries with economies in transition may continue to set GHG reduction targets in national, annual, and absolute terms under the vague terms of the accord, some analysts and policymakers argue that the first developing countries to take GHG mitigation commitments might be well served by a system based on per capita income or per capita emissions; such a system might be both more equitable and more likely to gradually expand international participation and strengthen commitments over time.[11] The accord does not attempt to standardize any such approaches among countries, but it does note that Annex 1 countries should commit to economy-wide emission targets for 2020.

The EU position has been quite vague regarding GHG mitigation commitments by developing counties, while the U.S. position is clear. EU officials tend
to argue that some form of participation by developing country emitters is necessary, but specifics are lacking. Politically, EU officials have been reluctant to call
for substantial emission mitigation from developing country emitters—at least
until the United States shows more willingness to cut its emissions substantially.

On the U.S. side, climate policy leaders in Congress and the Obama administration tend to be clear that they expect meaningful commitments to be made by
countries such as China and an often unspecified number of other non-OECD
countries. For their part, Chinese representatives have not ruled out the possibility of China making some form of GHG mitigation commitment in a post-Kyoto
agreement. However, Chinese representatives have repeatedly stated that countries such as the United States and Canada would need to do substantially more
in terms of curbing their own emissions before China would consider accepting
aggressive or mandatory energy efficiency or GHG mitigation commitments. The
Chinese government also opposes any international verification of possible commitments on grounds of national sovereignty.

Joint mitigation mechanisms, including international permit trading, joint
implementation, and the clean development mechanism, present a different set
of challenges for U.S. negotiators. In general, the existing mechanisms are
designed to afford states and firms opportunities to achieve given GHG mitigation goals (and international development objectives) as efficiently as possible
while conducting policy experiments from which to learn over time. All three
mechanisms have developed substantial public and private sector constituencies
over the last decade, and all have led to an enormous amount of assessment and
lesson-drawing in recent years. Together they also have attracted substantial capital investments. For example, the clean development mechanism grew from
sixty-one emission reduction programs in 2004 to more than 4,000 programs in
various stages of development at the end of 2008.[12] Such rapid growth has added
to CDM's substantial administrative difficulties and delays, but it also illustrates
the growing number of individuals and firms that see economic opportunities in
the program. In contrast, the JI program is substantially smaller, in part because
its costs are higher than costs under the CDM.

While among many analysts and environmental activists the mechanisms remain
controversial in both theory and practice, there appears to be little appetite among
participating states or firms for ending them entirely. CDM and the growing set of
cap-and-trade schemes seem especially well institutionalized in both the public and
the private sectors. The mechanisms have not engendered much opposition within
the Obama administration or Congress, either. Yet the institutional development
required to expand participation in the mechanisms and to ensure their effective
and efficient operation remains complex and controversial, presenting a host of

design and implementation challenges and raising the prospect of growing regulatory and transaction costs if the mechanisms are to be substantially scaled up.[13] Furthermore, because the rules, administrative procedures, and programs associated
with the mechanisms have developed while the United States has remained outside
the Kyoto framework, some aspects of "the details" may incur substantial opposition among U.S. officials and private sector interests.

For many U.S. policymakers, views about forest issues, adaptation, and financing and capacity building revolve in large part around questions of the generation
and distribution of necessary material resources. In Copenhagen, U.S. policymakers pledged to increase U.S. climate change–related assistance to developing countries and pledged to try to encourage others to do so. The Copenhagen Accord
adopts some of that language, noting that developed counties will try to jointly
mobilize $100 billion a year by 2020. The accord's references to financing call for
the establishment of a Green Climate Fund to raise resources for ongoing and new
projects and institutions related to adaptation, capacity building, forestry, GHG
mitigation, and technology development and transfer. In general, industrialized
countries did not commit to specific figures in the accord. Furthermore, the details
of capacity building, financing, forestry, and adaptation issues are likely to be unfa-
miliar or little understood in Washington, outside of a small group of people with
long-standing commitments to climate governance.

As the international community struggles to address climate change under a
post-Kyoto agreement—be that the Copenhagen Accord or some other agreement—many developing countries, which typically have fewer resources to adapt
to a changing climate than industrialized countries, face major mitigation and
adaptation problems.[14] Perhaps the most significant of these social justice concerns to U.S. federal policymakers, beyond whatever ethical issues they raise, may
be the growing sense that the political and social ramifications of climate change
may negatively affect U.S. national security interests around the world. Those
concerns are expressed in the National Intelligence Council's 2008 classified
National Intelligence Assessment about climate change and U.S. security, and
national security analysts testified on the issue before Congress.[15] Some of the
same concerns about the potential for climate change to exacerbate international
security challenges are addressed in the council's public report *Global Trends 2025:
A Transformed World.*[16]

Money, Justice, and Global Climate Cooperation

From a global equity perspective, the situation of many comparatively vulnerable
developing countries and peoples gives rise to critical procedural and distributive
social justice issues.[17] Procedural justice refers to the ability to fully partake in collective decisionmaking processes focusing on mitigation and adaptation issues
(including under the UNFCCC), while distributive justice concerns how climate
change affects different societies and people differently. Both types of justice issues

engender intense debate and invoke substantial interstate differences in global negotiations. Acrimonious debates and disagreements between industrialized and developing countries about both types of justice issues were also on display in Copenhagen, and the debates are set to continue.

For many developing countries, procedural justice relates to how international climate change policy is formulated and how their interests are taken into account. Many governments—particularly those of smaller countries—face multiple problems engaging actively in multilateral environmental negotiations and assessments.[18] Those problems include having fewer human, economic, technical, and scientific resources than leading industrialized countries with which to either prepare for international negotiations or implement resulting agreements. The significant differences in capacity between wealthier and poorer countries risk skewing international assessments, debates, and decisions in favor of the perspectives and interests of the most powerful countries. As international negotiators seek to design and implement new agreements and programs—and U.S. officials seek to shape those efforts—representatives of developing countries raise procedural justice concerns and related capacity issues.

Simply put, adaptation to ongoing and accelerating climate change requires the investment of significant resources, as does building international climate governance institutions. Annex 2 of the UNFCCC currently lists twenty-three countries and the EU having committed themselves to provide "new and additional financial resources" to developing countries for addressing climate change issues (Article 4).[19] While helping especially vulnerable countries and local communities facing significant challenges as a result of climate change should be a priority for many in the international community, funding needs and requests have greatly outnumbered the financial resources that so far have been made available by UNFCCC Annex 2 countries and international organizations. Funding for adaptation therefore is set to be a major issue under the UNFCCC and in future political and economic forums. In addition, while joint mitigation mechanisms offer opportunities to raise and distribute private sector capital, it is less clear that adaptation offers similar opportunities.

Therein lie major challenges for the Obama administration and Congress, governing during a recession and period of slow growth and unprecedented budget deficits: raising the funds needed for adaptation and capacity building, including funds to create incentives for engaging in sustainable forestry and reducing greenhouse gases in ways that are acceptable to U.S. officials and citizens. Chapter 2 of this volume suggests that many U.S. citizens express willingness to pay something to protect the climate, yet how much they would like to contribute to addressing international needs remains unclear. For example, the inclusion of forest issues in the post-Kyoto debates has been hailed by many as a potential step forward for efforts to simultaneously reduce deforestation, mitigate climate change, and support sustainable economic development in forested regions. Yet, like addressing adaptation and increasing international, national, and local capacity building, developing incentives for protecting forests in accordance with such goals is likely to require substantial resources.

If political leaders and citizens in the United States are to mitigate and prevent the most catastrophic impacts of climate change, they must make difficult choices regarding the capital needs of institutions in developing a serious and effective system of global climate governance, as noted by President Obama in his inaugural address. In Washington, within UN forums, and in capitals around the world, the need for substantial funding for global climate governance raises a host of challenging questions. Are the resources to be transferred from North to South? Are they to be raised (and spent) in some internationally defined and institutionalized arrangement and written into a treaty? The Copenhagen Accord largely skirts those sticky questions by including vague, collective promises about increasing international assistance of many kinds while avoiding the details about where the money is to come from and how it is to be managed.

Most treaty secretariats—indeed, most UN programs—have very small budgets and staffs. Yet the record of industrialized states in living up to financial pledges like those in the Copenhagen Accord is not impressive. Also, should funds be administered through existing international institutions, such as the World Bank or the Global Environment Facility? Will the U.S. Congress and the American people agree to any arrangement involving large international resource transfers? If they will not, it is difficult to see how resource-intensive issues such as adaptation, financing and capacity building, and information and assessment can really be effectively addressed in a post-Kyoto agreement, unless policymakers can devise creative ways to raise and distribute funds from the private sector through market creation and joint mitigation mechanisms. It is certainly possible that at least a portion of the funds raised by auctioning allowances in a U.S. cap-and-trade scheme could provide funding for international programs, but that would be controversial in Congress and public debate—and it assumes that a cap-and-trade bill with an auctioning provision will one day pass.

Continental Climate Politics: Multilevel Options in the Neighborhood

The arrival of the Obama administration, with its stated interest in cost-efficient GHG mitigation, brought the U.S. interest into closer alignment with that of both the Canadian and Mexican governments. Unlike Europeans, who have launched ambitious continental climate governance institutions while they have deepened continental economic integration, the United States and its North American neighbors have largely ignored that option. Fifteen years after the creation of NAFTA, the Canadian, Mexican, and U.S. markets are increasingly integrated economically. However, there has been strikingly little bilateral or trilateral

Table 13-2. *North American and Global GHG Emissions*

Measure	Canada	United States	Mexico
Total emissions (CO_2 equivalent)			
1990	599 megatons	6,109 megatons	383 megatons
2004	758 megatons	7,074 megatons	643 megatons[a]
Increase since 1990	26.5 percent	15.8 percent	67.9 percent
Per capita emissions (tons CO_2 equivalent) (2000)	22.1	24.5	5.2
Global ranking of per capita emissions (2000)	7th	6th	76th
Population (2000)	31 million	280 million	100 million
Percent of total global emissions (2000)	2.0 percent	20.6 percent	1.5 percent

Source: Henrik Selin and Stacy D. VanDeveer, *Changing Climates in North American Politics: Institutions, Policymaking, and Multilevel Governance* (MIT Press, 2009).

a. Mexico figure is for 2002.

cooperation around climate change.[20] The 2009 meetings of Canadian, U.S., and Mexican leaders—dubbed the Three Amigos Summit by some in the media—demonstrated some increased, at least rhetorical, interest in reinvigorating climate change and energy cooperation among the three countries.

Roughly tracking their respective economic sizes, U.S. annual GHG emissions dwarf those of Canada and Mexico (see table 13-2). Canadian per capita emissions are similar to those in the United States and thus comparatively high among industrialized countries, while Mexican per capita emissions are less than one-quarter of those in the United States and Canada. Emissions in all three countries have grown substantially since 1990 (the UNFCCC base year) and since the adoption of the Kyoto Protocol in 1997. Unlike the United States, however, both Canada and Mexico ratified the Kyoto Protocol. As a developing country, Mexico has no commitment to reduce emissions under the protocol. U.S. refusal to ratify Kyoto left it outside the Kyoto mechanisms, which in turn substantially reduced Mexican interest in pursuing bilateral cooperative mitigation programs as well as resource transfers to Mexico.[21] Although Canada committed to reducing its emissions by 6 percent of 1990 levels, national emissions are roughly 25 percent higher than they were in 1990—a result of economic growth, lack of any serious federal attempt to curb emissions, and unwillingness on the part of a number of provinces to take any action.[22]

Beyond the general trend toward greater continental economic integration and trade in goods, cross-border trade in energy resources and electricity is common, as is cooperation among environmental organizations at both the federal and local levels in Canada, Mexico, and United States. Furthermore, interaction and cooperation on national environmental policy is quite common across the U.S.-Canadian border in a host of issue areas besides climate change.[23] With climate change issues, however, cooperation and emulation on environmental policy are even more common among subnational jurisdictions (including states, provinces, and municipalities) and within the private sector and civil society.[24] That stems, in part, from the fact that all three states are federal and assign a substantial set of environmental policy functions and authorities to the states/provinces, although the exact mix of authorities and functions varies substantially among the three.

According to a minimal definition of multilevel governance—actors operating across horizontal and vertical levels of social organization and jurisdictional authority around a particular issue—a multilevel model is emerging in North America.[25] Many initiatives also involve collaboration among U.S., Canadian, and Mexican public and civil society counterparts. Examples include the Climate Registry, which includes most U.S. states and several Mexican states and Canadian provinces, and the Western Governors Initiative, which attempts to engender climate mitigation cooperation between U.S. state leader California and Canadian provincial leader British Colombia. Furthermore, many such efforts are getting more ambitious over time in terms of their mitigation goals. Yet because federal governments have been so inactive, North American multilevel climate change governance consists of a multitude of generally uncoordinated efforts that have adopted different goals over different time frames and applied a multitude of different political and technical means. However, there are signs of increased standardization of technologies used and harmonization of policies across initiatives and jurisdictions.

States, provinces, municipalities, and firms use an increasingly standardized set of processes, from processes for doing inventories of GHGs and developing action plans to those for coordinating policy actions with other jurisdictions.[26] The untapped benefits of increased cooperation on North American climate change include gaining policy learning opportunities, capturing economic efficiency gains, cooperating to meet adaptation challenges, and leveraging greater global leadership.[27] Continental coordination tends to occur within institutions created to achieve coordination, like RGGI, as greater numbers of actors learn from and emulate previous initiatives. Learning from others also reduces costs, unlike starting from "square one" every time. This kind of coordination is much different from the more directed multilevel governance that might arise from coherent federal and/or continent-wide leadership on climate change. For example, without federal action, the regulatory distance between local jurisdictions that take action and those that refuse to do so is likely to grow, with policy laggards' emissions likely to continue to increase.

All three North American states are engaged in UN-sponsored global climate change negotiations, and Canada and Mexico also face calls from many international and domestic actors to do more to combat the growing threat of climate change as well as its implications and associated challenges, such as severe urban air pollution. In all three, some domestic public and private sector actors are well in front of federal policy. As a developing country in the Organization for Economic Cooperation and Development, Mexico is coming under increasing pressure to make GHG mitigation commitments of some kind. Canada, having been internationally lauded for its Kyoto ratification in the face of U.S. opposition, now faces the prospect of official noncompliance when the treaty's 2012 deadline passes. Canada's GHG emissions growth since 1990 also presents the country's leaders with substantial political and practical challenges.

If federal authorities in Canada, Mexico, and the United States are to constructively cooperate in taking action on climate change at either the national or the global level, they must increase their bilateral or continental cooperation. Among the options for federal officials is to cooperate at the continental level in issue-specific areas such as renewable energy investment, development, and distribution[28] or to seek greater political consensus or institution building within NAFTA bodies.[29] That may involve different combinations of federal and subnational climate change politics and policymaking efforts.[30] Four general combinations of high or low federal policy engagement with high or low subnational involvement in continued climate change governance can be outlined.[31] The four scenarios are not collectively exhaustive and within each combination exist several possible sets of detailed policy developments. The four scenarios are as follows:

—*federal inertia* (low federal engagement, low subnational policy involvement), wherein federal inaction continues and obstructs or contributes to declines in subnational action

—*federal resurgence* (high federal engagement, low subnational policy involvement), wherein aggressive federal action subsumes or eliminates subnational leadership

—*bottom-up expansion* (low federal engagement, high subnational policy involvement), wherein federal inaction continues, as does the kind of bottom-up climate change policymaking that has become commonplace among many states, provinces, municipalities, firms, and civil society organizations

—*complex multilevel coordination* (high federal engagement, high subnational policy involvement), wherein subnational policymaking continues even as federal climate change action becomes more aggressive in attempts to reduce GHG emissions.

The increase in U.S. federal officials' rhetorical commitment to increasing climate change mitigation and renewable energy development suggests that the scenarios entailing continued U.S. federal inaction appear less likely than they once seemed. However, federal climate change policy action requires more than increased rhetorical support for more stringent climate change policies: it requires those policies to be actually enacted. Mexican federal officials remain likely to embrace at least some aspects of shared continental and/or global climate governance if it holds the prospect of driving additional investment in Mexico. In contrast, the 2008 Canadian federal elections did not produce noticeable change in terms of climate politics, though Canadian political observers often note that U.S. reengagement in international climate change policymaking and institution building would likely induce greater Canadian engagement. Leadership from the Obama administration and an increase in the ability of Congress to pass meaningful GHG mitigation policies and confront adaptation issues could be expected to "change the game" in Ottawa and Mexico City and thus potentially at the continental level.

Changing U.S. federal domestic and foreign climate policy holds the potential of changing climate policy dynamics across the North American continent. "Federal resurgence" includes a number of possibilities for more aggressive federal policymaking in conjunction with a decline of subnational policy efforts. Federal policy may override all, or large portions of, existing and ongoing subnational policymaking by effectively setting national policy "ceilings" (see also chapter 14, this volume).[32] In so doing, federal policy may limit the innovations and potentially larger ambitions of some subnational policies. However, federal resurgence may also lead to the setting of such aggressive GHG reduction goals and technical standards that few public or private entities would choose to exceed federal policies. If federal policymakers set relatively high standards, subnational policy implementation would accelerate, but desires to formulate additional policies may very well be much reduced, at least in the short term. Two or three of the continent's federal governments could also work together to accelerate federal efforts in ways that exceed existing initiatives by subnational leaders.

While all four scenarios remain possible, "complex multilevel coordination" may be the most likely outcome in the near and medium terms if more aggressive federal policy is enacted. Federal policy expansion may take place separately in each of the three countries, but if any two (or all three) of North America's federal states become more serious about climate change mitigation, it is in their common interest to attain emissions reductions via the most efficient and effective means possible. It is that shared interest that should induce greater cooperation on continental climate change and energy policy. For example, irrespective of whether cap-and-trade schemes are enacted at the federal level exclusively or if regional schemes such as RGGI and the Western Climate Initiative move forward, officials, firms, and citizens share an interest in such schemes efficiently achieving the defined GHG reductions. It would make sense for policymakers at multiple levels of government to facilitate the trade of emissions allowances across borders and/or across schemes.

In all three North American states, there is likely to be substantial debate about which governance levels are the most appropriate for enacting and implementing specific policies—and about what roles are best played by public, private, or civil society actors. To that end, the European Union's greater experience with multilevel continental climate change governance, including debates about "subsidiarity," may offer important lessons for North American efforts.[33] North American multilevel climate change governance offers states and provinces continued opportunities to act as important laboratories for policy innovation that can shape subsequent federal and/or continental policymaking. Yet public and private sector actors also share an interest in the harmonization of many climate- and energy-related standards across economies and societies, preferring regulatory uniformity over regulatory fragmentation. However, because subnational actors can continue to develop a wide range of climate change and energy policies within their jurisdictions, regulatory differences are likely to persist (or even continue to grow) across North America.

Furthermore, local officials and private sector representatives are likely to compete over which standards and policies do—and do not—get uploaded to the federal and continental levels. Leader states and provinces and their representatives in federal legislatures hoping to reap "early-mover" advantages have strong incentives to compete to have their specific standards and programs adopted in federal and continent-wide policy initiatives. Consequently, debates about differences between and advantages of various policy approaches may increasingly be heard in Washington, Ottawa, and Mexico City as pressures grow on federal policymakers to develop more aggressive national standards. At the same time, many state, provincial, and municipal officials will take strong action to protect their authority from the federal government in many areas of climate change and energy policymaking.

International Coalitions of the Willing, Worried, and Opportunistic?

The failure in Copenhagen to achieve a significant global agreement on how to reduce GHG emissions or address many critical adaptation issues may encourage U.S. policymakers to turn to international engagement options involving more ad hoc arrangements among interested states or groups of states. Myriad choices, opportunities, and challenges face U.S. federal authorities. For example, how might U.S. federal officials and programs engage EU member states and policies, including the Emission Trading System? If, for example, the United States seeks a leadership role on climate change mitigation and/or adaptation issues, to what extent should it attempt to coordinate its efforts with those of leading states in Europe? It is possible that goals could be set and achieved within transatlantic relations that cannot be achieved through global cooperation.[34]

In addition to engaging climate change policy leaders in Europe, ad hoc coalitions could be organized on many other bases or around a host of common challenges. U.S. policymakers might reach out to federal states besides Canada and Mexico, for example, to engender increased multilevel cooperation as all levels of government seek to achieve GHG reduction and address adaption. Large federal states such as Australia, Brazil, and the Russian Federation offer a host of cooperative opportunities. U.S. leadership might also afford opportunities for greater programmatic cooperation across the Asia-Pacific region, either through existing regional multilateral institutions, such as Asia-Pacific Economic Cooperation and the Association of Southeast Asian Nations, or through newly constructed joint programs. The Bush administration launched some such initiatives, but they lacked serious funding and commitment, and they were explicitly designed to facilitate rather small-scale voluntary programs and pilot projects.

Growing Chinese GHG emissions are of particular concern in Washington and around the world. Should U.S. authorities develop more systemic climate change cooperation with Chinese authorities (as the Earth's two largest national emitters) in parallel to the ongoing negotiations under the UNFCCC? Some of the dangers of such ad hoc bilateral and multilateral efforts include the risk of undermining or further complicating negotiations within the UN forum and the challenge of making commitments that may be seen as precedent setting within the global talks. Yet, a post-Kyoto agreement cannot realistically hope to curb the worst impacts of global climate change without both U.S. and Chinese participation and implementation. Because they are perhaps the two most critical states, bilateral engagement seems both prudent and wise. Furthermore, each country's domestic market offers enormous opportunities for the other's firms and researchers.

Like the United States, major emitters across East Asia (including China, Japan, South Korea, and Taiwan) face the challenge of slowing and then reducing GHG emissions in societies that have millions of citizens with high-consumption lifestyles and growing energy demands. Similarly, all such states must develop "greener" technologies and deploy them rapidly if the dual challenges of mitigation and adaptation are to be addressed. Shared challenges hold the potential for shared solutions and joint institution building. Such valuable, shared interests (and responsibilities) offer tremendous opportunities for cooperation between the two states and between subnational policymakers and jurisdictions and myriad private and civil society actors. In addition, bilateral transnational engagement offers the added potential of increasing knowledge and understanding of Chinese policies, interests, and developments among U.S. policymakers and publics—and vice versa.

Integrating Multilateral amd Multilevel Climate Politics

As the epigraphs that open this chapter suggest, global climate change poses substantial global and national risks across multiple and often interrelated realms— economic, political, social, ethical, and security. Recent reports from the IPCC and the U.S. National Intelligence Council confirm that fact. Yet, as Secretary of State Hillary Clinton suggests, international challenges require international solutions, offering opportunities to build joint institutions for mutual benefit. One might add that none of the options discussed above—global, continental, or ad hoc—are likely to offer comprehensive international climate governance solutions. It is more likely that all three approaches must be pursued in some measure if global GHG emissions are to be slowed, capped, and reduced and if the substantial adaptation challenges posed by the twenty-first century's changing climate are to be met.

Leading U.S. subnational actors are well-connected with climate change policymakers in Europe, Canada, and other countries. California is a global climate policy leader, along with cities such as Portland (Oregon), Toronto, and New York City. Governments around the world can learn lessons from these North American leaders, just as North American jurisdictions can draw lessons from abroad. Similarly, advocates of the EU's negotiating position with the UNFCCC process extend well beyond Brussels. The EU's global leadership sets the tone for leaders around the world, including many climate policy advocates in Washington, Ottawa, and Sacramento. Furthermore, the Kyoto Protocol experience has raised awareness around the world about the importance of engaging the U.S. Congress, particularly the Senate, in ongoing and future climate governance debates and agreements. The actions of the United States therefore are likely to attract the attention of public, private, and civil society actors from around the globe.

A related opportunity for U.S. engagement in international climate change policy can be found in the substantial experience of U.S. cities, states, and firms in developing and attempting to implement their own climate change mitigation and adaptation policies. A host of network-based organizations has already emerged, linking cities, states, and provinces; civil servants; professional organizations; and industrial sectors across borders. The U.S. "laboratories of federalism" do not generate experiments and lessons for U.S. consumption alone. Where climate change is concerned, the world is watching them—and they must enhance their capacity to learn from abroad if the challenges of climate change mitigation and adaptation are to be met. Last, as a number of chapters in this volume suggest, none of the discussions of the challenges of GHG mitigation or climate change adaptation in U.S. domestic and foreign policy should be taken to mean that the authors are certain that U.S. federal institutions can actually respond in time to avoid catastrophic changes. That verdict is still out.

Notes

1. Netherlands Environmental Assessment Agency, « Global CO_2 Emissions : Increase Continued in 2007 » (www.mnp.nl/en/publications/2008/GlobalCO2emissionsthrough 2007.html).

2. See chapter 14, this volume.

3. See chapter 14, this volume, and Miranda A. Schreurs, Henrik Selin, and Stacy D. VanDeveer, *Transatlantic Environmental and Energy Politics: Comparative and International Perspectives* (Aldershot, U.K.: Ashgate, 2009).

4. Ibid.

5. Simone Pulver, "Climate Change Politics in Mexico," in *Changing Climates in North American Politics: Institutions, Policymaking, and Multilevel Governance,* edited by Henrik Selin and Stacy D. VanDeveer (MIT Press, 2009).

6. For examples of this enormous literature, see Joseph Aldy and Robert N. Stavins, *Architectures for Agreement: Addressing Global Climate Change in the Post-Kyoto World* (Cambridge University Press, 2007); Joseph E. Aldy and Robert N. Stavins, "Climate Policy Architecture for the Post-Kyoto World," *Environment* 50, no. 3 (2008), pp. 6–17; William Pizer, "A U.S. Perspective on Future Climate Change Regimes," *Resources for the Future* RFF DP 07-04 (February 2007); David G. Victor, "Toward Effective International Cooperation on Climate Change," *Global Environmental Politics* 6, no. 3 (2006), pp. 90-103.

7. This list is also included in Henrik Selin and Stacy D. VanDeveer, "Global Climate Change: Kyoto and Beyond," *Environmental Policy,* 7th ed., edited by Norman Vig and Michael Kraft (Washington: CQ Press, 2009), pp. 265–85.

8. For a detailed treatment of state positions and preliminary analysis of the summit's outcomes, see the daily reports and the conference summary, "Summary of the Copenhagen Climate Change Conference," *Earth Negotiations Bulletin* 12, no. 459, pp. 1–29 (www.iisd.ca/climate/cop15/).

9. Ibid.

10. For detailed discussion of the EU positions, see chapter 14, this volume.

11. Aldy and Stavins, *Architectures for Agreement;* Aldy and Stavins, "Climate Policy Architecture for the Post-Kyoto World," pp. 6–17.

12. Nathanial Gonewald, "China and India Dominate Rapidly Expanding CDM Program," *Greenwire* (December 12, 2008).

13. See chapter 5, this volume, for detailed discussion of both the historical development of cap-and-trade schemes and the associated institutional complexities.

14. Adil Najam, Saleemul Huq, and Youba Sokona, "Climate Negotiations beyond Kyoto: Developing Countries' Concerns and Interests," *Climate Policy* 3, no. 3 (2003), pp. 221–31.

15. Thomas Finger, *Statement for the Record before the Permanent Select Committee on Intelligence and the Select Committee on Energy Independence and Global Warming,* U.S. House of Representatives, June 25, 2008.

16. National Intelligence Council, *Global Trends 2025: A World Transformed* (Government Printing Office, 2008).

17. W. Neil Adger, Jouni Paavola, and Saleemul Huq, "Toward Justice in Adaptation to Climate Change," in *Fairness in Adaptation to Climate Change,* edited by W. Neil Adger and others (MIT Press, 2006).

18. Pamela S. Chasek, "NGOs and State Capacity in International Environmental Negotiations: The Experience of the Earth Negotiations Bulletin," *Review of European Community and International Environmental Law* 10, no. 2 (2001), pp. 168–76; Ambuj Sagar and Stacy D. VanDeveer, "Capacity Development for the Environment: Broadening the Scope," *Global Environmental Politics* 5, no. 3 (2005), pp. 14–22.

19. The twenty-three UNFCCC Annex 2 countries are: Australia, Austria, Belgium, Canada, Denmark, Finland, France, Germany, Greece, Iceland, Ireland, Italy, Japan, Luxembourg, Netherlands, New Zealand, Norway, Portugal, Spain, Sweden, Switzerland, United Kingdom, and the United States.

20. Henrik Selin and Stacy D. VanDeveer, "Continental Climate Governance Challenges for North America," *Issues in Governance Studies* 30 (Brookings, 2009).

21. Pulver, "Climate Change Politics in Mexico."

22. Peter J. Stoett, "Looking for Leadership: Canada and Climate Change Politics," in *Changing Climates in North American Politics,* edited by Selin and VanDeveer.

23. Philippe Le Prestre and Peter Stoett, *Bilateral Ecopolitics: Continuity and Change in Canadian-American Relations* (Aldershot, U.K.: Ashgate, 2006); Barry G. Rabe and Stephen Brooks, "Environmental Governance on the 49th Parallel: New Century, New Approaches," working paper (Washington: Woodrow Wilson International Center for Scholars, 2010, forthcoming).

24. Ibid.; Henrik Selin and Stacy D. VanDeveer, *Changing Climates in North American Politics: Institutions, Policymaking, and Multilevel Governance* (MIT Press, 2009).

25. Selin and VanDeveer, *Changing Climates in North American Politics*.

26. Nicholas Lutsey and Daniel Sperling, "America's Bottom-Up Climate Change Mitigation Policy," *Energy Policy* 36, no. 2 (2008), pp. 673–85.

27. Selin and VanDeveer, "Continental Climate Governance Challenges for North America."

28. Ian H. Rowlands, "Renewable Energy Politics across Borders," in *Changing Climates in North American Politics,* edited by Selin and VanDeveer.

29. Michele M. Betsill, "NAFTA as a Forum for CO_2 Permit Trading," in *Changing Climates in North American Politics,* edited by Selin and VanDeveer.

30. Barry G. Rabe, *Statehouse and Greenhouse: The Emerging Politics of American Climate Change Policy* (Brookings, 2004); Barry G. Rabe, "States on Steroids: The Intergovernmental Odyssey of American Climate Policy," *Review of Policy Research* 25, no. 2 (2008), pp. 105–28.

31. Henrik Selin and Stacy D. VanDeveer, "North American Climate Governance: Policymaking and Institutions in the Multilevel Greenhouse," in *Changing Climates in North American Politics,* edited by Selin and VanDeveer, pp. 305–26.

32. Benjamin K. Sovacool and Jack N. Barkenbus, "Necessary but Insufficient: State Renewable Portfolio Standards and Climate Change Policies," *Environment* 49, no. 6 (2007), pp. 21–30; also see chapter 14, this volume.

33. Miranda A. Schreurs and Yves Tiberghien, "Multilevel Reinforcement: Explaining European Union Leadership in Climate Change Mitigation," *Global Environmental Politics* 7, no. 3 (2007), pp. 19–46; chapter 14, this volume.

34. For more detailed discussion of European-U.S. climate relations and the potential benefits of greater transatlantic climate policy cooperation, see chapter 14, this volume.

14

Multilevel Governance and Transatlantic Climate Change Politics

HENRIK SELIN AND STACY D. VANDEVEER

I was brought up with a firm belief that when the world needed leadership—from the World Wars and the Cold War to the fight against terrorism—we have counted on the United States for leadership. That leadership has been severely lacking in the climate negotiations.[1]

—Connie Hedegaard, Minister of Climate Change and Energy,
Denmark, October 2008

Few challenges facing America and the world are more urgent than combating climate change. My presidency will mark a new chapter in America's leadership on climate change that will strengthen our security and create millions of new jobs in the process.[2]

—Barack Obama, President-Elect, United States, November 2008

At the G-8 meeting in July 2009, President Barack Obama joined the leaders of other large economies for the first time in support of the goal of keeping the world's average temperature from rising any more than 2 degrees Celsius (3.6 degrees Fahrenheit) above pre-industrial levels. Doing so will require a steep reduction in greenhouse gas (GHG) emissions from the United States and other high-emitting countries over the first half of the twenty-first century. However, the weak and contested Copenhagen Accord from December 2009 failed to produce a detailed plan of implementation for reaching that goal, and global negotiations continue. The failure to agree on a strong global deal can, in part, be attributed to the unwillingness of the U.S. Congress to set national mandatory GHG reduction goals before the Copenhagen meeting, as well as a host of other factors. Nevertheless, the United States can be expected to expand domestic GHG regulations over the coming decades.

Over the past ten years, the European Union (EU) has emerged as a vocal leader in global climate change politics, in large part filling a political vacuum left by the absence of the United States. The EU consists of twenty-seven member states, and a few more countries are likely to join in the near future.[3] The population of the EU-27 is close to 500 million, which is to say that roughly one in fourteen people in the world live in the EU. The size of the EU economy is equal to that of the United States: $12 trillion. GHG emissions in the EU-15 (that is, the fifteen countries that were EU members in 1997, when the Kyoto Protocol was adopted) fell by 2.2 percent between 1990 and 2006. During the same time period, U.S. national GHG emissions increased by 14.7 percent.[4] While European politicians and citizens hope for much more constructive U.S. engagement on global climate change mitigation in 2010 and beyond, as promised by President Obama, they also wonder about the future of U.S. national and state-level policy and GHG emissions.

As climate change policymaking and implementation continue to develop in both Europe and North America, there is a growing interest among both analysts and practitioners in the possibilities for expanded transatlantic cooperation. Many EU climate change policy goals have been developed and transferred in a top-down fashion from EU organizations to domestic authorities and firms for implementation.[5] In contrast, as highlighted throughout this volume, U.S. climate change politics in the early years of the twenty-first century has been characterized by a bottom-up expansion of a plethora of municipal and state initiatives in the face of lagging federal policymaking and standard setting.[6] Despite their differences, as U.S. federal, state, and municipal policies expand alongside European climate change policies, there are increasing opportunities for transatlantic cooperation and lesson learning, as North American and European states share many multilevel governance challenges.

This chapter examines climate change politics in the EU and the United States from a multilevel governance perspective, taking into account the fact that policymaking advances simultaneously across multiple jurisdictions and regulatory levels. That creates many avenues for transatlantic interaction involving a large number of national and local governments, firms, and advocacy groups. The following discussion briefly outlines major EU policy responses to climate change, followed by a discussion of four multilevel governance issues of great importance to effective climate change policymaking and implementation in both the EU and the United States. The chapter ends with a discussion of the importance of the EU and the United States in global climate change politics and GHG mitigation as well as the future of transatlantic climate change governance as the EU and the United States seek to meet national, regional, and global GHG reduction targets.

European Union Climate Change Policy

EU climate change policy dates back to at least 1991, when member states adopted measures to limit carbon dioxide (CO_2) emissions and improve energy efficiency. Current climate change policy is formulated under the Second European Climate Change Programme, which began in 2005 (replacing the First European Climate Change Programme, which ran from 2000 to 2003). Programmatic efforts address a wide range of issues related to GHG emissions and energy production and use. Many of them focus on developing policy responses for meeting EU targets under the Kyoto Protocol by 2012 as well as on laying a common legal, regulatory, and administrative groundwork for more aggressive future action in the areas of GHG emissions trading, renewable energy, transportation, energy efficiency, and technology development. These initiatives seek to transform EU member states into low-carbon societies as an integral part of achieving sustainable development.

Climate change policy in the EU is formulated by the European Commission (the administrative bureaucracy), the Council of Ministers (government officials from each member state), and the European Parliament (members elected directly by citizens in each member state). Legislative proposals put forward by the European Commission are negotiated and passed by the Council of Ministers and the European Parliament. The Council of Ministers decides environmental policy based on qualified majority voting, but most climate change policy to date has been passed unanimously. However, energy supply and taxation issues are still largely decided domestically by each member state. As a result, member states have widely diverging mixes of energy generation (some are strong supporters of nuclear power while others oppose it) and eco-taxation schemes (some member states have adopted carbon taxes while others have not).

EU climate change policymaking is guided by a political agreement that global average temperatures should not rise more than 2 degrees Celsius above preindustrial levels. The EU, which pushed hard for the inclusion of the +2°C goal in the Copenhagen Accord, considers it critical to meeting the policy objective in the United Nations Framework Convention on Climate Change (UNFCCC) of preventing "dangerous anthropogenic interference with the climate system." Scientists have predicted that in order to avoid exceeding the +2°C target, atmospheric GHG concentrations must be stabilized below 550 parts per million by volume (ppmv); current concentrations, which are above 390 ppmv, are increasing by approximately 3 to 4 ppmv annually. On the basis of those data, EU officials

Table 14-1. *EU-15 Burden-Sharing Reduction Targets and National Changes in GHG Emissions, 1990–2006*

EU-15 member states	Burden-sharing target	Percent change in GHG emissions, 1990–2006
Austria	−13	+15.1
Belgium	−7.5	−5.2
Denmark	−21	+2.1
Finland	0	+13.2
France	0	−3.9
Germany	−21	−18.2
Greece	+25	+27.3
Ireland	+13	+25.6
Italy	−6.5	+9.9
Luxembourg	−28	+1.0
Netherlands	−6	−2.0
Portugal	+27	+40.7
Spain	+15	+50.6
Sweden	+4	−8.7
United Kingdom	−12.5	−15.1
EU-15	− 8	−2.2

Source: European Environment Agency, Annual European Community Greenhouse Gas Inventory 1990–2006 and Inventory Report 2008 (www.eea.europa.eu/publications/technical_report_2008_6).

argue that global GHG emissions may continue to increase until around 2020 but then must be curbed.[7] Many EU goals therefore identify 2020 as an important benchmark year for local, regional, and international policies that effectively begin to reverse the continuing growth in GHG emissions.

Under the Kyoto Protocol, the EU-15 took on a collective target of an 8 percent reduction below 1990 levels by 2012. Eight of the ten countries that joined the EU after the Kyoto Protocol was adopted also have Kyoto targets. The EU-15 divided up its Kyoto target in a 1998 burden-sharing agreement (see table 14-1) under which several relatively wealthy member states took on more aggressive commitments so that less wealthy member states could increase their GHG emissions as part of their efforts to expand industrial production and economic growth. As a result, member states are working to fulfill a host of varying national GHG reduction targets by 2012. As global negotiations continue regarding commitments under the UNFCCC, the EU is likely to continue with the formulation of collective targets coupled with internal burden-sharing approaches for meeting those targets. However, many (if not all) negotiations to set individual member state targets under a burden-sharing agreement may be politically contentious.

While the EU-15 moves to meet its Kyoto target with measures that are now in place or that will be implemented before 2012, significant differences exist in national GHG emission trends. As shown in table 14-1, only three countries

Table 14-2. *Kyoto Targets and National Changes in GHG Emissions for EU Member States Joining after 1997*[a]

Member state	Kyoto target	Percent change in GHG emissions, 1990–2006
Bulgaria	–8	–38.9
Cyprus	None	+66.0
Czech Republic	–8	–23.7
Estonia	–8	–54.6
Hungary	–6	–20.0
Latvia	–8	–56.1
Lithuania	–8	–53.0
Malta	None	+45.0
Poland	–6	–11.7
Romania	–8	–36.7
Slovakia	–8	–33.6
Slovenia	–8	+10.8
EU-27	…	–7.7

Source: European Environment Agency, Annual European Community Greenhouse Gas Inventory 1990–2006 and Inventory Report 2008 (www.eea.europa.eu/publications/technical_report_2008_6).
   a. Ten states joined in 2004 and 2007.

among the EU-15 were below their burden-sharing target by 2006: France, the United Kingdom (UK), and Sweden. While Belgium and Germany may also meet their targets by 2012, many EU-15 countries are set to miss theirs, and some by quite a wide margin. A main reason that the European Commission can argue that existing and planned measures will enable the EU-15 to meet its target by 2012 is that three major emitter countries—Germany, the United Kingdom, and France—"carry" many other members. EU-27 GHG emissions were down almost 8 percent between 1990 and 2006. Most countries joining in 2004 and 2007 have had significant drops in GHG emissions (see table 14-2). For the eastern European countries, the drops are largely a result of economic restructuring as they moved from highly energy inefficient, centrally planned economies to more market-based, capitalist systems.

Current EU climate change policymaking and implementation is guided by a set of "20-20-20" goals adopted in 2007 to be met by 2020: reduce GHG emissions by 20 percent; increase the share of renewable energy to 20 percent; and improve energy efficiency by 20 percent. The EU has also formulated a goal to increase the share of petrol and diesel consumption from biofuels to 10 percent. The GHG reduction goal for 2020 will be implemented largely through the EU Emission Trading System (ETS), the world's first public, mandatory GHG emissions trading scheme, modeled in part on U.S. trading schemes for SO_2 and NOx emissions. The ETS was formally launched in 2005 and currently is in its second phase (2008–12).[8] It covers more than 11,500 major energy-intensive installations across all member states, although most regulated entities are located in a few larger member states (Germany has more than 20 percent of all ETS allowances).[9]

The third phase of the ETS (2013–20) will gradually shrink the EU-wide cap, incorporate a growing number of emission sources (including aviation) and greenhouse gases (nitrous oxide and perfluorocarbons), and include a gradual increase in national auctioning of emission allowances (which have hitherto been given out free to participating installations by member states). The ETS also has been expanded to include non-EU members such as Norway and Lichtenstein, demonstrating that other states can participate in the ETS as they attempt to reduce their emissions. Efforts to increase the share of renewable energy include an attempt to create an internal energy market—European energy markets have historically been largely domestic, subject to different national controls and subsidies—and support the expansion of renewable energy sources (although member states continue to differ about whether nuclear power should be included in these efforts). Measures to improve energy efficiency focus on setting standards for infrastructure (including building codes) and products (including cars).

Multilevel Climate Change Governance in the European Union and the United States

EU climate change governance is developing simultaneously at the regional, national, and local levels, involving a multitude of public and private sector actors as well as a wide range of civil society representatives. As the Obama administration and the U.S. Congress continue the political and administrative processes of expanding federal climate change policy, they are wise to draw lessons from the EU's more extensive experience with multijurisdictional climate change policy-making, which extends well over a decade. Furthermore, possibilities for the EU to learn also will grow as more ambitious federal and local climate change policy is adopted in the United States. Four multilevel governance issues of transatlantic relevance stand out, although the specific form of the lessons may vary because of institutional and political differences between the EU and the countries of North America. Nevertheless, all these issues are likely to be important on both sides of the Atlantic.

Set Policy Floors, Not Ceilings

A first important issue concerns the design of regulations and standards in a multilevel governance structure such as that of the EU or the U.S. federal system. A major distinction should be made between the setting of policy "ceilings" and policy "floors."[10] If they adopt policy ceilings, higher-level authorities explicitly limit what lower-level jurisdictions can do; in contrast, if they adopt policy floors, they set minimum requirements for all lower jurisdictions, but they do not restrict the ability of those jurisdictions to exceed the requirements if they choose to do so.

In the EU, regional environmental policies typically are formulated as floors because many directives set minimum standards that more ambitious member states may exceed domestically.[11] The policy floor approach is also used in many U.S. environmental areas involving states, including water quality, hazardous substances, and brownfields.

Setting common environmental and human health standards at the top of any multilevel governance structure has several political and practical advantages. It ensures that every person living in a lower-level jurisdiction is afforded the same basic protections. In addition, the formulation of common minimum standards—which may also be gradually strengthened over time in response to developing scientific understanding and the introduction of cleaner technologies—prevents a "race to the bottom." That is, a common standard set at the top and applying equally to all lower-level jurisdictions means that a firm cannot decide to relocate from one jurisdiction to another within the same governance structure simply to avoid compliance. In fact, as seen in both the United States and the EU, lower-level policy leaders may use the need for harmonized standards as leverage to raise the bar in lagging jurisdictions, instead creating a "race to the top."[12]

The experiences of both the EU and the United States suggest that climate change policy in both should focus on setting policy floors rather than policy ceilings. Policy floors have at least two practical benefits. First, it is easier to convince lower-level climate change leaders to support expanding EU and U.S. federal standards if they do not think that such standards will seek to pre-empt higher standards that they have already in place or that are under development in their jurisdictions. Second, setting policy floors allows for policy experimentation and innovation across a multitude of jurisdictions. That benefits EU countries, U.S. states, and municipalities on both sides of the Atlantic that want to learn from each other, as policy ideas are diffused horizontally and vertically in both Europe and North America as well as between the two continents.[13]

Combine Policy Flexibility with Enforcement

A second issue concerns the degree of flexibility that lower federal jurisdictions have in meeting mandatory targets set at higher levels of authority. In the EU, climate change directives (and to a much lesser degree, regulations) give member states the freedom to select different means of implementation, depending on their political, economic, and cultural circumstances. Similarly, the United States gives a high degree of freedom to states to implement and enforce federal environmental policy. Such flexibility should also apply to climate change and related energy issues. The more freedom that lower-level jurisdictions are given to design their own detailed implementation plans—for example, in the area of promoting renewable energy production and consumption—the more local political and economic factors can be considered and the more multilevel policy experimentation is promoted.

The ability of EU member states to design domestic policies and implementation measures to fulfill regional targets results in a plethora of domestic policy developments. That has helped some member states make progress in reducing GHG emissions while maintaining solid economic growth. For example, between 1990 and 2006, the United Kingdom reduced national GHG emissions by 16 percent even as its economy grew by 45 percent. Similarly, during the same time, Sweden cut national GHG emissions by 9 percent while increasing its gross domestic product by 44 percent. EU leader states have long focused on both the supply and the demand aspects of energy issues, using different mixes of energy sources based on domestic conditions and public opinion. Lessons from those states can be applied across Europe and non-European jurisdictions, including the U.S. states and federal government.

Since the early 1990s, successive Swedish social democratic and conservative governments have initiated a host of measures targeting energy use and consumption, including the following: introducing CO_2 taxes on fossil fuels; subsidizing the expansion of domestically produced biofuels and wind power; and giving rebates to consumers buying biogas and electric vehicles or vehicles that emit less than 120 grams of CO_2 per kilometer. Swedish authorities, like those in other leader states, also focus on improving energy efficiency in buildings and expanding public transportation systems, while introducing congestion fees for driving in urban areas. Leader states, moreover, institutionalize their efforts. For example, in 2008 the United Kingdom created a new Department of Energy and Climate Change. Political efforts also are complemented by public awareness campaigns about climate change and possibilities for individual action. In the United Kingdom, that includes the web-based initiative ACT ON CO_2.[14]

Along with providing flexibility in the design and implementation of policy, ensuring enforcement in multilevel systems also is critical. An effective multilevel system requires all jurisdictions to meet their obligations to fulfill collective goals. That is, in part, ensured through top-down monitoring and enforcement in collaboration with lower-level jurisdictions. For example, the EU's Emission Trading System—a critical instrument for meeting regional GHG emission reduction targets for 2012 and 2020—is administered through the European Commission, which has the competence to take political, economic, and legal action against derelict member states, including by initiating formal infringement procedures through the European Court of Justice. The European Commission has, however, sometimes refrained from taking such measure to avoid upsetting powerful member states acting to protect their national interests.

During the first phase of the ETS, many member states set generous national caps and asked the European Commission for more allowances than needed to cover actual emissions; moreover, allowances were distributed for free. That weakened the ETS and resulted in a collapse in emission prices in 2007. More recently, however, the European Commission forced several member states to submit revised allocation plans with lower requests for allowances, which increasingly will be subject to auctioning. The ten U.S. states that created the Regional Greenhouse Gas Initiative (RGGI) learned from those mistakes, collectively auctioning off more than 90 percent of all allowances. Observers, however, express concerns that RGGI covers only a limited number of installations and that the cap is not low enough to effectively reduce CO_2 emission levels and drive investments in renewable energy and energy conservation. See part 2 of this volume for further exploration of these issues.

As U.S. federal policymakers move to establish mandatory standards to be monitored by federal agencies, they face many challenges similar to those encountered by the European Commission in balancing political considerations with effective enforcement. Such challenges are present in, for example, the creation of a national GHG emissions trading scheme and the setting of national mandates on renewable energy generation. The U.S. government will develop these kinds of policies only after many states have already taken individual and/or regional action. For example, the existence of RGGI (and other developing regional emission trading schemes) presents both obstacles and opportunities for federal policymakers and regulators seeking to design and implement a national cap-and-trade scheme involving the fifty states, in which public and private sector actors have partially diverging interests, preferences, and experiences with such issues.

Consider Issues Related to Burden Sharing and Redistribution

A third issue arising from EU climate change action, one also related to issues of policy flexibility and enforcement, is the centrality of a burden-sharing agreement facilitating EU goal setting. If the fifteen EU member states with a collective GHG emission target under the Kyoto Protocol were required to also meet identical national reduction targets, it would have been much harder and more expensive for the EU to move ahead with policy developments at the pace that it has. The acceptance by European domestic and regional political leaders of differing emission targets among member states based on their different energy profiles and levels of economic development made it not only possible to move ahead in the years immediately following the adoption of the Kyoto Protocol but also to design subsequent policy instruments such as the EU ETS.

The EU political burden-sharing negotiations in the 1990s, however, were difficult. The negotiations concerned both the size of national targets and the collective commitment that the EU-15 should (and could) accept under the Kyoto Protocol. In fact, ambitions were lowered on several occasions as lofty goals were squashed by the political realities of maintaining consensus among fifteen member states.[15] For example, in the mid-1990s the EU-15 pledged to cut its GHG emissions by 15 percent, but that goal was reduced to 8 percent during the Kyoto Protocol negotiations as several members, including the UK, France, Spain, and Italy, argued that a 15 percent cut was prohibitively expensive and unrealistic and that it would not be matched by other industrialized countries. Subsequently, several member states fought to reduce their national reduction targets under the 1998 burden-sharing agreement.[16]

Any future EU burden-sharing negotiations to implement EU-wide climate change and energy targets adopted in regional and global forums are also likely to be contentious. Major member states like Germany and the United Kingdom, which took on relatively large reductions under the 1998 agreement and are on track to meet or exceed their national goals, may not be willing (or able) to do so again after 2012. Many other EU-15 countries also are well above their targets. Furthermore, eastern European members that saw large drops in GHG emissions after 1990 because of the reconstruction of their economies face significant challenges in shifting toward becoming low-carbon societies as they seek to increase industrial production and consumption. Collectively, that raises important questions of how EU members will be able to continue their tradition of burden sharing to stay on track to meet all 20-20-20 goals by 2020, yet burden-sharing agreements are nevertheless likely to remain useful.

Although the issues and challenges confronting North American and European nations are not identical, the EU's experiences in developing and implementing burden-sharing approaches are relevant to the United States as the federal government expands climate change regulations and mandates. Since its inception, the United States has been home to contentious debates and relations between the federal government and state governments competing for legal authority and resources, as highlighted in chapters 3 and 4 of this volume.[17] Nevertheless, the U.S. states implement many federal environmental laws, they issue more than 90 percent of all environmental permits, and they conduct more than 75 percent of all environmental enforcement actions. Furthermore, the states can control GHG emissions through the many policy areas in which they have regulatory competence, including the generation and distribution of electricity, transportation infrastructure, land use and planning, agriculture and forestry, and waste management.[18]

U.S. federal climate change policy may involve many burden-sharing and redistribution issues. For example, a federal cap-and-trade scheme will require identifying which kind of GHG emissions and emission sources are to be regulated, setting caps on state emissions, and agreeing on how much the caps are to be reduced over time. Similarly, federal mandates on renewable energy generation must identify which energy sources are to be recognized as "renewable," as states receive energy from widely different fossil and non-fossil sources of fuel. States will furthermore demand and compete for federal dollars to implement new federal policies, including funds for building their institutional and technical capabilities for monitoring and oversight. Financial issues also include the possible return to states of funds generated from auctioning allowances under a national GHG trading scheme to be used for public benefit purposes.

In the EU, burden sharing was accepted as a way not only to facilitate collective decisionmaking but also to allow less economically developed member states to increase their GHG emissions in the short run as they pursued multiple development policies (often with EU financial assistance) to close the wealth gap with more affluent members. That approach may seem much too "socialist" for some U.S. policymakers and observers, but critical redistribution issues between economically different regional areas will nevertheless be part of U.S. climate change politics. As leader states compete to have their preferred climate change standards adopted at the federal level, laggard states are likely to resist more ambitious federal policies. Federal and state policymakers therefore would do well to think seriously about how formal or informal burden-sharing approaches could be used to address distribution issues in the U.S. context.

Expand Transatlantic Collaboration at Multiple Levels

A fourth issue concerns opportunities for closer transatlantic collaboration, including between EU member states, U.S. states, and U.S. and European municipalities. European experience offers information and inspiration as U.S. leader states such as California, New York, and Massachusetts expand their climate change policies with respect to transportation, renewable energy, and energy conservation. For example, several European countries have experimented with feed-in tariffs in the generation of renewable electricity (see chapter 8, this volume). Moreover, as explored more fully in chapter 7 in this volume, European policymakers have also gradually strengthened vehicle emission standards and actively promoted the use of energy-efficient cars, resulting in fuel economy rates in Europe that average over 40 miles per gallon; in contrast, average U.S. rates average approximately 21 miles per gallon. In addition, many European countries have long set aggressive energy efficiency standards for buildings and implemented energy taxation schemes.

As noted in chapter 6 of this volume, EU member states and national officials have much greater experience than their U.S. counterparts in the area of carbon taxation (although efforts to establish an EU-wide carbon tax failed in the 1990s because of lack of consensus among all member states).[19] Since 1990, when Finland became the first country in the world to institute a carbon tax, several European countries have followed suit, even though the design and effectiveness of carbon taxes are still debated.[20] Carbon taxes play an important part of several European governments' efforts to reduce fossil fuel use, promote renewable energy development, cut energy demand, and encourage energy efficiency upgrades, which may be attractive to at least some U.S. states. European experience also demonstrates that carbon taxes and emission trading schemes can operate in tandem. That is, the discussion about taxes and other regulatory instruments, including cap and trade schemes, is not an either/or proposition, as some of the recent U.S. debate seems to suggest.

U.S. states at the forefront of GHG mitigation efforts also are finding novel ways to reduce GHG emissions that may be emulated in European capitals and cities. For example, twenty-nine states had adopted some kind of mandatory renewable portfolio standard by late 2009 and many states also are seeking other ways to "green" electricity generation. The goals of several of these initiatives are more ambitious than the EU goal of 20 percent renewable energy generation by 2020. For example, New York has set a goal of 25 percent by 2013. In 2008, California governor Schwarzenegger proposed a 33 percent goal by 2020, expanding on the current goal of 20 percent by 2010. As more U.S. states—most of which have GHG emissions at levels comparable to those of large or medium-size EU member states—take action in the areas of energy generation and consumption, new and promising opportunities for transatlantic technical and political collaboration open up.

There already is ample opportunity for U.S. and European leaders to discuss climate change issues and learn from each other. Officials from Washington, Brussels, and the capitals of EU member states meet regularly at the Conference of the Parties to the UNFCCC; they also may exchange views in the United Nations General Assembly High-Level Dialogue on Climate Change, Clean Energy, and Sustainable Development, initiated in 2006, and at G-8 and G-20 meetings. However, such top-level interaction is only part of the story. In addition to the increasing instances of direct interaction between European and U.S. state officials, new transatlantic networks are rapidly growing, many of which bypass the formal (and sometimes restrictive) channels between Washington and European capitals.[21] Members use these networks and associated organizations to share knowledge and policy ideas beneficial to both the United States and the European Union.

One noteworthy trend in interaction through extra-governmental channels is the development of memorandums of understanding between European countries and U.S. states. For example, UK prime ministers and ministers between 2006 and 2008 signed four such agreements with governors from California, Florida, Wisconsin, and Michigan. Although the memorandums are not legally binding—U.S. states are constitutionally prohibited from entering into treaties with foreign jurisdictions—they allow for exchanging policy experiences and best practices, promoting public awareness, collaborating on research and technology development, and facilitating trade in low-carbon technologies. For example, officials from California and Sweden signed a memorandum of understanding in 2006 to collaboratively develop bioenergy, particularly biomethane, for transportation fuels and other uses.

Another major example of the development of new transatlantic networks related to climate change is the International Carbon Action Partnership (ICAP), which held its first meeting in 2007. ICAP was created to share best practices in designing and implementing GHG cap-and-trade systems. Founding members include the European Commission, several EU member states, and a multitude of U.S. states working on emissions trading issues under RGGI and the Western Climate Initiative (WCI). Other jurisdictions and organizations may join in the future. Such collaboration not only supports the diffusion of policy ideas and lesson learning as increasingly more local, national, and international GHG cap-and-trade schemes are established, but it may also bring the operation of separate trading systems closer together. That may facilitate linking or even merging different trading schemes in the future, although doing so will require careful analysis and planning.

A growing number of U.S. and European cities also are expanding collaboration in both old and new forums. Many municipalities on both sides of the Atlantic are long-standing members of the Cities for Climate Protection program operated by the International Council for Local Environmental Initiatives. More recently, the Clinton Foundation launched its Clinton Climate Initiative, which works with twelve large European and twelve large American cities. This initiative is linked with the C40 Cities program, an association of large cities around the world seeking to accelerate efforts to reduce GHG emissions. Several other municipal networks also connect policy efforts in the United States and Europe. These networks seek to diffuse information about mitigation and adaptation efforts and to build local capacity in important policy areas, including building codes, transportation, and waste management.

The Future of Global and Transatlantic Climate Change Politics

In global climate change politics, the ultimate objective is not to enact more climate change policy; it is to bring GHG emissions down to levels that limit significant disruptions in the climatic system and minimize serious and costly socioeconomic effects. Nations and subnational entities all over the world are announcing new climate change measures at a growing pace, but to date very few jurisdictions have actually achieved notable GHG reductions. It remains unclear how many will be able to do so by 2020, a point identified by many scientists as critical for meeting the goal of preventing the global average temperature from rising any more than 2 degrees Celsius above preindustrial levels. So it is worth stressing that formulating more aggressive climate change policy is important, but effective implementation and actually reducing GHG emissions are even more critical.

As discussed further in chapter 13 in this volume, EU-U.S. collaboration is essential to the successful conclusion and implementation of any robust post-Kyoto agreement. Even if the United States takes on a more constructive role in global negotiations in 2010 and beyond, President Obama faces many interrelated challenges with respect to international and domestic climate change politics. As he took office, he voiced support for the goal of returning U.S. GHG emissions to 1990 levels by 2020. In the run-up to the Copenhagen meeting, that position was changed to cutting GHG emissions by 17 percent from 2005 levels by 2020, which was on par with the goal in the bill that passed the House of Representatives in fall 2009. That goal, however, is significantly different from the preferred EU target for industrialized countries for 2020. Moving forward, EU and U.S. GHG reduction targets need not be identical, but they must be mutually acceptable to U.S. and EU officials and tolerable to the European and American publics.

In multilevel governance systems, the ability to meet collective GHG reduction goals is determined by the capacity of most (if not all) jurisdictions to find ways to bring down their emissions. The ability of self-identified leaders in both the United States (such as California and Massachusetts) and the EU (for example, Sweden and the United Kingdom) to sustain their positions is increasingly determined by their willingness not only to adopt ambitious goals, but also to maintain declines in GHG emissions over multiple cycles of domestic economic contractions and expansions—and over the course of successive political administrations. In addition, lagging EU member countries (like Spain and Portugal) and U.S. states (such as Nevada and Arizona) with significant increases in GHG emissions over the past two decades must take serious measures to reverse their growth trends. That is, policy measures increasingly must translate into actual reductions in greenhouse gases.

Consideration of the four issues discussed earlier can help cut GHG emissions. The setting of policy floors rather than ceilings encourages support from policy leaders and promotes policy experimentation. Allowing for flexibility in implementation permits lower-level jurisdictions to base their measures on local conditions while the political and legal ability to use comprehensive mechanisms for monitoring and enforcing compliance gives EU organizations and the U.S. government oversight. Addressing burden-sharing and redistribution issues creates opportunities for reaching agreements on policy goals among a large number of jurisdictions in different energy and economic situations. Finally, expanding transatlantic cooperation across governance levels helps to diffuse policy ideas and knowledge on a host of issues, which may help drive down GHG emissions in both Europe and the United States.

It is important to note that North American and European societies are only at the very beginning of political efforts to address climate change. Much remains to be done to bring down anthropogenic GHG emissions to levels that do not significantly disrupt the climate system, thereby causing widespread economic and human damage. Much also remains to be done in the area of climate change adaptation. While some critics continue to believe that the short-term costs of aggressive mitigation are too high, a growing number of analysts and policymakers argue that early action will be less costly for societies than coping with severe climatic changes in the future.[22] In addressing critical mitigation and adaptation challenges, the United States and Europe share many common interests and problems. Certainly, there will be political and practical differences between them on specific issues under the UNFCCC and in other forums. Yet there is also room for extensive multilevel transatlantic collaboration and lesson learning on a host of important mitigation and adaptation issues.

The Obama administration and Congress face many challenges in expanding and implementing U.S. climate change policy in a federal system characterized by well-organized state interests. Many near-term efforts will be about catching up with Europe, including in the area of GHG emissions trading. However, the EU also faces significant implementation issues with respect to expanding and strengthening the Emission Trading System, increasing the production of renewable energy, and bringing down transportation emissions. Policymakers in both Brussels and Washington are well-advised to expand their lines of communication because climate change policies in the United States and the EU are likely to move toward convergence (even if they do not align perfectly) over the next decade, especially given recent policy developments and statements in Europe and the United States. Increased communication is critical not only for amending transatlantic relations strained during the presidency of George W. Bush but also for successful cooperation under the UNFCCC.

Finally, future transatlantic relations in the area of renewable energy generation and the development of low-carbon technology will be characterized by competition in international and domestic markets. Over the past decade, Europe—together with Japan and increasingly also China and India—has become a leader in green technology production, including wind power and solar power technology. Many U.S. policymakers and commentators hope that more aggressive U.S. climate change policy and federal GHG emissions standards will spur American technological development. There were record levels of financial capital moving to such projects all over America in recent years. Hopefully, such competition will spur non-U.S. firms to develop even cleaner technologies and help drive down their prices. That would benefit not only the United States but the entire world.

Notes

1. "Negotiating a New International Response to Climate Change: The Prospects for COP-15 in Copenhagen 2009," speech at the Grantham Research Institute on Climate Change and the Environment, London School of Economics, October 1, 2008 (www2.lse.ac. uk/publicEvents/ events/2008/20080819t1155z001.aspx)]. Hedegaard is now the EU's first Climate Action Commissioner.

2. Juliet Eilperin, "Obama Sends a Message to Governors on Climate Change," *Washington Post*, November 18, 2008 (http://voices.washingtonpost.com/44/2008/11/18/obama_ sends_a_message_to_gover.html).

3. The EU is engaged in formal membership negotiations with Croatia, the Republic of Macedonia, and Turkey. Additional countries are expected to apply for membership over the next decade or so.

4. Environmental Protection Agency, *Inventory of U.S. Greenhouse Gas Emissions and Sinks: 1990–2006*, US EPA #430-R-08-005 (Washington: 2008); European Environment Agency, *Annual European Community Greenhouse Gas Inventory 1990–2006*, Technical Report No. 6/2008 (Copenhagen: 2008). The EU-15 refers to the fifteen countries that were EU members in 1997, which adopted the Kyoto Protocol and accepted a collective reduction commitment: Austria, Belgium, Denmark, Finland, France, Germany, Greece, Ireland, Italy, Luxembourg, Netherlands, Portugal, Spain, Sweden, and the United Kingdom.

5. Miranda A. Schreurs, Henrik Selin, and Stacy D. VanDeveer, "Conflict and Cooperation in Transatlantic Climate Politics: Different Stories at Different Levels," in *Transatlantic Environmental and Energy Politics: Comparative and International Perspectives*, edited by M. A. Schreurs, H. Selin, and S. D. VanDeveer (Aldershot, U.K.: Ashgate, 2009).

6. Henrik Selin and Stacy D. VanDeveer, *Changing Climates in North American Politics: Institutions, Policymaking, and Multilevel Governance* (MIT Press, 2009); Barry G. Rabe, "States on Steroids: The Intergovernmental Odyssey of American Climate Policy," *Review of Policy Research* 25, no. 2 (2008), pp. 105–28.

7. European Commission, *EU Action against Climate Change: Leading Global Action to 2020 and Beyond* (Brussels: 2007).

8. Jon Birger Skjærseth and Jørgen Wettestad, *EU Emissions Trading: Initiating, Decision-Making, and Implementation* (Aldershot, U.K.: Ashgate, 2008).

9. European Commission, *EU Action against Climate Change*.

10. Henrik Selin and Stacy D. VanDeveer, "North American Climate Governance: Policymaking and Institutions in the Multilevel Greenhouse," in *Changing Climates in North American Politics*, edited by Selin and VanDeveer; Benjamin K. Sovacool and Jack N. Barkenbus, "Necessary but Insufficient: State Renewable Portfolio Standards and Climate Change Policies," *Environment* 49, no. 6 (2007), pp. 21–30.

11. EU member states may set higher domestic environmental protection standards as long as they do not restrict the functioning of the common market. The European Court of Justice has established that domestic restrictions on environmental grounds may be justified as long as they are nondiscriminatory and proportional. A member state may, in the absence of common marketing rules, restrict the import and use of a particular product in order to meet domestic environmental standards as long as such restrictions apply equally to domestic and imported products. The national restriction must also be proportionate to the identified environmental policy goal and be the least trade-restrictive option for achieving that goal. See Henrik Selin and Stacy D. VanDeveer, "Politics of Trade and Environment in the European Union," in *Handbook on Trade and Environment*, edited by K. P. Gallagher (Aldershot, U.K.: Edward Elgar, 2009).

12. David Vogel, *Trading Up: Consumer and Environmental Regulation in a Global Economy* (Harvard University Press, 1995); Henrik Selin and Stacy D. VanDeveer, "Raising Global Standards: Hazardous Substances and E-Waste Management in the European Union," *Environment* 48, no. 10 (2006), pp. 6–18.

13. Schreurs, Selin, and VanDeveer, "Conflict and Cooperation in Transatlantic Climate Politics."

14. See http://actonco2.direct.gov.uk/index.html.

15. Loren R. Cass, "The Indispensable Awkward Partner: The United Kingdom in European Climate Policy," in *Europe and Global Climate Change: Politics, Foreign Policy, and Regional Cooperation*, edited by Paul G. Harris (Northampton, U.K.: Edward Elgar, 2007).

16. Nuno S. Lacasta, Surajee Dessai, and Eva Powrosolo, "Consensus among Many Voices: Articulating the European Union's Position on Climate Change," *Golden Gate University Law Review* 32, no. 4 (2002), pp. 351–414.

17. Paul E. Peterson, *The Price of Federalism* (Brookings, 1995).

18. Barry G. Rabe, *Statehouse and Greenhouse: The Emerging Politics of American Climate Change Policy* (Brookings, 2004).

19. Marcel Braun, "The Evolution of Emissions Trading in the European Union: The Role of Policy Networks, Knowledge and Policy Entrepreneurs," *Accounting, Organization and Society* 34, no. 3–4 (2009), pp. 469–87; Skjærseth and Wettestad, *EU Emissions Trading*.

20. Monica Prasad, "Taxation as a Regulatory Tool: Lessons from Environmental Taxes in Europe," paper prepared for the Tobin Project conference "Toward a New Theory of Regulation," Yulee, Florida, February 1–3, 2008 (www.sociology.northwestern.edu/faculty/prasad/Taxation_3_25_08); William D. Nordhaus, "To Tax or Not to Tax: Alternative Approaches to Slowing Global Warming," *Review of Environmental Economics and Policy* 1, no. 1 (2007), pp. 26–44.

21. Schreurs, Selin, and VanDeveer, "Conflict and Cooperation in Transatlantic Climate Politics."

22. This is a core argument in the report by Nicholas Stern, a former chief economist with the World Bank. See Nicholas Stern, *Stern Review on the Economics of Climate Change* (London: Her Majesty's Treasury, 2006). For a critique of Stern's arguments, see Robert Mendelsohn, "Is the *Stern Review* an Economic Analysis?" *Review of Environmental Economics and Policy* 2, no. 1 (2008), pp. 45–60. Dietz and Stern offer a rebuttal to Mendelsohn in Simon Dietz and Nicholas Stern, "Why Economic Analysis Supports Strong Action on Climate Change: A Response to the *Stern Review's* Critics," *Review of Environmental Economics and Policy* 2, no. 1 (2008), pp. 94–113.

15

Conclusion

BARRY G. RABE

The very idea of modifying the temperature of the planet by adjusting the mix of gases that are released into the atmosphere ranks among the most ambitious undertakings ever considered by human beings. An avalanche of scientific evidence demonstrates strong links between greenhouse gas emissions and climate change but can offer only sophisticated estimates, not a precise prediction, of what impact various concentrations of these gases may have on future climatic conditions. Even the seemingly more straightforward issue of measuring the cost of various policy options to reduce emissions is far more complex than is generally acknowledged. In late 2009, the Congressional Research Service reviewed seven separate economic analyses of the cap-and-trade provisions of climate legislation that had passed the House of Representatives in June and concluded, in bold print, that "long-term cost projections are at best speculative, and should be viewed with attentive skepticism."[1] Calculation of benefits from various policy interventions, whether measured in terms of global temperature or other factors, such as conventional air pollution or dependence on imported oil, are even more imprecise.

Amid such uncertainty, efforts to govern the climate lumber forward. This book examines the challenges of climate governance, with an eye toward what a constructive U.S. role might entail. It considers lessons from subnational innovations, federal and intergovernmental policy options, the capacity of existing institutions to play a viable role, the views of citizens, and ways in which the United

States might join forces with other nations. It draws heavily from the social sciences, which have largely been peripheral players during the decades of debate on this issue in international forums, in Congress, and in statehouses around the nation. The National Conference on Climate Governance, from which this volume is drawn, was designed to consider the capacity of the nation to govern climate change and to explore a wide range of options in coming to terms with the sobering intergovernmental policy puzzle that it has created. These chapters have emerged from the participants' deliberations with a series of ideas that can contribute to the nation's capacity to develop future policy initiatives that are plausible and can be implemented in a cost-effective manner over the long term.

One possible starting point for a review of U.S. policy options, a 2005 Sense of the Senate resolution, has largely been forgotten but remains the official position of the Senate on climate change. The provision was included in section 1612 of the Senate version of the 2005 Energy Policy Act but disappeared in conference, surfacing later in the form of a resolution. Before that, the prevailing Senate statement on climate change was the widely quoted Resolution 98 of July 1997. Better known as the Byrd-Hagel resolution, in recognition of cosponsors Robert Byrd (D-West Virginia) and Chuck Hagel (R-Nebraska), the resolution passed by a 95-0 vote. It was widely seen as a repudiation of the Clinton administration's approach to the Kyoto Protocol given the protocol's failure to secure emission reduction commitments from developing nations and its lack of direction on possible next steps.

In vivid contrast, the 2005 Sense of the Senate resolution began by acknowledging the impact of accumulating greenhouse gases on climate change. It then stipulated that

> Congress should enact a comprehensive and effective national program of mandatory market-based limits and incentives on emissions of greenhouse gases that slow, stop, and reverse the growth of such emissions at a rate and in a manner that—
> (1) will not significantly harm the United States economy; and
> (2) will encourage comparable action by other nations that are major trading partners and key contributors to global emissions.

The 2005 resolution not only passed with a 54-43 vote but did so with an equal number of Democratic and Republican sponsors. In fact, the majority included votes from a number of senators who did not normally take strong environmental positions or possess a track record that favored action on greenhouse gas reduction. This resolution underscored the severity of the threat posed by climate change and presented basic principles to guide future policy. In short, it represented an unusually calm and coherent legislative voice—especially when weighed against the babble of congressional conversations on the matter over thirty-five years—that offered a reasoned plan for future action.

A Basic Policy Infrastructure for Climate Governance

Consistent with that resolution, this book has scrutinized a number of fundamental governance challenges that must be addressed in order to maximize the likelihood that any future U.S. climate policies will be thoughtfully designed and effectively implemented. Taking the steps detailed below would reflect the intent to establish a viable infrastructure for governance policies to reduce greenhouse gas emissions steadily over the coming decades and to promote comparable steps abroad. Taking these steps would not be as dramatic as setting a numeric target for atmospheric concentrations of greenhouse gases or pledging to reduce emissions by a certain amount by the middle of the twenty-first century. But doing so would demonstrate adherence to the core elements of effective governance and prepare the United States to be a constructive player in meeting what promises to be a long-term challenge.

Develop Institutional Capacity

Any effort to confront climate change will require collaboration and transparency across institutional boundaries. A number of states have established promising climate policies by actively encouraging and developing key units of government, including agencies representing environmental protection, energy, agriculture, and transportation as well as by coordinating efforts between executive and legislative branches. Top staff members have joined leadership teams that cut across traditional boundaries, creating networks that allow for cross-unit collaboration. Indeed, many of the most successful examples of climate policy to date, measured in terms of early implementation and emission reductions, come from U.S. states, European Union member states, and local and other subnational governments around the world that have begun to take seriously the daunting challenge of climate change. Their collective experience offers models for best practices and a set of guidelines for the development of U.S. federal institutional capacity for climate governance.

BUILD AGENCY CAPACITY

Effective governance need not involve a far-reaching reorganization of executive branch institutions or creation of mega-agencies, as was the case when the hurried response to terrorism within the United States after 9/11 led to the creation of the unwieldy Department of Homeland Security. Indeed, many scholars and practitioners at the conference advised against any such massive consolidation of administrative agencies. But the federal agencies and departments that are likely to participate in climate change governance are clearly not prepared to assume a leading role in collaborating with other units. The systematic weakening of EPA in recent times is cause for particular concern, given its likely assumption of major responsibilities under many possible scenarios. Moreover, one key partner, the Department of Energy, has been decimated by the loss of many key staff members and absorbed by the task of distributing massive amounts of energy-related economic stimulus funds over the 2009–10 period. Sobering questions arise about the preparedness of those and other federal units to assume a constructive role in climate governance, and careful capacity building will be required if they are to effectively implement any future climate policies and establish viable links with other partners in a federal network of allied institutions.

This type of institution building is neither glamorous nor easy. It requires unusual cooperation between the executive branch and Congress to provide needed resources, revisit traditional roles, and actively recruit the most talented staff available. Given the complexity of the undertaking, the decision to establish a "czar" without well-defined links to other executive units, Congress, or the states is suspect. Such hierarchical models have generally not been successful when attempted in states and EU nations, and often they can obscure the larger governance challenges that lie ahead and will be faced by subsequent administrations. The federal government will be in the climate change business for decades to come, so now is the time to think seriously about how to prepare various units and staff for taking a constructive role. The National Academy of Public Administration has shown considerable expertise in exploring new approaches to environmental governance and could be tapped for an advisory role. A number of state government officials could transfer their expertise to federal institutions and regional offices, perhaps building on the Obama administration's 2009 decision to appoint two former state environmental agency directors to pivotal EPA positions.

ESTABLISH A VIABLE EMISSIONS REGISTRY

A reliable and accessible database on greenhouse gas emissions is an essential building block in any viable climate governance strategy. It is stunning that more than a decade after the negotiations on the Kyoto Protocol, data on emissions of carbon dioxide and other greenhouse gases from individual sources are still so inexact. Most of the emissions data noted throughout this book are based on official estimates, usually provided by EPA or international authorities rather than derived from any form of mandatory reporting. Emissions reporting has been required for more than two decades for hundreds of environmental contaminants released in the air, on land, and in water, and it is generally recognized as among the most important U.S. environmental policy innovations ever conceived. Creation of the so-called Toxics Release Inventory (TRI) through 1986 legislation that built on early state experimentation established a reliable baseline of data for subsequent policy interventions. It also performed an important function in that the information, which was released annually to the public, has led to many public and private efforts to reduce emissions following the public embarrassment that accompanied its disclosure. With some important exceptions, GHG emissions data in the United States and many other nations are still based on a mix of estimates and some limited reporting programs. Indeed, at least part of the early performance problems of the European Union's Emission Trading System is attributable to the absence of reliable emissions data, which complicated the process for allocating carbon allowances and overseeing compliance.

Congress should remedy the data gap with legislation to develop a reliable and verifiable national inventory of releases of carbon dioxide and other greenhouse gases. It should be formally linked with the TRI, as has been proposed in periodic bills, and produce an annual emissions scorecard by source, industry, state, and region. EPA has been working on a disclosure process in response to a congressional call for such a step that was tucked into a 2007 appropriations bill, but the agency has advanced haltingly while numerous states, regions, localities, and non-profit organizations have forged ahead with their own versions of a disclosure program. Their efforts lack any coordination or integration and suggest the very real possibility that competing registries and databases may emerge and unnecessarily complicate policy implementation. Moreover, it is not at all clear that the threshold for reporting under the proposed federal program is sufficiently low, given the need to secure broad participaption, or that clear and reliable provisions for verification will be established.

Legislation to produce a robust registry has been introduced in recent Congresses but has largely been ignored amid more high-profile climate policy debates. With a proper framework and mandate, a national inventory could be developed through collaboration with the very states and other entities that have already made progress in this area, thereby establishing a trustworthy national database that could prove invaluable for any number of policy options and provide a model for the world. Such an inventory could also provide a baseline of data by which to evaluate other promising strategies that might inform citizens about the climate and energy impacts of various behaviors.

BUILD ANALYTICAL CAPACITY IN CONGRESS

The challenge facing Congress in crafting effective climate legislation would be considerably easier had the Office of Technology Assessment (OTA) not been eliminated in 1995. OTA provided a unique institutional forum for cutting across traditional government departments and academic disciplines to produce highly credible analysis of many issues with enormous salience to climate change. A relatively straightforward step for Congress would be to revisit the OTA model and design a successor institution with an explicit charge to examine policy and technological options on climate change and related areas such as energy, transportation, agriculture, and environmental protection. This new institution could provide valuable input to both the executive and legislative branches and also offer guidance in ensuring the integrity of all climate-related research commissioned by the federal government, including a protocol for data archiving and access.

When OTA received a charge from a congressional committee, it frequently consulted actively with state and local governments on their experiences with various related issues and displayed a unique ability to reach a broader public with many of its reports. In many instances, OTA hearings and sessions to review draft reports were unusual events that achieved a considerable degree of deliberation and often weighed the pros and cons of competing policy options without the rancor so common in congressional hearings and floor debate. A number of state governments have established their own versions of OTA to develop climate analysis expertise and establish networks across traditional department and agency boundaries. Indeed, a newly reconfigured OTA might also include an explicit charge to consider state experience in a meaningful way in assembling advisory boards, undertaking studies, and reviewing reports and recommendations.

An immediate assignment for such a new entity would be to explore ways to use the kinds of emissions data published in a federal registry to better inform citizens of how their daily actions consume energy, generate greenhouse gases, and impact them financially. The availability of technology in certain vehicles that provides detailed information to drivers on how their behavior affects gasoline mileage is an illustration of one way in which citizens might be given more information about the consequences of their behaviors. Although such technologies do not mandate any particular response, they may well serve to elevate awareness and encourage more efficient use of energy. As economist Richard Thaler and legal scholar Cass Sunstein have noted, "What if a way could be found to ensure that people see, each day, how much energy they have used?"[2] The options are potentially infinite, from stickers on new vehicles that specify anticipated fuel costs to home thermostats that estimate monthly energy bills depending on the level of air conditioning or heating that is used. A reconstituted OTA would be uniquely suited to undertake a credible review of such options and many others, including a review of state and local best practices that might warrant federal emulation. Given Sunstein's prominent position in the executive branch as head of the Office of Information and Regulatory Assessment in the Office of Management and Budget, an agency building on the OTA model could provide a significant opportunity for collaboration across the executive and legislative branches of the federal government.

Technological Infrastructure: Reinvent the Grid

The increasing state policy focus during the past decade on expanding the share of electricity from renewable sources has underscored the inadequacy of the existing grid system. This issue will only intensify if the United States continues to generate electricity from an increasingly diverse and decentralized set of sources.

Thus far, Congress has focused on ways to funnel funding through a maze of subsidies, incentives, and loan guarantees to virtually every electricity source imaginable, most notably through its 2005 and 2007 energy bills. States also have begun to follow this path, in some cases picking anticipated technology winners and losers through a range of financial assistance and regulatory programs. This approach reached new levels during House development of the American Clean Energy and Security Act in June 2009, with members of the 111th Congress tripping over each other in trying to find new ways to underwrite the costs of competing electricity and energy sources, given the incredible attraction of awarding benefits to targeted sets of constituents. This pattern only accelerated in the Senate, where expanding subsidies to sources such as nuclear energy and offshore drilling for fossil fuels emerged as a possible way to broaden support for a massive climate bill.

Looming over any transition to alternative energy sources is the challenge of overhauling the national system for distributing electricity, known in simple terms as "fixing the grid." The absence of a reliable national infrastructure poses a range of impediments to full development and deployment of competing technologies and also raises national security concerns.[3] One option for Congress is to look closely at what is needed to allow for a modernized distribution system that encourages integration from multiple sources and regions and also permits full and secure involvement by promising low-carbon technologies that are currently stymied by their limited connection to distributional channels.

In many respects, a grid-based infrastructure initiative could be legitimately framed as an effort to foster new economic development and allow for more open and active competition among various technologies in shaping the electricity system of coming decades. Rather than exploring ways to subsidize every conceivable energy technology, Congress would instead follow the playbook from interstate highway legislation of the 1950s to make the case that national electricity infrastructure is a national priority. The federal government could then generate and allocate the revenues necessary for the task, finding ways to work in partnership with states and regions. Just as federal gasoline taxes underwrote much of the cost of developing the interstate highway system, the federal government might pay for such a project by imposing costs on electricity consumption.

Begin to Price Carbon

There appear to be two proven methods to achieve a significant reduction in carbon emissions. One entails economic collapse, whereby energy consumption can drop markedly in short order, especially as a result of huge declines in emissions from the manufacturing sector. Eastern Europe in the early 1990s and the industrial Midwest in the late 2000s are obvious cases in point. These are models to be avoided. A second method involves explicit pricing of the carbon content of fossil fuels to deter consumption. That builds on long-standing scholarly literature that focuses on imposing costs on externalities and has a diverse following among policy analysts and commentators who tend to agree on little else. The politics of cost imposition, whether through some form of tax or auctioning allowances under a cap-and-trade regime, is fraught with peril. But carbon pricing offers predictability and transparency concerning future energy costs, provides a clear deterrent to consumption, and creates a pool of revenues that governments can either return to their citizens through a tax rebate or dividend check or use to underwrite national projects such as an electricity distribution system worthy of the modern era.

One initial step in this direction would be for Congress to back away from its penchant for engaging in distributional sprees across all sectors of the energy industry and instead work to make the existing federal tax code less carbon friendly. It could begin with a "carbon audit" of the federal tax code, perhaps the first task for a reconfigured OTA, to begin to cut through the many layers of energy tax subsidies and incentives that continue to be piled onto the existing tax code. The House Ways and Means Committee has shown continued interest in this question, and Representative Earl Blumenauer (D-Oregon) has issued a call to "make the tax code carbon neutral." According to Blumenauer, "the tax code values wasteful and dirty energy generation by 5 to 1—if not more—over clean, renewable technology."[4] Careful analysis would be needed to verify that charge, but a carbon audit could indeed help make the case to repeal a range of subsidies and then perhaps channel the funds to other activities of broader benefit, such as those noted above.

One active model here is the 1986 Tax Reform Act, which saw a unique cross-partisan coalition agree to repeal a laundry list of specialized tax provisions in exchange for reduced tax rates for millions of Americans. Such an exercise in concentrated cost imposition is not an easy step to take politically, and once the legislation was enacted subsequent Congresses and presidents succumbed to pressure to restore many specialized provisions and add new ones in the process.[5] Nonetheless, an effort to achieve a more carbon-neutral tax code might reduce current subsidies that actually promote greenhouse gas emissions and contribute to clarification of the way that the federal government sets carbon price signals through tax policy.

In turn, Congress could use its considerable fiscal powers to establish a tax based on the carbon content of electricity and other energy sources. Such a tax could be phased in, perhaps functioning in a fashion similar to the British Columbia carbon levy or taxes in operation in some portions of the European Union. An alternative would be a cap-and-trade program that auctioned all of its allowances in an open market, similar to the approach used for electricity in the ten Northeastern states that form the Regional Greenhouse Gas Initiative. The revenue could be returned to the public through rebate or refund, as is done in British Columbia and some European Union member states—an approach that is consistent with proposals in the 111th Congress by such House members as John Larson (D-Connecticutt) and Bob Inglis (R-South Carolina) and senators Susan Collins (R-Maine) and Maria Cantwell (D-Washington). The funding also could be divided between direct revenue returns and designated projects such as national energy infrastructure.

The national recession, of course, gives pause in launching any new cost imposition strategy, but such a step could be phased in gradually, sending a clear signal to all Americans and to the world that the United States is serious about reducing its carbon imprint and encouraging both energy efficiency and use of cleaner energy. It also could base future increases in a carbon tax on rate of emissions growth in order to produce greater predictability in terms of total emission levels. At the same time, the creation of a carbon tax need not preclude consideration of a cap-and-trade regime. Many European nations, including all of those that have been the most successful in reducing emissions in recent decades while also fostering considerable economic growth, feature some blending of domestic carbon taxation with participation in the EU's Emission Trading System, a cap-and-trade program. In such a system, the tax serves as a floor below which prices will not fall, sending very clear cost indicators to citizens as well as electricity producers, vehicle manufacturers, and other industry sectors.

Take Federalism Seriously

The considerable body of experience and talent in climate governance at the state and local levels can be tapped as Washington becomes increasingly serious about climate change. But federalism does not mean that the national government can treat states and localities as minor league farm clubs, occasionally borrowing their ideas and personnel while acting as if the U.S. system were ultimately unitary in character. As Paul Posner said during the National Conference on Climate Governance, "states are not viewed as a kind of co-governance conspirator in this. They're viewed, if anything, as 'thank you very much for your innovations. Now let us go to our national market, and we'll maybe let you back in.'" Such a view, which has been evident in many congressional hearings to date, misses opportunities to learn from the best (and worst) practices at the subnational level and to consider carefully the optimal longer-term distribution of responsibilities among the different levels of government.

A top-down approach to climate policy is dangerous, as Elinor Ostrom, the 2009 Nobel laureate in economics, has noted.[6] It risks eviscerating early state innovations and capacity while exaggerating the extent to which an ill-prepared federal government can walk in and take control of a playing field as vast as climate change. During the conference, Susan Gander of the National Governors' Association noted that "we've almost moved beyond that laboratory stage. We're in full-scale production at the state level. And I think that really complicates what will need to happen in the federal government, and certainly provides an amazing foundation for what to build upon." Done constructively, collaborative federalism could combine the strengths of various states and policy alternatives, resulting in a dynamic federalist response to climate change.

Each climate policy option presents a different intergovernmental puzzle, yet all offer some opportunity for federal and state sharing of burdens. In the area of carbon taxation, for example, federal and state strategies could coexist as they do in other areas of shared authority, such as excise taxes for cigarettes and gasoline. Indeed, a federal pricing strategy supports continued state experimentation with policies that reduce energy use and emissions, rewarding early and effective subnational actors through a reduced tax burden. Essentially, each area that could be included in the area of climate policy allows for careful crafting of an intergovernmental partnership, perhaps taking, as Martha Derthick notes in chapter 3, a "compensatory" approach that builds systematically on the strengths and weaknesses of the different levels of government.

Take a Fresh Look through a Commission

At first glance, any proposal to establish a commission to study an issue and deliver policy recommendations might appear to be simply a tactic to delay congressional deliberation. But continuing state experience shows that various forms of commissions and task forces have played significant roles in guiding development of state climate policy. Such entities usually take their charge from a state governor, who often seeks fairly broad representation and requests a menu of policy options. Commissions often are formed following some initial step in policy development, and they are designed to establish a longer-term agenda. Of course, there has been considerable experience with such entities in Washington, including those that produced a far-reaching reform of Social Security in the early 1980s, a process to close surplus military bases in the 1980s and 1990s, and a comprehensive review of what led to the events of 9/11 and how the federal government might respond. States such as California are also returning to this model in order to get a comprehensive view of their difficult fiscal situations and explore taxation options that make sense given the evolution of their economies since earlier periods.

Political scientist Larry Diamond has recently made the case for expanding the use of federal commissions, particularly on those issues over which partisan divides have been severe and significant intergenerational challenges are involved. "With something as complicated and consequential as entitlement reform or fighting global warming, it is unreasonable to expect Congress simply to vote a set of recommendations up or down, with no right of amendment," says Diamond. "But a bipartisan commission consensus on basic principles could give key members of Congress the courage and the political insulation to do what is right by claiming—honestly—to their offended constituents that it was 'the best reform we could get.'"[7]

More broadly, such a body might serve to reduce some of the melodrama that has tended to engulf political discussions of climate change, explore ways to find nonpartisan common ground, and begin to address some of the challenging governance issues that are likely to emerge.

A commission would present an opportunity for the president and Congress to convene a distinguished group of leaders to outline a viable long-term strategy to address climate change. It need not preclude congressional hearings or the kinds of policy steps noted above. But a commission might begin with the 2005 Sense of the Senate resolution and draw especially on individuals with real expertise in climate policy formation and implementation, namely state and local government and corporate leaders who have taken initial steps in this area over the past decade. Whereas federal legislators can speak only in hypothetical terms about climate policy, a growing number of state governors and legislators, mayors, and corporate leaders can draw on real experience. Assembled into a commission, they could serve as an invaluable resource to Congress and the nation. Issues of federalism under any future federal policy could be a central focal point for such a body. Ironically, a majority of members of Congress now reside in states where legislators from both parties have long since begun to develop climate policies tailored to their particular economies and polities. Perhaps the time is nearing when federal legislators can begin to catch up with their statehouse colleagues. That would enable them to begin the process of becoming a constructive partner with other branches of the federal government and other levels of the federal system on an issue likely to remain prominent on all agendas for decades to come.

Cultivate Allies

During much of the first decade of the twenty-first century, the United States was derided in capitals around the world for its seeming indifference to climate change coupled with its outsized contribution to global greenhouse gas emissions. The year 2009 began with a new lease on life in some respects, as the world witnessed new U.S. engagement on this issue. State government experience shows that the governments of many other nations (and units within those governments) are keen to collaborate with U.S. partners. That possibility was well illustrated by the response to Barack Obama's first visit as president to a foreign country, Canada—the largest U.S. trading partner. That visit launched serious discussion of a "clean energy dialogue," which quickly took on a full North American perspective through expanded collaboration on this issue with Mexico. Given the enormous scope of climate change, virtually every point of U.S. engagement with other nations or international bodies on the issue creates a unique opportunity to find common ground. This kind of work may be far more constructive, at least in the near term, than assuming that the next round of international summitry, whether in Copenhagen or Cancun, will crack the cosmic egg of climate change once and for all and produce a seamless global climate regime. It is imperative for the United States to seize these opportunities for cross-national and cross-continental partnerships.

Learn from Prior Experience

On one level, climate change presents a uniquely complex set of technical and policy challenges. At the same time, it also constitutes an intergenerational challenge of the sort not easily dealt with by existing federal institutions. Nonetheless, deliberations at the National Conference on Climate Governance frequently returned to prior instances in which the U.S. government succeeded in putting longer-term considerations ahead of short-term political obstacles. Indeed, a number of contributors to this volume have written extensively about some of those cases and drew on that experience in considering climate change. Examples include the deregulation of various sectors of the economy and far-reaching tax reform legislation in the 1980s, the historic agreement in 1983 to extend the financial viability of Social Security, and the 1990 enactment of the Clean Air Act Amendments, among others. In all of these cases, an expert consensus emerged to define the problem at hand and to outline ideas to guide a viable policy response. In many instances, such policies were carefully crafted and are widely viewed as having met their key goals.

State experience in climate change over the past decade or more suggests that such action is not beyond the capacity of U.S. political institutions, even in the current era and on as complex a matter as climate change. But transferring any state's experience to the national level requires more than just a formula for securing the requisite number of congressional votes to "do something." Indeed, a worst-case scenario would entail congressional enactment of climate legislation that was deeply flawed and beyond the capacity of existing institutions to implement, ultimately proving costly to citizens, further damaging U.S. credibility on this issue, and doing little or nothing to reverse the growth of U.S. greenhouse gas emissions. Such a scenario is entirely possible given the realities of American politics and the profound complexity of the issue. That is why serious attention to the details of effective governance, however complicated or unpleasant, is indispensable.

Notes

1. Larry Parker and Brent D. Yacobucci, *Climate Change: Costs and Benefits of the Cap-and-Trade Provisions of H.R. 2454* (Washington: Congressional Research Service, 2009), p. 116. The report further noted that efforts to anticipate costs of such a bill "are fraught with numerous difficulties that reflect more on the philosophies and assumptions of the cases reviewed than on any credible future effect." It should be noted that this analysis, like many of the economic analyses of HR 2454, focused only on the cap-and-trade components and so did not address the hundreds of pages that added still further complexity.

2. Richard H. Thaler and Cass R. Sunstein, *Nudge: Improving Decisions about Health, Wealth, and Happiness* (Yale University Press, 2008), pp. 193–94.

3. For a detailed analysis of this issue, see North American Electric Reliability Corporation, *Electricity Industry Concerns on the Reliability Impacts of Climate Change Initiatives*, November 2008 (www.nerc.com/files/2008-Climate-Initiatives-Report.pdf).

4. "House Panel Drafting Tax Reforms to Promote Low-Carbon Energy," *Carbon Control News*, May 3, 2007 (http://carboncontrolnews.com/). For a thoughtful review of federal government energy funding, see Environmental Law Institute, "Estimating U.S. Government Subsidies to Energy Sources: 2002–2008" (2010).

5. Erik M. Patashnik, *Reforms at Risk: What Happens after Major Policy Changes Are Enacted* (Princeton University Press, 2008), chapter 3.

6. Elinor Ostrom, "A Polycentric Approach for Coping with Climate Change," World Bank Policy Research Working Paper (Washington: World Bank, 2009); Justin Lahart, "Nobel Looks outside Markets," *Wall Street Journal*, October 13, 2009, p. A3.

7. Larry Diamond, "Comment," in *Red and Blue Nation?* volume 2, p. 302.

Contributors

Christopher Borick
Muhlenberg College

Martha Derthick
University of Virginia

Kirsten Engel
University of Arizona

Marc Landy
Boston College

Pietro Nivola
Brookings Institution

Paul Posner
George Mason University

Barry Rabe
University of Michigan

Leigh Raymond
Purdue University

Walter Rosenbaum
University of Florida

Ian Rowlands
University of Waterloo

Henrik Selin
Boston University

Stacy VanDeveer
University of New Hampshire

Index

ABC surveys on global warming and energy measures, 29, 48, 49

Acid rain, 102, 103–04, 247–49. *See also* Clean Air Act Amendments (1990)

ACT ON CO₂ (UK public awareness campaign), 343

Adaptation strategies, 15, 21, 204–26; current developments, 219–20; engineering and construction, 222; future developments, 349–50; insurance, 207–09, 221–22; low-impact development techniques, 222–23; market forces and risk, 206–09; obstacles to, 209–11; reform proposals, 221–23; regulatory failure, 211–18; Rocky Mountain West and, 218–19

Adler, Jonathan, 65

Administrative Procedure Act, 235, 251

Agriculture: general circulation models (GCM) and crop yields, 211; and soil conservation, 79

Agriculture Department, U.S., 274

Air Quality Monitoring Group, 300

Alaska: gas tax, 141; as plaintiff in climate change litigation, 233

Allowances under cap and trade: private ownership of, 102; RGGI allocation, 108–09, 115. *See also* Auctions

Allstate and home insurance, 208

Alternative energy: clean coal technology, 48; public opinion on, 45–48; subsidization of, 263–64. *See also* Nuclear energy

American Clean Energy and Security Act (ACESA, proposed 2009): and "Blueprint for Legislative Action" (USCAP), 280; and clean energy targets, 187–88; cost estimates for, 150, 297, 353; criticism of, 175–76; description and status of, 7–8, 13, 19, 91, 92, 104, 112, 219–20; and EPA role, 287; and funding of technological infrastructure, 359; and governance, 302; House consideration of, 10, 278–82; Larson's support for, 132; and revenue distribution, 113, 115

American Enterprise Institute, 127

American Geophysical Union, 4

American Highway Users Alliances, 152

American Recovery and Reinvestment Act (2009), 263–64

American Wind Energy Association (AWEA), 183, 184

Amtrak, 165

Arceneux, Kevin, 25

Arctic ice, melting of, 210

Army Corps of Engineers and New Orleans, 213–14

Aspen Institute, 301

Atkinson, Alan, 206

Auctions: and cap-and-trade policy, 117, 279, 360; EPA as decision maker for, 91; and EU ETS, 106, 341, 343; and